Russia's Sputnik Generation

**Indiana-Michigan Series in Russian
and East European Studies**

Alexander Rabinowitch and William G. Rosenberg,
general editors

Russia's Sputnik Generation

Soviet Baby Boomers
Talk about Their Lives

Translated and edited by Donald J. Raleigh

INDIANA UNIVERSITY PRESS
BLOOMINGTON AND INDIANAPOLIS

This book is a publication of

Indiana University Press
601 North Morton Street
Bloomington, IN 47404-3797 USA

http://iupress.indiana.edu

Telephone orders   800-842-6796
Fax orders   812-855-7931
Orders by e-mail   iuporder@indiana.edu

The paper used in this publication meets the minimum
requirements of American National Standard for Information
Sciences--Permanence of Paper for Printed Library Materials,
ANSI Z39.48-1984.

Manufactured in the United States of America

Library of Congress Cataloging-in-Publication Data

Russia's sputnik generation : Soviet baby boomers talk about their lives /
translated and edited by Donald J. Raleigh.
      p. cm. — (Indiana-Michigan series in Russian and East European
studies)
  Includes bibliographical references and index.
  ISBN 0-253-34725-4 (cloth : alk. paper) — ISBN 0-253-21842-X
(pbk. : alk. paper) 1. Saratov (Russia)—History—20th century.
2. Saratov (Russia)—Social conditions 3. Saratov (Russia)—Biography.
4. Interviews—Russia (Federation)—Saratov. 5. Oral history—Russia
(Federation)—Saratov. 6. Soviet Union—History—1953–1985. 7. Soviet
Union—History—1985–1991. I. Title: Soviet baby boomers talk about
their lives. II. Raleigh, Donald J. III. Series.
  DK651.S4R87 2006
  947'.43—dc22   2005026057

  1 2 3 4 5 11 10 09 08 07 06

To the memory of my mother
Lorraine P. Raleigh

Like history, memory is inherently revisionist and never more chameleon than when it appears to stay the same.

RAPHAEL SAMUEL, *Theatres of Memory*

Contents

Acknowledgments   xi

Introduction   1

1 "Sasha the Muscovite" | *Aleksandr Aleksandrovich Konstantinov*   24

2 "Back then I really wanted to join the party" | *Natalia Valentinovna Altukhova (maiden name Pronina)*   55

3 "We grew up in a normal time" | *Natalia P.*   87

4 "Our entire generation . . . welcomed perestroika" | *Arkadii Olegovich Darchenko*   120

5 "I saw the life of my country, and thereby my own, from a variety of perspectives" | *Natalia Aleksandrovna Belovolova (maiden name Ianichkina)*   154

6 "It's very hard to be a woman in our country" | *Olga Vladimirovna Kamaiurova*   187

7 "I came to understand things, but only gradually" | *Aleksandr Vladimirovich Trubnikov*   220

8 "People have lost a great deal in terms of their confidence in tomorrow" | *Gennadii Viktorovich Ivanov*   253

Selected Bibliography   281

Index   287

Acknowledgments

I wish to extend my sincerest gratitude to the eight individuals who gave me permission to translate and publish their interviews or excerpts from them in this volume: Aleksandr Aleksandrovich Konstantinov, Natalia Valentinovna Altukhova, Natalia P., Arkadii Olegovich Darchenko, Natalia Fedorovna Belovolova, Olga Vladimirovna Kamaiurova, Aleksandr Vladimirovich Trubnikov, and Gennadii Viktorovich Ivanov. They good-naturedly supported this project, generously shared photographs as well as memories with me, and patiently responded to my subsequent queries. I also thank the twenty-two other members of School No. 42's Class of '67 who likewise let me interview them, and who facilitated this project in various ways, especially Vladimir Nikolaevich Kirsanov, who provided me with contact information for many of his classmates. If I had not mistakenly pressed the pause button on my tape recorder during part of my interview with him, he would have been included in this anthology, for he has an absorbing story to tell.

I am indebted to my Saratov colleagues and friends. Members of the History Department at Saratov University assisted me in immeasurable ways during my visits to the city, especially Velikhan Salmonkhanovich Mirzekhanov, Nina Ivanovna Deviataikina, Anatolii Ilich Avrus, Arkadii Arkadievich German, and Nikolai Mikhailovich Malov. Igor Krutikhin duplicated school textbooks for me. The former director of School No. 42, Igor Andreevich Molchanov, helped me find members of the Class of '67, and put me in touch with several of the school's teachers. Klara Eduardovna Starshova, who taught the group, shared her memories with me. Denis Belousov, a graduate student at the university, did valuable preparatory work before I arrived in Saratov during the summer of 2004. Iosif Vladimirovich Gorfinkel searched out apartments for me to rent and made sure I put aside work long enough to enjoy the Volga and the restorative powers of the Russian *bania*. His wife, Liudmila Mikhailovna Aleksandrova, fed me until I ached.

The University of North Carolina generously funded my research. Grants from the University Research Council and the Spray-Randleigh Fellowship program helped defray costs for travel and transcription. A Chapman Fellowship from the Institute for the Arts and Humanities during the Spring 2004 semester allowed me to translate and edit most of the interviews and to discuss my work with colleagues across the disciplines. The research fund that came with the fellowship made it possible for me to travel to Saratov during the summer of 2004 and paid for transcribing some of the tapes resulting from that trip.

I would like to express my appreciation to others as well. I initially translated two interviews for the students enrolled in my undergraduate writing seminar (History 90) in the spring of 2003. Insisting they wanted to read more, they urged me to "put out a book of interviews." Beth Millwood at UNC's Southern Oral History Project shared her expertise, always finding time to answer my queries and to steer me in the right direction. The project's director, Jacquelyn D. Hall, encouraged my move into oral history and gave me the opportunity to discuss several translated interviews with her graduate students. William R. Ferris also took interest in this project from the start. Yasmin Saikia acquainted me with her experiences conducting oral history in South Asia. Marko Dumančić served as a research assistant during an early stage of the project and in this capacity reviewed several of the transcriptions. Louise McReynolds, Rósa Magnúsdóttir, and Janet Rabinowitch read my draft introduction, providing invaluable feedback. Chad Bryant put aside work on his own manuscript to look over the revised introduction.

I was fortunate to employ two excellent transcribers who worked on the tapes with great care. My first transcriber, Katya Karelina, involved her entire household in the project, conveying not only her own but also her family's impressions of what members of the Sputnik generation had to say. Before moving to Finland, Katya found a skilled and dedicated replacement, Olga Kotik. I am pleased to acknowledge their arduous efforts.

Finally, I owe a special thanks to Janet Rabinowitch, director of Indiana University Press, for encouraging me to produce this book; to assistant sponsoring editor Rebecca Tolen and managing editor Miki Bird for overseeing its publication; to Emmy Ezzell for helping me to minimize the risk of losing important image data as I prepared the illustrations; to Eric Schramm for carefully copyediting the manuscript; and to Sharon A. Kowalsky for compiling an excellent index. I also appreciate the efforts of the five not-so-anonymous readers who evaluated the proposal for the press, offering many helpful suggestions in the process: Barbara Engel, David Hoffmann, Peter Holquist, Adele Lindenmeyr, and Richard Stites.

At every step along the way, Karen and Adam made this project a family affair.

I likewise cherish the friendship, support, and encouragement of old friends, Stan and Barbara, who always come through for me when the going gets tough, and of new friends, Doug and Lois, who joined them along the way.

My mother, Lorraine P. Raleigh, died the week that I finished putting the final touches on the manuscript. I dedicate this work to her loving memory.

I take full responsibility for any errors that readers may encounter.

Russia's Sputnik Generation

Introduction

On October 4, 1957, a Soviet R-7 intercontinental ballistic missile lifted off from the Baikonur Cosmodrome in Kazakhstan with a 184-pound polished silver sphere called Sputnik ("Traveling Companion"). The size of a beach ball, the world's first artificial satellite contained two beeping radio transmitters that allowed observers to track its orbit. A decade earlier, the RAND corporation had foreseen that the launching of the first artificial satellite to orbit the earth "would inflame the imagination of mankind, and would probably produce repercussions in the world comparable to the explosion of the atom bomb." RAND was right. A dazzling public relations victory, Sputnik's appearance demonstrated, according to the *New Republic,* that the USSR had "gained a commanding lead in certain vital sectors of the race for world scientific and technological supremacy." Future Sputniks, informed *Newsweek,* "would be able to sight and even photograph just about every point on earth."[1] Worse yet, cautioned the *Chicago Daily News,* "the day is not far distant when they could deliver a death-dealing warhead onto a predetermined target almost anywhere on the earth's surface."[2] As the title of a recent study called it, Sputnik was "the shock of the century."[3]

Other Soviet successes and "firsts" in space followed hard on the heels of Sputnik, fanning fears that "the Russians" were beating the Americans at what we believed we did best. Technology, after all, had become the deciding factor in the Cold War superpower competition since 1949, when the Soviet Union had ended the U.S.'s nuclear monopoly. Less than a month after the alarm caused by Sputnik, the USSR put into space the much heavier 1,120-pound

---

1. Cited in Matthew J. Von Bencke, *The Politics of Space: A History of U.S.-Soviet/Russian Competition and Cooperation in Space* (Boulder, Colo.: Westview Press, 1997), 18–19.

2. Cited in http://www.centennialofflight.gov/essay/SPACEFLIGHT/Sputnik/SP16.htm.

3. Paul Dickson, *Sputnik: The Shock of the Century* (New York: Walker, 2001).

Sputnik II, which carried on board scientific instruments and a dog named Laika.[4] On April 12, 1961, Soviet science propelled the first man into space, Iurii Gagarin. In 1959, three Soviet space missions, Luna 1-3, sent back to Earth images of the far side of the moon. The Soviet space program also launched the first space flight with more than one cosmonaut aboard. It accomplished the first space walk. And it boasted the first woman in space, Valentina Tereshkova.

The launching of Sputnik inspired tremendous fears in the West, but enormous confidence in Soviet citizens, for the triumph complemented the "thaw" in cultural life, robust economic growth, and rising living standards that characterized the country follow-ing Joseph Stalin's death in 1953. His successor, Nikita Sergeevich Khrushchev, who remained in power until his opponents ousted him in 1964, publicly denounced the "crimes" of the Stalin era at the Twentieth Party Congress in 1956, contributing to the heady optimism in the Soviet Union at the time. Not surprisingly, given the Cold War competition between the superpowers for the hearts and minds of the Third World, Soviet propaganda capitalized on the world's shocked reaction to Sputnik's launching, depicting the achievement as but one of many spectacular technological advances underway in the USSR. "We are living in a remarkable period," boasted Soviet aviation scientist Karl Aleksandrovich Gilzin. "Under the firm but friendly guidance of the Soviet people, armed with the latest scientific and technical achievements, deserts are receding, age-old virgin lands are being ploughed up, rivers are finding new courses, and the world is miraculously changing its face." Lest there be any doubts regarding what this all meant, Gilzin reminded read-ers that "life for the Soviet people is daily becoming more prosperous and more satisfying."[5]

Although it dealt a blow to American prestige throughout the world, the launching of Sputnik did not prove Soviet technological superiority beyond the moment,[6] and may ultimately have been a

---

4. This "achievement" did receive mixed reviews. Its detractors nicknamed Sput-nik II "Muttnik" because Laika became the first casualty to space exploration when the satellite overheated.

5. Karl Gilzin, *Sputniks and After,* trans. Pauline Rose (London: Macdonald, 1959), 23.

6. How Sputnik's launching surprised the world can be understood only in its Cold War context, for Soviet scientists had not kept secret their plans to launch a satellite. Nor had the United States, which, as part of the United Nations–sponsored International Geophysical Year, announced its intention to lift into space its first artificial satellite, Van-guard, as early as November 1957. Although Vanguard had fallen eight months behind schedule, the U.S. government could have launched it before Sputnik if this had been

Pyrrhic victory of sorts for the USSR. For one thing, the achievement, as a Soviet defector involved in the country's space program opined, "suddenly imposed on the Soviet Union . . . the heavy [i.e., financial] burden of being a power in space."[7] Moreover, the crisis of confidence in the American way of life and values caused by the USSR's success in space galvanized the United States into action as it began to "reinvent itself."[8] Sputnik led to massive new funding to promote research in science, technology, and engineering, one consequence of which was the development of microelectronics and ultimately the computerization of our lives. It brought about the creation of the National Aeronautics and Space Administration (NASA), charged with winning the space race.[9] And it overhauled American education. Many observers insisted that Soviet schools outperformed American ones, that Ivan knew more than Johnny. Some critics even blamed child-rearing expert Dr. Benjamin Spock and educator and philosopher John Dewey for the perceived scientific lag that had allowed the Soviet Union to pull ahead in the space race.[10] As a result, Congress passed the National Defense Education Act (NDEA) in 1958 to address what it perceived as a "critical national need." This meant more and better scientific equipment, foreign language study, new math, student loan money, fellowships for PhDs, the introduction of honors courses "to meet the Soviet challenge," and efforts to teach American students to think independently, ostensibly so that they would never fall susceptible to what the popular imagination feared as Soviet-style mind control. It meant the rapid expansion of Russian and East European

---

a priority. But President Dwight D. Eisenhower saw Sputnik as a way to establish the principle of freedom of space. This was a main concern of his because government and military officials and select defense contractors were developing a top-secret spy satellite that would allow the United States to detect all Soviet missiles. See Von Bencke, *Politics of Space*, 7, and Dickson, *Sputnik*, 2, 11.

7. Leonid Vladimirov, *The Russian Space Bluff: The Inside Story of the Soviet Drive to the Moon*, trans. David Floyd (New York: Dial Press, 1973), 53.

8. Von Bencke, *Politics of Space*, 29, and Dickson, *Sputnik*, 224.

9. As then Senator John F. Kennedy put it, "We cannot run second in this vital race. To insure peace and freedom, we must be first." In May 1961 President Kennedy announced that the United States would up the ante in the superpower competition by sending a man to the moon and back within the decade. See Von Bencke, *Politics of Space*, 2–3, and Dickson, *Sputnik*, 4, 6.

10. Susan Jacoby, *Inside Soviet Schools* (New York: Hill and Wang, 1974), 16. Jacoby is highly critical of the spate of books appearing in the aftermath of Sputnik's launching that exaggerated the benefits of the Soviet educational system (see p. 3). One example of this genre is Arthur S. Trace, Jr., *What Ivan Knows that Johnny Doesn't* (New York: Random House, 1961).

studies programs at the country's major universities.[11] Later, under President John F. Kennedy (1961–63), it meant a new emphasis on physical fitness.

But what about the "Sputnik generation," those who began school in the USSR the year the first artificial satellite was launched, and who completed their secondary education in 1967, when the country celebrated the fiftieth anniversary of the October Revolution that brought the Communists to power? Born in 1949 and 1950—after demobilization of the Red Army, famine, rationing, and martial law had come to an end, and the Soviet government affirmed that "reconstruction" had been completed—its members represent the first generation conceived during a return to "normality" following World War II. Depicted by the Soviet government as the Great Patriotic or Fatherland War (1941–45), the conflict took a devastating toll on the country and its people, leaving 27 million dead, including 17 million civilians; cities, infrastructures, and villages ruined; and countless people homeless, injured, and/or otherwise aggrieved. Some observers have estimated that the war destroyed as much as one-third of the country's national wealth. The sheer magnitude of Soviet losses—U.S. war casualties, in comparison, amounted to 407,000 deaths—makes Sputnik's launching all the more impressive and menacing.

A central moment in the evolution and legitimization of the Soviet system, the war also determined how the country's people and leaders viewed the world and lived in it—especially, for our purposes, those who parented members of the Sputnik generation. Although the USSR's political and economic structure remained largely intact, "a complex of hopes and expectations prompted by the sacrifice of the great victory led to major changes in Soviet society,"[12] as we shall see below. The outcome of the war likewise guaranteed that the rest of the world, particularly the West, would fear the Soviet Union as the other superpower. This was ever more the case as the USSR, before the end of the decade, established control over most of Eastern Europe and manufactured an atomic bomb,

---

11. Dickson, *Sputnik*, 227, 232. See also Robert F. Byrnes, *Soviet-American Academic Exchanges, 1958–1975* (Bloomington: Indiana University Press, 1976).

12. Elena Zubkova, *Russia after the War: Hopes, Illusions, and Disappointments, 1945–1957*, trans. Hugh Ragsdale (Armonk, N.Y.: M. E. Sharpe, 1998), 51. Amir Weiner situates the war at the very crux of the evolution of the Soviet system. See his *Making Sense of War: The Second World War and the Fate of the Bolshevik Revolution* (Princeton: Princeton University Press, 2001).

and Chinese Communists consolidated their power over the world's most populous nation.

The defining experiences of the USSR's Sputnik generation differed appreciably from those of their parents. These "Soviet Baby Boomers" grew up during the Cold War, but in a Soviet Union that increasingly distanced itself from the so-called excesses of Stalinism. Unlike earlier generations, whose success in transforming the country into the other superpower was tempered by shortages, deprivations, famine, arbitrary terror, relentless mobilization of people and resources, and a horrific war with its many telling consequences, the postwar generation benefited in untold ways from years of peaceful, evolutionary, organic development. During this generation's childhood and young adult years, the Soviet leadership dismantled the Gulag labor-camp system, began to rule without terror, promoted Soviet-style consumerism, and opened the country in teaspoon-size doses to the outside world. Reaching middle age when Mikhail Sergeevich Gorbachev carried out his revolution of perestroika between 1985 and 1991, its members had to negotiate the bumpy transition from Soviet-style communism to a Russian-style market economy.

In short, the Sputnik generation came of age at the zenith of Soviet socialism, only to see the system crumble some three decades later. We have yet to understand fully why this remarkable transformation occurred, but ironically much of it had to do with the Soviet system's very success at effecting social change, whose byproducts included rapid urbanization and a concomitant rise in the number of educated professionals.[13] Between 1940 and 1980 a "remarkable reversal" took place in regard to the relationship of one's age to level of support for the Soviet system. On the eve of World War II, the younger generation in the USSR had voiced the greatest enthusiasm for their country. But by 1980, when our Soviet Baby Boomers were thirty years old, things were the other way around. Moreover, education became another crucial factor determining attitudes and social position: the higher the educational level achieved by the younger generation, the weaker their backing was for the regime, with the exception that support for the system increased with income level.[14] Indeed, in the decades following Stalin's death

---

13. See, for example, Moshe Lewin, *The Gorbachev Phenomenon: A Historical Interpretation,* expanded edition (Berkeley: University of California Press, 1991).

14. James R. Millar, ed. *Politics, Work, and Daily Life in the USSR: A Survey of Former Soviet Citizens* (New York: Cambridge University Press, 1987), x–xii.

people turned their attention away from the priorities of the state to private concerns such as family and friends, owing, in part, to the system's failure to reward its population adequately. The pursuit of new aspirations created a Soviet mass culture shaped by education, the media, and contact with the outside world. As a result, not that long after the excitement and confidence prompted by Sputnik, the state experienced a "gradual loss of authority over all strata of the population," breeding apathy and cynicism. Although the shifting attitudes did not necessarily result in a questioning of the basic values of the Soviet system,[15] some Western observers noticed a certain malaise at the time. "After fifty years the Soviet Revolution has lost its momentum," claimed sociologist Alex Inkeles. "It has exhausted its imagination and shows no marked signs of potential vitality for the immediate future."[16]

The Sputnik generation, whose lives were shaped by the events of the last fifty years and the times in which they lived, is only now being opened to historical inquiry: until the collapse of the Soviet Union in 1991, the postwar period in the country's history had been largely the domain of political scientists and sociologists. Because its perspectives can shed light on the history of the Soviet Union in its final decades and in the first post-Soviet decades, I decided to consider the life experiences of this critical generation of people who, for the most part, had remained faceless and even unstudied up until now. Few firsthand accounts exist for the postwar period in English, and those available tend to have been authored by political dissidents or, later, by prominent public figures during the Gorbachev years. The idea of interviewing people who otherwise would probably not have left a formally documented record of their lives appealed to me because Russian citizens are talking about their past and trying to make sense of it, and I saw obvious benefits in listening in.[17] To be

15. Vladimir Shlapentokh, *Public and Private Life of the Soviet People: Changing Values in Post-Stalin Russia* (New York: Oxford University Press, 1989), 13, 63, 153, 170.

16. Alex Inkeles, *Social Change in Soviet Russia* (Cambridge: Harvard University Press, 1968), 60.

17. Few oral histories about Russia have appeared to date. Among them are Deborah Adelman, *The "Children of Perestroika": Moscow Teenagers Talk about Their Lives and the Future* (Armonk, N.Y.: M. E. Sharpe, 1991); Daniel Bertaux, Paul Thompson, and Anna Rotkirch, *On Living Through Soviet Russia* (New York: Routledge, 2004); Barbara A. Engel and Anastasia Posadskaya-Vanderbeck, *A Revolution of Their Own: Voices of Women in Soviet History*, trans. Sona Hoisington (Boulder, Colo.: Westview Press, 1998); Larry E. Holmes, "Part of History: The Oral Record and Moscow's School No. 25, 1931–1937," *Slavic Review* 56 (1997): 279–306; Richard Lourie, *Russia Speaks: An Oral History from the Revolution to the Present* (New York: Edward Burlingame Books, 1991); and David L. Ransel, *Village*

sure, remembering has its own sociopolitical and historical context in each country. In the case of the Soviet Union, remembering had been dangerous.[18] As a result, a project such as this could not have been carried out before the country's opening.

The result is this book, comprising life story interviews with eight members of the Sputnik generation. Rather than selecting people randomly or attempting the impossible task of trying to identify a cross-section of the country's population, I chose individuals who are historically and contextually connected and who belong to a social stratum that has played a key role in the Soviet Union and in Russia today, members of the urban professional class or intelligentsia, that is, those with a higher education. I opted for a cohort of people who attended, and in 1967 graduated from, School No. 42, located in the provincial city of Saratov. I picked this group to interview because its members are well educated, articulate, and remain loosely networked, and because they grew up not in privileged Moscow, but in an important provincial center.[19] Like much of the country, Saratov was physically off limits, that is, closed to foreigners from "capitalist" countries and thus to many direct outside influences until 1990. Members of this cohort have yet another feature in common: School No. 42 offered intensive instruction in English at a time when its students had no real chance to meet native speakers and practice their language skills. Nonetheless, the appearance of these elite magnet schools in the 1950s symbolizes the country's opening amid the changing battlefields of the Cold War and a domestic climate of exhilarating optimism, while their graduates represent a microcosm of the Soviet Union's professional,

---

Mothers: Three Generations of Change in Russia and Tataria (Bloomington: Indiana University Press, 2000). One of the most popular practitioners of oral history in Russia is Svetlana Alexievich. Her account of the nuclear reactor accident at Chernobyl has appeared in English as *Voices from Chernobyl*, translated and with a preface by Keith Gessen (Normal, Ill.: Dalkey Archive Press, 2005).

18. Daria Khubova, Andrei Ivankiev, and Tonia Sharova, "After Glasnost: Oral History in the Soviet Union," *International Yearbook of Oral History and Life Stories*. Vol. I, *Memory and Totalitarianism* (New York: Oxford University Press, 1992), 89. Luisa Passerini remarked that "ideology had replaced historical memory." See her "Introduction," *International Yearbook of Oral History and Life Stories*. Vol. I, *Memory and Totalitarianism* (New York: Oxford University Press, 1992), 8. My thinking on collective remembering as an active, social, and dynamic phenomenon is also informed by James V. Wertsch, *Voices of Collective Remembering* (New York: Cambridge University Press, 2002).

19. Friendship in the Soviet context by necessity required a high level of trust and confidence, as a result of which most people's friends came from those they knew since childhood or for a long time. See Vladimir Shlapentokh, *Love, Marriage, and Friendship in the Soviet Union: Ideals and Practices* (New York: Praeger, 1984), 245.

educated urban class. Moreover, I feel an affinity toward this group because I was born in 1949 and graduated from high school in 1967, too. Further, I have visited Saratov fourteen times since 1990, mostly to research a book on the Russian Civil War in the Saratov region,[20] an experience that made it easier for me to locate and identify with my subjects and to navigate their microworlds.

Opening in 1954, School No. 42 enrolled pupils from the second grade through their high school years. The school's class of 1967 comprised fifty-six students divided into two groups of roughly equal size, groups A and B.[21] Group A was formed in 1958 when the children were second graders, and group B the next year. Two-thirds of the members of the class are female (thirty-eight of the fifty-six graduates). Six of the graduates have died; several others have suffered strokes or other debilitating illnesses. Five live abroad (one in Germany, one in the Netherlands, two in the United States, and one in Israel), and five in Moscow. The whereabouts of two others who left Saratov have been impossible to ascertain. Although several pupils ended up at No. 42 because it served as a neighborhood school as well as a magnet institution for the entire city, most who attended did so because their parents actively sought to enroll them there. Social standing thus played a central role in shaping the makeup of the school's student body, comprising children of Communist Party and government officials or of the cultural and technical intelligentsia. More of the former were concentrated in group A; more of the latter were found in group B. Only a handful of children—no more than 10 percent—came from working-class families. In sum, this project deals with privileged elements of Soviet society that may have had different expectations than less-educated and less–well-connected people. The Baby Boomers I interviewed may not be ordinary, but they are certainly representative of the country's urban professional class.

It is much harder to determine the class's ethnic or national composition, because, when enrolling children, administrators re-

---

20. See my *Experiencing Russia's Civil War: Politics, Society, and Revolutionary Culture in Saratov, 1917–1922* (Princeton: Princeton University Press, 2002). My interest in Saratov actually dates to my graduate student years, when I wrote a dissertation on the Revolution of 1917 in Saratov, later published as *Revolution on the Volga: 1917 in Saratov* (Ithaca: Cornell University Press, 1986).

21. Specialized schools for mathematics, science, and foreign languages began to open across the USSR in the 1950s. Saratov boasted a magnet school for mathematics and English, and later a third school specializing in French.

corded the nationality indicated on a child's birth certificate, which was not always an accurate indicator of one's ethnicity.[22] According to school records, all the students were Russian by nationality, except for five Jews, one Ukrainian, and one Moldavian. Yet my conversations with members of the class suggest that as much as 18 percent has some Jewish lineage. Several others are half Volga German, and one has a Tatar surname. The loose generalization that can be made from the data is that the ethnic composition of the school roughly corresponded with that of Saratov, except that Jews were overrepresented and the city's Tatar population underrepresented. This profile was less the result of conscious policies than of the overall educational levels achieved by these two communities: Jews represented, by far, the most highly educated national group in the Russian Federation.[23]

I located and interviewed thirty of the fifty living members of the class of 1967 over four summers between 2001 and 2004, when they were in their early fifties. Conducted in Russian, the interviews range in length from sixty minutes to three hours. Exploring the margins between the political, the personal, and the professional, I employed open-ended interview techniques to uncover my informants' remembered experiences and to reveal how Soviet society operated at an everyday level. I tried to involve my informants as collaborators by asking them what *they* believed I needed to know about them in order to shed light on the five wide-ranging questions that interested me most. First, who and what shaped my informants' worldviews while they were growing up? Second, what do my Soviet Baby Boomers' life stories tell us about what constituted the "Soviet dream" of the Sputnik generation, and ultimately about the relationship between the expansion of the private sphere after 1953, the delegitimization of ideology, and the fate of the Soviet Union? Third, what do we learn from the interviews about daily life in a "closed" provincial city? Fourth, how have my informants negotiated the challenging transition to a post-Soviet Russia following the collapse of communism in 1991? Fifth, how have their lived experiences both reproduced and transformed Soviet and Russian society after 1953? In other words, how do their personal stories help us comprehend cultural transmission across generations?

---

22. Soviet citizens were issued passports, which indicated nationality, when they turned sixteen. At that time they could select the nationality of either parent.

23. Jacoby, *Inside,* 154–55.

The result is a book that treats the broad sweep of Soviet and Russian history during the past half-century and that has the feel of a class reunion to it. The great value of the interviews is that they not only provide information about events, processes, causes, and effects, but also reveal what these issues mean to the people who experienced them. By helping us appreciate how members of the educated urban class in today's Russia—and beyond—understand the remarkable transformations of the past half-century and how the changes have impacted their lives, the narratives give human expression to otherwise remote historical developments.

In this regard, oral history is a highly appropriate approach to take to accomplish the task at hand. An interdisciplinary methodology, oral history draws from other disciplines including anthropology, folklore, cultural studies, and psychology. I began my work by interviewing people, by creating primary sources that otherwise might never have been recorded. Afterward, I hired a native speaker to transcribe the tapes. I reviewed the transcriptions for accuracy and then translated them. I also edited them, deleting repetition, questions that led nowhere, and a variety of false starts and fillers. I considered whether my informant had reason to withhold or modify the story, and also the context and site of the interview, matters that I discuss in my prefatory remarks to each.[24] But I stop here, leaving it up to readers to interrogate the texts for multiple meanings, tropes, patterns, stories that have become common property, silences, ideologies, embroidered myths, and emotional overtones. Consideration of these issues allows readers to grasp how the interviewees make sense of the world, and to uncover the historically conditioned structures of society as exhibited by representative individuals composing it. By examining the narrative structures of these eight texts, readers can identify patterns and contradictions as they construct their own narrative out of the fragments, one that is more instructive, perhaps, than any single reality can be. In sum, the reader can create a story that no lone individual could tell and embed it in larger historical narratives of Cold War, de-Stalinization, "overtaking" America, opening up to the outside world, economic stagnation, dissent, emigration, the transition to a market economy,

---

24. Oral history is normally put together in one of three ways: the single life story approach; a collection of stories (such as this volume); or cross-analysis. In effect, I am asking readers to begin cross-analysis. See Paul Thompson, *The Voice of the Past: Oral History* (New York: Oxford University Press), 204–205.

the transformation of class, ethnic, and gender relations, and global-ization, among others.

In effect, I invite the reader to contextualize and historicize my informants' memories. A montage of images rather than a snapshot of the past, memory is malleable, dynamic, and historically con-ditioned. Because an individual's values and beliefs evolve owing to personal experience and changes within a larger sociohistorical context, there is an inherent element of historical revisionism in oral narratives. Simply put, people tell their stories in different ways throughout their lives. This book, then, is not only about specific historical events, but also about what they mean to Russia's Sputnik generation, now middle age, *today.* Interpreting what they experi-enced with the cultural repertoires available to them, they, among other things, told me about childhood pastimes, favorite books and movies, the popularity of the Beatles, foreign radio broadcasts, cloth-ing fads, influential teachers, best friends, careers, spouses, children, parents, foreign travel, and even marijuana use. I learned their at-titudes toward the outside world, what factors shaped the formation of their identities and gender perspectives, how they understood the launching of perestroika, what they thought of Gorbachev and Yeltsin, what role, if any, English played in determining the life choices they made, why they might have decided to emigrate, and what life has been like for those who did so. Ready for recall, some of their memories were seemingly archived and rehearsed,[25] but others clearly had not been given voice before.

Ultimately, I selected for inclusion in this volume eight inter-views, four each from men and from women, which together I deem representative of the wide array of experiences, lifestyles, and views of the larger collective. I could have rationalized select-ing any combination of the thirty interviews I carried out, for each of them proved illuminating in its own way. As a colleague remarked in regard to her own experience interviewing well over a hundred individuals for a study on American history, "I leave each interview feeling as if someone had given me a gift."[26] What about the gifts I

---

25. These terms are used in Jaclyn Jeffrey and Glenace Edwall, eds., *Memory and History: Essays on Remembering and Interpreting Human Experience* (Lanham, Md.: University Press of America, 1992), 124.

26. Interview with Beth Millwood of the Southern Oral History Project conducted by Nina Ivanovna Deviataikina, University of North Carolina, Chapel Hill, January 5, 2005.

did not publish in this collection? They include those from a doctor who works for the police, who found renewal in life by starting a second family with a trophy wife; a star pupil and Komsomol activist who wanted to study in Moscow to become a diplomat, but was discouraged from doing so because of his Volga German heritage; a physicist whose daughter married an American and now lives in the United States; a private businessman who made—and lost—a fortune during perestroika; a Jewish student who changed his surname to avoid discrimination; a favorite of the group crippled by a stroke and now an invalid; an award-winning teacher who shared some school secrets with me; a woman who hosts her own television show; the daughter of the editor of Saratov's Communist Party newspaper, whose own daughter now resides in Israel; a woman who lost her life savings—and temporarily her dream of owning her own apartment—during the Yeltsin years; a college teacher of English who never mentioned that she is Jewish; another teacher of English whose husband visited Chapel Hill, North Carolina, as part of a sister city delegation; a woman whose spiritual search led her first to astrology and then to the Church of Scientology; a woman from working-class origins who lost her son to cancer; a professor of medicine now living in Moscow; and an engineer who, unlike so many other informants, had only positive things to say about today's youth.

A few words are in order about the context and the times in which the Sputnik generation grew up and practiced adulthood. Located in the eastern tip of Russia's fertile black-earth (*chernozem*) zone, Saratov oblast (region) is roughly the size of South Carolina. Lying on the western bank of the Volga River, the city of Saratov became the eleventh largest in the Russian Empire on the eve of World War I. A major river port and rail center, Saratov processed and shipped throughout Russia and Europe agricultural products produced locally. At the time the Sputnik generation was born, the city's population had grown to 473,000. A decade later it had risen to 602,000, and swelled to 763,000 by 1970. It increased to 816,000 in 1975 and to 887,000 the year Gorbachev came to power.[27] New neighborhoods arose in Saratov's outlying regions, often in the vicinity of industrial enterprises. In 1952 trolley buses began running

---

27. Today the oblast occupies second place in Russia (after Krasnodar) in the volume of grain production, and the city, with a population just over 900,000, ranks fifteenth in population.

down the major thoroughfare, Lenin Prospect. In 1965 an auto transport bridge was completed across the Volga. An embankment was built along the riverbank. Sitting atop Sokolov Mountain that rises over the city to the north, Victory Park, which commemorates World War II, opened in 1975.

Saratov's industrial significance expanded during the period as well. In 1951 the city began to manufacture "Saratov" refrigerators, which became prized throughout the Soviet bloc. Its factories and plants produced YAK-40 airplanes, machine tools, gear-cutting machines, industrial glass, ball bearings, synthetic fibers, trolley buses, chemicals, gas, electronics, and space communication equipment. Because many of the plants had ties with the Soviet military-industrial complex, the government closed the city to Westerners.[28] The skilled workers and professional specialists employed by these factories received certain perks, such as higher wages and priority housing, but they became particularly vulnerable after 1990, when many of the enterprises, newly privatized, shut down or gropingly retooled.

Within the USSR, Saratov enjoyed the distinction of being a leading cultural and educational center. Saratov University, which opened in 1909, had roughly 9,500 students when members of the Sputnik generation attended it. At the time, the Saratov Polytechnic Institute enrolled about 15,000 students, and the Saratov Medical Institute another 5,500. In the first half of the 1950s, Iurii A. Gagarin, the first person to orbit the earth, studied in a Saratov technical school, which later was renamed in his honor (the school is mentioned in the interview with G. V. Ivanov). In April 1961 Cosmonaut Gagarin completed his space flight by parachuting into a field near Saratov, further firing the imaginations of members of the Sputnik generation, now entering their teenage years.[29] Although no Westerners visited the city after it closed, Saratov oblast developed a special exchange relationship with Slovakia, then part of Czechoslovakia, and the city of Saratov with Bratislava, Slovakia's capital. The year our Baby Boomers graduated from college, school children

---

28. The Soviet government did not issue documents shedding light on when cities were closed to foreigners. Most Saratovites report that the city closed in the early 1950s, or perhaps shortly after World War II. Be that as it may, exceptions were occasionally made for foreign Communists and others, at least until sometime in the early 1960s.

29. This information is drawn from http://www.saratov.ru; http://www.russian americanchamber.org/regions/Saratov; G. A. Malinin, *Saratov: Kratkii ocherk-putevoditel'* (Saratov: Privolzhskoe knizhnoe izdatel'stvo, 1974).

from Slovakia visited Saratov, but the city did not reopen to the rest of the world until 1991.

To help readers navigate the interviews, I would like to sketch a typical life trajectory of these Soviet Baby Boomers born in 1949 or 1950, usually in Saratov. The parents of those born elsewhere tended to have some connection to the city or region. The life stories of the thirty people I interviewed make clear that World War II created an itinerant society and considerable room for upward social mobility: the war scattered their parents across the Soviet Union, providing opportunities as well as hardships. As with earlier Soviet generations, the grandparents of the Sputnik generation played a major role in raising them, since roughly 85 percent of mothers in the Soviet Union worked at this time. Attitudes toward authority are shaped largely in the family.[30] Owing to the physical closeness of people resulting from an acute housing shortage—and the perils of historical memory—the family's role in determining attitudes appears to have been particularly profound, as many of the interviewees acknowledge.

The school experience probably came next. The interviewees began attending neighborhood schools in 1957, and enrolled in School No. 42 in second or third grade. The school itself moved into a new building, its current location, when the students were in fifth grade. Their school year began on September 1 and ended on June 1. They attended school six days a week, usually from 8:30 AM to 2:30 PM, a period divided into lessons of forty-five minutes. The amount of time devoted to the study of English increased to as much as 30 to 40 percent in the upper classes, when special foreign-language schools experimented in teaching some regular subjects in English, an experiment that did not yield the desired results. Nor did Khrushchev's efforts to channel students into the labor force to learn a trade before attending the university: young people found ways to circumvent this ruling, which his successors scrapped. Similarly, during the Khrushchev years the government extended its minimum educational requirements from eight years of primary school and two years of secondary school to eight years and three years, respectively. Under Brezhnev, it reverted back to ten years of required schooling, a ruling that affected the class of 1967, which became the first produced by the new ten-year curriculum.

---

30. Luisa Passerini, "Italian Working Class Culture Between the Wars: Consensus to Fascism and Work Ideology," *International Journal of Oral History* 1 (1980): 10.

The Soviet educational system provided a mechanism for the Communist Party to inculcate its ideology into the minds of the country's young people. Like all Soviet school children between the ages of six and nine, members of the Sputnik generation belonged to the Young Octobrists (*Oktiabriata*), named after the October (Bolshevik) Revolution of 1917 and founded in 1923–24. At age ten, they joined the Pioneers, the next level of children's organizations formed to replace the prerevolutionary scouting movement. Pioneers were instructed to study hard, to be honest, and to learn how to live happily with others. Senior to the Pioneer organization was the Komsomol (an acronym for the Russian name of the All-Union Leninist Communist Youth League), which catered to young people between the ages of fourteen and twenty-eight. Membership in the Komsomol, an auxiliary of the Communist Party and training ground for party membership, was far from universal in the country at large, but a high percentage of school-age children who had aspirations to enroll at a university joined the organization. Significantly, all thirty of the individuals I interviewed had taken part in the movement.

In addition to these national youth organizations, those attending School No. 42 joined "kruzhki," circles or clubs devoted to a specific academic interest, hobby, or sport. Many of the children also studied music, dance, or some other activity. They took private lessons to help them with difficult subjects or to make up deficiencies in their educational background if they enrolled in the school in a later grade. After school they often played in the courtyard of the building in which the students grew up. It was here that they learned the "facts of life" from older kids, smoked their first cigarettes, and experimented with alcohol. In the older grades they began to attend parties at each other's apartments. The boys remembered being interested in sports, electronics, music, and girls. Some of them played the guitar, strumming the melodies of the criminal underworld. Later, some of them mimicked popular singers and the so-called guitar poets Vladimir Vysotskii, Aleksandr Galich, and Bulat Okudzhava who, in the 1960s, began performing their songs to their own solo accompaniment on the seven-stringed guitar. Circulating on privately recorded tapes made possible by the state's mass production of tape recorders, guitar poetry represented the most popular form of counterculture activity in the Leonid Brezhnev period (1964–82). The girls remembered being interested in fashion, reading, music, and boys. Many made their own clothes, drawing on the skills they learned in a required home economics course taught at school. All thirty of the people I interviewed noted how much they read during their school years. Although televisions became household items for some, the interviewees had little to say about the new technology. Quite a few spoke fondly of the month they spent each summer in the upper grades at a camp on an island in the Volga. Others traveled with their parents, often south to the Black Sea. People recall positive memories better than negative ones (except for truly dramatic negative ones). Interestingly, everyone claimed to have had a happy or normal childhood.

Enormous changes came to the Soviet Union during the Khrushchev years when the Sputnik generation reached adolescence and young adulthood. Khrushchev's populist style and spasmodic reformism resulted in a new focus on agriculture, on improving the Soviet diet, on raising living standards, on extending social services, and on raising labor productivity and wages. Khrushchev likewise gave top priority to expanding housing. During their school years, many of those interviewed left communal flats—where their families often inhabited one room and shared kitchen and bathroom facilities with other families—for their own apartments. Between 1956 and 1965 about 108 million people nationwide moved into their own flats.[31] This is highly significant, because communal living had made it difficult for autonomous social groups to develop and sustain themselves.[32] Moreover, the new emphasis on improving living conditions helped to buoy the popular mood. Surveys conducted at the time capture the population's unprecedented optimism circa 1960, as the Sputnik generation entered their teenage years. In one survey, 73.2 percent responded that their living standards had improved, as measured in terms of higher pay, more goods, a better diet, a shortened workday, and better housing. Other surveys confirmed a sense of optimism and personal satisfaction. People took pride in their generation's patriotism, moral values, loyalty, and regard for the collective. Soviet youth aspired to serve their country by becoming top-notch specialists and "real" Communists. A whopping 96.8 percent believed that mankind could prevent nuclear war.[33]

31. William Taubman, *Khrushchev: The Man and His Era* (New York: W. W. Norton, 2003), 382.

32. Victoria Semenova, "Equality in Poverty: The Symbolic Meaning of *kommunalki* in the 1930s–1950s," *On Living through Soviet Russia,* ed. by Daniel Bertaux, Paul Thompson, and Anna Rotkirch (New York: Routledge, 2004), 66.

33. B. A. Grushin, *Chetyre zhizni Rossii v zerkale obshchestvennogo mneniia: Ocherki massovogo soznaniia rossiian vremen Khrushcheva, Brezhneva, Gorbacheva i Eltsina v 4-kh knigakh. Zhizn' 1-ia: Epokha Khrushcheva* (Moscow: Progress-Traditsiia, 2001), 84, 125, 178–79, 184, 189, 191, 192.

Where, then, did the apathy mentioned earlier come from? Khrushchev's policies had changed popular expectations. "In fact," maintains Khrushchev's biographer William Taubman, "he began the process that destroyed the Soviet regime, while at the same time undermining himself."[34] Indeed, Khrushchev sought results through what his detractors would later decry as his impulsive "campaignism," such as plowing up virgin land in the country's remote regions and planting corn in places it would not grow. As part of this effort to refashion Soviet-style socialism, he tinkered with democratizing and decentralizing the Communist Party, a highly unpopular move among the elite that cinched his ouster in 1964. So did other things, for by this time Soviet public opinion had turned against him as well. A string of serious setbacks in foreign policy, an unpopular attack on religion that greatly reduced the number of churches and opportunities to practice one's faith, and inconsistent cultural policies alienated the intelligentsia and the general population. On top of this, the Soviet economy palpably began to decline at the start of the 1960s, just when Khrushchev issued with considerable fanfare a new Communist Party program that not only claimed the USSR would surpass the United States in per capita production by 1970, but also boasted that communism would be achieved by 1980. The government's need to raise meat and butter prices in mid-1962 resulted in riots in Novocherkassk and other disturbances, which the leadership brutally suppressed.[35] Drawing on the archival record, Vladimir Kozlov has argued that paradoxically these manifestations of popular unrest demonstrated that people still held onto their belief in communism, and that the sharp decline in mass disorders in the Brezhnev era "signaled the ideological collapse of the regime and the decay of the entire Soviet system."[36]

Perhaps. But the majority of the people I interviewed at first looked favorably upon the Brezhnev leadership. As political scientist George Breslauer has shown, as an "intra-establishment consensus builder," Brezhnev avoided confronting the institutional interests of the Soviet system. He established authority by replacing his predecessor's reforms with Soviet patriotism and budgetary redistribu-

---

34. Taubman, *Khrushchev*, xx.

35. For a discussion of the Novocherkassk unrest, see Samuel H. Baron, *Bloody Sunday in the Soviet Union: Novocherkassk, 1962* (Stanford: Stanford University Press, 2001).

36. Vladimir A. Kozlov, *Mass Uprisings in the USSR: Protest and Rebellion in the Post-Stalin Years*, trans. and ed. Elaine McClarnand MacKinnon (Armonk, N.Y.: M. E. Sharpe, 2002), 314.

tions, throwing resources into the agricultural sector, wages, the development of Siberia, and imports of foreign food, clothing, and other goods. He also created a more predictable (and economically favorable) environment for politically conformist specialists graduating from Soviet universities.[37] This new so-called socialist legality, however, entailed putting an end to Khrushchev's anti-Stalin campaign and repressing dissidents. In addition, the improvement in living standards that many people experienced in the 1970s, as the Sputnik generation entered their twenties, masked signs of serious economic stress. A series of fortuitous circumstances—the world oil crisis of 1973, the rise in gold prices, and favorable terms of trade for Soviet raw material exports—had enabled the regime throughout the 1970s to earn hard currency to spend on satisfying consumer demands through imports. What the state could not supply, the flourishing black market or second economy often could. Both party officials and the population at large, to quote Kozlov, "sought individual happiness and used the numerous holes and gaps in the disintegrating system to further their own well being."[38] Moreover, by the late 1970s, the once vibrant Brezhnev had morphed into a stroke-stricken old man whose actions and utterances became the target of vicious new jokes.

In the meantime, the Brezhnev leadership appealed to Soviet patriotism and enhanced its indoctrination efforts to gain support from the country's young and impressionable generation that had not known terror, war, or deprivation first-hand. Besides exposing the country's youth to official organizations such as the Komsomol during the 1960s, the government, aware of the impact of social change and politics, stepped up the study of Marxism-Leninism, party history, and Soviet law while the Sputnik generation attended school. Yet informal learning at home and outside school often limited the effectiveness of these measures: a good number of the thirty people I interviewed noted that, already as young children, they knew that some topics could not be discussed openly. Moreover, the repercussions of the thaw in cultural life, the release of Gulag prisoners, and the publication in 1962 of Aleksandr Solzhenitsyn's novella about the labor camps, *One Day in the Life of Ivan Denisovich*, reminded people of the dark chapters in the Soviet past and the

37. George W. Breslauer, *Gorbachev and Yeltsin as Leaders* (New York: Cambridge University Press, 2002), 7.

38. Kozlov, *Mass Uprisings*, 314.

shortcomings of the Soviet present. So did foreign radio broadcasts. The BBC began broadcasting to the Soviet Union in 1946; the Voice of America began the next year and Radio Liberty in 1954. Soon thirty nations beamed alternative radio signals at the Soviet population.[39] Although difficult to catch owing to the state's attempts to jam their reception, they became accessible to those who acquired a VEF, a popular and portable multiband receiver previously known as the Spidola, produced in Soviet Latvia. Members of the Class of '67 who listened to foreign broadcasts did so because of their fascination with Western music, or because it gave them something to boast about among their peers, confirming sociologist Vladimir Shlapentokh's observation that access did not necessarily change people's views, which remained "impervious to new information which was deeply at odds with official information."[40] But the state frowned upon, and sometimes even persecuted, those who listened to "the paid instrument and servant of Wall Street" and other Western broadcasts, revealing the growing gulf between the regime and many of its citizens, who saw nothing subversive about Voice of America, the BBC, and/or German Wave, the three broadcasts to which most of the Saratovites recalled listening.

Getting into college represented the next major milestone for the Sputnik generation. All but a few of School No. 42's class of '67 enrolled somewhere that fall, belonging to the roughly 12 million young specialists who would graduate from college and enter the workforce between 1965 and 1982.[41] Paralleling national trends, the most popular majors among them were physics, medicine, English, and technical subjects. A gold medalist from the class was admitted to Moscow State University, the country's premier institution, to study biology. The rest went to Saratov University, the Saratov Medical Institute, the Saratov Polytechnic Institute, the Saratov Pedagogical Institute, or the Saratov Law Academy. At the time the local university did not offer an undergraduate degree in English, so those who wished to continue their study of the language enrolled in the Pedagogical Institute. The few who had trouble with entrance

39. Liudmila Alekseeva, *U.S. Broadcasting to the Soviet Union* (New York: U.S. Helsinki Watch Committee, 1986), 8.

40. Vladimir Shlapentokh, *A Normal Totalitarian Society: How the Soviet Union Functioned and How It Collapsed* (Armonk, N.Y.: M. E. Sharpe, 2001), 141.

41. David L. Ruffley, *Children of Victory: Young Specialists and the Evolution of Soviet Society* (Westport, Conn.: Praeger, 2003), 2.

exams signed up for the evening division of the Polytechnic Institute or elsewhere. Everyone I interviewed attended college. At this time about 25 percent of high school graduates from regular schools in the USSR enrolled in institutions of higher learning. Among one sampling of graduates of the country's 600–700 specialized schools, the figure rose to 65.7 percent.[42] The results from Saratov therefore underscore the selectivity and remarkable academic success of School No. 42 and its graduates.

A few interviewees remembered responding critically to the Soviet Union's invasion of Czechoslovakia in August 1968, which took place at the end of their first year of college, but the overwhelming majority of the thirty people I interviewed admitted that they accepted the government's official representation of the event. This is not surprising: the Sputnik generation received a heavy dose of ideology in college, where they were required to complete courses in political economy, dialectical and historical materialism, the history of the Communist Party of the Soviet Union (CPSU), and the fundamentals of scientific communism.[43] Moreover, as part of the general process of socialization, they took part in "voluntary" work brigades sent to collective farms and construction sites during the summer to help bring in the harvest or to build something. During their university years the government, still reeling from what it saw as a dangerous reform movement that had prompted the Soviet invasion of Czechoslovakia, cracked down on individuals and informal groups opposed to official policies. Not confined to the country's twin capitals of Moscow and Leningrad, the so-called dissident movement manifested itself in Saratov, but admittedly to a lesser degree; however, some of the interviewees had not heard of the arrest in 1971 of a group of students at Saratov University who had formed an independent Marxist reading group, one of the best-known chapters in the local dissident movement. To be sure, such dangerous activities attracted few followers. Young people focused on getting an education, having fun, falling in love, establishing careers, and other everyday concerns. All but one of the thirty people with whom I met found spouses during their university years or

---

42. John Dunstan, *Paths to Excellence and the Soviet School* (Rochester, Great Britain: NFER Publishing Co., 1977), 101.

43. More than half of those who taught these courses at Saratov University in 1974 had no special training in the subject. See Mervyn Matthews, *Education in the Soviet Union: Policies and Institutions since Stalin* (London: George Allen and Unwin, 1982), 125.

shortly thereafter. Many of them divorced, a procedure made easier as the result of a 1966 law. Graduating from college in 1971 or 1972 (depending upon where they enrolled), some members of the Sputnik generation went on for graduate degrees. Those who did not pursue advanced degrees repaid the government for the education it provided by spending two years working where the state needed them. Several served in the army. Quite a few of those whose jobs did not require security clearances joined the one million Soviet citizens a year who traveled as tourists to Eastern Europe in the 1970s.[44] Six of the thirty people I interviewed joined the Communist Party, but two of them did so during the Gorbachev era once reform had already begun. In each case, the parents of those who became party members also belonged to the CPSU. Significantly, most of the interviewees remembered being critical of the Soviet Union's invasion of Afghanistan at the end of 1979, suggesting a tectonic shift in attitudes since the USSR crushed the reform movement in Czechoslovakia in 1968.

The glasnost revelations and economic chaos accompanying Gorbachev's perestroika and the subsequent collapse of the Soviet Union in 1991 created unprecedented challenges for members of the Sputnik generation, now in their forties. Catastrophic economic conditions through the late 1990s compelled many of them to change jobs, even careers, or take on additional work to make ends meet. These wrenching circumstances strained family relations, especially as the Baby Boomers had to deal with aging parents and with helping their own children get established against a backdrop of corruption, political instability, and the psychological impact of the country's breakup and loss of superpower status. But the new environment also provided opportunities, especially after the economy began to rebound at the end of the 1990s, as the Sputnik generation turned fifty. Some traveled abroad for the first time. Others took a spiritual journey. Roughly as many who had joined the Communist Party earlier now emigrated, either by marrying foreign men or by taking advantage of their Jewish ancestry.

Statistically speaking, members of the Sputnik generation were about two-thirds of the way into their life stories when I interviewed them. What are we to make of their lives so far? Here, as well as

---

44. This figure comes from Stephen Kotkin, *Armageddon Averted: The Soviet Collapse, 1970–2000* (New York: Oxford University Press, 2001), 40.

in the introductory remarks to each interview, I have avoided suggesting what conclusions should be drawn from these narratives,
because that would limit what readers might otherwise see. For
this reason, I return to the wide-ranging questions I posed earlier
in this introduction to help readers unpack the meaning of the life
stories.

- First, who and what shaped my informants' worldviews while
  they were growing up? (How do they evaluate their school experience and childhood as part of Russia's Sputnik generation?
  How "free" were they coming of age in the Soviet Union?)
- Second, what do the Soviet Baby Boomers' life stories tell us
  about what constituted the "Soviet dream" of the Sputnik generation, and ultimately about the relationship between the expansion of the private sphere after 1953, the delegitimization of
  ideology, and the fate of the Soviet Union? (What role did ideology play in their formative years and beyond? What generalizations can be made about the differences between the interviews
  of men and women?[45] How does each gender characterize the
  other? What generalizations can be made about marriage as an
  institution, about divorce rates, and about Soviet/Russian family
  life based on these interviews? How did nationality affect some
  of the interviewees? Why did or didn't the interviewees join the
  Communist Party?)
- Third, what do we learn from the interviews about daily life in
  a "closed" provincial city? (How important was English in determining the life choices members of the Sputnik generation
  made or in shaping their attitudes or in facilitating their careers?
  How did they relate to the outside world, back then and now?
  Did they fear nuclear war?)
- Fourth, how have my informants negotiated the challenging
  transition to a post-Soviet Russia following the collapse of communism in 1991? (How do members of the Sputnik generation
  account for perestroika? How have their lives changed since?
  How do the interviewees assess Gorbachev, Yeltsin, and Putin,
  and why?)

---

45. It has been argued by psychologist Carol Gilligan, among others, that the interviews of men and women differ in that men usually have more to say about public events
and about what they do, while women discuss issues reflecting who they are. Women
operate from a social context—most often the family—while men are more autonomous.
See Carol Gilligan, *In a Different Voice: Psychological Theory and Women's Development* (Cambridge: Harvard University Press, 1982).

• Fifth, how have their lived experiences both reproduced and transformed Soviet and Russian society after 1953? In other words, how do their personal stories help us comprehend cultural transmission across generations? (How do the accounts differ and what do they have in common? What is unique about each interviewee? How does each present him/herself? What silences are noticeable in the interviews? How do people talk about the past and their role in it? How do they describe their parents' generation, or that of their children? What issues appear to be most important to them? What positive things do they have to say about the Soviet experiment? Does anything seem Soviet or Marxist about their thinking today? How does the Soviet experience constrain and enable post-1991 efforts to establish a democratic political system and a market economy, and to negotiate a new set of relations with the rest of the world?)

≋✿

A note is in order about usage. To make the interviews more accessible, I have dropped the soft and hard signs from Russian geographic terms and surnames because they do not help the uninitiated to negotiate the pronunciation of these words. However, I have applied the Library of Congress transliteration system elsewhere.

1. "Sasha the Muscovite" | Aleksandr Aleksandrovich Konstantinov

June 19, 2002, Moscow

It's hard to be on time in Russia, even for someone like me who habitually shows up early. But on this occasion the fault was all mine; I erred in deciding to walk from the red line's University metro stop in southwestern Moscow to campus so that I could embrace my nostalgia. Moscow University, after all, had been my home during the 1974–75 academic year, and once again for the first half of 1986. Reminiscing as I made my way toward the facility's main building, one of the city's "wedding cake" skyscrapers built in Stalinist Gothic style familiar to most readers, I realized that, over the years, I had not paid attention to the layout of the university's science complex. Asking for directions eventually helped me locate the building I needed to find, but only after I had been given wrong information by eager, though misinformed, passers-by. In short, I violated a basic rule of practicing oral history: I arrived late.

I regretted this even more because I desperately wanted to make a positive impression on my would-be informant. There was something about how I located him, about his instant appreciation of what I sought to accomplish, and about our flurry of e-mail exchanges in the preceding weeks that heightened my expectations. I had begun working on this project the previous summer, when I interviewed two members of the class of '67 living in Saratov. One of them intimated that Aleksandr Aleksandrovich Konstantinov had left Saratov to attend Moscow University and that he "taught somewhere in Moscow." My subsequent sleuthing over the Internet back home in Chapel Hill, N.C., located an A. A. Konstantinov at Moscow University, but identified him as director of the university's orchestra, and not as some variety of biologist, which I expected him to be. It was June 6, 2002. I clicked on the link. Seconds later it opened to reveal a photo of a man sporting a tuxedo, with long salt-and-pepper hair pulled back into a ponytail. Hastily composing a message to him in Russian, I confused the number of the Saratov school with another in Moscow (why don't they name schools in Russia after people?): "Please excuse me for disturbing you. I'm looking for A. A. Konstantinov who graduated from School No. 20 in Saratov in 1967. Are you he?" A reply came within a few hours: "Thank you, I, A. A. Konstantinov (Aleksandr Aleksandrovich), indeed graduated from high school in Saratov in 1967, but from School No. 42, the so-called English school. I would be most pleased if I can be of service or of interest to you, and I'm obviously very curious to know what's up. All the best, Sasha Konstantinov." In the coming days we actively corresponded via e-mail. Since I planned to arrive in Moscow in mid-June when he was scheduled to leave for a conference in Australia and New Zealand, he urged me to phone him as soon as I got settled.

Aleksandr Aleksandrovich pretended not to notice that I showed up late to his research laboratory on the evening of June 19, 2002. Dressed in cut-offs (until recently it was not culturally acceptable for Russian men to wear shorts), a T-shirt, sandals, and the same long hair I had seen in his picture on the Internet, he looked like he belonged more in Madison or Berkeley than in Moscow. Soon we were comfortably ensconced with mugs of green tea in his director's empty office. I set up my Marantz cassette recorder and began firing away with questions.

I wasn't sure whether Aleksandr Aleksandrovich's concise yet thoughtful answers betrayed his training as a research scientist or my ineptness as an interviewer. As it turned out, the interview represented but the first stage in an on-going dialogue. After the interview he reflected further on his responses via e-mail, and also responded to follow-up queries. I incorporated this additional information into the text of the conversation that follows.

As an enthusiastic proponent of my project, Aleksandr Aleksandrovich helped me locate former classmates, scanned his school-days photograph collection for me, and read my translation of his interview. We kept in touch through e-mail and telephone conversations and met again in Moscow in June 2004, and in Saratov a few weeks later. As a result, I learned a great deal more about him. He travels extensively. He meditates. He prefers red wine. He reads Proust while vacationing. He's a film buff. He follows U.S. politics. In many respects his lifestyle and tastes do not seem that far removed from my own (although I read lowbrow fiction when on vacation), yet they differ from those of some of his classmates. Even as a child growing up in Saratov, he was called "Sasha the Muscovite," because he came from the capital and was "different." However, "Sasha" Konstantinov fulfilled his classmates' every expectation: one of two gold medalists to graduate from School No. 42 in 1967, he went on to pursue a brilliant academic career as a research scientist at Russia's premier university. "He was in a league of his own," "He knew as much as some of the teachers," "We all knew he'd end up at Moscow University," "He was an accomplished violinist and could have gone on to make a name for himself in music"—these are some of the things his classmates confided in me. His favorite teacher, Klara Eduardovna Starshova, confirmed that he was special. She illustrated this by recalling a probing observation young Sasha had made that forced her to confront one of her own deepest convictions. When she remarked to him that "the USSR doesn't want war," he replied, "It actually needs conflict to keep the system going."

How did Aleksandr Aleksandrovich's family shape who he is? How similar was it to the families of his classmates? How does he assess his student years at Moscow University? Are there questions that he appears hesitant to answer? Do his attitudes differ from those of his classmates? Although he never felt completely at home in Moscow, despite the fact that the city had done so much to determine his way of life, what is "Muscovite" about him?

My parents are Natalia Sergeevna Konstantinova, maiden name Iurkevich, born in 1919, and Aleksandr Stepanovich Konstantinov, born in 1917. They both graduated from Moscow University, where they met. My mother's first husband was a friend and classmate of my father's. They all hung out together. Then the war began and Oleg disappeared without a trace. His name was Oleg Lipin, and he evidently got killed. After the war my mother married my father, Aleksandr Stepanovich Konstantinov. I was born in 1949. At first we lived in Moscow. My father, who had been taken prisoner dur-

Aleksandr Aleksandrovich Konstantinov, July 2004.

ing the war, underwent some sort of verification as a result of which he managed to avoid being sent to the labor camps.[1] However, he wasn't allowed to remain in Moscow. He told me he was given a choice: move to Baku, Saratov, or some other town—I don't remember which—and he chose Saratov. He's a hydrobiologist and something of an ichthyologist. There's a fishing industry institute in Saratov and he went to work there,[2] and later became a professor and chair of the biology department at the Saratov Medical Institute. I moved to Saratov when I was three or four years old.

Were your parents Communist Party members?

No, never.

What about religion?

No, neither of them was religious. I'm not sure, but perhaps Mother was baptized. However, I wasn't.

Tell me a bit about your friends and about your childhood interests.

---

1. During the Second World War, Soviet citizens taken prisoner of war were considered traitors. The government sent many Soviet POWs who later returned to the USSR to labor camps in the Gulag.

2. The All Union Research Institute of the Fish Industry.

I had some childhood friends back in Moscow when I was very young. We grew up together on Pokrovka Street, but afterward I maintained little contact with them. My closest friends were those I made in school. They're perhaps closer than those I made at the university. We had a very good class, and as a result those with whom I attended school back then became my good friends such as Kolia Khabarov and Sasha Virich.[3]

How would you describe your childhood?

You know, I was something of a prodigy. I began to read at an early age, at four, and began to play the violin when I was five. I've always loved to learn, and therefore I attended both school and a special music school with great pleasure. To a certain degree it was a happy period in my life, because I found school interesting. I always made friends with the older boys who lived on my street. I lived in several places in Saratov, in rowdy enough neighborhoods, but I was on good terms with everyone, except for the fact that the kids were usually older than me, and because of that sometimes made fun of me, but in a friendly way.

What year did you begin attending School No. 42?

At first I began school somewhere else, School No. 9, located then on Solianaia Street. When I finished second grade it was announced that School No. 42 would begin admitting third graders. The first class enrolled there the year before and was called the A group, and our group, the B group, was enrolled in the third grade. Apparently, my parents heard about this and insofar as I was an A student I had a good chance of getting admitted. I went for some sort of interview and everything went well, except for the fact that I mispronounced the letter "sh." They told me that they might let me in if I was able to correct this. I went to a speech therapist and repeated "sh-shilly-shally and sh-shiney shoes" [laughing]. And it turned out that they admitted me that fall. Since I was born in '49, and started school when I was eight years old, this would have been back in 1957.

Tell me about your favorite teachers, your favorite subjects, your friends, and what you did in your free time.

In general the teachers were quite good at the school, and I, of course, had my favorites. For the first two years we had a homeroom

---

3. Nikolai Aleksandrovich Khabarov and Aleksandr Grigorievich Virich live in Saratov today. I located and interviewed both.

teacher, Aleksandra Sergeevna, a pleasant woman, whose surname I no longer remember. Beginning in fifth grade we had different teachers for each subject, and, again, I had my favorites. There was Klara Eduardovna Starshova, teacher of English, who was a real friend to our group. We had a good teacher for history, Albina Ivanovna, who at one point was supposed to become principal, but for some reason it didn't work out. We had a good teacher for chemistry, Rosa Vasilievna. We had good teachers for mathematics, biology, and physics. Actually, all the teachers were excellent. Except for a few individuals, they were all interesting. For a time, we had a great geography teacher, who temporarily replaced our regular teacher, who was quite boring.

How politicized was the instruction?

It's hard to say. It seems to me that in comparison with other schools, it was far less politicized. That is, it all depended upon the teacher. Our teachers for English and for chemistry, for instance, were so reasonable that there was no politicization. Even the historian there was so trusted that . . . However, when a new teacher of history showed up in the ninth grade she proved to be Communist to the core. She wasn't mean, but it was awful, and the contrast was so obvious. The other teachers were intelligent.

How important is it that you learned English as a child?

You know, it's hard to overemphasize its importance. The situation was like this. My parents held different views when it came time to discuss what I should study. My father said that I needed to study all sorts of serious subjects, whereas my mother was more practical. She said that I absolutely had to learn English well. It turned out to be very important. Although I didn't realize this at the time, it played a determining role in my entire future. So, they sent me to the English school. I believe that, to a significant degree, I was able to work independently as a scientist because I know the language fluently. I could get by without supervisors. It made it simpler for me to communicate with colleagues and to write articles in English for international journals, and this took me to an altogether different level.

What changes took place in the school during the years you attended it?

I didn't notice any especially important changes.

To what extent did your friends affect you while you grew up? Can you give me some concrete examples?

That's hard for me to say. If I were going to be altogether open with you, I'd have to say that I felt that I influenced them more than

May Day celebration circa 1965. Konstantinov is carrying the banner.
He recalls being scolded afterward for wearing tight-fitting jeans.
Courtesy A. A. Konstantinov.

they did me. I was something of a leader in class. I saw that there
were all sorts of people around us and I knew who was good and
who was bad. There were some kids who were patently bad, and I
realized this.

*How would you describe the school, its pupils, their class and national
makeup?*

You know, regarding nationality, astonishingly enough, I made
it to the university before I realized that there was such a thing as
antisemitism. Despite the fact that it existed, we somehow didn't
notice it. This essentially was the only problem regarding nationality that there was. True, the Tatars also existed as a somewhat aloof
community, but at the time we generally didn't know this.[4] As far
as I can tell now, the company we kept at home was mostly Jewish. My father worked at the Medical Institute, and many of our

---

4. The Tatars form the second largest nationality in Russia today and one of the
largest in the former USSR. Their language belongs to the Turkic family, and most Tatars
are Sunni Muslims. Many live in Tatarstan, with its capital up the Volga River in Kazan,
a constituent republic of the Russian Federation, or in neighboring provinces such as
Saratov.

acquaintances were professors from there. Apparently they were all Jews. But I understood this only much later. They were all nice, likeable people. On the other hand, on the street kids called sparrows "Yids." The word sparrow was not in vogue, but I didn't know what the word "Yid" meant. This was normal, since everyone spoke that way. In my view, nationality problems didn't concern people at all. As regards class composition, we had two parallel groups that graduated in 1967. They represent a rather amusing case, because, well, again, perhaps my recollections are incorrect, but the parallel A group was formed earlier. The school was an elite one, and the A group was made up not so much of people with connections as of people of privilege, among whom were several children of party officials. For instance, if I'm not mistaken, the class included the daughters of the two party secretaries, one of the city committee, the other of the oblast committee. They formed a sort of nucleus around which an elite group was fashioned. The group also included the children of trade officials. When they selected our group, we, too, came from the privileged stratum, but we were not of their ilk. Our group included my friend Sasha Virich, who was the son of the main architect in town. Kolia Khabarov was the son of an artist at the opera theater. There were quite a few children of university professors. Our class came more from the intelligentsia and the other one more from the political elite. But some apparently came from the most needy families too.

Did they end up in the school by chance?

You know, I can't say for sure. The school was a municipal one, School No. 42. Therefore it's hard for me to say. But there clearly were a few kids from underprivileged families who somehow got admitted, perhaps through acquaintances. There also were children of the state security organs, two or three to be sure, whose parents were in the KGB as far as I recall. You know, though, no one was interested in such things. However, the fact that there were children of the oblast party elite in the A group somehow made itself felt.

What else can you tell me about groups A and B or about school life in general?

Well, another difference between the A and B groups concerned what we today call gender relations. As far as I know, up until the tenth grade, relations between boys and girls in our group were quite innocent, with perhaps one exception. But if we are to go by what people said back then, a select group of "golden youth" in the A group beginning in the seventh or eighth grade began to throw parties with alcohol and perhaps even sex. I also forgot to tell you that one characteristic feature of our and other Saratov schools at the time was what we might call their deep criminalization. What I mean by this is that some of the boys were connected to city gangs, sort of like *West Side Story.* Your prestige at school—in the restrooms where the pupils smoked—was dependent on who your "protectors" were. I was protected since the "king" of the riverbank neighborhood nicknamed the "Italian" lived in our building and was friendly to me. This gang world was a fact of life for us boys. Relations were never determined one on one, but during a conflict each person involved called upon his lads for support. Sometimes a conversation was enough to settle things. At school Matveev, who was two or three years older than me, was "king." Everyone feared him because of his criminal ties. They began to respect me in school after he told one of the older boys in the bathroom not to touch Konstantinov because "the Italian's behind him."

This sounds like my high school on Chicago's South Side! Can you tell me a bit about what you did in your free time?

There were all sorts of hobby groups that were an important part of our personal development. For example, for many years I belonged to the chess section and the ballroom dancing group at the Pioneer Palace. Several of us from school went there. I also belonged to a photography hobby group at school. There was something specifically "Soviet"—in the positive sense of the term—about these activities: the leader of each hobby group had authority and was trusted. There was one other wonderful thing. Each summer from the time we reached eighth grade, our school sponsored a summer camp on an island in the Volga. We lived there in tents for almost a month. I recall how delighted all of us were with the camp. It meant freedom for us, especially from our parents!

By the way, how did your parents react to the fact that they had to leave Moscow for Saratov and how did their reaction affect you?

I think their reaction was appropriate. Generally, they raised us in a politically open atmosphere since childhood. I remember one of the first times we left for Saratov by train, shortly after Stalin died. I recall that I went out into the car and told everyone that they'd soon remove Stalin from the mausoleum. And my father, who had been the one who had told me that, grabbed my shoulder and said, "Hush." Thus, in a political sense, everything was clear.

As children, we're not terribly interested in politics, but your childhood corresponded with some momentous events in history such as the Twentieth

Summer camp on the Volga, approximately 1966. Konstantinov is on the right. *Courtesy A. A. Konstantinov.*

Party Congress in 1956 at which Khrushchev denounced the Stalin cult, the Cuban Missile Crisis, Khrushchev's ouster in 1964, the Siniavskii-Daniel trial,[5] and so on. Do you recall how your parents reacted to some of these events?

Yes, of course, I remember well. As for the Twentieth Party Congress, it was clear that Stalin was, one might say, a monster, and it was wonderful what Khrushchev did.

What about at school?

That was before I attended school. But in my opinion when we were in school there were no nostalgic memories of Stalin as there are now. Everyone knew that Stalin was God knows what and thank God that all of that had come to an end. I was in school during the

---

Cuban Missile Crisis. I remember it well. I didn't know about it, but on my way home from school the newspaper *Izvestiia* was posted somewhere on a fence. And it contained an article, "How *The Times* Got into a Fix." I remember that very well. There was a fake photograph in the [New York] *Times,* which allegedly depicted Soviet soldiers and bases in Cuba. That very same paper, that is, *Izvestiia,* the next day wrote about the "wise" decision to remove our rockets from Cuba. Everyone got a kick out of this. We didn't realize that we had been on the verge of war. I, for one, didn't know. But I remember the article in the paper. I also remember well, since I read it, an article that appeared about Siniavskii-Daniel, "Turncoats." My grandmother knew Siniavskii at one time when she taught literature and was close to literary circles. She told me what a wonderful man he was, and for this reason we had no doubts whatsoever at home about what had happened.

How did your parents react to Khrushchev's removal?

As far as I recall, Khrushchev's ouster most likely distressed us. As far as I recall, it was understood as some sort of reversion toward a tougher policy. Perhaps I'm wrong. My mother saw how Khrushchev abruptly left Pitsunda[6] for Moscow, for she had been vacationing there at the time. We all understood, of course, that Khrushchev was no saint. He was crude, and that episode with the artists[7] was simply [outrageous]. But, nonetheless, he was seen as someone who accomplished much. We didn't yet have a feel for the new people, for Brezhnev and the others.

Did the kids at school discuss politics? Or was it something that they avoided?

It was something that simply didn't interest us, except for anecdotes about Khrushchev. As a result, the only sort of conversation that there might have been would have poked fun at something that wasn't right.

What did you think about Lenin at the time?

Of course, it's hard for us now to recall what it was like back then, but it seems to me that when we attended school we mostly looked upon Lenin as a figure imposed on us from above. Besides this, many probably were under the impression that Lenin, unlike

---

6. Pitsunda, in the Soviet republic of Georgia, is where Khrushchev and other members of the leadership vacationed in government villas.

7. Konstantinov is referring to Khrushchev's tirade at an exhibit of avant-garde art that opened in November 1962 at the Manezh Exhibition Hall across from the Kremlin.

Stalin, was a good man, so to speak, who wanted the best. As was apparent, however, things didn't turn out or else he ran out of time. Well, things turned out, but not as expected. Of course, people nevertheless looked upon him with some skepticism because he was forced on us. Basically, they didn't think much about this. I got serious about Lenin only later when I began to read his writings at the university. It seemed to me that he was very smart and more sincere [than I expected]. And then I understood that he was less dreadful than Stalin.

What about the KGB? What did you think about them?

We knew that the KGB existed. This didn't concern us at all at school. In my opinion there were no special feelings toward them. However, during the Siniavskii-Daniel trial, we were already older then, their existence began to interest me. But as far as I recall it simply wasn't something that we thought about.

What were your attitudes back then toward the West?

Toward the West? That's really hard to recall. We formed our ideas of the West mostly from caricatures in newspapers. The American was always depicted as Uncle Sam, with a striped flag and with striped pants. Moreover, there was also the English lion. I don't recall how they depicted the French, but the three always were drawn together. Regarding what I really thought, I probably had some sort of prejudice. It's hard for me to recall. I probably believed that there were people there who, generally speaking, weren't interested in our country's well-being. After all, the pressure on us was strong. But it's hard for me to recall how it actually was. On the other hand, there was interest and curiosity. Mother attended the first American exhibition in Moscow.[8] Of course, it made a huge impression on her.

What did she say about it?

She had a lot to say about it, but that was a long time ago. The organization of scholarly research amazed her. From what I remember, she told us about the system of grants, about American kitchens,

---

8. In the summer of 1959 the United States opened an exhibit in Sokolniki Park, while the Soviet Union opened one in New York. In the American exhibit's seventy-eight-foot-high geodesic dome, a huge screen showed alluring slides of American life that conveyed a real sense of technological superiority, thereby undermining Soviet propaganda. At this exhibit, Vice President Richard M. Nixon and Khrushchev angrily debated the virtues of their respective countries. This episode is often called the "kitchen debate" because it took place against the backdrop of an American dream kitchen in a model ranch house.

American cars, and the general style—light-hearted, cheerful, open. That was so long ago that I of course don't recall the details. But on the whole, insofar as our family was, as they said back then, intellectual, our attitude toward the West was [an open one].

What did your mother do?

My mother also graduated from the biology department here at Moscow University. My father settled down into a job in Saratov through a fellow biologist. My mother first went to work there, I think, as a lab assistant, then as an associate, and later in the Department of Virology at "Microbe," a large anti-cholera institute, the leading one in the USSR. She settled down there, and managed the Department of Virology or something of that sort. By the way, it would have been impossible to have had in Moscow or Leningrad an institute dealing with such dangerous infectious diseases.

Aleksandr Aleksandrovich, I want to understand what shaped the formation of your worldview at that time. What else do I need to ask you in order to understand this?

First of all, I think that probably more than anything else the formation of my worldview had lots to do with my parents. Then I'd say my grandmother, who was also a very interesting person. She lived in Moscow. My mother, after all, was a Muscovite. My grandmother taught literature. First in Riazan,[9] then in Moscow. At one time she worked with Krupskaia.[10] She was a graduate of the philosophy department. She was an SR.[11] There's a real story there. By the way, my great-grandfather, her father, was fairly well known as the person who wrote Vladimir Ilich Lenin's favorite song, "Exhausted by the Hard Bondage." His name was Grigorii Aleksandrovich Machtet. He was a fairly well-known writer, a friend of Korolenko.[12] Secondly, apart from my grandmother, I also had a nanny who lived in our home and who, to a significant degree, was like a mother to me. Consequently, association with her played a big

---

9. A Russian province and provincial town in central Russia on the Oka River southeast of Moscow.

10. Revolutionary and educator Nadezhda Konstantinovna Krupskaia (1869–1939) was married to Vladimir Ilich Lenin.

11. The Socialist Revolutionary (SR) Party was Russia's most popular political party during the Revolution of 1917. Its populist program held that the peasants, industrial workers, and the radical intelligentsia would make revolution in Russia.

12. Vladimir Galaktionovich Korolenko (1853–1921) was an author of short stories and a political activist. He denounced the Red Terror associated with the Bolsheviks during the Russian Civil War.

role in my life. And, thirdly, I'd have to mention reading. I began reading when I was four years old, and I read a lot. I think that also influenced me a great deal.

Please tell me more about your nanny.

On my mother's side of the family our relatives came from Riazan. They were members of the gentry and, accordingly, there were country people who, as it were, came from their former estates or villages. And my nanny, as far as I remember, was the daughter of Auntie Fenia, whom I later visited in the village of Dediukhino, some ten miles from Riazan. She was simply taken into the home and hired by her former Riazan masters. I don't think she was any more than eighteen years old when she showed up at our place. Since then she's lived many, many years in Moscow, then in Saratov, and now lives once again in the Riazan countryside.

Did your classmates have nannies, too?

I don't think so. It was pretty rare. She was called a "maid." Few had them. It wasn't accepted. But it was more common in Moscow.

How did she influence you?

If we look upon this as a myth, then she influenced me like Arina Rodionovna influenced Pushkin.[13] Such is popular belief. Of course, the things she told me greatly differed from what my parents had to say. She had an altogether different view of things, a different perspective. Moreover, she was critical of my parents. Therefore, I saw some things in them from her point of view, for instance, the oppression of one individual by another. I saw this in how my parents treated her. It was not nice, and I always defended her, of course. It was a form of obvious social inequality. It's an important, interesting circumstance.

Was she religious?

Although she wasn't really religious, she went to church and had Easter cakes consecrated. It was more of a superstition, but she had respect for the church.

I understand. But didn't she have you baptized?

No, not as far as I know.

How did you understand the fact that Saratov was a closed city?

---

13. Aleksander Sergeevich Pushkin (1799–1837) is considered Russia's greatest poet. His nanny, Arina Rodionovna, is credited with nurturing him emotionally and with entertaining him with folktales and gossip.

You know, there was an expression that Saratov was a closed city, but we didn't fully understand what that actually meant.

When did you first meet foreigners?

Foreigners? I can't remember if I met any in Saratov. It was more likely later, most likely at the university.

How would you characterize your generation? How does it differ from that of your parents and from that of your children?

I say this with the benefit of hindsight, but it seems to me that we had less built-in fear. As compared to 1937, which for them was drenched in blood.[14] In spite of all that we endured, we didn't experience that. We didn't know real repression. We knew that as punishment for hooliganism we could get into trouble, but we didn't see this as something that was systemic, whereas our parents had every reason to think otherwise. And generally there also was great openness.

Did you sense Western influence in your lives at that time, say in the realm of music, fashion, literature, and/or religion?

Evidently, not much. Of course, Western music interested us, but there practically wasn't much of it, because the Beatles, who represented a revolution in music, hadn't yet reached us while we were in school. It was only at the university that I came into contact with them, and by then the fad had already faded a bit. There were some random tapes of rock music or something of that sort. But this forbidden, well-off, interesting life in the West attracted us.

Did television influence you?

We didn't have a television for a long time.

What about travel?

There wasn't that much of it. I studied a great deal and also studied music. That, too, was very important for me. And I traveled during the summer. Mother took us to the same place in the south for many consecutive years. But there were no major trips.

You graduated in 1967 and then enrolled at Moscow University?

Yes.

Did you get married?

Yes. My wife was Tania Okuneva. We went to school together and were in the same class. She enrolled later, I think in the sixth grade, when she transferred there. We essentially met at school and understood we loved each other as we were about to graduate. We

---

14. The height of what is known as Stalin's Great Terror, or purge.

Konstantinov dancing the frowned-upon "Twist" with his future wife, Tatiana Okuneva, in 1966, in a school in Briansk oblast. They traveled to the district along with several others from School No. 42 to trace the footsteps of local partisans during World War II. *Courtesy A. A. Konstantinov.*

got married toward the end of my university years. We had two children, but got divorced ten years ago. She now lives in the United States. She was, I can now say, one of the two or three finest human beings that I have had the privilege to know. I was attracted to her in the first place because she's an extremely nice person. She's kind, responsive, full of energy, and attentive, an altogether wonderful person.

Do your children live in Moscow?

No, my son, he's twenty-four, is with her in America. My daughter is older, around thirty, and she's in Germany. She went there to study. She's a flutist, but I don't think she's a flutist anymore. I think she received German citizenship and spends most of her time there, but she visits occasionally.

How was your former wife able to leave?

She left with her husband, who also worked here.

What did your wife do?

She graduated from the philology department at the Saratov

Pedagogical Institute with a specialty in teaching English, mostly to children. After our move to Moscow, she gave private English lessons to preschoolers and also worked in our institute as a secretary to our director, Academician Skulachev. I arranged for her to work here back then.

I have another question that perhaps is a bit harder to answer. What shaped the formation of your self-identity?

Reading above all. Yes, reading. Among the most serious things, of course, there was Dostoevsky, it all began with him. Dostoevsky. Tolstoy. Sartre when I was at the university. And later there were others.

Can you give me some examples of how these writers affected you?

That's a really tough question. It's hard to provide such examples, but as a child I developed a real complex. I got the message in dealing with my nanny that I was selfish and mean. Moreover, my father was rather rigid. I tried to suppress these character traits, but apparently without success [laughing]. However, I at least always tried to be attentive toward people who were more spontaneous, and I thought that they possessed some sort of internal truth that I lacked. I was driven by the mind and they were driven by the soul, by the heart. For example, my wife, Tania, was very loving, and I always tried not so much to imitate her, as to be more like her. In order to understand who you are it's essential to know how the world is ordered, and you do this through reading.

You ended up in Moscow in 1967, and in 1968 the invasion of Czechoslovakia took place. What was the reaction among your fellow students and acquaintances?

All my friends, of course, were outraged. That was the case. My cousin, Sergei, we learned, attended a meeting at his institute at which a resolution was carried to the effect that they supported the invasion of Czechoslovakia. "Does everyone agree? Okay, I see everyone agrees." But Sergei raised his hand and said, "I'm sorry, but I disagree." Afterward, they, true, didn't expel him from the institute, but for a long time he held the lowest jobs. Moreover, I learned that several people demonstrated on Red Square. Later I met a few of them. Of course, we listened to the radio about what was happening.

When did you begin to listen to foreign broadcasts?

When radio receivers became available. You needed a good receiver such as a Spidola,[15] and there weren't many. But we listened in the dormitories.

Was that widespread or just among your friends?

That was determined once again by what kind of radio you had. Some had the money to buy good ones.

Did it seem to you that the students who studied the natural sciences were more politically aware than their counterparts in the humanities or is it hard to say?

It's hard to say. We had little contact with people in the humanities, although we were of the opinion that people in the natural sciences had a more sober view of things and were more politically aware.

What about samizdat *or other dissident literature?[16] Did you read any and, if so, when?*

My mother had a typewritten text of Gumilev and some other banned writers.[17] Regarding political *samizdat,* I date my encounter with it to my Moscow University days. I might be wrong about the chronology, but my grandmother gave me to read a typed version of Grigorii Pomerants;[18] however, that was during one of my visits to Moscow during my late school years in Saratov. Saratov was sort of desolate in this regard, but not Moscow. When I was a second or third-year student at Moscow University Tania Lavut, now in the U.S., joined our circle. Her father, Aleksandr Pavlovich Lavut,[19] an altogether wonderful man, was and remains a well-known dissident. Therefore we read just about everything. I remember one time when they arrested him and searched his place. For a long time I held on to a briefcase with Aleksandr Solzhenitsyn's *Gulag Archipelago* and many other dissident works.

---

15. Later known as the VEF, the Spidola multiband receiver was made in Latvia and could be used to listen to foreign radio broadcasts.

16. *Samizdat,* translated as "self-publishing," refers to typed, mimeographed, and even handwritten manuscripts that circulated clandestinely in the Soviet Union at this time.

17. Lev Nikolaevich Gumilev (1886–1921) was a major poet of Russia's Silver Age and husband of poet Anna Akhmatova. The Bolsheviks executed him during the Civil War and banned his writings.

18. A Soviet dissident who authored philosophical essays.

19. Lavut was a member of the first human rights association, which appeared in 1969, the Initiative Group for the Defense of Human Rights. For many years Lavut helped the Crimean Tatars in their struggle to return to their homeland (they were one of the "punished peoples" forcibly exiled during the Second World War).

Did your attitudes toward the West change as an adult?

Well, I learned a great deal more about the West as an adult. It wasn't so much a matter of my attitudes changing as it was of my attitudes forming, I would say.

What were your attitudes toward Eastern Europe back then? Did you get to travel there? Take part in a student work brigade?

Yes, the first time I went abroad I was in East Germany, after my sophomore year at the university. I was part of the biology department's agitation brigade,[20] which meant that I played music there. We were rewarded for our good schoolwork, for our successful presentations, with a month-long trip to the GDR.[21] It was very interesting to travel there. Afterward I was in the GDR several more times. I also traveled to Poland before I visited the West. Everything was far more serious in the GDR than it was back home. We did everything with humor and they were so serious about things. For instance, we visited different cities when we were in Germany. In one of them our group leader was an energetic German with blond hair, your stereotypical German. We noticed some train cars that had "Reichsbahn" [Imperial Railroad] written on them. We were surprised and asked him "How can this be? This is a socialist country, yet you have 'Reichsbahn' written on your train cars." He replied, "I don't know. I think that we Germans don't understand such things" [Konstantinov imitates a German accent]. As a result, we realized that people there were far more "in the dark" than we were. It was just the opposite in Poland. Poland was a free country. The people had a sense of humor and one that was uniquely Polish.

What about China? What were your attitudes toward it? Both during and after the "great friendship?"

You know, the "great friendship" was like a stock phrase. Then there were the incidents over Damansky Island and the others.[22] Yet this was so far away that the attitude of most, up until now, is slightly, well, not exactly racist, but they think the Chinese are funny. This attitude remains unspoken, but back then it definitely existed.

---

20. The oldest one of its kind in the country, the biology department's agitation brigade did not involve itself in propaganda work, but represented an elite group of student amateur performers. During winter and summer vacations, groups of fifteen to twenty-five students gave concerts, often in far-flung regions of the country.

21. GDR is the acronym for the German Democratic Republic, the official name of the East German state.

22. In March 1969 armed confrontations took place with China on Damansky (Chenpao) Island, located in the Ussuri River.

What about Cuba?

About Cuba, well, we knew that Cuba existed, that there was a charming man there, Fidel Castro, with a beard, who was able to speak for six hours without a break. Initially people felt that the Cubans were a heroic people, yet not for long. I don't recall if that was while I was in school or later. But there wasn't any kind of special feelings about the place.

After you graduated in 1972 did you immediately enroll in graduate school at Moscow University?

Yes.

When did you first come into contact with foreigners at work?

Contacts began rather early, since all the scholarly literature with which we deal is in English. If I'm not mistaken, a congress of biophysicists took place here in 1972, I forget which one, but there were many foreigners with whom we came into contact. Perhaps even before then. No, before then there weren't any contacts. Probably the year I wrote my senior thesis. When was that? That was in 1972. That's when I had my first contacts. And afterward there have been so many.

Were these early contacts superficial ones, or . . .

Yes, superficial ones. Generally speaking, contacts with foreigners began earlier, when I lived in the dormitory. There were some foreigners who studied with us, but they were mostly from somewhere in Africa. There were some interesting people in the dormitories with whom we became acquainted. There was Mark Brayne, an interesting guy, who taught me how to play the guitar. He later became a correspondent with Reuters and, if I'm not mistaken, he still works with them somewhere in Asia.[23] He was a very pleasant and interesting fellow. There also was a Frenchman, Bernard Kreise, who played a recorder in the Moscow University orchestra. He was a philologist who became a translator of Russian literature. But real professional contacts with foreigners started up after that first conference somewhere in Dresden, probably in 1976. It was there that I began to meet people whose articles I had read.

You found work at Moscow University afterward?

Yes, I wrote my honors thesis here, then enrolled in graduate school. As soon as I finished, they hired me, and then promoted me and promoted me. It all took place here.

---

23. For over thirty years Mark Brayne served as foreign correspondent for Reuters and the BBC World Service. More recently Mr. Brayne runs Dart Europe, a global resource for journalists who cover violence and trauma.

Marxist writings underscore the importance of economic development. How did you at that time understand your standard of living and the fact that many items were hard to obtain?

You mean living conditions? We didn't know who was responsible for this, but we understood that the world is ordered such that some are richer and some are poorer. Those who "had contacts," that is, sales clerks and party functionaries, well, that's a separate story. But the rest, those of us who worked, well some were simply luckier than others. The attitude about this was like in Dostoevsky, that there are people for whom life is a struggle, people who are humiliated and aggrieved. We felt sorry for them, helped them as we could, but we were all stuck in this together.

When you were in the GDR and Poland you undoubtedly noticed that the living standard there was higher.

Yes, but that was later, after we had left school.

But how did you understand the difference?

Even though they were in Eastern Europe, they nonetheless were "foreign countries." And all the "foreign countries" in the West were richer than we were. This was well known from conversations, therefore it didn't come as much of a surprise.

Did many of those who attended college with you go abroad? Was it only to Eastern Europe initially?

There were several of us who studied together as sophomores who went on the trip, four from my class, and we were all in the agitation brigade. Gradually others began to travel, and this was already nothing out of the ordinary by then. That is, the first trip was interesting, but later ones became routine.

Were you instructed how to behave before you traveled?

I can't recall exactly; however, there probably was some sort of briefing. We had a group leader. Of course, there was a briefing. And there even was an incident on one of our trips when they censured a girl in our group who, I believe, behaved too freely during the trip. But the first real briefing of this sort that I remember occurred when I traveled to Italy. I got called in. That was in 1980. It was my first trip to a capitalist country and, by the rules back then, we all got called in by the Central Committee of the CPSU [Communist Party of the Soviet Union]. I got summoned too. There was a Central Committee instructor named Chebotarev. I remember it well. I remember the long corridors, the rugs, the green walls, and the plain black letters in which their names were written. And I remember that man, Chebotarev, and the way he looked at me. We had to read some sort of instructions, after which I had a discussion with this instructor.

Were there any limitations on your association with people? Were some things forbidden?

I carefully avoided reading it, but I think there was the phrase that if, during a trip abroad, we ended up in a train compartment with a person of the opposite sex, we immediately had to register a protest. I remember this [laughing]. But I don't recall what else was written there. If we became suspicious about something we were supposed to inform our group leader. I even recall that on the second day of the trip to Italy—there was a conference there—I really wanted to sleep and missed the opening and showed up late. One of the members of our group insistently asked, "Why did you show up late? How did you get here? And why didn't you advise anyone about this?" I thus came to understand that he was put in our group to look after us. Others explained to me that there had to be two of them, one obvious, the other clandestine, one dumb one, as it were, and one smart one. This one was the obvious one. The stupid one collected information about everything, and the smart one only about what was important.

Did your travel companions try to guess who the secret informant was?

These weren't travel companions but members of a delegation. When we traveled to the GDR no one gave a second thought to such things. I didn't know and I don't think that anyone in our group did either. But the group leader this time kept an eye on us.

The fact that you lived in Saratov and then returned to Moscow gives you an interesting perspective from which to judge things. What did Muscovites think of people from the provinces and, when you lived in Saratov, what did Saratovites think of Muscovites? You're a Muscovite insofar as you were born here, but then returned to study already as someone from the provinces. How did you understand the difference?

First of all, when I moved to Saratov as a kid they called me "Sasha the Muscovite." That naturally didn't go unnoticed. People felt that Muscovites were privileged people. Muscovites, and those from Leningrad, too, were people from the two capitals, and people looked up to them. When I arrived at the university, about half of my class was from Moscow and the other half was made up of nonresidents. We lived in the dorms. Everyone in the dorms was a nonresident. The Muscovites kept a bit to themselves. They kept to their own company, and didn't mingle much with us. But I don't recall any patronizing behavior on their part. I don't believe that was an issue. They simply kept to themselves, that's all. They had gone to school together, or hung out for some other reason.

The fact that you settled down in Moscow, of course, played a role in your

*life. Can you imagine how your life might have turned out had you gradu-
ated from Saratov University and remained there to work?*

That's hard to say. When I went to school it was understood from
the start that I would finish school in Saratov but afterward enroll
somewhere in Moscow, either at the university or at the conservatory. Probably things would have turned out altogether differently
had I remained in Saratov. Of course, it's impossible to really carry
out scientific research there. Despite this, I consider Saratov my
hometown and I remain an outsider in Moscow. That is, I live here,
true, but the city remains "other." I probably would have ended up
teaching somewhere.

Did your parents remain in Saratov?

My father soon made it back to Moscow, too, when I was an
undergraduate, I think. He began working at the ichthyology department in the School of Biology at Moscow State University. It
was headed by his former dissertation advisor, an influential person
who could land him a job and arrange for a living permit for his
family members, including myself.[24] In fact, that's how I became a
Muscovite again. But he and my mother subsequently divorced, and
later, after I had already graduated from the university, we acquired
a cooperative apartment in Moscow.[25] Then my mother moved here
too.

*Aleksandr Aleksandrovich, during the Gorbachev era they called the
Brezhnev years a period of stagnation. What did you think of Brezhnev and
how would you evaluate his years in office? Did it seem to you that you were
living during a period of stagnation?*

No. Attitudes toward Brezhnev were somewhat positive. People
thought that he was a kind man. At one point it even seemed that
there were some reformers, such as Kosygin,[26] who was seen as a
progressive leader. There was the sense that nothing was changing—neither for the worse, nor for the better. And people didn't see
this as necessarily bad. There was considerable stability, and this,

---

24. The Soviet government had introduced the practice of living permits (*propiski*) in
order to control the flow of people to attractive urban centers such as Moscow. Without
a permit, one could not obtain an official job.

25. During this period Soviet citizens were allowed to purchase apartments in co-
operatively run buildings.

26. Aleksei Nikolaevich Kosygin (1904–1980) became chairman of the USSR Council
of Ministers, or prime minister, in 1964. He sponsored the so-called Liberman reforms,
which sought to give economic managers greater autonomy.

perhaps, was a good thing. No one harbored illusions that things might change, even in fifty years.

How did you relate to the problem of human rights back then? After all, the issue got a great deal of attention abroad.

My reaction was twofold. First, on its own merits, of course, it was understood that things here were bad in that regard. But the way the Western radio stations discussed the matter always seemed a bit artificial to us, because they harped over and over again on the same thing. Besides—and this too is important—everything was said with an accent, and this strongly affects you at a subconscious level. All the while it seemed that this was something artificial. But when our own people [native speakers] began to broadcast, we had much more faith in them.

How did you react to the invasion of Afghanistan?

The invasion of Afghanistan was seen as an absurd stupidity. People weren't indignant as they were in the case of Czechoslovakia, but simply astonished by such extraordinary stupidity. No one actually knew what had transpired in Afghanistan. It was clear that there was some sort of racket going on there that had nothing to do with us, and that political and geopolitical concerns prompted us to [invade]. But to invade the country, of course, was simply appallingly absurd. I remember that this was clear to everyone. I can't recall encountering a single individual who supported it.

In all societies myths help unite people. Tell me about the myths that sought to unite Soviet citizens.

I'm afraid that my ideas about this appeared much later in life and that I'm projecting onto the past that which I realized later. But one of the more interesting myths, perhaps, concerns the great deal of respect that people accorded the world of thieves and criminals. People projected onto them a kind of "Robin Hood" mindset and believed that justice prevailed among them. That was a major element of the myth. I now see that we also borrowed a great deal of slang, words, and attitudes from the criminal world. This was very noticeable. Second, perhaps, was what people repeated both then and now about our spirituality, that, despite political coercion, we read, are interested in what really matters, and show contempt for the mundane questions of everyday life and for material things. This scorn for consumerism also existed.

What about the cult of the Second World War?

Yes, of course, there was certainly that. There was a great deal of respect for everyone who took part in it. The first cracks in this myth took place when someone argued that it hadn't been necessary to involve so many people in senseless assaults, to lead people into battle regardless of obstacles when things could have been done otherwise. Then someone said that perhaps the Germans weren't responsible for the starvation during the blockade of Leningrad, but Stalin, who senselessly held onto the city. I can't recall who made that point. But such questions began to surface. And later people looked upon the myth of the war somewhat differently.

During the Brezhnev years they began to build BAM.[27] You were already in graduate school at the time, right? Did people you know take part in the railroad's construction?

No, I think that people's attitudes toward it were tongue in cheek. Nevertheless, there were some who went to the construction site. We understood that there were two sides to the matter, the official one and the personal one. There were people who sincerely thought otherwise, and they exhibited real interest, courage, and probably some romanticism.

Did you know any people like that?

[Laughing:] No. There were no such people among my acquaintances.

I forgot to ask about the Komsomol. You told me that you had been something of a leader in school. Where you a leader in the Komsomol, too?

Well, I was proud to be an Octobrist and a Pioneer.[28] I knew the meaning of the three points of the [Pioneer's] tie and all that. But with the Komsomol it was like this. It had nothing to do with politics, but it was a sign of maturity, and therefore it was very important who was enrolled first in the Komsomol. It was a matter of prestige. They didn't take me straight off, and I got offended and didn't join

---

27. The construction of BAM, the Baikal-Amur Magistral Railway, began in 1974 with much fanfare, and soon involved more than a half million Komsomol members. Heralded as the "path to the future," this last great Soviet-era construction project proved a highly wasteful and poorly run endeavor.

28. Soviet school children between the ages of six and nine belonged to the Young Octobrists (*Oktiabriata*), named after the October (Bolshevik) Revolution of 1917 and founded in 1923–24. At age ten, children joined the Pioneers, the next level of children's organizations formed to replace the prerevolutionary scouting movement. Pioneers were instructed to study hard, to be honest, and to learn how to live happily with others. Senior to the Pioneer organization was the Komsomol (All-Union Leninist Communist Youth League), which catered to young people between the ages of fourteen and twenty-eight. Membership in the Komsomol, an auxiliary of the Communist Party and training ground for party membership, was far from universal, but a high percentage of school-age children who had aspirations to enroll at a university joined the organization.

the organization for a long time. I enrolled, I think, only in the tenth grade or at the end of the ninth grade and, to be frank, partly out of practical considerations. At home they told me that I had to join. I wasn't happy about this, but I enrolled anyway, and simply didn't give the matter much thought. It was already late.

Did you join the Communist Party?

No. They asked me to join. But, as was considered proper back then, I said something to the effect that I was not "worthy," that it was too early for me to consider it. And when they asked me again I said that I don't like to subordinate myself to others and didn't want any problems over the issue of democratic centralism.[29] Afterward they stopped bothering me. One might say that I respectfully declined.

Did this negatively affect your career?

No. They always considered me as someone who was a bit unreliable in that regard, but they overlooked this because I was an accomplished professional and didn't display any offense over this. I found the right words to convey the point that I believed that this was simply not my thing.

Several people whom I interviewed noted that although it was hard for them to explain, they nonetheless knew that there were themes about which it was best not to speak and that from an early age they learned how to "read between the lines." I sense that this was also part of your experience. But I don't understand how people came to intuit this. Can you explain this to someone from a different country? When Stalin died you knew, already as a young child, that it was best to keep your mouth shut.

That indeed is a difficult question to answer. You have to think about and try to understand how such nonverbal things made themselves felt. It was clear that there were things that were best not spoken about. This was already obvious to me when I attended school. It was understood that if you expressed doubts about Lenin's inviolability, for instance, there would be serious consequences.

Would you have answered my questions differently had I asked them before the fall of communism?

In terms of my candidness?

Yes, and in terms of how you might have evaluated certain things.

I don't think that my reaction to the points that we've covered

---

29. Technically, party organs allowed discussion of most matters until a resolution was carried, at which point all party members were expected to back the party line.

so far would have been that much different. True, later I began to understand some things more deeply and from another perspective. In regard to how candid I might have been, I would have taken a good look at you and decided whether or not you were someone I could trust. And I probably would have opted to answer some things openly and would have said that it was best not to discuss others. But, of course we couldn't have imagined back then how things would turn out and that we would be able to speak freely and openly. Although now, it appears, new times are setting in.

Each and every personal history helps me better understand the course of Soviet history. To what extent did the path your life took reflect more global processes?

I don't thing that there are things in my life that reflected the collapse of the Soviet Union. I led my life independent of such things. In regard to the argument that the Soviet Union had to break up, I'd point out that we didn't know when this would take place or how. But I do have one very clear memory. Schiller wrote a wonderful historical essay about Sparta and Athens, and when I read it I understood that Sparta was very much like the Soviet Union, and Athens was very much like the United States and that for the very same reasons that Sparta lost to Athens, the Soviet Union would lose to America. Everything hinged on brawn instead of brains. An empire not founded on a realistic basis cannot survive for long. But, of course, I could not fathom that this would occur so quickly.

In what ways has your life changed since the collapse of the Soviet Union? How would you evaluate the changes?

A sharp decline in the prestige of our profession took place. This was deeply felt, and it, of course, fundamentally affected my life and the lives of many whom I know. Before that, it was clear how my career would progress: I would defend my dissertation, then, perhaps, become a corresponding member of the Academy of Sciences, then something else, and all this would take place smoothly. Then everything fell apart, and people were left to their own devices. They had to hold their own throughout all of this. That is, there was a loss of valuable reference points. That which formerly had seemed so obvious to us had vanished. I see this very clearly in the example of my father and his younger son, who said: "You're nothing but a miserable little professor. Who cares?" And he said this to him, the smartest of people, someone highly respected at work. Such cheap material interests penetrated our lives. Of course, this strongly affected our lives and we ended up in an awful situation. At times we swam and swam toward shore only to see it recede still further, or else we had to start out on our own, not knowing how accurate our navigational equipment was. This perhaps was the strongest sensation. Things could have been worse, for I had the chance to continue my professional activities, but this opportunity was closed to many. There's another important circumstance that appeared in the course of all this. Before, a certain way of life, which later came in handy, was being perfected in the Soviet Union, perhaps absurdly and incorrectly. However, I must say to you with some sadness, and this might be offensive to you as an American, that I now have the impression, as do many of my friends in the States and here, that in the States a certain social order is beginning to emerge, which much more fully embodies that which once existed in the Soviet Union. Except that we had, you might say, a dilettante's approach, whereas there everything is done more professionally. That is, this postdemocratic period might come to resemble Sparta. I also had this feeling.

More than a decade has occurred since the collapse of the Soviet Union. At first transition periods are always difficult and complicated. But have you gotten accustomed to the new way of doing things?

You know, ultimately nothing has changed that much in my life except in regard to my family life. I didn't suffer from lack of money. My needs are modest. Therefore, I didn't have any major problems. Rather, I observed all this as if from the outside.

How do your children differ from you? I have in mind here their generation.

Perhaps my children are not an appropriate topic because my son has some health problems. He's a fine young man, but he has a neurological problem that defines him more than his generation does. But to answer your question, I'd say that perhaps it's their practicality. I can detect this, for instance, in my daughter. In contrast, it seemed to us that our generation was more concerned with ethical questions. They're more practical than we are and rightly place greater value on important, practical things. Or so it seems to me.

Please tell me about your interest in music and how you evaluate this part of your life. The fact that you could have studied at the Moscow Conservatory in and of itself meant that you had quite a choice to make.

Well, yes, but ultimately there wasn't much of a choice, because they explained to me toward the end of my school years that my technique had already fallen behind that of the Moscow Central

Music School (CMS). Without graduating from the CMS, it would have been hard for me to get into the Moscow Conservatory and I would have had to attend a music college here instead. Yet it was all but certain that I'd get into the university. Moreover, there was the altogether stupid notion that, when it comes to art, one cannot be a mere artisan, whereas in academia one can [laughing]. Well, this, too, in part, played a role. Of course, things could have turned out differently, but straight off I can't say for sure.

But you continued with music, right?

Yes. There's a university chamber orchestra and I've been play-ing in it since 1967. Next year we'll celebrate our thirty-fifth an-niversary. Belonging to the same group for thirty-five years, as you know, is a lot. For the past ten years I've directed the orchestra. That takes half my time and is half my life. And most of my friends are there. Music means a great deal to me.

You mentioned that you're about to depart for Australia. Do you travel a lot?

Yes, a good deal. I went abroad to the West for the first time in 1980 to attend a conference. Then I traveled to one or two con-ferences a year, sometimes three. I have rather good professional contacts and I often get invited to conferences. Later I received my own grants. Twice a year I travel to the United States for a month, usually in the summer and winter, to the University of Illinois at Urbana-Champaign. In addition, I received a grant from the Howard Hughes Medical Institute, and it annually brings together all the participants in its programs for yet another conference. This year it will be in Australia. So, all in all, it depends upon the availability of free time. There's money for travel.

Did the problems during the early days of perestroika affect these trips? Did they continue?

At the start of perestroika? Yes, travel abroad became simpler at some point. It also became simpler with the appearance of comput-ers. Before computers, you had to have six copies of your character recommendation, a document called a *kharakteristika,* signed by the Komsomol leader, trade union leader, and head of the Communist Party at the institute, strictly in that order, and then by the same three officials at the university level, using carbon paper. They could make you return even if there was a single typing mistake, and the next party meeting might be a month and a half away. Incidentally, this was their "Catch-22." They rarely turned down people directly, but made you return over and over again for signatures. Then, with the appearance of computers, things were simplified.

How would you assess Russia's post-Soviet leaders, Boris Yeltsin and Vladimir Putin?

I've always liked, and continue to like, Yeltsin as a person. But I've never taken a personal liking to Putin, although, when I first heard him on the radio—his manner has since changed—his speeches sometimes stirred up trust in me. However, when you see him on TV that trust somehow vanishes. On the other hand, Yeltsin openly gave up running the country after his second [parliamentary] elections, well, essentially, soon after the first elections, handing things over to those around him, to a significant degree to thieves and intriguers.[30] Putin is young and healthy and actively promotes a strategy. But it's an altogether different matter whether this strategy of special operations is an agreeable and inspiring one. [Here I have in mind] the explosions in Moscow, Dubrovka, and Beslan, the war in Chechnia, and the rehabilitation of Stalin.[31] I'm sort of under the impression that Putin more or less duly implements the policy of a certain strategic center set up, apparently, within the state security organs.

What do you think are the greatest changes that have come to Russia since 1991?

It's hard to say, insofar as a retrograde process is underway and it's not altogether clear which of the changes will turn out to be lasting ones. But, so far, freedom of speech on a personal level continues to exist. It's also important to mention that, even when openly using force to solve political problems, the state tries to observe the semblance of legality. It seems to me that this, in and of itself, is important, although the trials during the Great Terror of 1937 also went through the legal formalities. One of the most important changes that has come to public consciousness, well, certainly to my own, although it seems like it's true of others, too, is, perhaps, a sobering up, perhaps extensively so, in regard to the notion that the post-Soviet authorities are striving to improve people's lives and that "good" politicians can come to power. I'm reminded of the end-

---

30. In September 1993, President Yeltsin dissolved the Russian parliament and called for elections to a State Duma, which were held in December 1993, and again in December 1995.

31. Here Konstantinov refers to the widespread speculation in Russia and abroad that agents of the Federal Security Service, the successor to the KGB, played a role in the explosions, blamed on Chechen terrorists, of apartment houses in Moscow in September 1999; in the seizing of hostages at Moscow's Dubrovka Theater during a performance of the musical *Nord-Ost* in October 2002; and in the hostage-taking and siege of a school in Beslan in September 2004, all of which resulted in extensive casualties.

ing of the marvelous epoch film by Fassbinder, *Berlin Alexanderplatz,* about interwar Germany, where after each misfortune and crisis "our hero," an ordinary person, grows wiser, stops believing others, and no longer lets himself be fooled.[32] But [history shows us that] he then goes ahead and votes for Hitler.

One final question. How would you assess the current state and future of Russian democracy?

An obvious rolling-back of democracy is underway. It's clear that this is the most important element of the strategy of [the Putin] administration, which keeps the appearance of democratic procedures for foreign policy reasons. It seems to me that it would suit the administration just fine to return to the late Soviet system under Brezhnev, so as to start over the country's transformation but this time along a different trajectory. However, I don't think that we're speaking here of returning to an authoritarian structure of the Stalinist type. Not that long ago, Gaidar, who makes few public appearances these days, calmly commented on what's taking place.[33] He said that as far as he's aware, the Chinese model of gradual liberalization of the economy under the unwavering control of the party and security police is to Putin's liking. I think Gaidar is right.

So much has changed in Russia compared to the Brezhnev days. Unfortunately, I'm afraid that, while we're grieving over the abortive democratization of Russia, a postdemocratic epoch is emerging throughout the entire Western world. Political and economic oligarchies are actively struggling to limit the freedom of the majority of the population in order to make the democratic system more controllable. In particular, this is one of the main goals of [George] Bush's antiterrorist campaign in the U.S., in addition to external expansion. Therefore, I fear that the caricaturized version of controlled democracy in Russia will gradually be realized but in a much more viable form in the U.S., and then in Europe. Thus, perhaps the course of the current administration in Russia, no matter how sad it may be, is a course of outstripping, one aimed at that same goal in the future.

---

32. Rainer Werner Fassbinder's 1980 miniseries is the longest narrative film ever shot. The hero, Franz, representative of the German nation, easily falls under the influence of others.

33. Egor Gaidar is one of Russia's first post-Soviet prime ministers, known as one of the main architects of the country's transformation to a market economy via shock therapy that drove the Duma to rebel against President Yeltsin in 1993. Ousted in December 2002 to appease conservative politicians, Gaidar formed his own political party, Russia's Democratic Choice.

2. "Back then I really wanted to join the party" | Natalia Valentinovna Altukhova (maiden name Pronina)

July 3, 2002, Saratov

A member of Saratov's School No. 42's A group, Natalia Valentinovna Altukhova (maiden name Pronina) took her degree in economics at the Saratov Polytechnic Institute (today the Saratov Technical University). She later completed her candidate's degree (roughly the equivalent of a Ph.D.) at the Moscow Economic-Statistical Institute. Natalia Valentinovna taught most of her career at her alma mater, the Polytechnic Institute, until the mid-1990s. At that time she accepted a position at the Saratov branch of the Moscow State Commercial University, where she currently heads the Department of Economics and Management. Many of her classmates made career changes after the collapse of the Soviet system, usually for economic reasons, and I assume that is what prompted her to do so. Cheerfully agreeing to be interviewed, she arranged to have two students pick me up from my apartment to take me to the Commercial University. She also saw to it that I got back to my apartment afterward.

Early July is a busy time at institutions of higher education in Russia, and I could tell from the flurry of activity and bustle in Natalia Valentinovna's office on the morning of July 3, 2002, that she spent more time with me than she could probably spare. Gracious throughout my visit, Natalia Valentinovna kept my teacup filled and plied me with sweets, not taking "no" for an answer. I regret that she would not allow me to photograph her, then or later, despite my entreaties. Natalia Valentinovna struck me as being not only a highly resourceful woman, but also as a person who generally got her way.

Born on April 20, 1949, Natalia Valentinovna spoke rapturously about the benefits of spending her early years in a remote part of the country, yet proved reluctant to supply the specifics. She thumbed through a worn family photo album, calling my attention to one or another physical attraction, and this only heightened my curiosity. Her reference to the Russian heartland as "the mainland" implies that she grew up in Siberia, somewhere in the Russian Far North, or perhaps on Sakhalin Island. For some reason, I got the impression that she might have been raised in the Magadan area, site of a cluster of infamous Gulag camps. This silence in her account made me wonder why her parents worked there and what they did on the job. Be that as it may, the fact that she moved to Saratov when she was a girl of eleven or twelve made her something of an outsider at School No. 42.

An energetic, confident, no-nonsense, direct woman, Natalia Valentinovna proved to have plenty to say. She provided me with rich detail about her childhood interests, about School No. 42, and about the cultural climate of the 1960s. My only informant to attend the International Moscow Youth Festival of 1957, she remembered the spontaneous interactions of Soviet citizens with foreign visitors, and made some discerning comparisons between the open climate of the Khrushchevian thaw and the far more controlled one of Moscow in 1980. She spoke frankly about her failed marriage, about a damaged friendship, and about how her life has changed since the collapse of the Soviet system. The day after we met, Natalia Valentinovna phoned me to say that our conversation had brought back a flood of memories. Since our interview, she had thought of several topics that we had not touched upon, which she believed had also defined her school-age experience. She mentioned the Cuban Missile Crisis and the fear of being on the brink of war. She mentioned the space race and the heady optimism that came from the Soviet Union's launching of Sputnik in 1957. And she mentioned decolonization in Africa and the emergence of newly independent countries whose shedding of the yoke of colonialism served as grist to the Soviet propaganda mill's extolling the relentless march of socialism. Shortly after putting down the receiver, I realized the extent to which these same concerns had also made an indelible impression on my own childhood on Chicago's South Side.

Although not uncritical of the Soviet system, Natalia Valentinovna had plenty more to say about its positive features, despite her disappointment in not being invited to join the

Communist Party. What specific attributes of Soviet life does she appreciate? How can we account for these attitudes? How might admiration for the old system color her understanding of some issues—and her answers to certain questions I posed? What does she choose to criticize either openly or implicitly?

My mother was from Saratov and my father from the town of Michurinsk. It's exactly halfway between Saratov and Moscow. Earlier, when Papa was born there, it was called Kozlov. My father came from a working-class family, and so essentially did my mother. But her family was a bit—well, her mother, that is, my grandmother, was a white-collar worker. She graduated from a gymnasium before the Revolution [of 1917].[1] However, after the Revolution she had to work as an ordinary typist. After graduating from the institute, my mother was assigned a job in one of the regions. It was there that she met Papa and where I was born. As regards influence, it was Papa, unquestionably, who exerted the greatest influence on me. He was an extraordinary man. There are few people like him. And although I didn't try to emulate him, it turned out that way anyway, because he was an example. Mama spent more time with me, but in my view she had less to do with shaping my life.

How, specifically, did your father influence you?

He distinguished himself by his exceptional capacity for work. Such attitudes toward work were not that common. That is, it was not just a matter of his showing up at work and of putting in time, but of doing something really well, something of high quality, something constructive. He distinguished himself in that he continued to learn new things his entire life. As long as he lived, he learned. Apparently, this was passed on genetically—perhaps not. And now, I, too, am always trying to master something new. I see this as a positive trait [laughing] that comes from him. I could teach the same subject all my life. I could pick a topic—although this is harder to do in economics—but there are such disciplines where you can teach the same old thing. However, each year I pick a new subject and master it because doing so interests me. As a result, I understand

---

1. A prestigious secondary school in tsarist Russia that provided a strong classical education and prepared its graduates for university study or for professional careers.

young people better, and it's easier for me to work with them. This, I think, comes from Papa. My mother, of course, also left her mark. She worked with me each day before the fourth grade to make sure that I did my homework accurately. Maybe it was she who instilled in me a love of learning. Or maybe that came from Papa, too. I'm not sure, but I think it came from Papa. Well, that's it regarding my parents. I have no brothers or sisters and there never were any. On my father's side I have some relatives in Michurinsk, but I've never had any contact with them and don't know who they are.

And on your mother's side?

On my mother's side, well, she had a brother who died at age forty. It was very long ago and I was still a child, a relative child, I was still in school.

What did your parents do?

Both of my parents worked in the transportation industry deploying automobiles. They most likely held various jobs. Papa was a department head and Mama worked under him. That's how it was. They were both engineers in the transportation industry.[2]

How would you describe your childhood?

I had a happy childhood. Yes, an exceptionally happy childhood. Perhaps I didn't completely understand that at the time, but now I see that no one in Saratov had such a childhood. That's a hundred percent certain. And that's because the tiny little settlement where I lived was surrounded by Mother Nature. That really has an effect on a child. You could play wherever you liked, run about freely, associate with others freely, and be a child of nature, so to speak. Yes, a child of nature. Though they instilled in me human principles, norms, morals, rules of behavior, I was free . . . to go wherever I liked, to play whatever I liked. And when I arrived in Saratov I realized that children here simply didn't know how to run and play. We have some traditional Russian games such as lapta.[3] And there we really knew how to play. But here no one knew what lapta even was! They weren't at all interested in playing lapta. Then there was nature, all sorts of plants, grasses, and berries. It was quite amazing. All sorts of wild animals abounded. It was like a wildlife preserve. It was quite special.

---

2. In the Soviet Union the term "engineer" was used much more broadly than in the United States, often referring to skilled workers or white-collar workers with technical skills.

3. Lapta is a traditional Russian ball game.

You started school there, right?

Yes, I began school there. Of course, I was a Young Octobrist,[4] as was expected of us. Probably that interests you—even more so because I took part in its activities sincerely, very much so. I can't say that belonging to such organizations is a bad thing, because all the children were well looked after, and because they taught us some good things. They accepted me into the Pioneers in that same small settlement. This meant Pioneer campfires and wonderful songs. By the way, I was on a business trip to Penza and altogether by chance ended up in a hotel where some Americans were staying.[5] These Americans were young, literally no more than eighteen. They simply amazed me when they sang the song "Light Up the Dark Blue Nights with Campfires." Well, you know, I couldn't for the life of me imagine where they learned this. Apparently, they really liked the sound and the human accord that came from singing it. Singing bonds people. It creates a sense of belonging. And they enjoyed this. We lack this at present. That's a real shame. I really regret that we've lost this. Yes, I joined the Pioneers. And then I entered the Komsomol.[6] I did everything that I was supposed to do. In school I was even secretary of the Komsomol organization. There was such a period. I can't recall how old I was at the time.

Did your parents join the Communist Party?

No, my parents did not join the party. I can say that this was not by choice. That is, they didn't turn down an opportunity to join the party. They probably would have joined if certain conditions for doing so had existed. Moreover, when I finished school and began to work at the institute, the general situation was such that they mostly accepted into the party people from a working-class background. White-collar workers also joined, but they were the exception. And

---

4. Soviet school children between the ages of six and nine belonged to the Young Octobrists (*Oktiabriata*), named after the October (Bolshevik) Revolution of 1917 and founded in 1923–24.

5. Founded in 1663, Penza has a population of roughly 500,000 inhabitants and is the capital of Penza oblast, which borders Saratov oblast on the north.

6. At age ten, children joined the Pioneers, the next level of children's organizations formed to replace the prerevolutionary scouting movement. Pioneers were instructed to study hard, to be honest, and to learn how to live happily with others. Senior to the Pioneer organization was the Komsomol (All-Union Leninist Communist Youth League), which catered to young people between the ages of fourteen and twenty-eight. Membership in the Komsomol, an auxiliary of the Communist Party and training ground for party membership, was far from universal, but a high percentage of school-age children who had aspirations to enroll at a university joined the organization.

by then it no longer was for everybody. It wasn't that there was some sort of selection process based on lofty principles, no. The sorting out was of an altogether different character, but it did take place. It did. Perhaps you've heard about it, since you're a historian. Well, insofar as I was not known in Saratov for having eminent parents and, for the most part, made my own way in life, I didn't have the opportunity to join the party, although I very much wanted to. I can tell you that in all honesty, despite the fact that today attitudes toward the system have completely changed. But back then I really wanted to join the party. I considered it a cohesive collective, too. I was, well, utterly convinced that it was an ideal organization, that party membership did not confer privileges, but provided the opportunity to participate in improving things in the country. These were my sincere, altogether well-meaning, lofty convictions.

What interested you during your childhood?

Everything. I had a wide range of interests. From my earliest years Mama taught me how to embroider. It's not that she taught me, but that she insisted I learn. If you were a pedagogue and not a historian, you'd understand what I'm talking about. She'd give me a lesson. For instance, embroider so many of, say, some sort of rectangles, here, in various colored threads. And I could not go anywhere until I finished doing so. That's right. I would cry, get hysterical, and run off. They'd punish me, and force me to embroider. As a result, the first thing that I grew fond of was embroidering. That is, I finished my first piece of embroidery under threat of punishment. I was forced to. But I completed my second piece on my own free will, and because I wanted to. They were pillows. I still have pieces embroidered with counted cross-stitches. It's sort of a hobby. People offered to buy them for a handsome sum of money, but I couldn't [sell them]. By the way, the Americans I met also wanted to buy them [laughing]. Yes, in one gardening organization, I used to visit a horticultural organization. . . . It wasn't all that long ago, maybe ten years ago. And there we exchanged and showed each other our crafts. They invited Americans, who bought things. Several women sold whole canvases, hand-embroidered with counted cross-stitches. Do you know what I'm talking about? They offered good money, of course, in dollars, as one should, but I'll never sell mine. Perhaps only after my death [laughing]. But I don't think that my son will sell them. So, there was embroidery.

Then there was an altogether female hobby, sewing. We had a sewing club at school. Not a club, but an actual class. They called it "home economics." Probably no one has told you about this. They taught us how to cook and sew. Afterward, several of us really learned how to sew. I was particularly lucky and learned how. And later, when we lived through some rough times, during so-called perestroika, I even earned some money on the side sewing, and I am not at all ashamed of this. I'm really quite good at it. And that's from my childhood. Then I took a fancy to collecting stamps. Yes, it was an exceptional passion of mine. I had a really good collection, which people also repeatedly asked me to sell. As a result, I no longer risk keeping it at home. It's a good stamp collection, and not only of the Soviet period. Well, let's see, what else did I take an interest in during my childhood? What else are we usually drawn to in childhood? Of course, reading. I've read a lot since childhood. I began reading at the age of four, perhaps younger. I recall that I read to other children when I attended nursery school. Actually, I don't remember this. That's what my parents told me. But they always bragged about this, and that's how I remember.

What year did your family move to Saratov?

In 1960, and I enrolled in School No. 42 in 1961. It was like this. When we arrived here, "on the mainland,"[7] as we say, from our far-away settlement to central Russia, my father wanted me to receive a good basic education. His fundamental aim was that his child would receive a good education that would provide further opportunities in life. For this reason, he wanted to send me to a boarding school in Moscow. Mama was extremely opposed to this. To lose touch with her child? And then they sent me first to School No. 19. I attended that school for half a year, after which Papa decided that that's not how things should be. The very best school was School No. 42, but in order to go there you already needed to know the language. That was for fifth grade. I showed up in fifth grade but didn't know a single letter of the English alphabet. I knew only Russian. Therefore they hired a tutor for me. It was a teacher from our school, a former teacher, of course, because she already was quite old. Her name was Natalia Ilinichna. It was she who prepared me for School No. 42, and within two and a half months I learned the material necessary to

---

7. Soviet citizens living in remote parts of the Far North and Siberia or on Sakhalin—the regions where many labor camps were located—referred to the heart of the country as "the mainland." Although she was vague about the specifics, it appears that Altukhova's parents were employed as civilians perhaps near a former camp in Siberia.

enroll in fifth grade. I took exams, entrance exams. That is, I wasn't with them from first grade or from second grade, but from fifth grade. Yes, I passed the exams, very tough ones. Several teachers of English, the principal, and assistant principal were all present. I had to prove myself before them, so to speak. It was as it should be. I had to read, recount what I read, and answer questions. I had to demonstrate that I had full command of the material. There was no pampering. It was not easy to get admitted. But, nevertheless, things worked out. I'll tell you about my first impression of the school, since your interests are historical. They had just finished moving into the new school building. I didn't study at all in the older building. I don't even know where it was located. I showed up at the new building during its ceremonial opening. That was my first impression. And when I arrived there they had me line up. The entire class was lined up, and they found a place for me. Then someone asked me, "What's your name?" "Natasha," I replied. All of them began to laugh and said, "Oh! Our seventh Natasha!" Yes, in one class there was now a seventh Natasha.

I noticed that! What were your impressions of Saratov when you arrived there?

My impression was that it was a hot, dusty, dirty city. It didn't make much of an impression on me. Probably because during my childhood my parents took me with them to various other cities. I saw quite a bit for my age.

Can you give me some examples of places you visited?

Well, only in Russia, that is, the Soviet Union, of course, let's put it that way, only in the Soviet Union. I was in Moscow, and what is now St. Petersburg, then Leningrad, and in Odessa, Kiev, and Kharkov. Yes, I saw quite a bit. There are many fine cities such as these. For this reason, Saratov struck me as an ordinary town, with no distinguishing features. Moreover, life here was more complicated than from where we had come. After all, it's a city. You have to walk and cross the street where indicated. And why did I need that back then? Here you had to meet all the demands of your surroundings. For example, let's assume that back then people were in line waiting for a trolley. It wasn't a matter of a trolley pulling up and everyone getting on. No. Rather, a trolley would pull up and everyone would take turns getting on. And you had to hold on to all sorts of papers and not throw them out. I understand that you can't pitch them, and I still understand that. But back then I didn't. There are many other examples. You couldn't pick the flowers.

Was it hard to make friends and to have your class accept you at that age?

You know, it seems to me that several of my classmates still consider me an outsider. Mainly because I didn't join them until the fifth grade. Those who enrolled in second grade bonded. They exhibited much more of a sense of belonging to a group, although no one ever said anything to me about this or made it apparent. It's more on the level of intuition. The point is that I had a gap in my schooling. I went to School No. 19 for half of fifth grade, and later attended School No. 42, also from the fifth grade. That is, I was a bit older than the rest of them, a year older. In School No. 19 I had far more contact with the other pupils, even though there were many bosses' children there, too. Still, I had greater contact there, and, when I left, the children came to my house and asked me not to go to the other school. Some of them actually cried, but I didn't at all understand what this was all about. In School No. 42, no one would have cried had someone left. That, too, is a very important point, isn't it?

Yes it is. There were two groups, then, the A group and B group, right?

Yes, two groups, the A group and the B group. I was in the A group.

Was there any difference between the two? Or was it just by chance where one ended up?

None whatsoever. Although, of course, the A group considered themselves better. But probably the B group thought that they were better. When we get together, we of course say, "We're from the A group. The B group is worse." But worse in what way? After all, Konstantinov [from the B group] is now working in Moscow.[8] How is he worse? He was a great kid, an exceptionally talented fellow. I don't know what became of him now. And take Podolskii [from the A group].[9] He also was exceptionally talented. Both of them now live in Moscow. I don't think either one of them is worse than the other. Yet during our childhood we of course thought that we were better.

How would you evaluate the school's educational program?

I'll be honest with you. The school program was one-sided. I be-

---

8. Aleksandr Aleksandrovich Konstantinov (see chapter 1).

9. Evgenii Mikhailovich Meier, who later changed his name to Podolskii, is also mentioned in Aleksandr Vladimirovich Trubnikov's interview (see chapter 7).

An official photograph of the Pioneer unit in group B taken on Pioneer Day, May 19, probably in the fifth or sixth grade. *Courtesy A. A. Konstantinov.*

lieve they taught us English well, given the possibilities at the time. Those who taught us English hadn't been abroad, and naturally they had an accent, that's only natural. My first instruction in getting prepared for School No. 42 was from Natalia Ilinichna, who had lived in the American sector of Kharbin.[10] Then she arrived in the Soviet Union and eventually ended up in our school. It was she who prepared me. Therefore, when I started the fifth grade, the very first teacher I had began to tell me that I had an American accent, which was not acceptable. It was better to have a British English accent, because it's of course better. How is it better? Only a fool knows. But that's what they believed. I had learned by rote memory several expressions that she had taught me, which I automatically repeated. They remarked to me that it was better not to use those phrases. One had to use literary English as in our textbook. But our textbook was published in 1949. It was as old as we were. There were no

---

10. The Manchurian town of Kharbin had been a Russian city since its founding in 1898 as the administrative center for the Eastern Chinese Railway, a Russian enterprise. It ended up under Chinese sovereignty after the Revolution and remained part of the Russian diaspora community throughout the 1920s.

new textbooks. You can imagine what difficult, literary language it was written in. It was hard for us. We had to translate and learn all of it. But they learned English in Moscow from the same textbook. I just so happen to know that this was the case. I don't remember the authors, but I remember the textbook. We had English every day and English literature three times a week. We studied history, modern history, in English. I don't know modern history at all in Russian. Not at all. We even studied some physics in English, and geography. Therefore I don't know geography at all, either, not at all [laughing]. But it's interesting that the language program nevertheless was a good one. They prepared us well. It was easy for us to get admitted into a language college. Here it was the Pedagogical Institute. Even our C students got A's on their entrance exams and studied there without any problems. But we didn't want things to be so easy, no matter how strange it seems. We wanted something more serious. These were the sixties. They were interesting years. There was a heated debate in Russia between physics and poets regarding who was more important. After all, very serious literary currents appeared, such as poems, with real meaning, which we secretly circulated and learned by heart. Vysotskii made his debut, and we passed his songs around in secret.[11] Then there were the Beatles—but they were already on tapes. I first heard them on [homemade] recordings made from used chest X-rays that showed people's ribs. We played them and listened to them. It was really interesting. Later, when they began to perform officially in the mass media, say on television or over the radio, I was sometimes amazed at how clear they sounded. Even the words were comprehensible! That's how it was. I think I answered your question.

In your view, how politicized was instruction back then?

In my view, not at all. Not at all. Of course, there was "The History of the Communist Party of the Soviet Union." There, indeed, was such a subject, and we had to study it, as it should be, when party congresses were held and the resolutions they carried. But,

---

11. A Soviet cult figure, Vladimir Vysotskii (1938–80) became popular in the 1960s as one of the country's leading "guitar poets." His music circulated widely via underground tapes and a handful of official recordings. His tough-guy songs represented an appealing alternative to official sanitized culture, for his lyrics dealt with life in the raw. Vysotskii was also an acclaimed actor at Moscow's famous Taganka Theater, and appeared in Charles Bronson–like roles in numerous movies. Sustained gossip about his counterculture life style added immensely to the Vysotskii cult.

on the other hand, what does it mean to be politicized? Things are politicized now, too. By that I mean that if some event of major historical importance takes place in politics today, children study it. And the same was true for us. Of course, we studied the resolutions of party congresses in great detail. But this was less true in our school; they really didn't pay much attention to such things. I can say that, even though our principal herself happened to be a historian of the Communist Party. Her name was Echberger, Vera. Vera, Vera, yes, Vera Filippovna. It was hard to recall, but I remembered.

How important was it that you learned English as a child? Did this play a role in your life?

I often regret that it didn't. Not at all. At first I really worried about this. But the city was closed to foreigners; there were no foreigners at all. Contacts were completely, well, there were none. I myself tried. I tried to read a lot of literature. I checked out literature in the original and read it; there was very little of it available in our main library. Mostly novels. Not highbrow stuff, but lowbrow novels. I at least wanted to read them, so I wouldn't forget. But it turned out that, well, in general, I forgot a great deal. I can still understand. When I hear it on the radio or see films on television—we can now watch films without dubbing—I understand. Moreover, I think that if I began to speak, it would all come back, not immediately, of course.

Natalia Valentinovna, please tell me about your attitudes toward the West at that time.

I was really curious. I never thought that they lived better in the West. I can say that with assurance. Basically, I pay very little attention to such things in my life, both now, and back then. I try to live so as to make a life for myself, and that pleases me just fine. Do you understand? Everything suits me. And that very West, as you put it, it's the same as the East. It interested me simply because people there lived differently. I was interested in what people there thought, what poetry they read, and what they felt when they read it. That is, my interest was purely emotional, not rational. When I worked at the Polytechnic Institute, some thirty years I worked there and only recently moved here. I've been here for eight years, half time, not full time. It actually turns out to be quite a bit. But thirty years at the Polytechnic and while I was there I traveled abroad once, the only time, to Hungary and Czechoslovakia. They were socialist republics. There was nothing particularly special about them, yet I went out of curiosity, as a simple tourist. This was in 1978. Yes, 1978, ten years after the coup in Czechoslovakia.[12] And I went for the simple reason that I was curious. Well, I looked around and decided that people live about the same everywhere. After all, we're all people. Some might be smart, some might be dumb, some might have a sense of humor, some might lack one, some might be rich, some might be poor—it's the same in each country.

Did you encounter any anti-Soviet feelings connected to the Soviet invasion of the country when you were in Czechoslovakia?

Well, when I went there I remembered that it was the tenth anniversary, right? I was there on the very day when it had taken place. It was summer. They warned us not to go out. To draw our curtains if we were on the bus. They might throw stones. Don't interact with anyone that day. Before or after, please, but not on that day. An encounter took place by pure chance, an interesting one. I'll tell you about it. Well, we left the hotel to get some fresh air, although they told us not to go anywhere. Yet since I was much younger back in 1978, I, of course, went out. And while we were standing there a young man came up to us and spoke directly to me in Czech or Slovak. I'm not sure which. I told him I don't understand and he switched to Russian. "Are you really Russian? I thought you were locals." Well, a conversation got started about this and that and he began to say that in Czechoslovakia people live better than in the Soviet Union. Something to the effect that American buses are better than the Ikaris [Hungarian] buses we rode in. This really astonished me because I believed that it was simply impossible to be better than the Soviet Union. That's how I was raised, do you understand? In principle it couldn't be, because it simply was impossible. People say that in Russia. You know, when he began to speak it was like some sort of discovery. Yet how can one make such comparisons? Basically, it's impossible to make such comparisons. How could he say that everything was better there? However, there were no hostile demonstrations and no one [harassed us]. Just the opposite. When he learned that we were from Russia he behaved fine and during our entire trip they treated us exceptionally well. I can say that with certainty. They fed us well, entertained us, invited us to their homes, and treated us exceptionally well. There was absolutely nothing unpleasant. Even in Slovakia. Things were a bit

---

12. In August 1968 the Soviet Union and most Warsaw Pact countries invaded Czechoslovakia to put an end to the so-called Prague Spring, an attempt to create "socialism with a human face," a more open and benign system.

worse there. The conversations. But they treated us well. Even, you know, when you asked someone on the street in Russian how to get somewhere. There was an interesting case in Prague. We got a bit lost because we wandered about from store to store. It also was interesting. There were more goods there.

And how did you react to the fact that things were better there from an economic point of view?

Well, it wasn't that life was better there but that there were more goods. These are quite different things! You're intelligent! There can be lots of goods, but what if you can't afford to buy them? We were able to buy everything that was available in the Soviet Union. Do you understand? But they couldn't. So where's better? Things weren't so good there, and they weren't so good here. Do you understand? How can one say that it's better? In any event, my girlfriend and I walked out of a store, got lost, and asked for directions. Since she knew French and German, and I only English, I went first. She said, "You go ahead and ask, since we don't speak Czech." Well, I asked in English and they replied, "We don't understand," as they shook their heads. Their reaction was openly negative. Immediately afterward she addressed someone in German. They turned around and left, quite rudely. Well, we didn't bother trying in French, since there didn't seem to be any point in doing so. I said, "Well, you know, we nonetheless have to find our way back to Hotel Swan. Perhaps the word swan is the same in Czech." It turns out that it's very similar. Russian worked well. They escorted us back to the hotel when they learned that we were Russian. That is, they treated us well.

Let me return to your school years. What did you do in your free time?

First, we had lots of hobby groups. They don't exist today. There are very few in schools today. And if there are any, they're expensive. Not everyone's able to pay for them. Back in our time everyone could join as many as they'd like. I, of course, took part in the literature group. I also attended the one for math, but not regularly. And in regard to hobbies, I already mentioned some of them—I collected stamps and various labels, and enjoyed sewing, knitting, and embroidery.

And the Beatles? You mentioned . . .

Music, yes, music. The minute Papa took me to this school he hired a music teacher for me. He believed that a child needed to know how to play an instrument. I didn't attend a music school, but someone came to our place and gave me lessons. I wasn't very enamored with the idea. It requires a certain diligence that's difficult to maintain. It's hard to play the piano for two or three hours a day. But in the end, I was able to play something. I performed at some school assemblies, and even at some neighborhood and citywide children's concerts.

I'm curious to learn about fads at the time regarding music and clothing.

There were, of course, there always are, for each generation. In regard to appearance, the girls wore their hair teased back. It looked terrible. You probably know what that looks like. Has anyone else told you about this? We combed back all our hair. Well, the hair was combed back, with two small braids, tiny ones, or into a ponytail with large bows. Perhaps someone gave you some photographs. Many of us wore such bows. It was really stylish. But it wasn't allowed. It didn't matter that it was in vogue, for it was forbidden because we wore uniforms. I'm not against them; in fact, I'm all for them. Am I right? I think that uniforms discipline those who wear them and don't give you the opportunity to show you're rich. You can agree with me on this, can't you? Well, you see, we wore uniforms and teased hair was strictly forbidden. The principal herself would catch you when you came in, take you into the bathroom, wet your hair, and comb it out [laughing]. That's how it was. Regarding music, let's see. You know, Magomaev was popular. And Kabzon just appeared. Then Kabzon sang with Kristalinskaia very simple songs about everyday life.[13] Such as, I walked by, more likely, she passed by, he noticed, and began to wonder why she passed by. They were simple lyrics, but very popular. And the melodies were not very good. There were no Beatles yet. That was only on the sly, in the later grades, closer to 1965 or 1967. But we didn't have them before then. It was 1965, I think, when they brought the Beatles to me on the sly on the chest X-ray film that I mentioned.

I asked you already about your attitudes back then toward the West. What about toward China?

Toward China? Well, yes, that was an interesting period. For some reason we got along with China pretty well until all of a sudden. That was our policy. What's there to say? The leaders of the two countries befriended each other. Why be on bad terms? Things were fine as long as they were friends. And then when, so to speak, one of them was no longer around, disturbances began. Appar-

---

13. Singers Muslim Magomaev, Iosif Kobzon, and Maiia Kristalinskaia popularized Soviet and foreign pop songs in the Khrushchev era.

ently, these hostile relations stemmed from how the two countries' leaderships got along, not from the attitudes of ordinary people. We didn't understand. Therefore, attitudes toward China were, well, what's it to us? At political information sessions—each day we had such a session in class. Each day we had to sit through a session on political information. It wasn't so bad. For five or ten minutes the children themselves would discuss the most interesting events, read newspapers, and retell their contents. It was only natural, of course, that when relations with China worsened in connection with such interesting events there as the Cultural Revolution that all this found reflection in newspapers, and the subject was discussed at the political information sessions.[14] As concerns me personally, I once had contact with a young Chinese woman my age. That was in 1957 when Papa took me to Moscow to the International Youth Festival.[15]

Really? You were there?

I was at the festival and can compare it with the youth festival that took place in 1980,[16] where I took my son. There were two main differences. When I was at the first festival with my parents, of course, we lived in a good hotel in Moscow. And people of many different nationalities from different countries lived in the hotel. One day, it turned out, my parents went somewhere in the hotel, either to a café or to, wherever, for a break, and I met a Chinese girl in the hallway. Although we didn't understand each other's languages, we got along really well. We drew, cut out some dolls, and I had a very positive impression of the Chinese. As it were, both my parents and her parents were quite pleased that we got along. That was the kind of fleeting acquaintances that occurred. It's quite well known from various sources that later, when they studied at universities in Moscow, they behaved very well. I personally didn't have occasion to interact with these Chinese because I was young. But when they

---

14. A violent, disruptive initiative launched by Chinese Communist leader Mao Zedong during his last decade in power (1966–76) to renew the spirit of the revolution by mobilizing the country's youth and to keep China from following a Soviet path of historical development.

15. Participants remember the Moscow Festival of Youth and Students as a moment of great discovery. Thousands of foreign participants poured into the city, which took on a holiday appearance: Picasso doves of peace temporarily replaced the Soviet hammer and sickle and Western jazz underwent something of a rehabilitation.

16. Moscow hosted a second youth festival in 1985. Altukhova either has the date wrong or is referring to the 1980 Summer Olympic games.

studied in Moscow colleges they got along exceptionally well with Russians, whom they always called their "big brother," or perhaps their big sister. In the sense that we helped them out a great deal.

Your parents ended up at the festival . . .

By accident. They were on vacation. What sort of festival was it? You have to see documentary films from the time, because people danced in the streets! People of all nationalities. You'd be going along, say, and there'd be one nationality and you're of another. Then we'd join hands and dance. It was spontaneous. People wanted to do it, their hearts were in it, and it was interesting for them. The interaction was completely free, completely. But when I brought my son to the festival in 1980, it was altogether different. I brought him mainly so that he could see how people of different nations communicate and get along with one another. But it turned out not to be the case. It turned out that two men in civilian clothes followed each foreigner. It was impossible to make contact, let alone sing together and talk with each other. This is the difference.

Yes, a huge one. By the way, I'm curious what you thought of Lenin back then.

Well, he was an official leader, so to speak. What's there to say? Here's Uncle Lenin? No one, not even my parents, said that to me, and I never put those two words together back then. He was the head of state, the one who brought the country into the condition it was in, insofar as, they believed, Stalin continued his policies. That's how the propaganda had it. But how it really was I can't say, not even now. It's too complicated a question for an ordinary Natasha. He was our leader, that's all. We sang songs about him. But that's only natural, since he was head of state. Who else would you sing about? That's what sort of ideology we had back then.

You mentioned that you had been secretary of your Komsomol organization?

Not for long, and then only because I was a bit older. I joined the Komsomol before the others owing to my age. And therefore I headed up the cell, not in our school, but in our class. Yes, there was a small Komsomol cell in our class. But then others joined, and I, well, I never really was drawn to such work. It's simply my nature, I'm, well, not particularly political, I'm more spiritual and emotional.

Be that as it may, your childhood overlapped with many important political events. I understand that children aren't interested in politics, but how did your parents react, say, to the Twentieth Party Congress?

Not at all. I can say that for certain. Not at all. They weren't party members. That is, my parents were far removed from politics. They were sensible people, who were too far removed from Stalin. If they had been part of the apparatus, or in the Central Committee or something, then . . .

What about when Khrushchev was removed? How did they react to that?

Also not at all. Not at all! True, the question of who would become the new leader was posed, but . . .

Natalia Valentinovna, please tell me: how does your generation differ from that of your parents?

It differs in fundamental ways. Namely, well, I no longer remember exactly, but namely the period of the Thaw exerted a powerful influence—well, maybe not on everyone, but it did on me.[17] I read a great deal, heard a lot. Perhaps I learned a bit more about the lives of certain people. Therefore, it influenced me, yes.

How does your generation differ from that which followed it?

Once again, it differs fundamentally. The younger generation is more rational. In my view, those who came after us don't think about lofty matters at all. If relations between people were very important to us, then, for the generations that follow, the more recent it is the less this is true. To buy something cheaper somewhere, to deceive the person next door because he's easier to deceive. These are the attitudes being cultivated now. It's a shame. I work with young people. I see this, but I try to keep it from manifesting itself so much among them. I'm always upset in this regard. I'm concerned. It seems to me that if people were more honest, we'd be better off.

I have a question about your generation. Someone mentioned that it was more optimistic than that of your parents. Would you agree with this?

Yes, of course. We'd take part, for instance, in public demonstrations. This was quite common at the time, this collective spirit. We'd join in a demonstration, singing the entire route, dancing. We enjoyed it. But just try to raise the spirits of young people today for a sustained period. It's simply impossible. We were sincere, and we believed, for they told us that we'd achieve real communism. This was namely our generation, do you understand? Khrushchev said

---

17. The Thaw, named after writer Ilia Ehrenburg's novella of the same name (1954), refers to a largely spontaneous cultural revival in the wake of Stalin's death in 1953. This revival sought to rid Soviet culture of the worst aspects of Stalinism. This first in a series of thaws lasted from 1953 through 1956. Despite a party crackdown, writers, artists, and other cultural figures continued to test the bounds of the permissible. During his last years in office, Khrushchev promoted another thaw during his final de-Stalinization campaign.

we'd overtake America. Yes, that's what he himself said. "Today's generation of Soviet people will live under communism." I'll never forget this remark. It was drilled into me since childhood. But what kind of communism did we have? Yet we once believed in this. Don't get me wrong, we believed, because we saw that we were living better and better. We saw this with our own eyes.

That's an interesting point. Please tell me about your observations.

Well, specifically, twice a year there were sales. Only then! I'm not speaking about second-hand things, which are on sale these days. No, these were new items of high quality. Moreover, there was a strict certification procedure, although it wasn't called that. Poor quality goods were simply not put up for sale. There weren't that many things available and the assortment was not what it is today, but the goods themselves were of high quality. Now there are many things available, the assortment is undeniably a hundred times greater, but they're not of good quality.

We were speaking of your generation's optimism.

It existed, it still does. It manifests itself even now, when I take a look at our young people and see how much more pessimistic they are than my generation. We're far more optimistic. Of course, it's all up to the individual, and even among my classmates people differ in this regard. You've already carried out some other interviews and understand that we're all different. Although, of course, we're undeniably from the same generation. But we're nevertheless different. Have you already spoken with Vera Miachinskaia [a classmate]?[18] I ask because you'd perhaps see in her outright pessimism. It's simply a matter of her personal situation since childhood. Yes, we're all different. I haven't seen her for three years, although she was my closest girlfriend. About three years ago we stopped seeing each other altogether. I never went to visit her. As an adult she came to see me. And that suited me just fine. She'd visit and we'd have a cup of tea and chat about life's problems. But I don't even know how to find her. She graduated from the Saratov Medical Institute. She was happily married. But I divorced early on. I lived with my husband for less than a year. On the other hand, one might say that her husband died on her, for she was married all her life. I remember that she has two children and that her daughter is a biologist.

I forgot to ask whether religion played a role in your life.

---

18. I was unable to locate or establish contact with Vera Ivanovna Miachinskaia.

This is something about which the other children in my class don't know, but it played a role, of course. I have to say that I'm an atheist by nature, but an atheist in regard to official religion. For example, I don't care for the rituals that they perform when you visit church. I don't see any point in them. But my grandmother was a true believer. However, insofar as this was forbidden back then, she carefully kept this hidden. She was an Old Believer.[19] You perhaps heard of them or know the fabulous and well-known painting of Boyarina Morozova?[20] Well, my grandmother was an Old Believer and her father was an elder in the Old Believer church. That is, it was a deeply religious family. But the times were such that my grandmother married a Chekist![21] He came from an altogether different circle. They got married in church, where he showed up with a revolver! It's forbidden to enter a church with a weapon, but insofar as it was 1917 or 1918, the priest was forced to marry them [laughing]. But she kept it secret, very secret. I found out that she was a believer only after I had already finished school. That's right. In regard to me personally, well, I know that there's a higher power. It's simply that humankind is so imperfect, that we haven't yet come to know what exactly it is. We simply don't yet understand why some believe in one god and others believe in other gods. That's what I think. There is a higher power per se and it's wrong to sin because our higher power sees this and knows this. Yet I'm not afraid of this higher power. Just the opposite. I turn to it in need. I believe that there's something there. But it's not an official belief. Be that as it may, in regard to everyday life, I'm a realist and materialist, unambiguously so. Let's suppose that I have a meeting tomorrow. For me to go to church and pray to have the meeting turn out well, well I don't believe in such things at all. I believe that I need to prepare myself well for the meeting and if I do it's likely to go fine.

In 1962 Solzhenitsyn's novella, One Day in the Life of Ivan Denisovich, *was published in the journal* Novyi mir *[New World]. Did the children in school read it?*

---

19. The Russian Orthodox Church underwent a schism in the mid-seventeenth century, after which those rejecting reforms introduced by Patriarch Nikon continued to practice old rituals. The Old Believers comprised numerous subdivisions, which were persecuted by both the tsarist and Soviet states.

20. A masterpiece painted by Vasilii Surikov (1848–1916) in 1887, "Boyarina Morozova" depicts a prominent Old Believer and is on display in Moscow's Tretiakov Gallery.

21. A member of the Cheka, the first Soviet political police organization founded in December 1917, and precursor to the KGB.

Not at school, but I read it as soon as it came out. But the others—well, no. It was like this. My mother loved to read, and apparently did so quite a bit. You're using official data apparently, in saying that it appeared in *Novyi mir* in 1962, for a booklet circulated well before then. A small, thin one.[22] There was a man wearing a quilted jacket on the cover, drawn in black and white. He was running. I can still see it, I remember this well. Somehow a copy ended up in Mama's hands. Not for long, but during that time I managed to read it on the sly. A tiny pamphlet. And Papa literally, probably the very next day, threw it out because it was banned. He said she got it from someone. "Excuse me, but I flushed it down the toilet." Indeed. Everything was pretty open back there in the settlement.

What was your reaction when you read it?

I have to say that I am ambiguous about Solzhenitsyn. It's not worth talking about, but he has a lot wrong in the novella. He editorializes a great deal, and subjectively. In each of his works. I can simply take an example from one of his writings. It's actually from this one. Ivan Denisovich ends up in camp, where they steal his quilted jacket. And this, in the Far North, where the temperature drops to more than 51 below zero. I know this for a fact. Yet he's in an unheated barracks without his jacket! Can you imagine how cold that is? I know that when the temperature already reaches zero that people will freeze to death if they're not in a closed, heated building. But he survives. How can this be? I didn't understand. I don't believe it. I know that can't be. I'm—a realist. Or take this widespread example from the north. It's widely believed that if a man spits when there's a hard freeze—the same would be in your Alaska—it turns into ice before it hits the ground. Into ice. But that's a myth for those who don't have first-hand experience. It's simply not true. Yet he writes this. Why write such a thing when it spoils the work? Do you understand, it's a small point, but because of such small points I don't believe in what perhaps was in fact true. I simply don't believe it. I'm inclined to believe that he's more of a historian, since he examined a great deal of material, a considerable amount, and spent some time in that world. But it's not literature in my view. It's some sort of documentary work. And not always objective.

What about foreign radio broadcasts? Did you listen to them when you went to school?

---

22. This might have been an underground publication that circulated in the former campsites and beyond. It is also possible that Altukhova's chronology is wrong.

I probably don't have to answer that question. We were forbidden to listen.

I understand. Tell me what you thought of JFK and the Kennedys.

I like them even now. You know, when he was assassinated the entire country mourned as if he were one of our own. Do you understand? Evidently, it was his appearance. You can see for yourself that he looks Russian. Take a look at him. He's not a typical American. There's something in his looks that, well, in any event, if you were to dress him like a Russian and put him on the street, no one would notice that he's not one of us. He'd look like us. He wouldn't differ in the least. That's one thing. And, for another, his policies were kindly disposed toward Russia.[23] For this reason, well, perhaps this too was the result of how our propaganda worked. We liked him a lot and were really upset [when he was killed]. I even believed that one year they'd reveal the secrets behind his death. They told us that we'll find out in twenty-five years, and I thought, "Oh, how old I'll be when that time comes!" How I wanted to speed up that moment, how I wanted to know who and why. Although, by and large, what difference does it make?

What else shaped your worldview while you were growing up?

That's a tough question. I'd have to say that apart from school and my classmates there were other contacts, other people with whom I interacted, both my age and older. They were people other than my classmates. And as regards my classmates, well, we too, often got together, as a matter of fact, at Vera Miachinskaia's. A large group on every holiday. Maybe someone told you about it. It was a large group, not fewer than twelve people. Six girls and six boys. Just as it was supposed to be at that age. And this was on each holiday. We played records, there was a victrola. And a piano. Sometimes we played popular songs. They were simple things, with banal lyrics. Of course we ate, drank some alcohol, and danced. Yes, we danced. Danced and danced and danced. There were some teenage romances, too. It's only natural. Some girls liked certain boys and some boys liked certain girls. It's all quite normal. I can say that in my class all of us girls no doubt were in love with Sasha Trubnikov.[24] He had quite a few admirers. Practically all of us.

---

23. The Soviet public remained enamored with the glamour of the Kennedy White House and looked favorably upon JFK, despite the real threat of nuclear war that occurred during the Cuban Missile Crisis in 1962.

24. See chapter 7 for Aleksandr Vladimirovich Trubnikov's interview, which is also published in this collection.

How do you account for this?

You know, it's really impossible to explain. If you meet with him, you're supposed to, right? In appearance he doesn't make an impression, all the more today. That is, he's aged, and, you understand, changed. His appearance changed for the worse. But he had a certain inner charm, which was, well, he still has it today. The moment he starts to speak his appearance becomes altogether secondary. He was very smart and well read, and his voice had a very nice timbre, but mainly it was his inner charm. He played the guitar and sang Vysotskii. Just imagine. And this in addition to everything else![25] That's right.

Vysotskii's songs were first . . .

It was impossible to hear them, except among a small circle of friends. Although there was absolutely nothing prohibited in them. . . . Take, for instance, the song "And All Is Quiet in the Cemetery." From today's perspective it's unclear why it had such a magical effect on us. Well, it was probably mainly because all was quiet in the cemetery and all was quiet in the country. Do you understand? It has such words as everything was as quiet as could be and as proper as could be. And although there's nothing at all in the song that makes an analogy with the country at large, that's exactly how we understood it. That it's like a cemetery, see? We young people understood this as, well, a political song!

I see why. So, you graduated from school in 1967 and that fall enrolled somewhere?

Yes, in the Polytechnic Institute, where I majored in economics. I studied there for five and a half years because they extended instruction by a half year for our entire group. They trained us differently. We were trained not just as economists, but as economists in the area of computer-based management. They offered us additional training for a half year, after which I remained at the institute and worked there. I worked there and then enrolled in a target graduate program. I arrived in Moscow and spent three years there at the Moscow Economic-Statistical Institute. It's a good institute, not because I graduated from it, but because it offers a good basic education. Foreign students go there to study, even from developed countries. It's not easy.

What years were you in Moscow?

---

25. For example, Trubnikov received a gold medal as the best student in group A.

School's over! The last assembly before graduation, 1967.
Courtesy V. N. Kirsanov.

From 1980 through 1983. For three years. In 1983 I returned to Saratov and have worked here ever since.

What did it mean back then to live in Saratov? How did Moscow differ from Saratov?

The exact same way it does now. There's no difference between what was and what is. Muscovites live in their own special world. They don't live like the rest of the country does. That was true before, and it's true now, too. Both then and now people in Moscow are better paid and receive the best goods. It's exactly the same now. As regards education, I'm not so sure. I don't know the number of the school that my girlfriend graduated from, but it also offered specialized training in English. When she and I exchanged impressions, it was clear that our school was better. Our education was more serious. Our teachers were better qualified. Life is a bit better there, but the schools are better here. That's my deep conviction. I lectured and taught in Moscow universities and can compare the students, their work, and their graduates. I concluded that we're not lagging in any regard, even though we call ourselves provincial.

That's an interesting perspective. By the way, Natalia Valentinovna, what year did you get married?

Oh, that was so long ago [laughing]. Let's see, I'll simply count it out. Well, I graduated from the institute in 1972 and therefore it was probably in 1973 that I got married, for my son was born in 1974 and I got divorced in 1975. It's all so simple.

Although you lived with your husband for only a short time, I wonder how he might have influenced you or shaped your worldview.

He didn't have any influence whatsoever on me, because we got divorced. I believed since childhood, owing to my father, that apart from loving my husband and the like, I had to respect him. I had to treat him respectfully as if he were the head of the household. Well, perhaps this is too Eastern a variant. But that's what I believed, do you understand? It turned out, however, that I couldn't respect him for a variety of reasons. He drank heavily. That's a national sickness. It's even part of our mentality. Therefore, since I could not respect him, I could not live with him as a family. And I have to say that over the years I tried to make a life for myself—that's only natural for a woman to do. However, I haven't met a man whom I could respect as much as I respected my father. That's how things turned out. Perhaps that's also some sort of illness. I later read that there exists a psychological type, when, let's say, a child gets along with one of his parents so well that his or her personal life simply doesn't work out for this very reason. But I don't think this is a clinical condition. Nevertheless, I didn't meet the right man. Well, perhaps in some other life. There's not much one can do about it. After all, the main thing here is respect, and it's something I simply don't experience with the large number of men with whom I come into contact. So, my husband couldn't have any influence on me because I didn't respect him.

What shaped the formation of your self-perception, of your so-called identity?

That's very hard to say. Perhaps even now I don't have a clear sense of self. Therefore it's hard to say what shaped it. Well, I can't judge myself from the outside, neither subjectively, nor in any other way. I understood already as a child that there's no point in this. When I attended school, I believed that I was too tall. I'm talking about my height, do you get it? Therefore, it was really hard for me to accept that my height was actually below average [laughing]. I realized that there's no point in evaluating myself and never did it again. I'm not sure, then, what shaped me when I don't understand who I am. You see?

What role did gender play in your life? How did your being a woman shape your fate?

Yes, that shaped me. I fully understood already as a child that things are a lot easier for men. I say this not because I hate men. Not at all. I'm on good terms, so to speak, with many men at work. I didn't fulfill myself on a personal level, but at work or in regard to friends there's no problem. Indeed, I have a large number of male acquaintances with whom I'm on good terms. But I realize that in our times it's much harder for a woman. It's harder in many ways. If there's a family, then I'd have to do everything at home and free my husband of any responsibility, understand? That's the way it is, so it simply would be harder for me, right? And if a man and a woman contend for the same vacancy at work, the man gets it. That's 99.9 percent certain. In other words, women play a huge role in our society. Many work, actually just about all do, but it's much more difficult for a woman to achieve something. Such is our life. Perhaps this is a peculiarly Russian way of looking at things that stems from our communal order, from our primordial patrimonial system. Probably. Whoever is in charge is served by women. It stems from this. Once again, it's an Asian, an Eastern concept.

You said that you had wanted to join the Communist Party, right?

Yes, I wanted to. I sincerely wanted to, but conditions were such that they picked party members from among workers. I never was a worker. I have nothing against physical labor, but nowhere could I write on an application that I had been a proletarian. That already instantly limited my options.

Is it fair to conclude that you experienced a certain disappointment in this regard?

Yes, of course. Great disappointment. But if they don't take you, they don't take you.

Did your attitudes toward the outside world change as an adult? Toward the West? Toward China? Toward Cuba?

I don't relate to countries, but to people. And I know that there are good people in each nation, in each country. That's my take on this. Perhaps my generation feels the same way. It's a good question. There are people who, for instance, behave negatively toward immigrants from the south [Caucasus] who end up in Saratov.[26] They'll blurt out, "See! They come here and sell things and mess up our lives." I can't agree with this. I've been this way since childhood. I believe that there are decent people and dishonest people

---

26. Saratov has attracted an influx of Armenians (from Azerbaijan), Georgians, and Chechens who fled troubled areas in the Caucasus.

in each nation or nationality. And it's better to associate with the decent ones. That's all. In this regard there can be only one form of discrimination. As soon as I see that someone's dishonest, I try not to associate with him. What difference does it make what nationality one belongs to? In our class, for instance, you may have noticed that there were a large number of Jews.[27] I'm a hundred percent Russian, but I don't see any difference. But some kids in class did think there was a difference.

Was this felt in school? That there was some sort of difference based on nationality?

I know that many felt this way. Have you already interviewed Chemodurova?[28] Well, long after we had graduated from school, probably about five years ago, maybe six, she told me some things when I met her that I heard for the first time, in particular, that at school she felt that people treated her like a Jew. That is, they treated her differently than they treated Russians. I didn't notice this. I befriended her at school. We socialized often, and if there was some sort of dissatisfaction, or, say, some manifestation of negative feelings, they were not tied to nationality but to personal qualities. That's for certain! She was known for her peculiarities. We each have our quirks. And with her it was her personality. It's only natural that some people didn't like this, while others weren't bothered by it. In any event, I don't discriminate on the basis of nationality. Not at all.

Marxist teachings underscore the importance of economic development and the importance of economic issues in general. You're an economist. How did you understand the problems that plagued the Soviet system back then? The fact that there was a black market, that Saratovites had to travel to Moscow on so-called sausage trains in order to buy sausage, meat, and other things? How did you understand this as an economist?

Well, you know, speaking simply as a person, when you live in a certain world, do you really evaluate it? You can assess it only after you've already lived through it, as if you were viewing it from the outside. Back then I never thought about it in the manner that you formulated your question. But I did as an economist, of course. The point is that at the institute I had to study economic theories, Marxist and non-Marxist, and any economic theory is based on

---

27. Jews composed the second largest cohort in the school's class of '67, approximately 10 to 18 percent of the class.

28. Chemodurova is a pseudonym for a member of the class of '67 that she herself asked me to use.

economic development. Any, not only Marxist. Therefore, we of course studied the economy's shortcomings in great detail, in a very serious manner. The shortcomings were not secret. Even back then we were able to say what was wrong with our system economically. By the way, there's a negative side even today, not everything is rosy, you might say. The market system has enormous drawbacks. Moreover, this very market system that's developing here is doing so in a distorted manner. It's not the same as it is in America. Do you understand? Well, I had more than my share of traveling to Moscow to buy things. I lugged around enormous shopping bags. That's a given. However, that was already after I graduated from school, of course. That wasn't necessary while I attended school, because it was possible to buy everything locally. In 1967, for instance, I went into a deli and counted how many varieties of lunchmeat were available. I remember the exact number, again, from 1967. There were 167 different types of lunchmeat in the store on Kirov Prospect. The store was called "Sausage Shop." It was a specialty shop. But many people today say that things were always bad back then. It's not true. There was no problem getting lunchmeat. But back in 1963, I believe, there was no bread. Maybe someone told you about this.[29] They passed out rolls to us in school, and you had to stand in line for bread. Yet at the same time there were other goods available! You see, it's not true that we were swollen with hunger here. Not at all. That wasn't the case. If you're speaking about the fact that for a period of time the stores were empty, that was in the 1970s, when there was nothing in the stores. The stores were empty, but people's refrigerators were well stocked. Life was simply organized differently. You can't say that we have it so good now. It doesn't at all suit me, at my age, that we lack natural foods. It's all artificial. This doesn't suit me at all. In other words, I have to search out opportunities [to satisfy my needs] just as I did back then when I traveled to Moscow for food. Now I seek out opportunities to get hold of natural food products. So what's the difference? It's simply that life in Russia is a constant struggle. Maybe that's simply impossible for you to grasp. We don't live our own lives. We live the lives of those who are close to us, whom we must help get by and help support. That's the way it is.

---

29. Bread shortages took place at the end of the Khrushchev years, as many informants recalled.

Why is that the case?

It's simplest to say, of course, that I'm too far removed from this and don't want to go deeper into it. That would be the simplest. But to answer, well, I thought a bit about this and perhaps I won't tell you everything I think. However, it seems to me that this country is too big. Too big. It seems to me that at present we lack an aim and purpose. If before we had a goal, communism, even if it was an unobtainable one, we at least had a purpose. However, there's none now. The mass media search for a single goal, a national one. They search for what this purpose might be. That which is cultivated today, the revival of religiosity, is not really an aim. Moreover, I think that the head of the government exerted a negative influence on the intelligentsia when he [Boris Yeltsin], a party functionary, suddenly appeared in church and crossed himself. That's absolutely terrible. It's deceitful! You can call it what you like, but it's insincere. If this is insincere, how can you believe in other things he says or does? I don't think that he's a true believer. I'm not speaking about the one who is in power now, not about Putin. But it's basically not my job to figure out why we live this way.

Before perestroika, what did you think of dissidents?

You know, that's really a hard one, since there always have been people who were otherwise-minded and there still are. However, these very dissenters were charged in such a way that back then we didn't know what they were being prosecuted for. For example, everyone condemned Solzhenitsyn, but no one heard him or read him. Everyone denounced Bulgakov,[30] but no one ever read a word he wrote. That's how things were. And the main thing was that they were impossible to read because they weren't published.[31] Be that as it may, people found ways; after all, some people read them and drew their own conclusions. Naturally, I can now say that all of this was politicized, because I don't find any literary value in these works. None. It's not fiction. Therefore, how can you denounce

---

30. Mikhail Afanasievich Bulgakov (1891–1940) was a Soviet novelist, journalist, short story writer, and playwright who soon fell out of favor with the Soviet regime. Not allowed to publish his works, he petitioned the government in 1930 to let him emigrate, but Stalin turned down his request. In the decade or so before his death, Bulgakov composed his internationally acclaimed novel, *Master and Margarita,* which made him something of a cult figure among elements of the intelligentsia.

31. A sanitized version of Bulgakov's *Master and Margarita* was first published in the USSR in the 1960s in the journal *Moskva* (Moscow), but it may have been difficult to obtain in the provinces.

them? There's nothing in these works. No one is going to read them on their own. Except for a historian. But an ordinary person isn't going to read these books.

During the Gorbachev years they called the Brezhnev era one of stagnation. What did you think of Brezhnev?

It's my deep belief that there was no stagnation when I was born. I'm not sure what stagnation is. I had responsibilities my entire life, beginning with kindergarten. That is, I worked my entire life. I love my work, whatever work I'm involved in. I never work under pressure. I do only what I please. What sort of stagnation can there be when your entire life is wrapped up in work? What kind of stagnation? I don't understand. How did I relate personally to Brezhnev? You're interested in Brezhnev? During the early years he was a real leader and people thought rather highly of him. And life in some respects got better. That's not in dispute. They were positive toward him. But then this changed, apparently owing to the status of his health. Indeed, he was old and sickly. However, I had no personal opinion of him. Please understand that I can't take him personally. I'm not among those people, who, let's say, can fall for an actor or. . . . That is, he was somewhere at a distance, so I don't understand what kind of relationship I could have had with him. I can't judge his qualities, because everything that he, and for that matter, the next one said, was written by speech writers. These people don't write their own speeches. They read them. Ultimately, it's not really their ideas if they read them. So how could I relate to him? He read speeches, and we studied them. We discussed them in class, that's all.

Why do you believe perestroika took place?

It took place owing to the enormous influence of America. That's what I think. Many people in this country share this view. You have to understand that it wasn't a matter of Americans coming here and saying, "You have to launch perestroika." No, that wasn't the case. Of course not. And the typical person could care less about what we're doing here in Russia. You're interested, because you're a historian. However, if you were not a historian, but a biologist, you'd be interested in your sharks and that's it. Nothing else. Therefore, it's difficult to say in regard to perestroika what brought it about. I'm at a loss. I'm at a loss. I'm not going to say anything more about this.

Okay. Tell me what you think of Gorbachev.

Not what you think in the West. That's absolutely for certain. If, say, in Germany they hold him in high regard as the person who brought down the Berlin Wall, I've heard the views of people who were against this. There are people who are for him and those who are against him. If you're speaking about life here in Russia, well, of course we were given glasnost. In the early days we walked about stunned by this glasnost, because we didn't expect such things at all. We knew all these things, but it was a shock to be able to articulate them. Don't at all think, though, that they divulged something new for me. They didn't disclose a single thing that I didn't already know, absolutely nothing. They published, for instance, poems and songs that we sang on the sly. But we already knew them down to the last word. However, none of this had been allowed before, and then, all of a sudden, it was all published. That's what was important. The fact that we could now articulate what was usually not spoken about. As it was, everyone already knew everything.

There was nothing in particular that shocked you?

Well, you know, it's often said about those who gave their lives, say, for some sort of cause, that "they'd roll over in their graves three times if they could see how we live today." That's what's shocking. Inwardly, I rolled over thirty-three times, not in my grave, but while alive, from all the changes that have come to our life. But there's no escaping this. We don't get to pick our life; we're placed in it to live the best we can.

I'll return to this point, but for now I want to ask you about myths and beliefs. In all societies myths help to unite people. Tell me about the myths that united people in Soviet society before the Gorbachev era.

Well, the first myth is that we were building communism. That's a myth—a political myth, right? It's propaganda, but it strongly united people. It united many. Don't think that the masses of people opposed this. Everyone was in favor. Only an insignificant number of people at the beginning of Soviet power, before the stable 1950s, opposed the system. Back in 1937 some were opposed, but the over-whelming majority of people were in favor. And even some of those who fell into the meat grinder were not opposed to the system; they simply fell into it. The myth was that if it was Soviet, it was good. There was such a saying. But it was a myth. Indeed, goods were of high quality, but they were by no means the best. Yet we believed otherwise. This in particular united us, because we clearly knew what we wanted. We wanted, let's say, Soviet candy, Soviet butter, Soviet sausage, because they contained only natural ingredients. In general, it was not the best that could have been invented, but we were convinced it was. That's a myth.

How can the history of your life help me understand the fate of the Soviet Union? To what extent does your life reflect more global processes?

My life reflects them in all regards. To begin, you know exactly what are the main events that took place in my life. Not long ago we had a meeting of the academic council at the institute, at which one of the older people present, a professor, stood up and began to criticize our past life. It was like, "Well, in the Soviet Union, things were really bad. Everything was secret. We could speak openly only on the sly, in the kitchen." I don't agree with him at all. Not at all, because it was precisely back then that I received an education free of charge. Free. I, someone from a family of very modest means, turned out to be someone after all. My parents, if they were engineers today, could not afford to send me to college. That's for certain. They couldn't afford to let me join any study or hobby group. They couldn't afford to hire someone to give me music lessons or foreign language lessons. That's for certain. And later, I undoubtedly would not have been able to complete my dissertation, because these days all this costs a great deal of money. Real money. True, we have various ways to deal with this. You perhaps know that, in addition to everything else, you still have to grease people's palms. Moreover, in regards to medicine, I, as it were, twice was declared clinically dead. This was back in the Soviet period. If this were to occur today, I wouldn't be among the living. Perhaps my life isn't important to anyone apart from my child, but I wouldn't be alive today. Yet back then a doctor saved me and it was free. She saved me because that doctor had taken the Hippocratic oath when she finished med school, and she considered it her responsibility to save people. Simply because she was obliged to do so. That's no longer the case. Today she wouldn't even know who Hippocrates was. That's a real difference for you. It could well be that you're raised this way and don't understand the difference. But I do. Perhaps you pay your way your entire life, and therefore don't understand the difference. However, that's not true here. There was a time here when a person earning 100 rubles a month, maybe 120, sat with me at night, brought me out of it, and put me back on my feet and I'm alive today. When I brought her a bouquet of flowers, she said to me, "What are you doing? You don't need to do this! I did what I did because it was my job." That's what the Soviet period was. It had its positive qualities. There was a lot wrong with it, but there was a lot that was right. It's like today—there are some good things, and some bad.

3. "We grew up in a normal time" | Natalia P.

July 3, 2002, Saratov

I interviewed Natalia P. immediately following my interview
with Natalia Valentinovna Altukhova (Pronina). A heat spell
had descended upon Saratov, and since air conditioning remains rare in provincial Russia, I took Natalia P. up on her
offer to hold the interview in her apartment, which had a window air conditioning unit in the living room. When I contacted
her over the phone, Natalia P. had reacted with enthusiasm
to my request to meet with her, and she later proved to be
helpful and hospitable. Yet like several others whom I interviewed—only a little more than a decade after the collapse of
the Soviet Union—she requested some degree of anonymity.
She reviewed and corrected my records, providing me with
recent phone numbers for some of her classmates. She showed
me old photographs, and let me copy one of her as a young
girl clad in a ballet tutu. She offered me a much-appreciated
espresso, accompanied by platefuls of snacks. And she gave me
several books as gifts. But she forgot to tell me that she had a
pet rat, uncaged, that had free run of the living room. Comfortably ensconced in an easy chair reviewing my questions
while she brewed coffee in the kitchen, I had my concentration interrupted by the rodent, who jumped onto my lap to get
a closer look. I'm sure my reaction surprised him as much as
his inquisitiveness had startled me.

Open, introspective, and prepared to speak her mind, Natalia P. answered my questions in rich detail. Her recognition of
the malleability of memory and readiness to acknowledge how
the present shapes her view of the past revealed an almost
intuitive understanding of oral history in all its marvelous
subjectivity. The daughter of a professor of political economy,
Natalia P. made clear how important family was in shaping her
worldview and what it meant to be a young girl from a "good"
family. Offering invaluable insight into what she described as

growing up "in a normal time," her nostalgia was not naive, for there was plenty about this "normality" that she disliked or at least could see in a more critical light now. As a teacher and a mother, she had a particularly good vantage point from which to evaluate today's youth and what she believes was lost and gained as a result of the breakup of the Soviet Union. The economic transition hit Saratov hard, as the large and inter-connected complex of defense-related factories in the city shut down or fumbled to reinvent themselves. She recounts how these changes affected her own family—and others—providing both real challenges and new opportunities. Spontaneous and animated, Natalia P. told her story with so much intensity, even passion, that she seemed burned out at the end. I ben-efited from her sustained effort to explain not only the impor-tant milestones in her own life, but also those of her country. I likewise appreciated her ruminations about conspiracy theory, about the oft-mentioned Russian soul, and about subjectivity and human memory.

What was "normal" about Natalia P.'s childhood? What did it mean to be a girl from a "good" family in Saratov during the Khrushchev and Brezhnev eras? How does she understand the difficulties she encountered establishing herself professionally in Saratov? What values and attributes does Natalia P. ascribe to men and women? Is her son growing up in a "normal" time?

My father was twelve years older than my mother. As he liked to say, he was a participant in three wars: the war with Finland, the war with Japan, and the Great Fatherland War.[1] Unfortunately, we've been without him now for twelve years. I was born in 1950, when he was thirty-nine years old. He was, as they say, ready to start a family. Papa taught political economy at the Technical University.[2] He began working there in 1948, the year he defended his dissertation in political economy. He was one of the first to do so in the late

---

1. The Soviet Union launched a military campaign against Finland in November 1939, fought against the Nazis after Hitler's armies invaded the Soviet Union in June 1941, and went to war against Japan in 1945.

2. Formerly the Saratov Polytechnic Institute.

Natalia P., July 2002.

'40s after the war. My mother had a secondary education in the field of medicine and worked as a hospital nurse. The war began just when she turned sixteen. As a result, she completed school and throughout the war worked in hospitals caring for the wounded. There were many of them in Saratov. They married in 1948, and I was born in 1950. I also have a sister who is three years younger than me.

Are your parents native Saratovites?

Yes. Papa and Mama were born in Saratov. My father was a Communist by conviction, ever the more so because the subject that he taught was a social science that demanded an ideological approach. As he said jokingly, "I teach the political economy of capitalism. I don't study the political economy of socialism." When they would ask him questions, he'd say, "Don't make a fool of me. I only teach the political economy of capitalism." He was a very good lecturer. Back then they even taped his lectures as models and sent them to Moscow. You have to take into account the level of technology back then. Moreover, how shall I put it? Active forms of teaching as we now like to say were just getting underway. But for the times he was a very good specialist. My mother did not work after we were born. She took care of the household and of us. We were what are called girls from a good family, as we jokingly liked to say. And when our school was opened, the English-language school, in 1958, we enrolled in the third grade. The A group with twenty-six pupils had been formed the year before. I think it's interesting that before that I had gone to School No. 9, and that five or six members of our class, including Sasha Konstantinov,[3] who now lives in Moscow, enrolled in the special English-language school. Our parents were on friendly terms and even now remember each other fondly.

Well, what was my childhood like? You know, in recalling my childhood and projecting things onto my own child, who just this year graduated from the Law Academy, I see a big difference. Let's just say that we were obliged to listen to our parents, but this obedience came easily because they made reasonable demands on us. I knew, for instance, that I had to study hard and do well in school, not for the sake of good grades but for the sake of acquiring knowledge. We had lots of books at home. I read a great deal during my childhood. And we learned a lot from our parents, too. I remember that when Papa came home from work, we'd usually gather around him. He'd tell us what happened at work that day and what problems he encountered in his department. And we'd tell him about our day at school. That is, we knew what was going on in each other's lives. Analyzing this from today's perspective, I think that the totalitarian regime left its mark on my parents' childhood. For that reason, that's the same upbringing that we received. It's not that I felt some kind of awful strictness. I wasn't so afraid of my parents that I had to lie to them, let's say, so that they wouldn't punish me. For example, if I received a D in mathematics—I didn't do so well in that subject since I was interested in the humanities—I simply didn't do well. What should we do? Papa was very principled. To take the teachers a box of candy and to ask for their help as is customary today was absolutely unacceptable to him. I remember once when I got a C in math. My math teacher showed up and asked for his help in getting someone into the institute. He could have done that without any problem and in so doing improve my grade. Yet he dismissed her and wouldn't even talk with her. My mother tried to save the situation, do you understand? What else

---

3. See Aleksandr Aleksandrovich Konstantinov's interview in chapter 1.

can I tell you? I got to see a large number of performances in our Saratov theaters, in the children's theater. And when I was around six we began to attend ballets. During the summers we went south. My mother didn't work, only Papa, but as an associate professor at the Polytechnic Institute he could afford to take us on vacation to the sea. Our needs, once again when compared with the situation today, were modest enough. By the way, regarding material things, the families of only two pupils [in our group], I think, didn't belong to the so-called intelligentsia and were workers.

Were you aware of this back then?

You know, that question simply didn't interest us! It was only much later, when I was already grown up and when my mother and I recalled my school years that she'd say, "There were two pupils. . . ." They admitted them to improve the school's profile. They couldn't take children only of the intelligentsia. Our parents understood this. But we weren't at all interested in who one's parents were. We were all dressed modestly. There was no conspicuous consumption, there were no such possibilities, although back then an associate professor's salary allowed a family of four to live comfortably. Therefore, Mama didn't work. I remember a book, one that I still have, and one that my son enjoyed when he was a child. It's about prehistoric animals and it was published in Czechoslovakia. It was on sale in the "Friendship of Peoples" store, we had such a store on Radishchev Street, and it cost one ruble forty kopecks. After school—I was in the sixth grade, I was about thirteen at the time— I'd go to the store and admire the book. My parents gave it to me as a gift on New Year's or some other holiday, that is, on some sort of special occasion.[4] It wasn't that they regretted spending money on the book, but it simply wasn't the norm to spoil children with endless gifts. Not like we do, not like I do with my own child. And I repeat, this didn't harm me in the least. But my sister, well, she is three years younger. She went to an ordinary school, and things were altogether different with her, despite the small difference in age between us. There was already competition among parents there to see who could clothe their child the best, to see who could be cooler as they say. We weren't at all like that. Only later, having finished school, did I come to understand that one of our classmate's father

---

4. After the Soviet government discouraged the celebration of Christmas (which, according to the Russian Orthodox Church calendar, falls on January 6), the New Year became one of the most widely celebrated holidays.

was some sort of party official. There were some parents who were party officials and who were in power. All in all, I have but the very best memories of my childhood.

Regarding school, I'm once again afraid that my present impressions color [my recollections], that back then I perceived all this differently. Of course, there was discipline in our school. They were strict with us, but we girls thought this was all right. For instance, we couldn't wear short skirts. I remember that when our principal, Vera Filippovna, visited our class—we were about thirteen or fourteen—we had to show our hands and if she noticed that anyone was doing their nails she'd punish them. We weren't allowed to wear adult hair-dos. We didn't dare think about wearing makeup! Yet it was interesting to learn, because, first of all, our teachers were probably chosen on the basis of their pedagogical skills. From today's perspective, some of them undoubtedly used methods associated with the regime. The older ones were brought up before or during the war and weren't able to shed this. We had some really good young teachers of English. But our group wasn't so lucky, because they were constantly changing. The other group had more stability in regard to teachers. However, the young ones were marvelous. The very best memories I have are connected to the English language, of course, with the teaching of English literature. Well, sometimes it was hard going. We had homework. When we had a book to read, a work of literature, we'd be assigned, say, twenty pages [to read at home] and then we'd discuss them in class. Once we read, I no longer recall the author, *Lorna Doone.*[5] It's an absolutely boring, awful book with nothing to offer in terms of knowledge or information. But apparently they simply had enough copies to go around. By and large, there was a genuine problem with textbooks. For me it was real torture to read *Lorna Doone.* When we read *Jane Eyre,* for example, it was much more interesting and we recognized it as being such. I remember that in tenth grade we read Oscar Wilde's *The Portrait of Dorian Gray,* and then reread it during our first year at the Pedagogical Institute. This is altogether different language, an altogether different thing, and therefore we discussed it with great pleasure. When our class gets together today, even the guys, who, generally speaking, were not as diligent in their study of language as we women, remember how we used to listen to the tape of a story

---

5. L. D. Blackmore published this "romance" in 1869.

called *Billy Bobtail.* We still recall these stories! That is, the school provided us with a good, broad education, not a narrow one. We even studied art. They taught us how to sew. And after school I sewed a lot for myself.

Are you speaking of an after-school club?

Well, no, we had a class called Home Economics where we learned to cook and sew. And boys had "shop," where they learned how to make furniture, how to work with wood and metal. We also did something with metal, because I recall that we wore blue overalls. We sawed and turned lathes in the locksmith's workshop, too. In other words, this knowledge that they gave us basically came in handy. We were able to do a few things, to sew something, to make a salad. They taught us all that.

And what became popular during your school days in regard to music and clothing? You've already mentioned that you weren't allowed to wear short skirts.

Short skirts, well, mini-skirts came a bit later, when I was probably in my third year at the Pedagogical Institute and began practice teaching in the schools. My girlfriend and I arrived at School No. 42, and when the director saw us she said, "I don't understand a thing, but I won't allow you in those skirts!" Well, by then, she, of course, had grown old and frail. It wasn't that she locked horns with us, but that she tried to apply her restrictions in full measure. Perhaps she no longer had the strength, because the next generation no longer subordinated themselves to her. But there was a certain benevolent and pleasant atmosphere in the school. Let's see. What did we enjoy doing? We first got together at someone's apartment when we were in the eighth grade, when we celebrated New Year's. Practically all of us from the B group were there. We also went to a sport camp on the Volga. My parents didn't let me go. This totally distressed me. I didn't need their trip down south to the sea; I wanted to go to camp with my classmates. But my parents were strict and didn't let me go.

Why not?

I don't know. It simply wasn't permitted to ask why. If I were to, let's say, tell my son, well, I can't say to him, "I don't allow you." Well, for one, what right do I have to tell him he can't do something? He's already grown up. But if one of my parents said to me, "I won't let you," it wouldn't even have occurred to me to try to change their mind or to ask them why not. Not at all. Well, we also celebrated birthdays, but only in the upper grades. I remember, I think it was when we were in eighth grade that we went to the beach. There also was the camp that I wasn't allowed to attend. We celebrated birthdays. We celebrated them without alcohol, purely symbolically, with one bottle for everyone. A shot glass was all that it took to make us girls silly enough for the boys. You know, we talked about this when we got together for our reunion recently on June 14.[6] They managed to bring us up, the majority of us, with a strong sense of duty and responsibility, especially we girls, who were better brought up, let's put it that way. I feel this even now. Do you understand what I'm saying? If you have to do something, you simply have to do it. Some of this remains with me even today, and with the present generation. Since I work with young people, with today's generation, I'm in a position to compare. There is no doubt that there are students today with a very developed sense of responsibility. But more often than not these are students who have no one standing over them and who lack their parents' support. For example, it's the student who arrives from the village who has to make his own way. Do you understand? He knows that no one will help him and for this reason he studies from morning to night. He has a sense of responsibility. However, the majority of kids these days are spoiled by their parents. If they're turned down one place, the parents take them elsewhere to some other institution of higher education and make arrangements there. In other words, a sense of responsibility is unfortunately all too rare among today's young people. And they lack a real thirst for knowledge, today's generation, because they're pragmatists, they're rationalists. It's the times. We grew up in a normal time. I worked for three years at the Pedagogical Institute, then for thirteen years at the university, then for three years again at the Pedagogical Institute, which I left to go to work at our Law Institute. When I began to work it was already the period of the so-called Brezhnev stagnation. Khrushchev was in power until 1964 and through inertia they continued for several years with the "Khrushchev Thaw." When we enrolled in the Pedagogical Institute's Department of Foreign Languages I mostly studied my favorite subject. I really liked being a student. We had absolutely wonderful teachers. I didn't have a single "B" on my transcript. I was a straight-A student, because I really liked what I was doing. The first years after I began working were similar to my

---

6. Many members of the tight-knit B group hold a reunion each June or whenever former classmates now living elsewhere return to Saratov.

student days. But it's one thing being a student, and another being a teacher even at the same institution. It was then that all that was connected with ideology manifested itself in full measure. This was back in 1972, 1973.

But I'm getting sidetracked. There was this paradox. When we studied English there wasn't much to work with. But now there are audiocassettes, videocassettes, and native speakers with whom to practice, and fabulous textbooks, yet knowledge of the language is superficial. We learned without hearing a single native speaker. And what ancient textbooks we had! From the point of view of contemporary pedagogy, things were less than perfect. But we knew the language. We sometimes discuss this among ourselves, we specialists, when we talk about active teaching methods. We devoted a conference to this, and we remember how we learned back then without any active methods. Apparently, when you teach people who want to learn, all methods are good ones. But when you do things under constraints, no matter what it is, none of the methods is quite right. When we studied the country of the language we were learning we couldn't use the word "Christmas," because it's tied to religion. Now, when I lecture on the English language and speech practices, we take everything into account, because these matters are so interesting. Back then, despite the separation of church and state that still exists, back then, when religion was virtually banned, I couldn't even use the word "Christmas" in class. It was as if we didn't have Christmas here. It was absolutely under a ban at the Pedagogical Institute, but our university, which has always prided itself in being a university, well, there one encountered freethinking. At the university you could still find a way to somehow talk about it. Now we hold conferences dedicated to the celebration of Christmas, where we stage a Christmas celebration with our students. The times have changed!

Therefore, when we begin to argue about when things were better, back then or now, many sharply criticize the present and are nostalgic about back then when our economic situation was more stable. But I still recall what things were like at work. Back then I was pretty limited in the methods I could use and I always had to keep in mind what I could not say. I could not express my true thoughts. There was a lot of hypocrisy. Remember how we used to cry out "Glory to the CPSU [Communist Party of the Soviet Union]?" Well, on the one hand, everything that was connected to the party was ideological and hypocritical. It's very important to me that things are no longer that way. Let there be fewer varieties of sausage [in the stores]. It's not even that good for you anyway. We can eat porridge. On the other hand, the absence of the Komsomol, which also was a product of that political system, makes itself felt in a negative way. Young people must have "something to do." I try to make sense of our life today, our relations, say, with the West. Well, because we were a closed city, for all practical purposes we had no contacts with foreigners. But even in our closed system [at work] foreigners began to visit in 1995. We have some collaboration with the police in Germany and with the FBI, with the secret service. On the one hand, I see no fundamental differences between us. We think alike, we have the same human and moral values. We have the same problems. The problem between generations is probably a difficult one for you, too. As I always say when they begin to tell me that things weren't like this before, what do you mean by before? When primitive man hunted mammoths some probably charged ahead while others hid behind them. Some wanted a bigger and juicier piece to eat, while others were satisfied with a regular chunk. Yet generally our values and human nature have not changed. Human nature is refined through education. Young people need some constraints and organization during their childhood.

There's a problem here today. My mother didn't work but raised us. She returned to work when I was in eighth or ninth grade and my sister was a bit younger. Because of this she's entitled to a pension. But she receives a small one because she didn't work for that many years. She's now seventy-eight years old. I can help her out, so that's not the point. Papa worked, of course, but nevertheless he and my mother devoted a lot of time to us. I no longer work like I used to five or six years ago, but I still slave away from morning until night. They offer me work, and I simply can't refuse it. Sometimes I do it for the money, sometimes out of interest. I've now been teaching Latin for four years. I like it. At the same college, the Law Academy. I don't have any time or energy left for my son. Do you understand what I'm saying? We nevertheless had a good childhood. I consider our generation to be normal. Well, perhaps that's connected to the fact that our parents had time for us, even though they earned less. There's no longer a Komsomol, and young people are left to fend for themselves. The parents are either unemployed—and this gives rise to a mass of problems—or work from morning until night earning money. There's no time left for the children and we're undergoing a change of values. Whereas before we discussed whether or

not someone acted decently, we now think about whether or not
something is advantageous to us. It seems to me that this influence
came from the West. Our reality had been different. There was a
real leveling that took place. It didn't matter if you worked or not
because you'd nevertheless be paid practically the same. You could
earn a lot of money only in some criminal way. Now there is a legal
way to do so. If before our criminal code prosecuted "speculation,"
now it's called business. It's natural that even the legal code reflects
what's happening in society. There's no longer any article against
"speculation" in the criminal code, because business has been legal-
ized, and this amounts to people earning money by reselling things.
If before we manufactured things, now we resell them. What else
is there?

*You recounted in an interesting way how your generation differs from
the one that followed, but how does it differ from that of your parents?*

Well, I don't think we differed greatly, in any significant way.
First, our parents' generation lived through the war. Such an ordeal
is difficult for any generation. But that war was fought at a different
time. You can't compare it, say, to the war in Afghanistan or Chechnia today.[7] Back then they had their ideals in which they sacredly
believed, and they fought for those ideals. By and large they passed
on these ideals to us. I, therefore, think that there aren't any fundamental differences, although we're, well, we're more democratic,
we're freer, we're less inhibited.

*Why is that? After all, that's a major difference. What specifically shaped
your generation?*

It's a result of the times, of course. We grew up in different circumstances, in a different era. Nonetheless, ideology was something
we had to deal with when we were in school, right? And by the time
we became conscious adults this was no longer the case. Some things
were easier for us than for our parents, because when perestroika
began it was very hard for people from the older generation to accept it. The older you were, the harder it was to take. I don't know
if you knew the philosopher at the university, Iakov Fomich Askin?
He was a very smart man, a doctor of philosophy. About six or seven
years ago he committed suicide, he hanged himself, and left a note

---

7. Fearing that the Afghan government would move out of the USSR's orbit, the
Soviet Union invaded Afghanistan in December 1979. Russia went to war with Chechnia
in 1994–96 to prevent the territory's secession, and found a pretext to do so once again
in late 1999.

that read, "I no longer understand anything in this life. I can't live like this." He was a man of the old school, and it was hard for him to adapt himself. It was harder for my father to accept perestroika, because of the nature of his work, which was tied to ideology. As for my mother, well, women tend to adapt easier to change—although it was also hard enough on her, but for different reasons. We're younger, and our way of thinking is more flexible. Yet there were periods when things were challenging enough. At the beginning of perestroika and in the early 1990s it was hard to understand and accept what was going on in the world. My husband, for example, worked all his life at a factory in the military-industrial complex, where he earned good money compared to others. And all of a sudden he ended up unemployed, when the factory stopped functioning with the collapse of the Soviet Union, because all the parts had been produced in other union republics. It was hard for him to reorient himself, but now he does repair work; it's only our apartment that he's not able to fix [laughing]. It's terrible to bungle things! I ask him, "When do you plan to redo the apartment?" He replies, "When your child begins to speak English" [laughing]. He now makes a decent salary. By and large, I react fairly calmly to this; however, you can never earn enough money, since one's needs can grow without limit. Yet there is a certain level of need that each person determines for him or herself. My husband, of course, earns more, for example, than a professor, but his social status is lower. This also affected him. But nothing's perfect in life. Therefore, it was hard to accept what was going on. Take my sister, who was an engineer. There was a period when all of the factories were shut down and no one was working. She came to work where I do, and was paid piecemeal. She gave out uniforms. She had to change professions. We all lived through such a period, but young people, our students, are beginning to understand that they need practical knowledge and not just a diploma. If you don't have the skills, even if you manage to get a job somewhere, you simply won't be able to hold on to it. They'll fire you. Anyway, that's what they're beginning to understand.

There might be something of a paradox here. The teachers in your school, those who taught English, at least, probably were somewhat favorably disposed toward those countries in which English is spoken. On the other hand, instruction was politicized. What were your attitudes toward the West back then?

You know, it's hard for me to say. I adored Britain, but it was very hard to obtain any information that wasn't distorted. When we were older we understood that the information presented through the mass media did not always correspond to reality. As I said, I loved English, which I studied since the third grade, and because this became my profession, everything connected to Britain interested me. Well, my father lived my life and everything that he heard, say, about Britain, about the queen of England, he'd pass on to me. That is, Papa reinforced my interest in and love for English. America was simply too far away. Back then we learned British English. The first time I had to translate for Americans, they asked, "Did you study in Britain? You have a British accent." I'd reply, "What Britain could I have ever studied in? We learned through old textbooks." America was so far away, and when we were in school there was practically no information about it.

I recall that when I first visited the USSR in 1971 people were quite fond of the Kennedy clan. I remember being surprised by how many people asked about them. Do you remember this? I was about fourteen when Kennedy was killed. How did people here react to his assassination?

I do recall that. Keep in mind that Americans, after all, are very good at PR, as is customary to say today. Therefore, everything that you did, you did well. You showed us. You do so now. For you, the president is an ordinary person, with all sorts of family problems, someone you can feel sorry for, someone you can relate to. He's one of, and understandable to, the people. But here, well, now people understand this, but back then they didn't. [The leader] was an idol to whom everyone prayed. Therefore, if only on the human level, people, my father, well, I can give you an example. My son, Lesha, was young, so it must have been in the early 1980s, or just before. We didn't have a phone, but there was one at the entrance to our building. I went down to call him. Someone had told him, well, I began to speak and he interrupted me, "Can you believe what happened? They killed Olaf Palma!"[8] Papa didn't hear anything I said. He was an emotional man. "They killed him, the scoundrels killed him!" We reacted the same way when they killed Kennedy, who, after all, promoted détente.[9] There was a great deal of sympathy, of

---

8. Born in 1927, Sweden's controversial prime minister actively participated in international affairs on behalf of the Third World and helped to radicalize the country's Social Democratic agenda. These considerations made him popular in the Soviet Union. An unknown assassin killed him in Stockholm in 1986.

9. This is a popular view in Russia, even though relations with the Soviet Union during Kennedy's presidency remained strained.

course, and indignation on account of this from among the majority of the population. I'm not speaking of those they called dissidents, do you understand? It never even entered the heads of the majority of the population that the mass media could name as the assassin not the person who killed him, but for political reasons, let's say, Oswald or someone else. Not because they couldn't find him but because they had to substitute someone else because of politics.[10]

But did they mention here that Oswald had lived in the Soviet Union and that his wife was from Minsk? That many Americans thought that the KGB had recruited him and had something to do with the assassination?

No, there was no such information. None whatsoever.

Natalia P., how important was it that you learned English as a child? I realize, of course, that you teach English, but how do you evaluate its role in your life?

I can tell you that my father worked at the Polytechnic Institute and tried to convince me to enroll there. Although I was an obedient child, I didn't enroll there. Moreover, there's another interesting moment when I began to work. Mostly it was young women, but the daughters of party officials and generals who went to teach in the Department of Foreign Languages [at the Pedagogical Institute]. Therefore, it was extremely difficult for me back then to fight my way into a job there; it was practically impossible. I worked at the university for seven or eight years, but only part time. Later—and it wasn't because of my situation at work or because my father was a professor—I decided to write a dissertation. Back then there was no graduate training in the field in Saratov. My choices were Moscow, Leningrad, or Tver, located near Moscow, which back then was called Kalinin. But Papa insisted that I study political economy. Political economy didn't demand such a broad education, it was a social science. It was possible to take your candidate exams,[11] enroll in graduate school, and get to work on your dissertation. I even recall that he found a dissertation advisor for me, and a dissertation topic on the Council for Mutual Economic Assistance.[12] I passed my

---

10. Natalia P. appears to be under the influence of the numerous conspiracy theories surrounding JFK's death.

11. Students normally had to pass three exams before they could begin work on their dissertations (one on Marxism, a discipline exam, and a foreign language exam). It normally took three years, start to finish, to complete a candidate's (graduate) degree.

12. Founded in 1949 as a counterweight to the Marshall Plan, the council, known as COMECON or CMEA, included the Soviet bloc countries and later Mongolia, Cuba, and Vietnam.

exams and told him, "Papa, you can kill me if you like, but I can't study political economy." I left for Kalinin, as it was called back then. I took my candidate exams there; my dissertation advisor was in Moscow. She's still alive, she's quite old now, having turned eighty. She was also a consulting professor in Saransk, at Mordovia State University.[13] So, I was a graduate student in Saransk with a dissertation advisor in Moscow, but I ended up defending my dissertation in Lvov in 1986! Can you imagine how much I had to travel? I can think of ten representatives of my generation in Saratov with this specialty—Germanic languages. That's a lot. For other specializations, say linguistics or comparative linguistics, one can defend dissertations here at Saratov University. But in my specialty it was either Moscow, Leningrad, Tver, or later Odessa or Piatigorsk. There's something else that's interesting. When I considered which academic council to submit my dissertation to, back in 1986, there was a rule that dissertations had to include four quotations from the classical writings of Marxism-Leninism. But by the time I was ready to defend they only accepted dissertations with citations from five classics of Marxism-Leninism [laughing]. That's why I ended up defending in Lvov. Thus, I had to battle for my English. That was the only time I dared go against my father's wishes. And therefore I madly love my profession, although I'm very tired. My current position—I'm head of a department—this administrative position takes up a lot of my time and energy, and is hard on the nerves. That's how things turned out. What else can I do? I've been in that position already for eleven years. Yet the thing I love most, of course, is teaching.

I forgot to inquire about religion. Did it play a role in your childhood? And what about your grandparents? Did you know them?

Well, on my father's side, I didn't know them. They died before I was born. But my mother's mother taught us a prayer. And when Papa came home from work, I enthused, "Papa, Papa, look what I know!" and recited the prayer. There was such a scandal [laughing]! Papa really chewed out Grandma for, well, it wasn't that he was afraid that someone would find out, but he really strongly believed in what he did, in what he taught.

Your childhood overlapped with many interesting political events. As

---

13. Saransk is the capital of the Republic of Mordovia located in the European part of Russia in the Volga basin, north of Saratov. It borders Nizhnii Novgorod, Ulianovsk, Penza, Riazan, and the Chuvash Republic.

a child I was little interested in politics, but I do recall how my parents re-
acted. How did your parents react, say, to the Twentieth Party Congress, to
Khrushchev's denunciation of Stalin's personality cult? Did they discuss such
things at home or keep their thoughts to themselves?

You know, I think, well, of course I heard something about this,
but they did not discuss such things with us.

Had anyone been repressed in your family?

No. They didn't discuss such things with us. The only thing I
can recall is that we had a neighbor who venerated Khrushchev,
because he freed him [from the Gulag]. He was a very intelligent
and soft-spoken man.

How did your parents react to Khrushchev's overthrow? To the fact that,
at the end of his years in power, things worsened materially? Bread was even
rationed for a time.

Yes, I also remember this. But you know, here, too, you need
to keep in mind what kind of father we had. Mother suffered her
whole life from this, because when others were trying to obtain rugs
or crystal or other such things, Father. . . . You know, all things of
this sort were obtained through connections; none of it was available for sale in the stores. Being a university professor, he, of course,
could have developed all sorts of ties. However, he didn't pay any
attention to such things. Mother was always telling him, "People
drop in to visit. Can't you see? Look what old furniture we have!"
And he'd reply, "So? We have a wardrobe and you can hang clothes
in it. What difference does it make what kind it is?" Insofar as he
nonetheless earned enough money, he decided what to spend it on.
For instance, I studied music since I was six years old. There was a
music school at the House of Scholars, on Communard Street. There
was a ballet school there, so I studied ballet, music at the music
school, and something else. And then I got sick, it had something
to do with my heart. I was nine or ten. They took me to the doctor.
She examined me and said, "So, we have ballet, music, the English
school. Figure skating has become popular, too. Maybe you'll enroll
the girl there too?" She added, "She's simply tired." So they dropped
me from ballet, which grieved me greatly, because music was music,
solfeggio, choir. I couldn't stand it. But Papa never regretted spending money on such things, on books, on education, on tutors, on
music, on English lessons. I probably studied something else, too.
I no longer remember. Yet nothing that was connected with living
conditions interested him. Clothing, for instance. He paid so little
attention to such things, to what he wore—that was true of his gen-

Natalya P. in second grade in 1957 (*bottom row, far left*). A. A.
Konstantinov, wearing glasses, is in the middle of the back row.
Courtesy A. A. Konstantinov.

eration in general, since they had had so little. He told us how his
students once sent him a note to the effect that "it's time to replace
your jacket." He went out and bought a new one. Do you understand? Such things simply didn't interest him.

*I'd like to shift focus a bit. Did you read Aleksandr Solzhenitsyn's no-
vella,* One Day in the Life of Ivan Denisovich, *published in the journal*
Novyi mir *(New World) in 1962?*

Back then, no.

Did the other kids at school read it and talk about it?

Probably not. Perhaps there were a few individuals who read it,
but they didn't discuss it.

What about foreign radio broadcasts?

They were discussed. My family didn't listen to them, but others
certainly did. They discussed them and told others. I can't really say
that this was widespread; however, there were conversations on the
topic. Yet there weren't any in my home. As I've already said, you
have to keep in mind what my father did.

I understand. I've tried to make sense of what shaped the formation of your outlook on things. Therefore I asked about your parents, grandparents, religion, books, your knowledge of English, etc. What else do I need to ask you in order to understand the formation of your worldview? What else shaped you growing up?

It's hard to say. I think, however, that the most important consideration is the family. The basic foundations are laid in the family. Undoubtedly, evaluating things from today's perspective, I can see that perhaps the discipline was stricter than was necessary. But on the other hand, I was a girl. They told me what to do, and I did it. Back then I didn't question the appropriateness of their decisions. Perhaps children need such discipline. Each of us has his or her own personality and temperament. Such discipline is good for some, bad for others. Take even the situation at work, where people have to follow orders. Let's assume, for instance, that the militia, that is, the police, is part of the military. It's not every person who can feel at home in such a system. Some can subordinate themselves to orders; it's so important to understand this, that you must curb your ego, right? You have to keep your opinion to yourself, to hide it. Some are capable of doing so, others are not. This, too, probably depends upon one's personality. Of course, as a child I harbored some grievances against my parents, like all children. But I didn't experience any special anxiety. For the most part, my childhood memories are pleasant ones.

Were there conflicts, romances, or unusual sorts of behavior?

I understand your question. Well, I befriended one girl, and then another. It's possible that I took offense at something. There was a time when I thought that I was fat, that I was not pretty, that I was this or that. I remember that it seemed that no one understood me. At first the other kids didn't understand me, then the teachers didn't. This was less the case with the teachers. Except for mathematics. I had problems with the teacher. Yes, problems, but I can't say that they were all that important or that they were drawn-out conflicts. Back then I didn't especially befriend any of the boys. Or have a crush on anyone. Sure, I liked some of them, but there was nothing more than that.

After completing school in 1967 you enrolled at the Pedagogical Institute?

Yes. I studied there for four years, and finished in 1971. Back then a university education lasted for four years, not five.[14] After

---

14. This was true at the pedagogical institutes, law institutes, and elsewhere, but not at universities.

graduating I worked for a year at a research institute as a technical translator. I really disliked this job, despite the fact that it was
difficult to find employment there. It was considered a great place
to work. The pay was decent. However, I disliked it, so I quit and
went to work temporarily at the Pedagogical Institute part time. My
father was very much against this. But I really like teaching. And I
worked part time for more than ten years, until I defended my dissertation.

When did you get married?

Well, I now tell people in 1978. But that was for the second
time. I got married the first time during my senior year. We soon got
divorced. My husband was a dental technician, and his father was,
too. We had an awful romance. We were twenty years old when
we met each other and soon got married. We divorced because our
families were so different. His believed that it was possible to buy
and sell everything. That was how they saw things back then. Our
family was altogether different. And our being in love came to an
end over the fact that we were altogether different people, with an
altogether different upbringing.

How did your parents react to your getting married at that time?

They were distressed, but not over the fact that I got married.
Three days before the wedding they tried hard to talk me out of it,
to convince me that he's from the wrong family. The head of our
department at the Pedagogical Institute had a husband who was a
dental technician. Even she told me, "Natasha, don't get married.
A dental technician is a special caste of people, not only a profession. It's a way of thinking, a personality type. Don't go through
with it. Knowing you and knowing what it means to be a dental
technician—you don't have a clue—I know it won't work out." By
the way, it's interesting that, when I married again, gave birth, and
when my child was about ten I went to visit my mother. My son
and I were standing at the bus stop, when my first husband drove
by in his car and said, "Where are you going?" I replied, "To my
mother's." "Well, get in, I'll take you there." We were carrying some
heavy things. He said to me, "You know, I need to study English.
Find me a tutor." He had completed a technical secondary school to
become a dental technician, and that was enough for him. He made
very good money, ever the more so because he belonged to a family
of technicians. There was something he needed in America, or else
he was planning to leave for America, I no longer remember. I said
to him, "Gena, you know you're not a good student. Where am I

going to find you a tutor?" He replied, "But I'm going to pay good money." Well, there are some problems that money can't solve. He agreed, "Yes, there are things that money can't buy, but also things that you can buy with lots of money." My reply: "Gena, for a moment I thought you had changed." My son was sitting right there during this conversation and it never occurred to me that he would remember it. We arrived at my mother's, returned home, and a few days passed. My child, a boy, naturally always takes his father's side. He told him, "Papa, did you know that someone gave us a ride the other day? Mama's first husband?" How did he know? Well, it turned out that when I moved out of my parents' some pictures from my first wedding remained in some album or another. Not because I left them there on purpose. I simply gathered up all my books, and they were in one of them. And one morning we were sitting around and my child, who was quite young, ran up to me and cried out, "Mama, Mama, I found photographs where you and Papa are at a wedding." And he showed me those photos. My husband angrily replied, "Don't you see that that's not Papa?" My son answered, "No, how can it not be you? There's Mama, so you should be there, too." That was logical. Well, my husband got really annoyed. But when my son found out that I had had a first husband, it seemed normal to him. Anyway, he later told my husband, "Can you imagine, Papa, our Mama made fun of him and he didn't even know it." Can you imagine? I was dumbfounded! Since he lives nearby, I run into him every now and then and he tells me how he bought an apartment for his daughter or his latest car. And when we begin to exchange such news I think, "I shouldn't have divorced him." But after three or four minutes pass I think, "Oh no. How fortunate that I left him. I don't need a thing." Do you understand what I'm saying? Not long ago I saw him here, in Ilin Square and I said, "What are you doing here?" He replied, "I'm waiting for my bus." "Why a bus?" I ask. "Why not," he said. "I bought a bus that runs on route 53 and it makes money for me. I'm waiting for it to come in. I'll take the cash box and go home." He bought a bus! However, I haven't had any regrets in this regard for some time. I have a niece who got married recently who is experiencing problems. If I didn't understand such things when I was young, I now try to convince my son that a husband and wife should come from the same sort of families. They need to have common values, otherwise things will be very tough.

You met your second husband in 1978?

Yes, and we got married right away, a month later. We met on November 7 and got married on December 7.[15]

I wanted to ask whether or not you took part in work brigades or went to pick potatoes on state farms.

I did go to harvest potatoes, and my husband took part in a building brigade. He traveled a lot with them and with the leader of the brigades. He did so throughout his student days. His family was less well off, let's put it that way. His father, by the way, was the main engineer at our television station. Beginning in 1948, he built the station. He was a fanatic, was totally devoted to his work, and was a very hard-working man. But he and his wife divorced when my husband was eighteen or nineteen. Therefore, he completed technical high school, served in the army, and then enrolled at the institute. And while he was a student he traveled with the building brigades.

Did he participate willingly?

People wanted to take part, there was even some competition to get accepted, because they got paid very well.

And what about digging for potatoes?

We didn't get paid for that. It was, as we say, voluntary-compulsory. You know, it was possible to get out of it if you wanted, but it was actually quite fun. We really didn't overdo it, and it was such a diversion that it was okay.

You enrolled at the institute in 1967 and in 1968 the Soviet Union invaded Czechoslovakia. I realize that people didn't react to this publicly, but . . .

Yes. This went right by me altogether.

This was also the time of the dissident movement. I realize that here in the provinces such things were not particularly felt. But in 1991, I recall meeting a certain Romanov who got into trouble at the university in 1971 or 1972. He belonged to a small student group that ended up serving time.

When was that? In the 1970s? I really don't recall. Back then I didn't have anything to do with the university.

What about samizdat? Did it circulate in Saratov among the intelligentsia or not very much?

Well, generally, it circulated, but, once again, it somehow passed us by. You have to understand that it was all young women who

---

15. November 7 is the anniversary of the Bolshevik Revolution of 1917 and a major Soviet holiday.

studied at the Department of Foreign Languages. We were not at all interested in politics. We were basically interested in boys and in romance. And in studying. Therefore, samizdat didn't circulate among us.

Can you tell me what influenced the formation of what we today call your identity?

Well, of course, it was the opinion of those surrounding us and our parents. In any case, if it weren't the most important, then important enough was our parents' opinion. It's possible that I got upset when they bawled me out for something for which I wasn't at fault. But my parents' opinion was very important to me.

What about gender? How did your gender define your life? You said that it was all women who taught at the Pedagogical Institute and that you weren't especially interested in politics. How would your life have turned out differently if you had been born a man?

I generally haven't thought much about this. Now I hold an exclusively man's job at work. We have twenty departments and, for a long time, I was the only female department head. Can you imagine? More recently there was a period when there were three of us, but once again I remain the only one. There were two of us for a while, but the other one left on July 1 to begin work on her doctorate. I really didn't think about the fact that back then this was a woman's profession, a woman's department. Now, I very much would like to become a woman again, but I don't like emancipation. What is, is. It's too late.

I also wanted to ask you about travel. I first visited the USSR in 1971, and when I returned in 1974 to study at Moscow University, many of my friends and acquaintances and people they knew had begun to travel. Many of my friends, for instance, had been to Poland, Czechoslovakia, or Bulgaria. Academic tourism had even begun. Did you travel abroad?

Yes. The first time was probably in 1972, yes, in 1972, when I was in Poland and East Germany as a tourist with a youth group.

What impression did this have on you?

I was full of impressions, but by the end I was eager to get home. I loved Poland. Back then Poland really was a foreign country, not like it is today, a large Russian second-hand goods market. I really liked Krakow and the palaces there, Wawel.[16] I remember the absolutely indelible impression that the Catholic churches made on me. Ever the more so, since here I didn't go to church. For the most part

---

16. The royal castle and cathedral complex.

we hadn't any. Back then we didn't have any churches that were open. And the Catholic churches are far more magnificent than others. Of course, that museum in Germany, in Dresden, also made an impression. I can't recall what it's called. It's not just the old masters gallery where I saw all the reproductions. Back in school we studied the painters and the pictures from art albums. I think we studied them at school. In any case, we had art albums and encyclopedias at home, and I enjoyed art enormously. But it didn't make such an impression, [except for the fact that] "The Sistine Madonna" is so big. Besides, our excursion wasn't terribly interesting. We didn't have a real guide, but listened to headsets. We spent two weeks in Poland and eight days in Germany. All of us grew tired from so many impressions and therefore if everything was new and interesting in Poland, we were exhausted by the time we got to Germany. I think the museum is called Zwanzig.[17] It's there that they've assembled all sorts of jewelry, artwork, and porcelain. Insofar as I love that more, I ended up remembering it better. And in Potsdam we saw the hall where the conference took place.[18] A hall's a hall. It really didn't impress me. And then, in 1975, I was in Cyprus. I traveled with a tourist group as an interpreter to Cyprus and Syria. It was a youth group, part of whom were from Saratov. The others joined us in Moscow, and some were even from Georgia and Armenia. In Cyprus it was difficult to translate because so much was connected to religion. I simply didn't know the vocabulary in Russian, but they prompted me since we had Armenians and Georgians in the group who knew the terms. We relaxed on Cyprus. Of course I liked it a great deal. But the impression I got of Syria was of how dirty it was. I was afraid of the dirty dishes, all of it, the dust, the dirt, the unwashed fruit. But insofar as it was a new country for me, I found it interesting. Then I was supposed to travel to England. I no longer recall the details, but it was with a group of teachers, a tourist group, organized around a theme. I even filled out all the paperwork in June, and then it turned out that there was a cooling in relations with Britain. What year was that? 1979? We had some sort of disagreement with Thatcher.

It probably had something to do with the invasion of Afghanistan.

Well, perhaps that's it. I recall that there was some sort of conflict with Thatcher and that the trip was postponed until the fall, and by then I was already pregnant and therefore didn't go. Yes,

---

17. The museum is called Zwinger.
18. She is referring to the Potsdam Conference of 1945, involving Winston Churchill, Harry Truman, and Joseph Stalin.

it must have been 1979, since my son was born in 1980. To my
shame, I haven't traveled anywhere since. I recently looked at my
passport and saw that it had expired. It had been lying around for
five years. I haven't gone anywhere. Well, for one thing, in 1982
I began graduate work in Moscow. During the last year I had to
travel to Moscow, to my advisor, every weekend. That is, the sound
of the train even now . . . I was so tired of it all. Then I gave birth
when I was twenty-nine years old. In our understanding that's not
exactly old, but it's not young either. We really wanted a child. And
I was such a crazy mother that it was hard for me to be without
him even for a minute! But I studied in Moscow for four years and
had to leave him with my husband, and, how should I put it, all the
time I worried myself to death over him. Then, in 1986, I defended
my dissertation, then my father got sick, then me. My father died.
Then all of the traveling at the university connected to the Tempus
program[19] grants started up. But we don't have this where I work.
Of course, it was possible to get one by going to Moscow, but not
without extraordinary effort. For one thing, I don't like to have to
go begging and fighting my way. Second, I really didn't have an
urgent need to do so. By and large, though, it's always interesting
to travel, to visit some other city and to meet new people. About six
years ago a branch of our institute opened in Samara and there was
a time when I had to travel there every other month, even once a
month in order to see how things were going. In other words, I had
quite a bit of traveling to do in connection with work. Samara's a
large city. I really like it. It resembles ours. All the Volga cities are
alike in some ways. There's still a lot in Samara for me to see. For
instance, the last time I was there I didn't manage to see Stalin's
bunker.[20] I was also in Nizhnii Novgorod on business.[21] I really liked
it! Earlier I had traveled there by boat. It was a long time ago, and
we passed by the city. The city has really become transformed. The

---

19. A cooperative program in higher education between European Union members and partner countries such as Russia. Established in 1990 to respond to the new
opportunities made available by the collapse of the Berlin Wall, the program has since
been renewed three times. It greatly expanded the possibilities for academics at Russian
universities to travel and to host students and faculty from EU countries.

20. Known as Kuibyshev from 1935 to 1991, Samara served as capital of the Soviet
Union from 1941 to 1943 during World War II. A bunker was built there for Stalin in the
event he needed to evacuate Moscow. Today the city's population is 1,231,653, making
it larger than Saratov.

21. Located at the confluence of the Oka and Volga rivers, Nizhnii Novgorod is
Russia's third-largest city today (population 1,341,000) and is known both for its splendid
kremlin and for being the test site of Russia's market and democratic reforms.

kremlin there is beautiful, so well manicured and lit up. A lot has changed thanks to Nemtsov,[22] the shopping center, for instance. We had a great guide there. There's lots that we don't know about our own history. Well, each time I plan to travel somewhere, something prevents me from doing so.

What impressions did those trips make on you? The ones you made earlier? In 1972 you were in Poland. Society was more open there, there was more to buy, and people practiced their religion. How did you process this?

Well, of course, there was an abundance of things that we weren't able to buy, because we could exchange very little money. They had everything. After all, it was a foreign country. I remember that we were allowed to exchange a ridiculously small amount of money—a hundred rubles. Or was it thirty? I had wanted to buy some clothes, but decided not to buy anything. I sat in cafes, drank coffee, and simply observed what was happening. We also went to the movies. If I'm not mistaken, we even saw a film in English. It was either in Poland or in East Germany. We bought some exotic food items. That is, I wanted mainly to get to know the country.

Did you have any meetings with young people or only with administrators?

None that were planned, as far as I recall. No, there weren't any.

Did you have any discussions before you went abroad, especially for the first time in 1972? Did they warn you about how to behave? Were there informers in your group?

There undoubtedly were. But they did a good job since we didn't know who they were [laughing].

People have told me that there were always two of them, one who was obvious, and the other who was smart and discreet.

Yes, the other who was smart and discreet [laughing]. You know, for some reason I really didn't give the matter much thought. I was so disciplined, so. . . . Of course, in order to end up in a group like this you had to go in for an interview. They asked questions about the history of the country we would be visiting and about its overall development. They did tell us not to go out alone. That they did.

Did your attitude toward the West change when you became an adult, say in the 1970s and early 1980s?

---

22. The former governor of Nizhnii Novgorod oblast, Boris Nemstov (born 1959), had aggressively pursued market and democratic reforms at the local level. A member of the Russian government today, Nemtsov serves as chairman of the Federal Political Council of the Union of Rightist Forces (SPS).

Well, when I was in school the West was something far away, abstract. Something that was unreal, let's put it that way, because, after all, Saratov was a closed city and there were practically no contacts to speak of. I happen to remember when I arrived in Moscow in 1982, where I was a graduate student. There were foreigners there and I sometimes heard foreign speech merely by chance. For me, like for everyone else, it was as if they were from another planet, insofar as we were altogether different. Separated from each other. And gradually, when the city opened and foreigners began to visit Saratov even on personal invitations, I was sometimes asked by acquaintances to translate. Either someone came to visit or some sort of specialist on business. I translated, interacted with them, and naturally have an altogether different opinion.

Marxist teachings underscore the importance of economic development. Your father taught political economy, but, as he put it, of the capitalist world. Many believe, well, for that matter, Gorbachev himself said, that perestroika was necessary above all else to get the country out of economic crisis. How did you understand the fact that the economic system didn't work? That it was difficult to obtain things? The difference between Moscow and Saratov in regard to food supply? The sausage trains . . .

Well, with indignation, of course. I was a graduate student then and sometimes lived there for months, leaving my child with my husband and parents. I sent them endless packages of hotdogs and sausages through the train conductors. But please understand that I really didn't think about this all that much because back then, and now, I believe that a great deal of harm comes to our country because there are so many dilettantes. Economists and politicians who understand economics should run the economy, those who understand something about it. Everyone gives advice regarding how to fix things. Everyone knows. But when dilettantes begin to run things, when "cooks' children" begin to run things, as Lenin envisioned.[23] Yes, we were rightly outraged and dissatisfied, but what could we do about it?

What about Afghanistan? When we mentioned the Second World War, you pointed out that back then people had fought for something. But what about Afghanistan?

You know, I think that our military brass and politicians know all too well the particulars of that war, and that we, if we look at

---

23. During the Revolution, Lenin quipped that "any cook should be able to run the country."

things from today's perspective, don't have enough information to conclude whether it was a bad thing or a good one. That said, it's probably always bad to interfere in the internal affairs of another country. And, as a woman, well, any woman who has given birth is always against anything that might harm her children. I always say that if we had a female minister of defense, she'd have solved these problems a long time ago. But men decide things. Behind any war there's always money, big money, and the political ambitions of leaders, who think little of who might be affected by this. The people, ordinary people, rarely enter into the considerations of politicians, ours or yours. Right? However, for the most part, these political ambitions exist. Therefore, in order to answer your question, you need to know the country's history and traditions. I don't think I have the right to talk about this. But it's of course awful that they sent our people there, that our boys got killed, and that we wasted our strength and energy on this. What's going on in Chechnia is also awful.

Under Gorbachev they referred to the Brezhnev years as a period of stagnation, right? What did you think of Brezhnev?

What, indeed! He was in power for a long time and therefore at the beginning of his reign I evaluated him one way, and toward the end, when he could no longer put together a sentence, I saw him differently. Of course, toward the end of his years in office it was already obvious that the situation had gone so far that something had to give. Yes. Moreover, it was exactly during his tenure that the dissident movement appeared.

In all societies myths help to unite people. Tell me about the myths that existed in Soviet society before the Gorbachev era.

One myth was that we were the most powerful country in the world, that things were fine here and that everything in the West was terrible. Yet our life was generally quite stable back then, right? That which they began calling the period of stagnation was indeed stagnation, but life was quite stable. I was shielded from all external influences. My parents . . . true, I was offended that the daughters of party officials could get hold of some wonderful boots, and I couldn't, because back then it was necessary to "obtain" everything. There was nothing available in the stores. It was a shame, but we accepted this as a fact of life. That is, I can't say that I thought about this a great deal at the time, but only as I got older and things became even more stagnant. My son, I'm sure, thinks more about and sometimes expresses thoughts that I didn't articulate at his age. But that's probably to be expected, because they live in a different time and have to do everything for themselves. Things were decided for us, decisions were made for us.

Why do you think perestroika occurred? What caused it?

Well, probably the country had reached a critical state when something had to give. That's one thing. And probably the role of the individual in history is another.

The human factor [as Gorbachev put it].

Yes, the human factor. If there had been no Gorbachev, then perhaps someone else would not have been able to manage. And if no one had been given that power, things perhaps would have occurred later or else differently. The same way that things unfolded with Gorbachev in Foros.[24] If there had been someone else, perhaps things would have turned out differently and we'd still have Gorbachev. We see here the role of the individual, of the human factor, and also of chance, upon which much in politics depends. Yes, the role of chance probably also plays a role.

I remember how agitated things were, especially in connection with glasnost, when they began to fill in the so-called blank spots in history and tell all.

Yes, the blank spots. But I didn't like this, because I felt that if someone were a Communist, then he couldn't change his convictions in a flash. That means that he either was a bad Communist, or else he wasn't telling the truth now. And life suggests, more likely, confirms, that that's how it was. Of course, great hopes were placed on Yeltsin when he came to power. I remember how my husband and I argued over this until we were blue in the face. He believed in Yeltsin 100 percent, and said that now things would be different. I disagreed. Women are more realistic. Yeltsin, after all, came from the party elite and he was already of an age that it would be difficult to completely change. For one thing, even if he really wanted to, you understand, it's very hard for someone to change after holding office for so many years. For another, on the whole the people remained the same as before, the country remained the same, and the economy, well, let's say that in a few years time it's perhaps possible to make a real surge as they did in Korea, even in China. Still, it's impossible to change people's consciousness or educational or cultural level in a few years. It's possible to destroy things in a short

---

24. Gorbachev was at his holiday residence of Foros on the Crimean cost when his close associates launched a coup in August 1991.

time, but to create, to change things fundamentally, time is needed. Therefore, I didn't expect some sort of unusual leap forward. But we lived through some hard times when perestroika began. Things are far more stable now, far more so. Periods of great change are always accompanied by a downside. Nonetheless, and once again considering our upbringing, I nevertheless am a patriot of my country. We don't get to pick where we come from. It really doesn't matter whose mother was better or whose father is a minister or a street sweeper. It's a matter of chance who your parents are or which country you were born in. There are no such things as good countries and bad countries, good nations and bad nations. That said, there probably is such a thing as the elusive Russian soul. You Americans are greater realists and pragmatists, while we have our heads in the clouds. Not long ago there was a dissertation defense at the Law Academy during which one of the readers, a German-language specialist, said that, according to a study, the three words used most often in the Russian language are "soul," "fate," and "melancholy." I'm not certain how accurate this is, but Russian has a large number of synonyms for melancholy, unlike German, which has far fewer. I'm not sure about English. Language is always a spokesperson for a national culture and the soul of a nation or people. It's all very interesting. Therefore, we're different, and we should be different. We can't all be the same. It would be boring! Besides, we have a different history. Different roots. We have one, you have another. We must complement each other. In fact, I think we do so, because the disagreements occur between our leaders, not our people. For instance, when the events of 9/11 occurred, we were deeply shaken. But some people here said, "See, they bombed Yugoslavia, and interfered in our relations with Chechnia, and how are they going to get themselves out of this mess?" I'm convinced that the events of 9/11 are also puzzling. Yes, these events raised lots of questions in our country and throughout the world. Our people favor living in peace so that no one perishes. That goes without saying. You know, there's information circulating to the effect that your special services and the president himself knew of the danger but failed to take measures. Who knows what actually happened? Who knows?

How has your life changed since the collapse of the Soviet Union? You mentioned, for instance, that during the past four years or so a certain stabilization has taken place.

That's right. Let's see. Major changes during the past ten years or so. Well, I changed jobs. First, my father died in 1990. It was a great loss for me. He's absolutely irreplaceable. Then I had other things to think about as my son grew up. A child is a big responsibility. It seems to me that relations between parents and children are probably closer here than, well, I'm judging by the experience of my girlfriend who also went to School No. 42. She left and now lives in Portland. She had children here who were very attached to her when they were young. But they became greatly estranged there, because, as she put it, "that's the way of life." For whatever reason, her children simply aren't as close. We have closer relations, but they breathe down our necks. They live with us for a long time. This causes problems. Everything's connected. Some problems give rise to others. Well, this way of living, of course, involves tradition and the like. I like my present life well enough, in terms of work. I'm very self-contained. I'm at that age when I'd like to respect myself. It's not at all important to me whether my boss likes me or not, for instance. I know that I am respected and that people like me. But what's more important is to be in harmony with myself. Do you understand? I don't think that this is simply a matter of the times. I'm probably of that age. The older you get, the wiser you get. And I perceive things differently. Moreover, when I got seriously ill nine years ago I came to understand the real value of things. I no longer get all caught up in little things. I now know what are the most important things in life. Therefore, it actually became easier for me to live after I got sick, because, let's put it this way, I found out the value of life and death. I know what's important in life and what's not. My disposition, my attitude toward life, changed altogether and I'm much happier. What a paradox! But they say that God deals each of us only those cards that we're capable of handling. I'm so happy, knock on wood, that I'm still alive, that I can live and enjoy life, and not worry about the little stuff. For instance, we haven't been able to renovate the apartment. So what. I'll get through it. I now feel fine, although I of course understand that I'm not getting any younger and there's still so much I'd like to accomplish, to help out here or there, and to do a bit more of this or that. Before I used to think that I'd retire and would do all these things. I'd paint a picture. I'd . . . well, there's no time now left for anything; work takes up all my time.

Why did you change jobs?

It turned out that way. I worked at the Pedagogical University, not far from home.[25] My girlfriend worked there and she said: "Our

25. As a result of educational reforms introduced in the 1990s, the country's pedagogical institutes were elevated to the status of universities.

college opened up eleven years ago." It had been a secondary school, so there was no English department. Then they searched for someone to head up a department. And she said to me, "Natasha, there's an opening there. Maybe you should take it?" I replied, "Oh, no. I'm not going to work for the police. Why do I need that?" She said, "Come on. I already promised Fedor Andreevich that I'd send him someone.[26] Go ahead!" Well, I went, thinking, "Okay, my friend wants me to, so why not?" I showed up and had a talk with him. He told me, "Well, think it over." I thought to myself, "There's no way that I'd go to work there." I now work right near home, and that's further away. He called me the next day. "Well, have you decided?" I told him, "I'm not sure." Well, the pay was a lot higher there than what I had been receiving. He sent a car for me, and basically talked me into it. If it weren't for Fedor Andreevich, I wouldn't be there. Once again, the human factor. I also found it interesting. They didn't have a department, and I started one up from scratch. Everything that exists there now was created under my leadership. And for the most part we have a decent enough reputation in town. We know just about everyone and the department has a good reputation. Students from other colleges even come to study with us. In regard to this, I'm at times at odds with myself, because the role of an administrator is a complicated one. I have to get things done, but in such a way that people are okay with it. Here, and I'm sure it's common in America, too, you have to put up with a lot of foolish things at work, you have to busy yourself with who knows what. In addition, we have to subordinate ourselves to directives from both the Ministry of Education and the Ministry of Internal Affairs. We have a dual subordination. There's a lot of paperwork, a lot of administrative work. You want people to be satisfied at work, you want them to work well, to teach students, our cadets, well, so that the administration is satisfied. It seems to me that only a woman can plan like this. I've been there eleven years. Only three men remain in charge of departments. The rest have been replaced. That's because people usually serve for two terms, and we're elected for five years. So it's usually for ten years. I got elected to a third term in October.

How can the story of your life help me understand the fate that befell the Soviet Union?

Well, you know, in answering your questions, I tried, of course, to be sincere and candid. Nevertheless, I probably answered you

---

26. Fedor Andreevich Grigoriev, rector of the Saratov State Academy of Law.

through the prism of the present. I would say that we had a tranquil enough family life. I'd put it like that. There were no major upheavals. We probably ended up at the English school because there, at that time, one found children of the intelligentsia. If my husband had answered your questions, he undoubtedly would have done so differently, because he is a Kuban Cossack,[27] and his mother was dekulakized.[28] They were sent to Siberia, where the whole family perished. From the age of six she lived with total strangers. She mopped floors to survive. If you take me, well, I have a tolerant attitude toward religion. I believe that there's some kind of god in each of us. I don't know if there is a universal one who lives in heaven, but man must live by some sort of moral laws. If he doesn't obey those moral rules spelled out in the Bible, or, say, if he doesn't go to church, well, that's the last thing to worry about. But he must live by some sort of rules. If he doesn't, then God or else life will punish him for stealing or above all for betraying [others]. My mother-in-law is an ardent atheist. My father was an atheist because he was a Communist. She is an ardent atheist because, as she says, God would not have allowed such injustices as having people perish and having young children become orphans. Therefore, she can't stand to even hear about God, whereas people her age usually become more religious. What I'm suggesting here is that all this is a personal matter. It's probably difficult to put together a complete picture, because these stories of ours, nonetheless, remain subjective. She'd tell you the same thing from a different point of view. Take my husband, for instance. He has a tendency to exaggerate the slightest things or nuisances. I think that most men are like that. Women are different. By the way, I raised my son very democratically. I read Dr. Spock when he was born. He was completely free and I practically never punished him. Probably his upbringing was too democratic. But I'm pleased with my son. As for us, well, we had this episode back at school. Betrayal is probably the greatest sin of all. We had a classmate who very badly needed to receive a medal. When we

---

27. A branch of the Cossacks inhabiting the Kuban region in southern Russia. Probably a Turkic word, "Cossack" denoted freebooters of various Slavic and non-Slavic origins who inhabited Russia's borderlands and fiercely guarded their independence. By the end of the eighteenth century, however, they had been incorporated into the Russian empire, whose borderlands they now defended.

28. Dekulakization was the violent attack against peasants who resisted the state's collectivization of agriculture at the end of the 1920s. Although "kulak" (fist) heretofore referred to well-to-do peasants, the term acquired a propagandistic usage during the period and was leveled against any peasants opposed to government measures.

wrote our compositions [to graduate] the topics were generally not known beforehand. She found them out, but didn't tell anyone, even though it seemed that she was the life and soul of the class. It was her father who inadvertently gave her away. Even now we still discuss this. No one spoke with her at our graduation. That is, this was her betrayal. A different betrayal from someone else would have been perceived differently. And we had thought that she was the life and soul of the class, when she suddenly behaved this way. By the way, she now lives in America.

Have I asked you everything that you'd like to tell me?

I think so. Well, I'd say that I've tried to be sincere in my answers. Of course I had some really rough times in my life. That was when I couldn't settle into a decent job, because the daughters of the generals and party leaders got them. It was absolutely impossible to make one's way among them. But then I defended my dissertation, and all these generals' daughters knew that none of their fathers was making a fuss over them. Now they're in an unenviable position. The generals are all dead. Life somehow put everyone in her right place. I would have liked, though, for this to have happened sooner. I noticed one other thing. We by and large discuss this, too, whenever members of our class meet. All of us did very well in school. We had, I think, eight medalists out of twenty-six students. But it seems to me that those who received medals are less satisfied with their lives. Perhaps it has something to do with the high expectations that they had in school. They didn't fulfill them. It's as if they had gotten a medal in school and were expecting that this would take them far in life, but life, after all, is not like school. Perhaps school didn't prepare us well for the real world. Everything was idealized. That's probably how it was. We were such good and smart girls and boys. Yesterday, as a matter of fact, I met one of my classmates. She clearly didn't fulfill her potential. Although I think women obtain fulfillment from their family, their children, and their husbands, work also means a great deal to them. I, for one, have never been able to decide what role work and family should have for me. Even now, work plays an enormous role in my life. So does my child. I'm always trying to find some balance between the two. It's really hard. In addition, in Russia we women spoil our men. At first we shoulder all the responsibilities and then wonder why our men . . . stop being men. Yet it seems to me that emancipation is also a bad thing. Probably all extremes are bad. There's got to be a golden mean. Well, it's hard to find it. That's probably all that I have to say.

4. "Our entire generation . . . welcomed perestroika" | Arkadii Olegovich Darchenko

July 4, 2002, Saratov

Arkadii Olegovich Darchenko showed up at my apartment that morning with a ready smile on his face and a pile of old photographs from his school years. Upbeat and enthusiastic, he expressed great interest in my project and later helped me locate some of his classmates by supplying me with current phone numbers. Such information otherwise proved hard to come by, since no up-to-date phone directory exists for the city of Saratov. This was not only a matter of confidentiality: as the local telephone company purchased new equipment and upgraded its services, it needed to change local extensions and sometimes entire numbers. True, the city authorities offered a paid service that provided current phone numbers, but in order to obtain that information one needed to know just about everything else about the person in question: his/her date and place of birth, profession, and the neighborhood in which the person last lived. Moreover, there were long lines to deal with, and a need to return to the bureau a second time in order to learn the results of the search.

Arkadii Olegovich offered some invaluable observations as I explained the project to him and tested my equipment. I was still new at interviewing, and felt uncomfortable asking my informants to sign a consent form and tape disposal agreement that the Internal Review Board at my home university made me inflict upon them. Because I work with human subjects, I understand the rationale of this directive; but many of those who have emerged from a Stalinist past look differently upon my attempts to secure their signature on such documents. It was therefore a relief when Arkadii Olegovich signed the papers and joked about the similarities inherent in all bureaucracies. The very existence of the forms had made me apprehensive, because by this point in my project I had received several rejections from people I had hoped to interview; I worried that others might have a change of heart once they learned about the forms. But Arkadii Olegovich offered an explanation for his former classmates who had declined my request: those whose parents had been most intimately connected to the Soviet system were the most likely to have reservations about being interviewed. His remarks appear to have been right on target.

An articulate, introspective, optimistic, and focused subject, Arkadii Darchenko was born in Siberia and had some fascinating memories to share about his childhood there. He graduated from the B group of School No. 42 with a silver medal, after which he enrolled at Saratov University to pursue a career in nuclear physics, a popular field for outstanding students of his generation. His hard efforts and talent resulted in his being sent to Dubna. Located sixty kilometers from Moscow, Dubna was home to one of the Soviet Union's most prestigious atomic energy establishments, the Joint Center for Nuclear Research. It was there that he encountered a formidable obstacle that derailed his plans, forcing him to return to Saratov. This would not be the last time he had to regroup in so fundamental a way. As he points out in his interview, he had to change professions three times in his life, and his knowledge of English helped him cope with each of these trying moments.

Why did these ruptures occur and how did Arkadii Olegovich manage to deal with them? How might his Siberian childhood, and, later, his training as a research scientist, have affected his attitudes, outlook, and sense of identity? Why does he believe that his entire generation welcomed perestroika? How should we understand his remark that economics and objective reality determine consciousness?

Both my parents are from Saratov. Right after the war, my father studied at the Polytechnic Institute. My mother started out as a ballerina, but during the war she trained to become a nurse. After my father graduated from the Polytechnic Institute in 1949 they were sent to work in Siberia. My father worked as chief clerk at the construction site of a mine along the upper Enisei [River]. And,

Arkadii Olegovich Darchenko, July 2002.

as a matter of fact, I was born there in the town of Abakan.[1] We lived right in the settlement where the mine was under construction. It was not far from Shushenskii.[2] These were the very places where Lenin was once in exile. I grew up there and, no matter how strange it seems, since my generation learned about it only later, I remember the Gulag as it was. How each day they drove the inmates dressed in black pea jackets to work and back. How they escorted them with German Shepherds. I can still see it. Each day they led them first to work, and then back to camp. Moreover, when I later read Solzhenitsyn,[3] I could visualize the black pea jackets with their white checks. Yet I'm not from that generation; I wasn't supposed to [experience this]. It was sometime in '53 or '54, when I was four

---

1. Founded as a fortress in 1707, Abakan today is the capital of the Khasass Republic in south-central Siberia and has a population of 153,000.

2. The site of the Sayano-Shushenskaia hydropower station, the largest in Russia.

3. Darchenko is referring to Solzhenitsyn's *One Day in the Life of Ivan Denisovich*, published in November 1962, which describes a "normal" day in the life of a Gulag inmate in the early 1950s.

years old, and it somehow got carved into my childhood memory. And then, in 1956, my father worked off the time he had agreed to serve and we returned to Saratov. Here he continued working as a builder, as the main engineer at a construction enterprise. My mother worked as a nurse in a health clinic until she retired. That's about all regarding my parents.

What about your grandparents?

Regarding my grandparents, on one side they were also from Saratov, hereditary proletarians. They worked at a shipbuilding factory before the Revolution. And, on the other side, they came from the local merchant class. This is interesting, too. A certain Andronov, a merchant, was my great-great grandfather. My other great-grandfather was well known in his time. He managed the tsarist state's liquor factories in Saratov. His surname was Dyrchankov. My real surname thus was . . . changed.[4] Although I've never seen it, they tell me that in the town of Pugachev, where he lived, his house still stands and occupies a full city block. They tell me it's the home of that great-grandfather. So, in general, my family is local. By birth, I'm a Siberian, but I've lived here all the time.

What are your other memories of Siberia?

Absolutely tremendous ones, because of the natural beauty of the place. To me it was as things should be. It was normal. It's the only place I had seen. For instance, during the summer we swam in that same Enisei, when the temperature of the water was 12–14 degrees [Celsius]. We kids swam and thought that the water temperature was normal, that it couldn't be otherwise. The most amazing thing was the tall grass that you could get lost in. And the enormous mushrooms! They were so big! I remember how I would carry one whole mushroom with my arms wrapped around it. It was my size. They were colossal there. And in the Enisei, in the rapids, fish were jumping all the time. Such places! It's a real shame, but I later learned that they built a hydroelectric station right where we lived. It's not been preserved. But I remain terribly fond of the natural beauty there. One more thing. The weather was intensely cold. Including, well, something else is also carved in my memory. Inside the store there was vodka on the shelves, and something that looked like cotton was floating in it. I couldn't understand what it

---

4. In the early Soviet period those from the "wrong" class faced discrimination and often tried to hide their backgrounds. The Dyrchankov family may have changed its name for this reason.

was. They told me, "Yes, it's the water that's frozen inside." Inside the store! Minus forty or minus forty-five was the normal temperature. But there was no wind there, so we got along fine. And during that entire time, despite the bitter cold, I never got sick. I began to ail only after arriving in this climate [laughing]. That is, the climate there is very healthy. It's marvelous. Of course, I look back upon these things with a sense of amazement.

And the local people, were they from Siberia or from across the Soviet Union?

From across . . . that is, some were sent there on assignment. Those who ran things, the chief clerks, the foremen, they were sent there. It was a mandatory way of paying back the state [for one's education or training]. But the work force, for the most part, was made up of prisoners. They were mostly from Western Ukraine, so called followers of Bandera.[5]

People who fought against [Soviet power]?

Yes, basically. In general, I think, there were whole villages deported there. I'm not certain, but there were many.

What were your childhood interests?

When? There? Before I was five? I didn't have any! After I moved here I began to get interested in things. Yes, right after I started to go to school, physics became my thing. And that's understandable, since it was then that I saw the movie *Nine Days of One Year,*[6] about physicists and scientists. Back then there was a cult of physics. In sum, I knew exactly what I wanted to become, and where I'd go to college already as a child.

What kind of impression did Saratov make on you?

When I arrived, we lived with my grandmother on the banks of the Volga. For the most part, the city at that time, as I recall it, was roughly how it looks in photographs of old Saratov. There was no embankment, and no bridge. There were natural beaches right on the riverbank. There were huge barges with watermelons, which they unloaded simply by tossing them. Some of them fell into the river. We kids retrieved them and ate them. These were good times.

---

5. A Ukrainian nationalist, Stepan Bandera was freed from Nazi imprisonment in 1944 and allowed to head the struggle of Ukrainian nationalist forces against Soviet power. After the war, the Soviet government deported, exiled, and arrested many followers of Bandera's armed bands.

6. Directed by Mikhail Romm (1901–71) in 1962, the film depicted the conflict between old and new and featured a scientist who thinks independently, as well as sinister omens reminding viewers they lived in a dangerous, nuclear age.

But I didn't hold up well against the heat, because I wasn't used to it. I don't like the heat even now, because I got so used to the cold. But, basically, Saratov became my hometown. Especially that neighborhood, it's now Bolshaia Gornaia, approaching the bridge.[7] The very house in which we lived is still standing. It was very comfy and cozy. I liked it.

At first, you did not enroll in School No. 42.

Right. Only later. They gave my father an apartment and we moved from my grandmother's. It was on Second Dacha Street, and there I attended first and second grade in a local school, No. 76. Back then they enrolled pupils not in second grade, as they do now in the English-language school, but only in third. And then, at the start of third grade, I went there for an interview and enrolled.

Why there? Why did your parents want you . . .

Well, people understood that you needed a language. And I'm very grateful to them, in general, because I had need of the language all my life. I speak English now with great pleasure. I learned what I know back then, and it's helped me. They decided that it was important to receive an education beyond high school. I'm grateful.

Did your parents join the Communist Party?

No.

No? I also want to ask about religion. Did it play a role in your life?

You know, my parents aren't religious. But my grandmother was. My great grandmother, who looked after me when we first arrived here, was very religious. She, once, and, again, I'm very thankful to her, took me when I was five, right after we moved back [to Saratov] to church and had me baptized. I remember the fear I felt when I first entered the church! The frightening, scary-looking priest dunked me in the [font]. . . . That horror remains even now, but nevertheless, I'm baptized, and that's good. I have a very positive attitude toward religion. I, as they say, don't go to church every day, but I believe in God.

How would you describe School No. 42, its pupils, its social and ethnic composition?

Well, the [socioeconomic] level, in regard to families, was of course higher than the city average. Although there were a few from, as they say, a proletarian milieu. Regarding nationality, it's worth noting that we simply didn't think about such things back

---

7. Darchenko has in mind the suspension bridge over the Volga River linking Saratov to the city of Engels.

then. Even now I can't say with any assurance who belongs to what nationality.

Was there a difference between the two groups in your class, the A group and B group?

You know, when we enrolled they distributed us by chance. But ever since then it seems to me that we were luckier. We were, it seems, closer. Yet I'm not sure why. A large group of people couldn't all of a sudden simply by chance . . . no, things don't turn out that way. Apparently, we had good leaders who were able to unite us. I can't say who, because I don't remember. Each probably contributed something. But the friendship that's lasted among us for forty years is worth mentioning. Unfortunately, I see how the A group simply doesn't get together anymore, although there are some fine people among them, too. I like many of those in group A. I still see them and speak with them. For instance, Gorelik.[8] And there's Trubnikov,[9] the most colorful of all, who, unfortunately, is now in Israel. It would be interesting for you to meet with him! Well, I consider us lucky. Indeed.

And what about the teachers? Who were they?

As for the teachers, well, the school was somewhat privileged, and the teachers were very good. That is, the basic contingent was. Maybe in the middle classes there were some weak teachers. But they usually didn't retain them, because we had some interesting characters among the pupils. For instance, there was Konstantinov,[10] who could really mock a teacher, but, in general, no, they didn't hold on to the [weak ones]. Basically, the teaching staff was very strong. There were wonderful teachers of English, simply wonderful. We, beginning in the . . . already by the ninth grade we could converse freely in English. And without thinking. It was great! I've lost my oral skills, because I've had no practice. Conversational language [is] more difficult.

To what extent was the instruction politicized?

At school? Not at all.

Not at all?

Absolutely not.

---

8. Olga Iakovlevna Gorelik teaches physics at Saratov University. I interviewed her in 2002, but the interview is not included in this volume.

9. Aleksandr Vladimirovich Trubnikov; his interview is in chapter 7.

10. A. A. Konstantinov teaches at Moscow State University; his interview is in chapter 1.

What about the teaching of history?

You know, history was basically . . . it was all, of course, a bit politicized, all the textbooks. But it seemed to us that that's simply how things were. That's right. That's why it didn't seem political. Even the Pioneer movement.[11] We took it to be like your Scout movement. We were just hanging out. That is, we weren't at all politically minded when we attended school. That's altogether certain. That's how I remember it. It's more likely that things changed at the university when we had to study the history of the CPSU [Communist Party of the Soviet Union] and so on. But not at school.

You emphasized the importance of the fact that you learned English. How often did you make use of the language?

Practically all the time. I've already changed my so-called profession three times in my life. Whenever there's a fork in the road, life forces you to choose. My first profession was nuclear physics, and I worked in the international institute in Dubna. A foreign language was necessary there. Although there weren't any representatives from the so-called capitalist countries, there were from the socialist countries. There basically were two languages of communication: Russian and English. Therefore, already back then . . . then there were a ton of articles that I needed to read in scholarly journals. Finally, I earned some pocket money when I lived in the dormitory. I first studied for three years here at the university. After the fourth year they sent me to Dubna to study and to work. I worked in the neutron physics laboratory of Ilia Mikhailovich Frank, the Nobel Prize winner. We lived on our stipends, and, since many professors and others urgently needed information from articles, we worked as translators. That is, say it was necessary to have an article translated in a day, and the professional translator of articles on nuclear physics couldn't do it. That's how we earned money. That was the first time I needed English in my career. The second time was when I had to change my profession once specialists in Dubna were no longer in demand and I lacked a living permit. Thank goodness that now we don't [have to worry about such things, except in Moscow]. . . . I had to become an electrical engineer here [in Saratov]. Once again, there was an enormous number of articles to read. Then they began to use computers, and all the instructions were in English. Everything's

---

11. A Communist Party youth organization that catered to young people between ten and fourteen or fifteen years old. Virtually all school-aged children belonged to the Pioneers.

being done in English. And I worked long hours, traveled a lot with exhibits, and it turned out that I had to speak a lot, thank goodness, in English. That is, at all the exhibits I gave my commentary in English. Even in China, paradoxically. Well, when our professor presented a lecture on magnetic measurements to Chinese specialists, it turned out that there was no one to translate from Russian into Chinese. They had already forgotten their Russian. At one time, many knew Russian, but not now. Well, we worked out this system. He lectured in Russian, I translated into English, and a Chinese professor who graduated from a university in the USA translated from English into Chinese. Questions from the audience were translated three times. In sum, I needed English all the time. And now, once again, this time in connection with perestroika, the institute where I worked practically shut down. Well, it's open, but you can't work there, because they don't pay a thing. I changed my profession in 1995 and became a computer programmer, and English, well, I don't think any explanation of its importance is necessary. That is, I basically had need of the language all my life.

What was your attitude toward the West when you attended School No. 42?

You know, I never harbored a hostile attitude toward it. I never felt that we were enemies. Apparently, my family was normal. It all depends upon what children are taught. That's how it was. I was very interested, all the same, in seeing how other people live. Because what I saw, well, it made an impression and somehow seeped through. Why is everything different there? It was all fascinating. Let's just say that I was interested in other countries. I never viewed the West as an enemy. Never.

What was your attitude toward China at the time?

I was of two opinions toward China. Well, again, earlier we were taught that China was "brother number one." But then the events of 1968 took place:[12] "What enemies they all are, what vermin!" Yet now, after I've spent time in China, and saw the country, indeed I spent a lot of time there and was in six different cities. I now have enormous respect for them precisely because of their goals. It's the oldest of civilizations and one feels it in them. They already know things that we don't know. They accommodate overcrowding, noise,

---

12. Darchenko is referring to the Ussuri River crisis that actually occurred in 1969, a border clash in which the Chinese were determined to convince the Brezhnev leadership that they would not back away from armed conflict.

and so on. They're at home with themselves. We, it seems, still have a lot of growing up to do, a whole generation to go, in order to obtain that perspective. That's what surprised me about them and, in general, now I relate to them . . . with some apprehension. It's a very powerful nation and our neighbor to boot. And Siberia—is underpopulated [laughing]. Let's say therefore that my attitude is one of respect and fear.

Arkadii Olegovich, what did you think of Cuba back then?

Cuba? What brotherhood! Moreover, I managed to travel there. Again, I was with an exhibit. Sometime in 1993, I think, already after we had a parting of ways. Nevertheless, I felt that these people were very open and very friendly. Yes, they remained friendly. Once again, this says a lot about one's upbringing. When you walked along the street someone would run up to you and say, "Hey, Americano, give me a dollar." I'd say in Russian, "I'm not an Americano, I'm Russian." "Ah, Russo. Do you want a drink?" In general, they related differently. They were taught "Americano" is bad, and "Russo" is good. This, too, made an impression on me, these [stereotypes].

That's changed, by the way.

It's already changed? I spoke with some young Cubans at the time in English, who, by the way, didn't know any Russian. I already saw that they, how should I put it . . . and they said, "Well, it's great about perestroika; you're finally rejoining the rest of the world. We'll probably do the same thing." I think that things there probably are changing.

Were there any changes to the school program while you went to school?

When we went there? Major ones? No, when we went there the school program didn't change. But now I understand that our textbooks were politicized; however, at the time things seemed otherwise. Including literature. Even literature was politicized. That is, take Pushkin, who fought against the autocracy. How ridiculous! All this seems so odd. But there weren't any changes in the school program back then.

How does your generation differ from your parents' generation?

You know, probably less than our children from us. Most likely, our generation didn't differ at all from that of our parents. Back then we dressed exactly as our parents did. We had no concept of "young people's clothing." Well, I'm speaking about such superficial things. Then again, in character we were also most likely a repeat of our parents. But after us came a new generation that was completely different. This change can be seen, moreover, not only in Russia, but globally, it seems. I don't know how to account for this, but I consider us more like our parents. That's my opinion.

You mentioned clothing. Weren't there any fashions among young people?

Well, of course. Back then, toward the end of our school years, tight pants were the rage. And jackets with shoulder pads, but we weren't allowed to [wear them]. Our school principal was a mini-Stalin who dictated what we could wear. For instance, when girls came to school wearing earrings, she'd send them home immediately and tell them, "Come back without any earrings." We wore uniforms. Of course, people wanted to be fashionable, but it was difficult to get hold of such things. In general, it was impossible to buy them, and we needed to "get hold of" them. The meaning of "get hold of" is probably uniquely Russian [laughing].[13] Various fads passed through. Jeans, for example, came later. Probably at the university; we also had to "get hold of" jeans. But they're really comfortable and even now I mostly wear jeans. Thank goodness that it's no longer a problem getting them. So, yes, there were some styles of clothing that were popular, but not all that much back then. It was simply impossible to get hold of. . . .

What about favorite books and movies among young people at school?

There perhaps was nothing that, how shall I put it, appealed to everyone. You see, we were pretty well tracked by subject back in school. Some were inclined toward the humanities. Even though our interests differed, this did not keep us from being friends. And therefore, to say that someone liked something in particular and the whole class became engrossed in reading it, well, that simply didn't happen.

It's interesting that there was such a difference between the disciplines. Can you tell me more about this?

Now, perhaps, I'm able to understand it. For me, for instance, the film *Nine Days of One Year* was really special. The girls loved *War and Peace*, which Bondarchuk made.[14] I thought it was too long. But take another example. Of course we liked, well, we boys really liked the book *The Three Musketeers*. And the girls, more likely, preferred novels about love. Thus, there was no one book that was a hit

---

13. The Russian verb "dostat'" means to obtain, secure, or acquire with difficulty.

14. Born in 1918, Sergei Bondarchuk was a famous Soviet actor and film director. Critics consider his four-part *War and Peace* the most stunning historical epic made during the 1960s.

Arkadii Darchenko (*left*) and classmate Tatiana Okuneva, now of
Tempe, Arizona, sitting on a bench near a Moscow train station, in
1966. They had traveled to Briansk oblast along with several others
from School No. 42 to trace the footsteps of local partisans during
World War II. *Courtesy A. A. Konstantinov.*

with everyone. Although the Soviet film *Hamlet*, starring Smoktunovskii,[15] made the same impression on everyone. Here's a film that
probably everyone in the class loved. Even though we were only in
eighth or ninth grade. That is, we weren't quite grown up yet, but
the film made an impression. It probably was in 1965 or so. Apart
from this, we most likely all had different interests.

*Many exciting political developments took place during your childhood.
Although children usually aren't interested in such things, they observe how
their parents react to them. Do you recall your parents' reaction to events such
as the Twentieth Party Congress or Khrushchev's denunciation of Stalin's
personality cult?*

I'll tell you. They didn't react at all. Why? They were afraid to

---

15. Innokentii Smoktunovskii, a famous Soviet actor from the period, portrayed an
array of characters distinguished by their independent spirits. Director Grigorii Kozintsev
directed *Hamlet*, which featured a score by Dmitrii Shostakovich.

comment, especially since they had worked in the Gulag. That's right. They didn't discuss politics at home. My father never joined the party and was sensible, but my parents were afraid. They still are, by the way. They're alive, but remain apprehensive. Just in case. As they say, "Who knows what might happen?" But I recall that it was a real nightmare during the Cuban Missile Crisis, when at any moment bombs might be strewn down on us. I often dreamed of nuclear war and would wake up from my sleep in fear. That's how it was. If I'm not mistaken, such feelings were mutual. People probably reacted the same way in America. This fear, well, it often woke me up when I was no longer a tot. After all, the crisis occurred in 1957 or more likely, 1958.

Later. It was in 1962.

That late? Yes, I had already started school. But these childhood nightmares continued to haunt me. About a nuclear explosion and the like. It seemed that at any moment war might [break out]. . . . It was awful.

Khrushchev worked out a new party program; there were stunning achievements in space; Cosmonaut Iurii Gagarin landed in Saratov oblast; one of the slogans was to out-produce America by 1970 and to build communism by 1980. How did all this affect young people?

Back then we were too young and most likely too trusting. I was confident that we would truly achieve communism by 1980. Why not? Indeed, people believed that we were on the true path, and that soon we'd achieve it. But when we were a bit older, we realized that we're not heading in that direction. . . . Even during the Khrushchev years we understood. Yes, we knew that nothing would come of this, because there was this feeling that we should be getting more prosperous, yet things began to get worse.

At first things began to improve materially, right? It was noticeable?

Yes. It certainly seems that way. Significantly better. Well, although we lived in Siberia, we had our own home, of course. Well, we shared it, but it was a separate wooden house. Here people mostly lived in communal flats. And then, before your very eyes, they began to move us out of communal flats into our own. My father received a communal apartment in Saratov where we lived at first, but then we moved downtown, into our own place. People could see that a lot of new living space appeared and people began to live on their own. More things began to show up in the stores. And then, suddenly, what really put people on edge was that food, basic food items, began to disappear from the stores, including bread. We were still in school when they introduced rationing for bread. "How bad would things get?" people asked. Could Russia be left without bread? In sum, it all began already back then. We began to wise up. That's when we began to understand that this was some sort of illusion. And by the end of the 1980s we understood once and for all what was what.

Back then Saratov was a closed city. There were no foreigners. Did samizdat circulate here, despite the fact that Saratov was a closed city, or did this take place later?

A bit later. I read all the samizdat, but in Dubna. Things were freer there. It was an international institute and all samizdat literature circulated there. And a lot was brought into the country, books published abroad in Russian. I read Solzhenitsyn already at Dubna, before they began to publish him in Russia. And I read Bulgakov's *Heart of a Dog* for the first time.[16] If I'm not mistaken, it first was published in Russia about ten years ago or so. But I read it back then. Back then in Saratov we had minimal contact with foreigners. However, I recall that once there was some sort of teachers' delegation from Bristol in England. We were in the fourth grade at the time. Yes, there was some sort of delegation, and I remember that it was namely teachers. Probably of the Russian language. I don't recall exactly, but [that's] most likely. I do recall that they were from Bristol. Just once. We corresponded mostly with people from "brotherly" countries. That is, with Czechs, Slovaks, Poles. But to travel abroad, no, there was nothing like that.

What about foreign radio broadcasts? Did you listen to them?

Yes. As soon as I was able to figure out electronics myself. . . . We had a VEF.[17] I fixed the circuit, the wave band, so that they couldn't jam us. I made it more of a short wave band and they broadcast on it. Generally, I listened all the time. Yes, this was around tenth grade and afterward.

Do you think that others listened, too, but didn't talk about it?

No, we no longer were afraid. We were from a different generation. Well, I don't know if girls listened, too, but we often discussed what we heard in class, since we listened to the same things. Yes, we discussed it at school. We weren't afraid. No. That's our parents.

---

16. The early Soviet authorities deemed unpublishable Mikhail Bulgakov's (1891–1940) novella, which satirizes attempts to create the new Soviet man and woman.

17. A popular and portable multiband receiver produced in Soviet Latvia and earlier known as the Spidola.

We talked about it and we had our own opinions about things, and I think this was a good thing.

In other words, in this regard, your generation differs.

In this regard, yes. We lacked that genetic fear that was hammered into them. Basically two radio broadcasts reached us, Voice of America, in Russian, and Deutsche Welle [German Wave], also in Russian. The others didn't reach us. But the relay stations [for Voice of America and Deutsche Welle] were not that far away and our receivers were powerful enough that we could, how do you say, catch them.

What did your parents think of your listening?

They thought it was normal. They listened themselves [laughing].

How did you understand what you were doing, that you were listening to something that was banned yet weren't afraid?

We thought it was normal. Why? Well, I understood for some time already that I was going to study science, probably physics, and that this was a search for the truth. I understood listening to two points of view as part of that very personal search for truth. I realized that the truth lies somewhere in between. That is, both sides lie. In other words, you have to search for the truth. For that reason I saw listening to foreign broadcasts as normal. I never felt that I was some sort of freedom fighter. Not at all. It was simply interesting for me to know the truth. That's all. It was a view of the world. I'd put it that way.

You already mentioned that there were no clashes in school between nationalities.

None.

What about fights, first loves . . .

Sure, there were a lot of both. But we also were united in friendship. Each year, beginning with seventh grade, we spent a month together living in tents in a camp on the Volga. Not everyone went, of course. There were a few in the upper classes that didn't. But in our class a large enough group went practically each year. That, too, united us, by the way. After all, we did just about everything ourselves—cooked, procured things. That is, we went back and forth to purchase essentials, and took turns cooking. By the way, we cooked on open campfires. Under the supervision of two teachers, but in general we did things ourselves. And group work, it's the sort of thing that bonds people. Likewise, there were conflicts and romances, after all.

Teacher Igor Andreev-ich Molchanov served as chief cook during summer camp on the Volga in 1966. *Courtesy A. A. Konstantinov.*

Did you speak some English at summer camp?

You know, we didn't. I'll explain why. Everything is fine in moderation. In school they made us speak a lot of English much of the time. There were classrooms in which it was posted "Only English Is Spoken Here." And as a result, we probably were so sick of it that at camp we spoke Russian. Although they hammered English into our heads so that it became part of our subconscious. Sort of like you with Russian. That is, you don't translate when you speak. It was like that.

Did both groups go to camp?

No, it was mostly kids from group B. There were a few from group A, but it was mostly kids from B.

How did you react when they ousted Khrushchev? After all, you said that already while he was in power it was clear that communism . . .

I commented on his removal. I said it was about time. I thought that something might change, and wanted very much to believe that things would [laughing].

I asked these questions to understand what shaped the formation of your worldview while you were growing up. What else do I need to ask you in order to understand this? What else affected you? We spoke about your parents, for instance. Oh, and by the way, I forgot to ask whether your father or mother influenced you most, or . . .

My father. Namely in the independence of his views. That's to say, he could have achieved much more had he joined the Communist Party. He and I talked about this. He was the chief engineer and was the manager of a trust, rather, of a whole building association, but he couldn't advance any further. He's still alive and is retired. He was an excellent engineer. They wanted to promote him, but under one condition. . . . And he already told me back then that it makes no difference, that he wouldn't join the party. He told me that he was better off remaining in his current job. This independent worldview greatly affected me. I also never joined the party because, how shall I put it, I never accepted its ideology. Therefore, to sell yourself for the sake of getting ahead. . . . I had the opportunity to become chief engineer at the institute in Dubna, but I remained the chief designer. Even though it was a position lower, I still didn't join the party on principle.

What else shaped you, Arkadii Olegovich?

What else? Perhaps my coworkers in Dubna also had a strong influence on me, in part because I interacted not only with people from Russia, and I understood that people everywhere are the same. In general, they taught us that we're good and that over there they're bad. And in the middle were those from the brother countries.[18] But I understood that people are people, regardless of where they're from or regardless of their ideology. How shall I put it? There are good people and bad people everywhere. It doesn't matter where you're from. By the way, this greatly affected my political interests, there, while I was in Dubna. The free exchange of ideas with people from different nationalities. All that was really beneficial. To this day I maintain that the more people know about one another, the better the world would be. That's what I think. Hoorah [laughing]!

You completed school in 1967 and that fall enrolled in college?

Yes, immediately. I graduated as a silver medalist and therefore had to pass only a subject exam, that is, mathematics, two exams, written and oral. I enrolled in the physics department, of course.

---

18. That is, from the Soviet-bloc countries in Eastern Europe.

There were seven applicants for each slot, but I got admitted without a problem because I was a medalist in school. This is why I began to study my beloved theoretical nuclear physics. Because they took those who got in the first time around.

And after three years you . . .

I spent three years here, then they sent me away. There was a branch of Moscow University in Dubna, a theoretical nuclear physics department. It had a dormitory and that's where I lived. They promptly distributed us among the various laboratories at Dubna where we studied in the morning and worked on the accelerators afterward. In other words, we began working already at that time.

Your student years here in Saratov coincided with the invasion of Czechoslovakia in 1968 when you were a freshman. I understand that there was not much reaction, that people believed what they read. But were there discussions among students?

There were, there were. And opinion differed sharply. There was one false report released by the mass media that if we didn't invade Czechoslovakia, German tanks that were lined up on the border would have done so, and so on. Many believed this. They'd say, "Yeah, there's no disputing it, that's how it is. Otherwise, the German hordes would once again be at our border." But, the other half said that this was nothing but a lie, a canard. That it was, how shall I put it, another attempt at forcing them to accept socialism. I was one of those who agreed with the latter view. Although my uncle, my mother's brother, was a professional soldier. He belonged to the invading forces and commanded a regiment. He got burned there in his tank. They set it on fire and his legs got burned. In speaking to him afterward he always maintained that the invasion was necessary. But a soldier is a soldier. Undoubtedly, he couldn't see things otherwise, yet I told him that he had no purpose getting burned there. You shouldn't have been there [laughing]. Yes, all that left its mark, that is, it affected us for the better. We began to understand things about our country that were not all that good. For instance, I don't think it's right to invade another country.

When I was in Saratov in 1992, I met someone named Romanov. Back then, in 1971, the so-called Romanov affair flared up at the history department. I don't recall exactly how many people were involved, but a group of students formed a Marxist study circle to read Marx and to understand Marxism's origins better. They got arrested. Many members of the history department remember this. Was this discussed outside the department?

You know, more likely than not, this passed us by. I don't remember this. We discussed Marxism, but at the university and more critically, from the point of view of physics. That is, we searched for its logic and there wasn't any [laughing]. The Romanov affair passed us by.

You mentioned that instruction was more politicized at the university. That is, it was hard to avoid this?

You couldn't get around it. There was history of the Communist Party, at first for three years, I think. Then scientific communism. The very term! As one of us put it so well, "Why isn't there scientific physics or scientific mathematics?" What is "scientific communism?" Is there such a thing as "unscientific communism?" [laughing]. We saw it as a necessary evil. Unfortunately, we had to take quizzes and exams. There was no escaping it. We had to study it even if we were turned off by it. There was no getting around it.

And did they teach it in your department or was there a separate one for "scientific communism"?

The professors were members of the History Faculty, of its Department of Scientific Communism and History of the Party. They taught us too.

Just out of curiosity, do you remember who taught you these subjects?

Oh, the most colorful personality was Ilin.[19] Incidentally, he was the only one, perhaps, among those who taught communism, who had his own interesting point of view on everything. I always liked that a lot. We sympathized with him. I also remember Avrus.[20] He was also quite colorful, yes, very much so. Even now I exchange greetings with him when I see him on the street. We, well, I don't know if he remembers me. He knows my face, but he doesn't recall my name. But I remember him and am always glad to see him. And there were others cut from a different cloth, who droned on and on about this and that. Iakorev was like that.[21] There were others of this type. That is, as a group they were quite varied, too. Although we hated these subjects and made fun of them.

What styles of clothing were popular when you were a university student? Probably jeans?

Yes, they already appeared.

---

19. B. I. Ilin, author of a popular historical overview of Saratov.

20. Today Anatolii Ilich Avrus teaches twentieth-century Russian history at Saratov University. He has trained dozens of students, who staff universities and institutes throughout Saratov oblast and elsewhere in Russia.

21. N. A. Iakorev published articles on Communist Party activities along the Volga during the period of the Russian Civil War.

There was more Western music, than, say, the Beatles?

Yes, of course. By then there was everything. The fact is that good music appeared already while we attended school, already at school. Well, I don't know anyone from our generation who doesn't love the Beatles. Even now, I . . . I still have the Beatles' greatest hits. We grew up on them. Then there were the Rolling Stones, who also, well, by then we had everything. Generally, we liked all of it.

What about poet bards such as Vysotskii, Galich, Okudzhava?[22] Did you listen to them?

Yes, of course. Especially since all these songs also showed up at summer camp, on the Volga near Chardym.[23] By the way, several guys in the group played the guitar really well. They sang Okudzhava. Vysotskii was just making his debut. When we first heard his songs we didn't know whose they were, but we liked them enormously and all of us sang them. Each night, when it began to grow dark, we gathered around the campfires on the riverbank, in the sand, and sang until two in the morning. That was part of camp life. Thus, we grew up listening to these songs, to these bard-poets.

You moved to Moscow in 1971?

Well, already at the end of 1970. And I completed my studies there. I took some of my exams at a branch of Moscow University, but I was enrolled as a student here at Saratov University. I took additional exams here, I think, on some subjects that I studied there that weren't taught here. I took them together. For example, say that in Dubna there was neutron optics, but here there was solid-state physics. A professor here simply signed off that I had passed. I began to write my senior thesis as soon as I got there. And when I finished, it became the first chapter of my dissertation that I never completed, because I stopped being a nuclear scientist [laughing]. Well, yes, we went back and forth. I only showed up here for exams, but worked there.

And when you graduated, you returned to Saratov to work?

By the time I finished I was already married. You know, there's also an interesting story here. In the fall of 1971, during my fourth

---

22. Vladimir Vysotskii, Aleksandr Galich, and Bulat Okudzhava were poets who, in the 1960s, began singing their songs to their own solo accompaniment on the seven-stringed guitar. Circulating on privately recorded tapes, guitar poetry represented the most popular form of anti-regime culture in the Brezhnev period.

23. A resort area on the Volga located north of Saratov. The university maintains a camp there.

year—no, it was at the start of my fifth year. Well, I got married and on that very day left for Dubna and almost didn't make it because we had such a thing as work assignment back then.[24] If I hadn't gotten married when I did, they could have sent my future wife wherever they liked. Therefore, we officially got married so at least we'd get sent to the same place. How did this turn out? At first I went to Dubna where I studied. But then, when we finished the university, they assigned me back here, because the party had implemented a new policy whereby the best students had to teach physics in the schools. I was placed on the list of the ten best students. . . . But Academic [Ilia] Frank himself summoned me back to Dubna. However, they wouldn't let us go for a long time. We were nervous wrecks. I'd say, "They're waiting for me there." Well, the short of it is that, interestingly enough, the secretary of the party organization in Dubna helped me. Although I was not a party member and harbored all sorts of. . . . He turned out to be a decent person. I don't recall his name just now. Moreover, the rector back then said, "Not under any circumstances." The secretary of the party organization replied, "We have to treat him well, humanely." And with his help, he phoned the head of the oblast department of education and asked him to say that he turned down two students with wives. This astonished me, by the way. Yet things like that happened. And it helped a great deal. That is to say, my wife and I left immediately for Dubna, belongings and all. We rented an apartment and I worked there until the new year. And I worked, not for the money, but for the "love" of it all, since they accepted me temporarily and the pay, well, the pay was on par with our stipends. That's right! But my temporary living permit expired that winter, just before the start of the year, after which I needed a permanent living permit.[25] "We'll provide you with dormitory space, a salary, and the rest." However, just then they made it more difficult to obtain a living permit for Moscow. Dubna was placed in the same category as Moscow. And they absolutely refused to register those who had a temporary permit. I dropped in on them

---

24. A reference to the practice of *raspredelenie*, whereby the state assigned students to jobs at the completion of their higher education. The authorities sent students where they were needed, usually for two years, and sometimes to jobs that otherwise were difficult to fill. This was seen as a way of paying back the state for the free higher education it provided.

25. The Soviet state controlled population movement, especially to desirable locales such as Moscow, by introducing a system of permanent and temporary living permits (*propiski*).

a lot. I was received by the main general of the Moscow region. I had letters from Academic Frank and the like. The general told me "Oh, Frank, he's a distinguished scholar. But the law is the law. I'm sorry. You must gather your things and leave." Moreover, at work they'd say things like, "You know, you're probably the last young specialist left. That is, we're starting to die out. The problems with registration are keeping us from taking on others. We're starting to die out." By the way, that's what happened. Those who used to work there still do if they're alive. But there aren't any new ones since then, except for students who are there for two years after which they leave. It's terrible, of course. So I returned here once again with all my belongings, with my wife, and had to start over. That was in December 1972. We had left for Dubna in July. I worked there from July through November as a specialist and then returned here.

Was your wife a student?

Yes, she also studied physics, not nuclear physics, but chemical physics. She is from Saratov. We were born the same year.

How did she shape your worldview?

How? She made me more cultured [laughing]. I was probably fairly uncouth. She taught me good manners.

Was it common for students to take part in construction brigades or to help out on the farms?

Yes, of course, all of us did.

As volunteers, or was it required?

You know, in principle there's a great saying in Russian: "The harshness of Russian laws is mitigated by the fact that their fulfillment is optional." That's how it was. If we wanted to continue our studies, we had no choice. But you were always able to "get out of it" somehow, as they said. But we didn't. Why? I don't know. I guess we liked it. We took part in construction brigades and basically built things. That very same wife of mine, along with another woman the same size, pushed wheelbarrows full of mortar for fifty meters. That's altogether abnormal, since a wheelbarrow of mortar weighs a good sixty kilos, I think. Yes, in general, we took part in them, for at least two or three years. If I hadn't, well. There was even a competition to go to Siberia, I think to Angara.[26] We were really upset when we didn't get picked because of all sorts of intrigues.

---

26. Beginning in 1960, facilities in Angara, which had produced Soviet airplanes, began developing space rocket equipment. In the years that followed, local plants created a family of intercontinental ballistic missiles and space stations.

The older students got picked for it. And when I didn't take part in a construction brigade, I'd go to a sports camps near Chardym. I was on the fencing team, and still do sports. Each summer I had the construction brigade and training. I was always between things. We were all like that.

During the 1960s samizdat literature spread widely in Moscow and Leningrad. There was a lot of talk about human rights, and then relations with the West temporarily improved. How did these things affect you? Were they noticeable?

You know, here there wasn't any uproar over political events as there was in Piter and Moscow.[27] But within our milieu we always felt free to speak our mind. Nothing changed for us; we were always like that. We talked openly. Therefore, I really didn't notice any major change. As we saw things, we had our views and stuck to them. Our conversations were the same. That is, there basically wasn't anything special that set us apart.

In the 1970s it became easier to travel, at least to Eastern Europe. I studied in Leningrad in 1971 and many of the Russians with whom I studied by the middle of the 1980s had been to Poland, East Germany, Bulgaria, and the like. Did you travel somewhere?

I had top security clearance. Since I worked at the institute in Dubna and studied electronics I couldn't leave the country. I had access, well, I began to travel in connection with my work, but only after perestroika. It was about 1989 that I went abroad for the first time. And then I traveled a lot, as a specialist of the institute, with my projects. But before then it was impossible.

Did any of your friends or your parents travel abroad?

No. My parents couldn't because they lacked the money. It was fairly expensive. And second, it wasn't all that simple. None of my friends did either. Why? Because all my acquaintances came from the same circle. That is, if they didn't have top security clearance, they fell into the next category, but it, too, kept them from leaving the country.

Arkadii Olegovich, what forces shaped your personal identity?

You know, probably the fact that I had to start life over three times. The first time I was still young, and I could do it without much difficulty. But when I had to for the second time in 1995 it was really hard. Why? Because I was well known at the institute, I was, how

---

27. Piter is the colloquial name for St. Petersburg.

shall I put it, someone. And I left a nobody, a programmer trainee in a commercial firm. It was very tough going, and I didn't know that I had it in me to pull myself up once again. Now I'm affiliated with a large commercial enterprise as a specialist. I take delight in the fact that it turns out that I could do it. That is, the most important thing that I learned at school and then at the university was how to learn. That's the most important thing. Thank God. I don't have a low opinion of myself since I was able to retool myself three times.

What about gender, the fact that you're a man and not a woman? How has this fact shaped your life?

You know, a great deal. I still believe that the professions that I picked all my life are men's professions. Nuclear physics particularly so. It's not that women are inferior, but that they're different. They're more emotional, and emotion has no place in science. That's what I think. Moreover, emotion keeps you from concentrating on what's most important. What I mean is that when you add to this the distraction of taking care of the household and the like, you can see why. . . . I consider being a computer programmer also a man's profession. Although there are female programmers, it's simply not their thing. In the same way that being an electrical engineer isn't a woman's thing. And a nuclear scientist even more so. It's a guy thing even in regard to your health. All the radiation that we received . . . it affects women even more. So, all of my professions have been exclusively male ones, even back then.

But the women who worked in these fields, in nuclear physics . . .

We didn't take them seriously [laughing]. Maybe we were wrong, but . . .

Do you think that things were hard for them?

You know, that's not what I mean. Women are very smart. I have tremendous respect for many intelligent women who are much smarter than I am, but they're smarter in a different way. Women are simply not in a condition to give what it takes to be a programmer, for they're not able to concentrate as well on such things as programming or electronics. I'm not saying that they're not as intelligent as us. They're just different.

Did your attitudes toward the West, toward China, and toward the world in general change during the 1970s and 1980s?

My horizons broadened. Although I never looked upon any Western country with hostility, I have to admit that when I was a kid I wasn't fond of Germany. Like any Russian, I lost several relatives during the war. And this affects your view, of course. But now, how shall I put it, I think that's stupid. It would be like hating the French because of the war with Napoleon. All that's in the past. Basically, I've never seen anyone as an enemy, except, perhaps . . . well, yes, now, perhaps I strongly mistrust the Near East. Including Chechnia. Let's say that my attitude toward them is not the best. I don't think, for instance, that it's possible to really become friends with them. I consider all other countries normal, although I'm apprehensive about China. Once again, I'm apprehensive about the Eastern mindset. I'm quite, how shall I put it, loyal toward the West. Why? Because of its civilization. That very civilization that we lack and that will take us some time to acquire. Our general standard of living should be the same, but it seems to me that we're years away from this. That's what I think.

You had the opportunity to study in Moscow already as a student. The difference between Moscow and a provincial center such as Saratov was huge and remains that way. How did you feel about this? That Saratov was an agricultural region, yet people from Saratov had to travel to Moscow in order to buy meat?

For that same humiliating reason I don't like the existing state of things. I simply didn't understand why we had to travel 800 kilometers for sausage. It seemed to me that something was wrong with our country. The people were the same here and there. So, then, why in regard to food were things so different? Moreover, Dubna was altogether special. At one time Beria ran things there,[28] and this special status continued even while I lived there. The stores were of an altogether different sort. Even Moscow lacked things available in Dubna. At the very least you could always find essential food items there. For instance, you could buy a bottle of good Georgian wine for a ruble. Things were even better than in Moscow. First of all, there were always lines in Moscow and crowds. But not in Dubna. I wondered why the entire country couldn't live that way. By the way, you know, there's far more in Saratov now than [in Dubna] back then. Yet it seemed so special to us at the time! In general, we understood that this was a bunch of nonsense, I mean, a fluke, and that people shouldn't live that way. Again, we understood how things were, but this didn't turn us into active revolutionaries. We were busy doing our own thing. However, we understood that things weren't right.

---

28. Lavrentii Beria was head of Stalin's secret police from 1938 until his execution in 1953. In 1945 Stalin placed him in charge of developing the Soviet atomic bomb.

How did you react to the invasion of Afghanistan at the end of the 1970s?

I was really against it. Absolutely so. It was a repeat of the story with Czechoslovakia, I said, but on a larger scale. It was the same way with Czechoslovakia. They were suppressing people. I was in Dubna at the time and we listened to Czech broadcasts. And then the attitudes of the Czechs toward us Russians at Dubna took a sharp turn for the worse. We'd say to them, "Hey, what's up? We're not responsible." And they'd reply, "You're all, you're conquerors." It was possible to understand where they were coming from.

That is, there were discussions there?

Of course. Really nasty ones. Many of them simply stopped [having anything to do with us]. We had really gotten to be good friends there. After all, we were all young specialists with families. We invited each other over. Czechs, Bulgarians, Poles, Germans. Basically, just about everyone. There were no longer any Chinese, by the way. They'd been sent home. And then all of a sudden our relations with the Czechs drastically changed. They were particularly hostile to the Germans, who, the Czechs told us, behaved far more brutally than the Russians. "Russia, well, after all, you're Russians." But the Germans there began to introduce iron discipline. This became an everyday occurrence and was much disliked. So, I reacted with hostility to the invasion of Afghanistan. I reacted even worse, perhaps, to the fact that we began to fight in Chechnia in 1995. We should have simply cordoned them off. You should never fight against them. It's better not to. It's a mistake.

Under Gorbachev, the Brezhnev period was cast as one of stagnation. What did you think of Brezhnev and did your attitude toward him change?

No. That is, I was cynical toward him. Let's put it that way. At first we were still young and thought that, well. . . . And Brezhnev was young, too. Let's say that things changed starting sometime in the mid-1970s. The idiocy turned into a real avalanche of idiocy. When they began awarding him all sorts of medals and ranks and he no longer was able to speak clearly. We reacted negatively to all this. And stagnation, well, it's the most apt, the most fitting epithet. There was so much despair. Everything surrounding us seemed irreparable. Take television, for instance, which was unbearable. There were only one or two channels, and as soon as you'd switched them on you'd turn them off. Our "leading newspaper" *Pravda* elicited the same reaction. There was nothing but real despair. And the cinema was completely censored. Once some film was released. It was a typical one, some sort of hit about a group of Rockers. Oh, what crowds gathered! But they cancelled it. Western influence, that was the worst. . . . Yes, despair, literally despair. Then there was the unpleasant political and economic side of things. By this time I was already earning a decent living. Well, in the 1980s our son was born. The child grew. I wanted to buy him something and had the money. Chocolate, or something else. But no, I searched the entire town and wasn't able to buy anything. So, I came home and stashed away the money, this play money. Not in a bank. And you know what? It burned, and that's the way it was supposed to be, because it wasn't real money. The bills were nothing but tokens. They were never worth the amount of money indicated on them. For these reasons, the stagnation was real. It was awful. I'm happy that the period ended without bloodshed. It could have turned out violent, because things had reached the limit. I have to say that no matter what you think of Gorbachev, he's a great man because he was able to avoid bloodshed. There could have been a horrible civil war. Thank God things turned out otherwise. That's what I think.

You consciously turned down invitations to join the Communist Party, but did you ever meet real believers, true Communists?

You know, I didn't. As a rule, they were mostly careerists, and careerists in the most negative sense of the word. Demagogues. They'd lie to you and they knew that you understood that they were lying, and this encouraged them even more. Yes, it encouraged them. That was the downside. And what I don't like about our leadership today is that it's made up of the very same Komsomolites and Communists. Why aren't things improving? It's because of them. They don't let business-like people in. And they don't care what they're called. A Communist one day, and something else the next. They don't care as long as they're in power. As a result, I have a negative opinion of them. Although, as I said, I did encounter the secretary of the party organization who all of a sudden helped me, even though there was nothing in it for him. I'm not sure why. Perhaps he was one of the few committed Communists from the older generation. One of those who believed in everything. I understand how hard things must be for them if they're still alive. They can't, they don't want to admit that they were wrong. They invested their lives in this and they're really hurting. So much so that they really can't behave otherwise. They believed that they were right. I think that they back Ziuganov today.[29] Did they waste their lives for nothing? But those who see themselves as new Communists are something altogether awful. That's for certain. There were also groups of Communists who, let's put it this way, weren't like this at all. As a rule, they had served in the army. They had to join the party. They had to, so they did. They didn't think about it. Therefore, I'm neutral toward them. I can't say that I dislike all Communists, because there were all sorts. You see?

What did you think about all the commotion over human rights back then?

I knew, of course, that we simply didn't have any. But I never took part in demonstrations on this account. It's not that I was afraid. It's just that I'm not an active political sort. I was busy doing my own thing. However, I supported wholeheartedly those who—well, I supported Solzhenitsyn from the start, and Sakharov even more.[30] I respected Sakharov because, in Soviet terms, he had everything. That is, in Soviet terms he was like a millionaire in America. He was someone who consciously did what he had to do, even though he lost everything. In sum, I respected those people who struggled for human rights, but, in all honesty, I didn't myself. I did my own thing. Yes, it was a special category of people who were like that. They were political people.

What about the environment and ecological problems? Did people discuss such things?

No, it was, well, how should I put it, it was simply something that we experienced on an everyday basis. Take the Volga, for example. When we were in school and left for camp, we'd—it's hard to believe today—we'd drink water right out of the Volga. We'd go into the Volga and start to drink. And no one ever came down with anything. But then, you know, oil slicks began to float on the Volga. And fish got sick, because they dumped stuff into the river. It was industrial waste and the like. People accepted this as part of the rotten system that existed at the time. And it really was. It was as if

---

29. Gennadii Ziuganov is head of the new Communist Party of the Russian Federation founded in 1990.

30. Andrei Dmitrievich Sakharov (1921–1989) was a famous Soviet physicist and political dissident who received the Nobel Peace Prize in 1975. Exiled to the city of Gorky (today Nizhnii Novgorod), he was allowed to return to Moscow during the Gorbachev era and was soon elected a member of the Council of People's Deputies.

everyone dumped stuff into the river. I can't say that everything's fine now, but the Volga is much, much cleaner because they shut down many of the unproductive factories. In general, you'd have to say that what was in effect an economic misfortune was not altogether a bad thing. The factories that closed were unproductive, and they polluted more than they produced anything useful. I rubbed up against this industry for many years, almost for twenty-five. I saw the ineffectiveness of many factories. Therefore, when they shut them down, things became cleaner. The Volga became cleaner, the air became cleaner. It had been absolutely disgusting before. That is, we accepted all this as part of our overall, how shall I put it, standard of living.

Why do you think perestroika took place?

It had to take place. As I started to say, things approached the limit. I have to say that it's my opinion that, well, Gorbachev had some sort of special sense and understood that if he didn't start to change things from above, they would start to change from below. That is, everything collapsed and had rotted through. It was a very dangerous moment. Perestroika came just in time. God sent us two very interesting men. I can relate to Gorbachev in various ways, but he, indeed, came along just in time, as, I believe, did Yeltsin, despite all his shortcomings. I think there were two turning points, during which God gave us the very interesting and flexible Gorbachev and then the original Yeltsin. They came just in time. Therefore, everything was as it had to be, everything that took place. Perestroika had to occur.

Was this because of the economy or for a variety of reasons?

The fact is that economics determines everything, and objective reality determines consciousness. Yes, it all comes from the economy. Although there is such a thing as the "Russian character." That is, we'll never have the order that, say, they have in Germany. We're simply different. That's right. In many ways, Americans are more like us. In lifestyle, for instance. But they don't soil their own entranceways, as we do. It's basically a matter of the level of cultural development. We need several generations for that. It's like Moses leading the Jews out of [Egypt]. Probably, several more generations need to pass here. It's awful. That is, the general level [of civilization] is awful. But, how shall I put it, I believe that change will come, but not tomorrow. It's a very difficult process, I think.

You said that you first went abroad in 1989, right?

Yes, sometime in 1989 I was in Berlin. At the time the wall was still up, and they began to tear it down as soon as I left [laughing]. I arrived there in September. Yes, it was probably in 1989 that they tore it down.[31] I left and within three days they began to tear it down. I was in East Germany. The exhibit was an international one and there were people there from all over, not just from the socialist camp. There was a large exhibit hall right on Alexander Platz. It was an electronics exhibit. And there were people from all over, already.

What kind of impression did Berlin and Germany make on you?

Well, it was my first time abroad and it goes without saying that I found everything interesting. Second, I'd mention the German sense of cleanliness, which stunned me. That is, I understood why the Germans don't take off their shoes when they come home. Because the streets are cleaner than inside people's apartments. Each day, it simply shook me up. I'd be walking to work, to Alexander Platz along Unter den Linden, and they'd wash the streets, with soap and brushes! It was mind-boggling. No one here could even imagine it. That's what struck me. The third thing that struck me was the enormous quantity and quality of German beer. Our beer was terrible back then. I love beer. I drank a lot of good beer when I was in Dubna. And then I suffered for a long time. I drank to my heart's content for the first time there in Berlin. The general impression was, well, that the entranceways are as clean as their homes. We have a terrible scourge. Russia's shame is its entranceways and toilets. These two things are simply disgusting. Although things are beginning to change. I have to say that in those firms where I work the toilets are already up to civilized standards. Oh, the entranceways! They convey a sense of, well, a sense of cleanliness. And there's something else. People dressed differently. That is, I could spot a Russian in Berlin in a coat and tie three blocks away. By then I no longer dressed like that. They taught me how to dress casually back in Dubna. The Russians were in coat and tie. And everyone there was in light pants, sneakers, no matter what their age, bright shirts, and the like. It's really great! It's comfortable and convenient. Not like in Russia. It simply wasn't acceptable here. It's not that it was forbidden, but that it simply wasn't acceptable. Even now the older generation dresses funny in my view, but the younger generation. . . . So, my first impressions were very positive.

---

31. Berliners began tearing down the wall on November 9, 1989.

You traveled often after that?

Yes. Let's see, where was I? In Belgium, Cuba, and China. I was in five or six cities there, in five provinces. I was up north, in the south, just about everywhere. We sold some of our blueprints there. In vain, I wonder?

You've already told me a bit about China and Cuba. But what about Belgium?

Belgium, well, I was there only for a few days, it was a short exhibit, the same one. [My visit] came hard on the heels of my trip to Germany, about a year later. The quantity of technical equipment, in the stores, which I'm not indifferent to, simply blew me away. I stashed away money and in Germany by chance bought myself at a special store some decent audio equipment. But in Belgium, I went into a store and it had everything and it was all for sale. I was blown away. Things were worse off in [East] Berlin, but it had more than Russia. Still, it was a socialist country after all. I had not seen the West and then went there for the first time. I simply couldn't imagine the quantity of technical stuff, which I always loved and wanted, especially audio equipment. There was so much of it there! I was stunned by the abundance of it. Moreover, there was also the food scene, which interested me less. It was not the food, but the abundant technology. . . . My God, I thought, I can't believe how much they produce, and it's all so different. You can buy whatever you want. The colossal assortment. That was my first impression. Then I got used to it, that this was normal in the West. Where else was I? I was in Ireland for a short spell. I changed planes in Shannon. We did get off the plane to see the surrounding area. The climate and scenery amazed me. Ever the more so because it was in February and there was nothing but cold and blizzards here. But there in February the grass is green, the sheep are grazing, and there was a warm rain. Then it was Herder. I also stopped there in transit, in Canada. The climate was just the opposite there. But the cliffs of Newfoundland are quite interesting. It's more familiar, whereas Ireland. . . . So, I was in Germany, Belgium, Cuba, for more than a month, and spent a lot of time in China.

Glasnost accompanied perestroika and in many ways determined its outcome. How did you react to the flood of information and diversions at the time?

I was blown away! It was as if the floodgates were thrown open, and at first we accepted, we believed everything that we heard. But it gradually became clear that much of what was being said was a bunch of nonsense. People tried to present their own, well, the process of sifting through information began later. Back then it was looked upon as a breath of fresh air. People read everything and believed everything. Then much of what I had read in samizdat began to get published. It was as if glasnost were indeed for real. There was that peculiar naïveté during the first year or maybe two when I believed all of it, that is, all of the literature. But then you began to understand there was such a thing as yellow journalism, a radical press, and a normal press. That is, how shall I put it, we began to discriminate more. And now I trust only certain publications such as *Arguments and Facts*.[32] I consider many newspapers sensational and simply don't read them. But the first reaction was that this was real freedom, a breath of fresh air. It was great.

You've already told me what you thought of Gorbachev and Yeltsin and explained how perestroika affected your life in that you had to change jobs and the like. But what about the opening of Saratov, which officially remained a closed city until 1992? Was the change noticeable?

No, not really, no. I continued working during this time at the institute here. Despite the city's opening, no one visited for a variety of reasons. It's the building located on Theater Square, the large glass one, SNII, which produces measuring equipment. I worked there for twenty-five years, from an entry-level engineer to positions of authority. Even though I earn money elsewhere, I now sometimes drop in there about once a week, purely out of professional interest, and do what I formerly did. Well, I didn't see much change. The most I've noticed is on (Kirov) Prospect,[33] where there's a German flag, a consulate. I was happy to see this. But there's not much else.

And what about, well, I asked you earlier about how your generation differs from that of your parents. You replied that it differs more from the next generation. How, in your view, did perestroika affect the younger generation?

Probably a great deal, as a rule. But it was hard for us. I'll tell you why. Our children, probably those a bit older, grew up at a time when it was clear that you need money for everything. That is, to

---

32. *Argumenty i fakty* is a weekly tabloid with a huge press run, owing to its sassy tone and focus on human interest stories. The publication became especially popular during the perestroika era because of the many exposes that it published.

33. One of Saratov's major thoroughfares, Kirov Prospect was renamed German Street, its original name, during the early years of perestroika; however, many Saratovites continue to call it by its Soviet designation.

work "for the love of it," well, that's the other extreme, and that's foolish. They now see us as dinosaurs, as fossils, in the sense that well, "You still go to work for the same lousy wages. They can't do anything at your research institute. They pay nothing. What do you do there all day? Work?" I tell them, "Well, you know, I like it, it was my job, it was everything." "I don't understand," they reply. "I work only if they pay me." They're right. I'd also like it if a programmer was well paid. But that's not yet the case. However, for our kids, that's everything. That's how they've been brought up, the new generation, and no matter what I think of this, that's our objective reality. Moreover, for this life it's right. It's likely that our working for "the love of it" is a remnant of socialism, of the principle of distribution, of being equal. That is, you can work, or not work, and receive your due. But they already understand that if you don't work, you don't get paid. It's that simple. And if you work a lot, you might get paid a lot. That's good. That's how it should be and it corresponds to the laws of nature. That's right. Yes, they're different. That which we call cynicism might indeed be common sense, which we lack. The old ideas still linger. They're good ones, even wonderful ones. But they're the ideas of the sixties generation, right? And they're not for this life. For this reason we have to retool, too, and it's not easy. But what can you do about it? Life has passed us by. Our entire generation, and I speak for all of us, that is, for our class, welcomed perestroika. But it's been hard, really hard. That is, for several years we barely got by, almost all of us. Yet we survived, and didn't lose anyone. We all found ourselves. But at heart we're still . . . yes, it's been hard for us. Yes. And our children grew up under different circumstances. For this reason I think we're so different. Plus, young people's fashion—yes, we now have an understanding of this—well, it's not only about clothing but about music, cinema, and so on. It's as if they've followed a different path. We have few points of contact. Although, I'd have to say that my son, well, he's not like most. He just graduated from the mechanical-mathematics department at the university and also is a programmer. But, nonetheless, somehow there are fewer points of contact, although, in general, in principle, he and I get along fine. However, I see that they're different.

How can your life story help me understand the fate of the Soviet Union?

You know, that's a huge question. But there's something to it. I can't speak for everyone, of course, but I'd say, well, basically, that we went through this rupture—that we went almost literally from

Stalin[ism] to normal, developing capitalism. We still have far to go. Practically all of us went through the same thing, the people I came to know, those whom I care about. It was complicated enough, but we lived through this with the understanding that this was the deck of cards dealt us. We, how shall I put it, we simply couldn't escape it. And many of us, including me, are happy that we lived to see this other life. Unfortunately, we will not live to see the complete transformation of our society. But it's great that we've gone through what we have. It was hard, full of all sorts of difficulties, yet it gave life meaning. I wouldn't want to continue living as we had in the 1970s. Although everything was planned out like nowhere else, perhaps, on earth. I knew, for instance, that when I turned forty I'd be given a table clock, at fifty a crystal vase, at sixty a twenty-ruble raise, and that my pension would be 140 rubles. I knew exactly what to expect until I died. Now I'm not certain about anything and that's just fine [laughing]. That's life! Therefore, I think that our generation isn't a lost one and that it succeeded in accomplishing a good deal. True, many drank themselves to death, and others were broken. They couldn't handle things, and not out of ideological considerations. It's simply that socialism weakened many, they floundered, and weren't able to float to the top. Many simply gave up and sank to the bottom. There are such people. We're all different. It takes all sorts, but most are in the middle and they managed to survive it all. And the fact that many accepted this as normal and survived shows that we'll somehow make our way out of this. It seems to me that we were somehow able to pass on this optimism to the next generation, although, you know, they're more cynical. But we did it, yes, somehow we did it.

5. "I saw the life of my country, and thereby my own, from a variety of perspectives" | Natalia Aleksandrovna Belovolova (maiden name Ianichkina)

July 9, 2002, Saratov

An elite school that took pride in its academic rigor, School No. 42 sent all but a few of its students each year to Saratov's (and occasionally Moscow's) top colleges. Being admitted to a university's evening division, or having to sit things out a year before reapplying elsewhere, represented scenarios that brought acknowledged anguish to those few students who did not pass their entrance exams on the first try or who put off taking them. Early on in my attempt to locate members of the class of 1967, I spoke with one of its members who helped to put me in touch with others. When I mentioned Natalia Aleksandrovna Belovolova, my informant suggested that I not search her out, since "she was the only one in our group (A) who didn't enroll anywhere."

This remark only served to pique my curiosity. It also proved to be ill informed. I eventually tracked down a phone number for Natalia Aleksandrovna, contacted her, explained my intentions, and convinced her to let me interview her. We met in the apartment I rented that summer in Saratov.

Natalia Aleksandrovna's account mesmerized me from the start, undoubtedly because one of the first things I learned about her was that her mother and grandmother had been sent to the Gulag as part of Stalin's postwar campaign against "cosmopolitanism," a loose code word for Western influence. Raised by her great-grandmother until her mother's amnesty in 1957, following Khrushchev's denunciation of Stalin, Natalia Aleksandrovna opened up to me as if she had longed to tell her life story. (In fact, her request that I make a copy of the tapes for her daughter underscores this impression.) Her unpretentious and intimate manner made her a delightful

conversationalist, who talked about her life without any regrets and with a sense of dignity and even pride. Much about
her personal narrative distinguished it from the others I had
collected: her family background, her university experience,
and her two extended stays in Magadan oblast, where she and
her husband accepted jobs at higher pay in order to establish
themselves financially. (One also senses that they left Saratov
for Magadan because they wished to start married life on their
own, beyond the immediate reach of their respective families.
If this was the case, then the strategy appears to have worked,
for Natalia Aleksandrovna's marriage has not ended in divorce, unlike that of many of her classmates.) Living in distant
and isolated parts of the country and enduring both physical
and emotional hardship (her husband was expelled from the
Communist Party and blacklisted in the remote settlement
of Pevek), she emerged from the ordeal confident and open,
rather than broken or embittered. Although the trajectories
of her life differ in fundamental ways from those of her classmates, they reflect concerns that were all too much a part of
the Soviet political and social landscape.

From what perspectives has Natalia Aleksandrovna viewed
her own life and that of her country? What issues and experiences most shaped her attitudes as a schoolgirl, university student, and adult? How does she evaluate the Soviet experience
and the changes that have come to her life and to the lives of
her family members since perestroika and the breakup of the
Soviet Union?

I was born in March 1950. My mother worked, like all Russians
back then. She finished school practically the day the war began and
didn't go to college at that time. Even though Saratov was not occupied, it nevertheless was in the zone of military operations. There
was bombing here, because there was a strategic bridge. When my
grandfather left for the front my grandmother was frightened for
her family, for her daughter, and left with the evacuation to Central
Asia. They had to feed themselves there and find work somewhere,
right? Being an altogether young lady, my mother went to work
in a geological surveying expedition. I think it was an expedition
organized by a research institute in Leningrad. Mama told me how

she worked there in the most horrible of conditions. She caught a terrible case of malaria, and they let her go from the group. Nevertheless, she was in Central Asia when the war ended, and when she returned to Saratov her chance to study had already slipped by. No, that's not quite right. She attended the Law Institute for two years. For some reason—it wasn't discussed at home—she didn't finish it. Well, my mother had some artistic talents and was something of an artist. She could draw well, and she went to work at a design institute, first as a draftswoman and then as a technician. Then I was born in 1950. I practically didn't know my father, because my family broke up early on. I know that he was fourteen years older than my mother. Imagine the postwar generation; all the marriageable young men had been killed! Their marriage simply didn't work out and my mother raised me by herself. Our family had a really tough time. My mother was repressed. That was in 1952. I was left all alone.

Why did this happen?

There was a popular article in the legal code back then called cosmopolitanism.[1] It affected my mother, and my grandmother too. My grandfather was killed at the front and my grandmother married again. Her second husband, who helped raise me, worked for the NKVD,[2] for all that. Nevertheless, it was very popular to accuse people of cosmopolitanism back then. You probably know that the wives of some of the leading political figures in the country were repressed while they remained at their posts.[3] Well, my mother and grandmother were repressed, and my grandfather was dismissed from the NKVD. My mother was imprisoned until Stalin's death, when an amnesty took place immediately. She was amnestied, and then rehabilitated. During that time I was left with my great-grandmother, who was a very old woman. Well, and with my grandfather, too. Although he was a step-grandfather, he was there nonetheless. When they released Mama, I learned from her stories that she had been in camps in Vorkuta, in the Russian north. After she returned,

---

1. In Soviet public language, the term "cosmopolitanism" became a negative marker for someone who purportedly rejected Soviet values in favor of "reactionary" bourgeois ideology. A campaign to uproot cosmopolitanism began in 1948 following the founding of the State of Israel and had a distinctly, but not exclusively, antisemitic tone to it.

2. That is, for the political or secret police.

3. The most highly visible case of this sort involved Polina Semenovna Zhemchuzhina, the wife of Stalin's chief lieutenant, V. M. Molotov. Arrested in 1949, Zhemchuzhina remained in camp until 1953, while her husband continued to serve Stalin.

and my grandmother returned, having endured a serious heart attack there, well, she and my grandfather broke up. Thus I was raised in a family comprising my mother, grandmother, and great-grandmother. We even used to joke that we had a very large family: three mothers, three daughters, two grandmothers, two granddaughters, one great-grandmother, and one great-granddaughter [laughing]. But it was nothing more than four women living under the same roof. Well, as a child I came down with every illness there was. It was the postwar years, and then there was the fact that Mama's health had been undermined by her stay in Central Asia and the hunger and other deprivations she endured during the war, which were quite severe. Anyway, I attended School No. 42 from the second grade, when the school opened. I completed first grade at a regular school. School No. 42 was very prestigious back then, and Mama, as if to make up for that lack of maternal love that I experienced when she was away, well, she wanted to give me everything that she couldn't give me earlier. And I enrolled at that school and did well.

Why did your mother send you to the English-language school?

You know, at that time there practically were no special schools in Saratov. That was the only one. I'm not sure, but such schools were in fashion at the time and there also was the sense that we were involved in something prestigious. Then, too, I had been in the same class with other girls who also went there. But they were the daughters of the secretary of the oblast committee of the Communist Party and of the second secretary.[4] I think Mama wanted to make the point that I was as good as they were [laughing]. Maybe that's how it was. Maybe that's why she sent me there. That was in 1957.

What were you interested in as a schoolgirl?

It's hard to remember now. I don't think I had any what today are called hobbies. I did some needlework. Nor do I think that I had any passion for a specific subject such as mathematics. On the whole, there was no one thing that determined my various infatuations. Like all the girls, I wanted to become an actress and there was an acting club at school that I belonged to. I also went to a music school, even though I'm absolutely tone-deaf. But, once again, it was believed necessary back then to give a girl a good humanistic education. Back then people believed that that's how it should be.

---

4. The first secretary was the leading party official at the oblast level.

Group A, third grade. Natalia Aleksandrovna Belovolova (Ianichkina) is in the bottom row on the far right. *Courtesy A. V. Trubnikov.*

How would you describe the school, its pupils, and teachers? It goes without saying that it wasn't an ordinary school.

You know, back then when I attended school I couldn't have given you an assessment. But I can do so now with the benefit of hindsight. Moreover, I also have something to compare it to, since my daughter attended school and I was an involved parent. I was in frequent contact with the teachers and, when comparing these moments, I can say that our school differed fundamentally from the others. For one thing, the pupils with whom I studied represented the cream of the crop. Our school didn't have any of the serious disciplinary problems encountered in ordinary schools. There was no hooliganism, which in an ordinary school would be an everyday occurrence. In our school even the slightest stepping out of line would have been considered serious misconduct. We all agreed that our director, Vera Filippovna, maintained strict discipline, keeping watch over the moral and ethical side of things at school. I can even tell you a few funny incidents. Well, our industry developed, and with it, fashion. After the war, girls wanted to switch over to hose and pantyhose, right? The first one-size hose appeared, for example. And the income level of the pupils' parents allowed them to buy or "obtain" nylon stockings. But Vera Filippovna forbade this and we had to wear what everyone else wore, so that no one stood out. On the whole, she was probably right in this regard, at least in part. But as children, we thought this was unfair. She also made us carry our school bags on our shoulders so as to improve our posture. Of course, these were good intentions, but like all such things they're not always appreciated at the time. Now, of course, I realize what a good school we had. I'm not sure why, but for some reason I won't send my grandson there, whom I'm mostly raising. Everyone asks me, "Why don't you send him to School No. 42?" But I don't know why. Perhaps because I don't want him to go to a school that specializes in language. Yet our school gave us a very good education. Practically 90 percent of our class went on to college. Some got in through patronage, some without, some because they knew a lot, some because they had money. But nonetheless . . .

Who were your friends and what did you do in your free time? Can you tell me more about clothing? You've already told me about nylon stockings, but what about hairdos?

The school maintained a degree of asceticism that didn't allow us to "let our hair down." Of course, when there was a party at school, things were a bit different. Nonetheless, we were constrained and even knew that we shouldn't experiment and take liberties, because Vera Filippovna . . . In the higher grades we girls tried to make ourselves up. Back then I had a typical Russian face. I had light hair and dark eyelashes and eyebrows. How I suffered because of that! On ordinary schooldays we looked fairly nondescript, because our uniform consisted of a brown dress, a white collar, and a black apron. And even when the cut of these dresses was different, we seemed alike dressed in black and brown. But on special occasions we replaced the black aprons with white ones. Then we gradually began to change our hairdos. And whenever I did I suffered many humiliating moments, such as: "Go wash up. You're wearing makeup." "Yesterday you didn't look like that at all, but today. . . ." Of course I was different. I was wearing a different dress, and perhaps for this reason my face seemed more lit up. Besides, I was at a party, and behaved differently. Toward the end of our school years, just before graduating, Vera Filippovna eased up a bit. For the most part, I don't regret any of this. Because today the situation is like in America, where everyone wears to school whatever she chooses. Different income levels of parents determine how children dress, and this infringes upon many. The first year this was allowed girls dressed as if they were going to a discothèque. Then the racket died down and kids realized that they needed to dress comfortably, and not to stand out. Nonetheless, I'm not against uniforms. My grandson is now attending school. Let him wear a uniform, but one that gives him some flexibility. I don't think that uniforms detract children from the main reason they're in school.

Tell me about your teachers.

Favorite teachers? My favorite teacher taught literature. It wasn't that I loved literature so much, but that she was such a special woman. Once again, though, I need to make a comparison. At first we had a teacher who taught Russian literature, Valentina, Valentina Nikolaevna, I think. She was from the old Stalinist cadres. She would all but disrupt an entire lesson simply because it seemed to her that a girl's hairdo was not right or because her hair was braided, say, on one side. She would make the girl stand in front of the class and tell her that she wanted to pull her braid down to the base of her spine. Then Lidiia Vasilievna replaced her. She was more democratic. She'd express views that were not part of the school program, or tell us her opinion of an author, or of some situation. She was a bit sloppy as a woman, but she was my favorite teacher. I also had a favorite teacher with a beard who taught physics and who had lived through the war. He was a wonderful teacher and person.

What did you do in your free time?

I don't remember, because basically we didn't have much. We played sports. The entire class played basketball and held matches. That's about all I remember.

Were there any changes introduced in the school program while you went there?

You know, at first they wanted to make the school as much as possible a language school and therefore gradually began to introduce special subjects taught in English. They did this with history, with contemporary history, I think, and they began to do the same with physics by translating an ordinary textbook into English. But this was all done as an experiment, since for the most part our understanding of the language at that time was not deep enough to allow us to study physics. The result was neither English nor physics. We also had a special subject, English literature. By the way, it was taught by a teacher whom I'd also list as among my favorites. She was a young woman who had studied in England.

That was rare in those years.

It was, but Saratov, incidentally, back then had a sister-city relationship with Bristol, England. And our teachers went there. At least the head of the curriculum department did. I think Nina Vasilievna, our literature teacher, did too. Yes, delegations of teachers visited Saratov. There were no children. It was an exchange. I recall that our teacher had a pen on which was written "Greetings to Saratov from Bristol."

Saratov must have closed after this.

You know, those of us living in the city didn't feel that we lived in a closed one, do you understand? That's because if someone's work or profession required a trip abroad, they went. For example, Galia Kiseleva attended school with me.[5] Her father was the first secretary of the local union of trade unions. He traveled. They were in Africa and someplace else. Perhaps this was for appearances, but nonetheless some people could travel abroad. I don't know if you're aware of it or not, but I think it was in third grade when Iura Gusev joined our class. He didn't graduate from the school, and I'll explain why. He came to Saratov with his parents from Australia. They had a large family. As far as I understood it, one of his parents was sent to Germany during the war. From there they somehow, well, you're a historian and know that Soviet citizens who had been taken to Germany during the war were exiled to remote parts of the Soviet Union if they returned. I'm not certain how the Gusevs' fate unfolded, but they ended up in Australia. And sometime at the start of the 1960s when things were opening up the family came to Saratov. I'm not sure why to Saratov. Maybe they had some ties here. Because he spoke English better than Russian, he was sent to our school. Then the other children in the family, when they came of age, also attended our school. The father worked in some factory and since it was a large family the mother didn't work. The school helped this family out a great deal. We held school concerts, for instance, and collected money for the "curriculum fund," which went to the family for clothing and other things. So, Iura ended up attending school with us, but he didn't finish, apparently because he came from a large family, and, when he manifested some musical talent, he left to study at a military school specializing in music and graduated from there.

How often did foreign delegations visit?

---

5. Galina Viktorovna Kiseleva. I have been unable to locate her, but at one time she taught English at the Saratov Medical Institute.

Well, to be honest, I remember only one. And then probably when we were about to graduate from school, some sort of Englishman, I believe, visited and socialized with us. I think he gave some lectures at the university in all probability at that time. We somehow communicated. I even can recall what he looked like.

How important is it that you learned English already as a child?

Oh dear! You know, I have to say to my regret that I didn't learn English. I didn't continue with my language study, and we tend to forget things, including language. Moreover, I really lacked any passion for languages. Moreover, at that time I didn't have any opportunity to apply my language knowledge. The only newspapers we could read were *Morning Star* and *Moscow News*.[6] Generally, there wasn't any opportunity. . . . After all, we didn't think about our future. We were building communism! For the most part, considering how the political situation in the country unfolded at that time, we were unable to predict how things would turn out. Those who went to the Pedagogical Institute knew in advance that they would become teachers of English in the schools. But I lacked any desire to teach. The other option was to work in some factory as a technical translator. I didn't have any research talents either. So I went to the Polytechnic Institute.

You lived with a family of women. Who among them had the most influence on you, or is this difficult to determine?

You know, each of them did in her own way. I can now appreciate that each of them was very different. By the way, my great-grandmother's story has much to do with the history of Saratov. My great-grandfather came from a very poor village family, with a surname to match, Zalataikin [patched up]. The word for armor and patches share the same root. He was drafted, and back then it was for a very long time. He was already married to my great-grandmother. He was drafted because of his exceptional appearance: he was quite tall with broad shoulders. He served in a Grenadiers regiment in the Caucasus. And my great-grandmother followed him there. She was

---

6. *Morning Star* is a British Marxist newspaper founded in 1930 as the daily of the Communist Party of Great Britain. *Moscow News* was initially aimed at foreign workers who came to the USSR during the great industrialization drive of the first five-year plans. Shut down in the late 1940s, the paper reopened in 1956, after which its purpose was to inform the foreign community living in the USSR only about positive events going on in the country.

a respectful person and worked as a maid for the governor general of the Caucasus. It was there that my great-grandfather turned to revolution, and when it broke out he became a revolutionary. My mother has kept some documents, credentials from a revolutionary tribunal, some newspapers, and other old papers. Although he was semiliterate, he possessed some rhetorical talents. And in Saratov, I know from history and from my mother's stories, there was a movement called the Lopukhovskoe movement[7] in one of the villages, made up of army deserters. They sat it out somewhere in the forests. Well, my great-grandfather, by means of revolutionary agitation, led them out of the woods in large sub-units, that is, groups. During one of these so-called operations he got beaten to a pulp. Soon afterward he came down with consumption. Then came NEP. Was it in 1924?[8] Being semiliterate, he couldn't grasp this abrupt change in Russian history, do you understand? But since he was not without influence, some business circles approached him and he accepted NEP. He had some sort of fish business here. By and large he was rich enough. However, the lack of upbringing and education always make themselves felt. That is, he had money, not to spend prudently, but to blow. Then he apparently realized that he was sick and had little time left. He probably died in 1927 or in 1929.

My great-grandmother was also semiliterate, but the fact that she worked at one time in a manor house instilled some refinement in her. Life also made her very wise. There was an interesting moment when my great-grandfather, during one of his periods of revelry, picked up an abandoned male child in the yard of some sort of inn or hotel. My great-grandmother didn't have any children other than my grandmother. She once got knocked down by a horse-drawn tram. They operated on her after which she was unable to have children. My grandfather lamented that there was only one child at home and then all of a sudden this abandoned child appeared. He had no documents on him other than a note saying that his name was Kolia and that you shouldn't search for his mother.

---

7. The Lopukhovskoe movement was one of the local manifestations of a larger phenomenon known as the Green movement, consisting of armed peasant bands—deserters from the Red Army—who turned against Soviet power during the Civil War.

8. Introduced in 1921, not 1924, the New Economic Policy replaced the much hated requisitioning of peasant grain with a tax in kind and restored some legal private economic activity. The launching of the Stalinist industrialization drive at the end of the 1920s put an end to NEP.

This was during the famine in the Volga region.[9] Because the family had a decent enough income, my great-grandfather brought the boy home and said, "He's going to be our son." The family doctor, an elderly Jew, said to my great-grandmother: "Daria Andreevna, what are you doing? After all, you don't know anything about his heredity. Maybe he comes from a family of alcoholics, or of sick people, or of mentally retarded ones. How can you take in the child?" My great-grandmother got frightened and took the child back to the inn. When my great-grandfather returned from work he asked, "Where's Kolia?" When he realized what had happened he told her, "Go and don't return until you find him." She found him in an orphanage and brought him home to raise. Thus, when my great-grandfather died, she was left with two children.

My grandmother, if I'm not mistaken, was born in 1907, and was already of marrying age when Kolia appeared. She got married very early, but back then that was common. If I'm not mistaken, she was seventeen at the time. And soon my mother was born, in 1925, and little Kolia was raised more with my mother, since he was only a few years older than she. My grandmother was a very, well, her husband showed up at that time in my great-grandfather's life when he was materially well off and spoiled her. I wouldn't say she was a beauty, but she was a really interesting woman. She married, if I'm mistaken, the nephew of Konstantin Fedin.[10] But that wasn't my mother's real father. My grandmother's first husband was drafted into the army and never came back. He met another woman and married her. So she got married again, this time to Fedin's nephew. At home they used to have many books with dedicatory inscriptions, but the library was lost when Grandma was evacuated from Saratov during the war and had to abandon her apartment. When she returned, an official from the NKVD lived in the apartment. He wouldn't even let her in, and she had left everything in the apartment, the library, furniture, even some antiques. They were given a small apartment and had to start over from scratch. That's about all

---

9. The horrific famine that marked the concluding chapter to the Russian Civil War broke out in 1921 and continued in parts of Saratov province through 1924.

10. Writer Konstantin Aleksandrovich Fedin (1892–1977) spent his formative years in Saratov and is associated with the city, which is depicted in some of his prize-winning post–World War II works. Fedin is perhaps best known for his complex *Cities and Years* (1924), which experiments with time sequence and transitions from one narrative tone to another.

regarding my parents. That's why I'd say that each influenced me in different ways. Great-Grandmother was a woman of strict rules, while Grandma was more even tempered. She made friends easily and was something of a Scarlett,[11] living by the principle "Forget about it; I'll worry about it tomorrow." Then there's my mother, who had to endure so many ordeals. Imagine what it was like to end up in a Stalinist labor camp, leaving behind a two-year-old child. Right during the interrogation I got very sick. I probably had pneumonia, but they didn't let Mama see me. This is her story. She went on a hunger strike until they brought me to her. Nevertheless, as you know, both criminals and political prisoners were imprisoned together in these Stalinist camps. Mama was imprisoned in the same camp as Tatiana Okunevskaia,[12] a well-known actress. I think she's actually still alive. Those who live through extreme adversity often live longer than those who experience less in life.

Why, exactly, was your mother imprisoned, because your grandmother had married someone from the NKVD?

No. I don't know the whole story of why it occurred, but the family's material means were, well this was in the early fifties. They had lots of furniture and things that had been brought from Germany after the war. They bought some kind of furniture, and my mother began wearing clothing not seen elsewhere. And someone denounced them, and things began to unfold. Once again this turned out to be a kind of show trial, and that's why they imprisoned both a mother and her daughter. Both were repressed.

Because they liked Western things, crudely put?

Yes. Mama also told me how she managed to survive. Once again, it had something to do with upbringing. There were criminals among the imprisoned women. But she became an organizer of the camp's cultural life. Moreover, she could move about freely in and out of camp. When it was time to release her, they didn't let her go for a few months so that she could train her replacement. In this regard, we might speak of her successes.

She was released during a general amnesty. But how did she adapt to things in Saratov? Where did she work?

She returned to the same place where she had worked before, at the design institute. And, she managed to send me to an elite school.

---

11. A reference to Scarlett O'Hara from *Gone with the Wind.*

12. Okunevskaia (b. 1914) has published an autobiography, *Tatianin Den'* [Tatiana's Day] (Moscow: Vagrius, 1998).

There were no further consequences. That was in 1957, right after they denounced Stalin's personality cult.

What did they have to say about their experiences in the camps?

When I was young we didn't discuss it. It was only after I grew up. Then, too, back then I really wasn't interested in any of this. I can tell you in all honesty that I knew that Mother had been re-pressed, but back then we didn't use the term, which appeared much later. Back then I knew that my mother had been imprisoned, and I was ashamed of this. I didn't want to know a thing. It was only later, when I grew up and was able to reevaluate the situation, that I wanted to know.

What did you think of the West when you attended school? Many of your classmates mentioned their interest in the Beatles. Were you smitten by them, too?

Of course, and I still am. We made recordings on used chest X-rays. I recall the bell-bottomed trousers, too. We were already about sixteen at the time. You know, this wasn't out in the open, but something we did outside of school.

Did your classmates listen to Western radio broadcasts such as Voice of America and BBC?

They listened. I think they probably listened. I did too at home. Once again, though, back then I didn't pay much attention to what was said, but was more interested in saying that I listened to Voice of America. Ever the more so because it was jammed, and everything that's secretive and off-limits always elicits interest. But what they had to say didn't interest me at all. Maybe I was too immature at the time.

What did you think of China back then?

[Long pause.] Of China? You know, back then we didn't judge it from a political or ideological perspective, but from what was going on there. For instance, their Cultural Revolution seemed to us like vandalism. Take, for instance, the killing off of sparrows so that they wouldn't eat grain. That is, it's as if we didn't understand their domestic policies, but subjected their external manifestations to ridicule.

How does your generation differ from that of your mother?

We're probably less inhibited or something. That's how it seems to me. But at the same time we're products of our parents' upbring-ing. They had so many restrictions and for many years we were brought up on them too. As a result, we have a certain internal self-restraint. Nevertheless we're freer, but less so than our children.

Their generation differs a great deal. If we were raised strictly, then it sometimes seems to me that today's youth are completely unbridled because, after all, freedom is a deliberate necessity, as a classic of Marxism put it. Our freedom was realized in that regard and had limits. We then were given complete freedom, but a culture of systematizing this freedom has not yet been created. For this reason this freedom sometimes turns vulgar.

The years you attended school were a period of many achievements in space and other areas. Iurii Gagarin even landed in Saratov oblast.[13] Khrushchev formulated a new party program and unleashed slogans such as "Overtake America." How did you relate to all this back then? And did it seem that life indeed was getting better during Khrushchev's early years in office?

Basically, you're right. Yet I went to school in 1957 and don't remember much about the early period of my life. When I began to realize that these were the Khrushchev years, it was already the 1960s. The "Moral Code of the Builder of Communism" was posted at school, and we had to memorize it. You know, there was absolutely nothing wrong with this, since it's almost like the Ten Commandments. Gagarin's achievement was our greatest pride. For the most part we were raised to be proud of our country.

From a material point of view, did life get better at the time?

No, I can't say that. I simply don't recall. We didn't move into a new apartment. We didn't live in a communal apartment, but didn't move into a new flat. I can't recall any major improvement. I remember that in 1957 or 1958 there was a youth festival in Moscow. I recall there was some special event here, too. We didn't have a television, and back then people would visit their neighbors to watch TV. Even though Saratov is a provincial city, there were some mass outings, as they were called then, and the city was spruced up. I even recall sewing special dresses for the occasion. Mother looked like Lolita Torres.[14] That is, I remember that this was an event of national significance for our country. They probably held seminars and the like, too, but I simply don't know. There was dancing, fireworks, almost like a carnival. There's a park of culture and leisure in Saratov. Mama went there with her girlfriend, but didn't take me

---

13. The first human to orbit Earth, cosmonaut Iurii Gagarin parachuted into a field near Saratov in April 1961.

14. Argentine actress Lolita Torres (1930–2002) played leading roles in seventeen films and became popular among Soviet cinemagoers in the 1950s and 1960.

along because I came down with [laughing] the mumps. It was like a bit of a fling in our cultural life. Moreover, we began to get more information, not the kind you speak about in the kitchen in private, but public, open, information.

When was this? In 1961, after the Twenty-second Party Congress? Even Solzhenitsyn's One Day *was published in* Novyi mir.

Yes, and I read it, but much later.

What kind of impression did it make on you, especially since your mother had been in camp?

It turns out that my life unfolded in such a way that I, too, spent many years in remote parts of the country, but went there on my own volition. It was Magadan oblast, where, at one point the center of the Gulag was located. I met people there who spent many years in the camps. Some of them had sentences of twenty years or more. Others had lesser ones. I met people who lived there permanently. My husband taught in a technical school that had a wonderful director, an elderly man with the largest of libraries. He collected all kinds of literature on the subject. He gave me *Ivan Denisovich* to read and also told me to read Boris Diakov.[15] I don't recall what his novel's called, but it's also about that terrible period. Then a novel by Viatkin,[16] a local, Magadan author. It was a trilogy, *Man Is Born Twice.* After I read all this and spoke with people I was able to understand what they went through. It was then, by the way, that I began to ask Mama about her experiences. On the whole, I then understood why many things hadn't worked out in my mother's life. Mama was twenty-seven at the time of her arrest, at the peak of her creative as well as her physical, physiological, and moral potential. She was precisely that age when she ended up there. And when she was released, she didn't start a second family, although I think there were probably men in her life. She's not a nun, but she somehow was afraid that a man who might enter her life and that of her child could bring them harm. Maybe it's self-sacrifice, or maybe, I don't know, a form of egotism. To make a long story short, she didn't start a second family, and all the rest stems from this. All her life she had to drag me along, get me started in life so that I was

---

15. Ianichkina probably is referring to Boris Diakov's *Povest' o perezhitom* [A Tale of Survival] (Moscow: Sovetskaia Rossiia, 1966). He later published *Perezhitoe: Avtobiograficheskii roman v trekh knigakh* [That Which I Endured: An Autobiographical Novel in Three Parts] (Moscow: Sovetskaia Rossiia, 1987).

16. V. S. Viatkin wrote *Chelovek rozhdaetsia dvazhdy.*

not worse off than others, work, and so on. Well, in America children live apart when they grow up, but here the patriarchal family still largely exists. When I began my own family and left with my husband, Mama couldn't imagine that I could live separately. She believed that my husband and I went to work there under contract, and that we'd return to her. While we were there we saved money so that we could buy into a cooperative apartment house here, but Mama couldn't imagine how we could live without her and how she could live without us. As a result, we still live with Mama.

You finished school in 1967 and then enrolled at the Polytechnic Institute?

I didn't get admitted that first year in 1967 so I went to work with my mother at the design institute as a trainee draftsman. I was good at it, and quickly went through my apprenticeship. The next year I got admitted at the Polytechnic, but I enrolled in the evening division. After all, I was already working, and this gave me some material independence, although the pay was miserly. Nonetheless, for a young person to have her own money is already something, right? Moreover, I understood that my mother had a difficult time and I was blossoming into an attractive young lady. Mama wanted me to be well dressed and worked hard so that I could be. Since I was already working as a draftsman, I continued with this at the Polytechnic and graduated from the Department of the Natural Gas Industry. I graduated, but, again, with some breaks. I switched to the correspondence division because I got married. That was in 1971.

Did you meet your husband at the Polytechnic?

No, we had a vacation romance. We met at the Black Sea. Two of my girlfriends and I vacationed at a resort there and he and three of his friends were completing a drive along the Black Sea coast when we met. My girlfriend married his friend, and I married him, and both of them proposed to us the day after we became acquainted. It's quite an adventure story that, by the way, has already lasted thirty-one years!

Congratulations! Is he from Saratov?

No, he's from Donetsk.[17] He graduated from the Kiev Polytechnic Institute, was married, but was in the process of getting divorced. He

---

17. With a population of over one million inhabitants, Donetsk, formerly Stalino, is a large industrial town located in southeastern Ukraine well known for its heavy industry, especially coal and steel.

Graduation night, 1967. Natalia Aleksandrovna Belovolova
(Ianichkina) is on the far right in a pleated skirt. *Courtesy
T. A. Kuznetsova (Dumcheva).*

had a two-year-old child when we met. Within a month he visited
Saratov and asked Mama for my hand.

How did she react, especially since he wasn't from Saratov?

It turned out that when we met all of us spent four days together,
after which the fellows returned home. All of us took a strong liking to each other. They were great to be with. They sang and played
the guitar. They were intelligent lads who, after all, had graduated
from Kiev Polytech, really smart ones and not smart alecks. At first it
seemed like it would end in friendship. But we decided to drag things
out and return home through Kiev. We bought tickets for Kiev and
went to the post office to call my future husband, Viacheslav, who
was already back in Donetsk, so that he would come to Kiev so that
we could meet again. We told him to come to Kiev on such and
such a date, but he said, "No, return the ticket. The other Slava is on
his way to see you now." He's also named Viacheslav, the one who
married my girlfriend. "You come here to Donetsk. My parents are
inviting you." And Slava showed up the very next day. Viacheslav
had bought me a ticket to Donetsk. My girlfriend, Galia, phoned her
mother, who was a public prosecutor, and said, "Mama, the three of

us are coming home." Her mother said, "Thank goodness you're not coming back pregnant" [laughing]. Galia replied, "No, Mama, you don't understand. Me, Sveta, and Sveta's fiancé." Her mother said: "And what about Natasha?" "Natasha's going to her sweetheart's." "What? Come home, all of you, at once!" She ran off to my mother's—back then a telephone was a real luxury—and told her, "Dina, leave for Donetsk by plane immediately. One's going there, the other's coming here. They're up to something." Mama went to the airport and bought a ticket for Donetsk. My mother had decided to fly to Donetsk so that she could meet my plane when it arrived and prevent me from doing anything stupid. She had a very close girlfriend all her life who didn't have children, and I was like a child to her. They decided to go together. The flight to Donetsk was an early one, and she woke my mother up: "Dina, get up, it's time to go to the airport." "You know, I'm not going anywhere. What will be will be. I'm not going anywhere." And she didn't. Well, Viacheslav met me, introduced me to his parents, and proposed to me in Donetsk. A month later he arrived in Saratov, asked my mother for my hand, and we got married.

When was that?

That was in 1971, my last year in college. We got married in November 1971, and afterward lived on the phone, since we decided that I'd finish the Polytechnic and then move there. But things turned out differently, because his relatives came for a visit from Magadan.[18] It was his mother's sister with her husband and children. By then they had already lived there for a long time. In Ukraine such departures for the north were popular, because there were fewer job possibilities in Ukraine and less opportunity to make money. It's still the case. Well, we went to Donetsk to meet them, where they told us, "Make some money while you're still young and without children so that you can establish yourselves later. Come to Magadan." Back then salaries were twice as high there. Here salaries were low, even if you were a genius, and my husband graduated with honors. They had kept him at the institute, by the way, but since he had gotten divorced he moved to Donetsk and worked at the Donetsk Polytechnic Institute where he headed a lab. He took his Ph.D. exams and began working on his dissertation. Yet they somehow

---

18. Located on the Sea of Okhotsk's Nagaevo Bay in the Russian Far East, Magadan was the administrative center of one of the most notorious of Gulag camps. It has a population today of roughly 150,000.

talked us into it, and we left for Magadan in 1972. My mother was beside herself. The only thing that consoled her was our telling her that we were signing on for three years, in which time we'd earn enough money that would allow us to solve all our problems, or so it seemed to us at the time. And we left for the town of Susuman in Magadan oblast. It's basically the center of the gold mining industry. True, I never saw any gold, although we lived there the entire time, but nevertheless, it's an enormous mining complex. We lived for a short spell with our relatives but then received an apartment. I worked in the construction department, in my field of specialization. My husband taught at a mining technical school. For the most part things went okay. What played a large role in our lives was that we lived far away from his parents—and he had a father who was quite authoritarian—and from my mother, who loved to look after me. All the problems of newlyweds cropped up, since practically speaking we had had little time to get to know each other. We realized this the longer we lived together and had to deal with this without outside interference. Moreover, there were the extreme conditions of the Far North, with temperatures of 50 degrees below zero in the winter and freezing weather even in summer. Besides, it was a small town, where everyone knew each other. But we were young, and there was so much that was romantic in all this! I didn't pass up a single hunting trip before we had children. I traveled with the men and remember the cross-country vehicle packed with men and a dog. I bagged ducks, fowl, and all sorts of things. I went fishing with them. It was fantastic! Even the atmosphere. People rarely locked their doors, and some never did, keeping the key under the rug. When we left on vacation, for instance, we gave our key to some acquaintances simply because they didn't have nice enough living arrangements yet. It was a good time for us. And the foundation of our family was laid there. We've been married for thirty-one years. That's a long time, and life had its ups and downs, but the foundation was strong enough that we remain together.

Afterward you returned to Saratov?

Yes, we returned to Saratov because I was pregnant with my daughter. Somehow, to be honest, we didn't meet the minimum material goal we had established for ourselves, except that we earned enough to join a coop. Moreover, during our absence the building was completed, so we returned here to a new apartment, the one in which we still live. My daughter was born here. We had lived in Magadan oblast for almost five years, and my husband really didn't know Saratov. I no longer had any ties here. I had left when I was twenty-two. What ties could I have had? It's as if we returned to no-body. We had to find work again. We already had a decent living, but were faced with finding a job for only 130–160 rubles a month. My husband said, "You know, it's probably best to return to Magadan for a short spell." It's interesting what happened. We bought him a ticket, and got together with our friends and relatives for dinner in order to see him off. He had to fly to Moscow and from there fly to Magadan on another plane. But the flight to Moscow was delayed because of the weather. I think it was in January. No, that's not right. I got mixed up. I returned here, gave birth, and our daughter was already seven months old. My husband got seriously ill with excruciating lower back pain and his legs went numb. He was still there. I returned to him, leaving our daughter with Mama. I thought I'd go there for a month or two to reduce the length of his stay, but it turned out that I was there for seven months. My daughter was a year and four months when I returned. We were nothing more to her than a photograph on the wall. She didn't recognize us until she was alone with us in the room, without my mother. Well, we returned in September or October, it's not important, and planned to go back again in January. We thought that my husband would go first, and that I'd travel with my daughter in the spring when things warmed up. Because the flight was delayed, our friends didn't ac-company us to the airport to see my husband off. Once they had left, our daughter, Jana, despite the fact that it had been hard for her to get used to us, crawled up into his lap and threw herself around his neck. He was so deeply moved by this that he got tears in his eyes and he said: "Hey, why are we doing this?" "I agree." "But I won't return the ticket." I replied, "No problem." Then I went to the airport myself to cash it in and that was that. Thus ended the period in our lives when we couldn't decide whether or not to return to Magadan. That was in 1977. And it turned out that friends, my friends, who by this time occupied positions of some importance at work, well, I don't want to lie to you, this was a period of protectionism, when patronage opened many doors for people. And it was our friend who helped him. Then he linked us up with others who had been up north, his former classmates, who had spent several years in Dikson.[19] We befriended this group who had spent time together in Dikson. They helped him, and hired him for a well-paying job.

---

19. A tiny urban settlement on the Kara Sea in Taimyr (Dolganonenets) Autono-mous Okrug.

Although he was trained as a machine engineer, he went to work in the construction industry.

You mentioned that during the five years you spent in Magadan oblast that you read some literature and even met with former inmates. How did this affect you? You said, for instance, that you began to understand your mother better.

Well, first of all, I was in shock, because there's a saying in Russian, "You can't hide a mountain." And for how many years did they conceal this extraordinary period from people? And those who lived through this period, how many years were they silent? Yet what occurred probably took place namely because Russians are Russians. They say there's no smoke without fire. Some said that the events were falsified and didn't happen to anybody, while others said, "No, that can't be. There's got to be something to it." I encountered this first-hand. However, this was later, when people realized that something had indeed gone on. It simply can't be! But when we learned that it could be, it went against everything we believed in. That is, it was an outrage, a shock. It was also a shock that people resided in such places. It was simply a system of survival according to the principle, he who pulls through, survives. It's not that people experienced some sort of physical punishment, since being deprived of your freedom is already a punishment, right? But the punishment took place in awful conditions that didn't give people much chance for surviving. It was a form of extermination. Once we went hunting there in a valley. Nature there is breathtaking: hills, valleys, streams, marshes, and swamps. There were many camps there. And we're in a land rover and enter a valley and see something. It's as if entering the valley put things in perspective. We saw some fairly even rows marked by sticks. We got out of the car and went there. It was a burial place. There was a marker with a faded inscription, "A-76," "B," that is, with the prisoners' numbers. For the most part, the burial place was poorly covered with soil. That is, it's permafrost, Magadan oblast, where you need either Japanese or American equipment to dig a ditch, for you can't go deep by hand. Therefore, there was nothing more than a shallow ditch in the permafrost, strewn lightly with clumps of dirt, which in time got washed away. It was a rather sad sight to behold.

I've tried to understand what went into the formation of your worldview. That's why I asked about your childhood, parents, and school. What else shaped you? It's obvious that the time you spent in Magadan also did. What else do I need to ask you to understand this?

Let me think for a moment. Well, in my youth I ran into a situation that shattered my ideals. Well, maybe that's going too far, but I experienced great disappointment and great distress. I worked at the design institute and attended school in the evenings. I was a member of the Komsomol at the design institute, which was large with many students. When someone finished the institute he was still of Komsomol age. Therefore there were lots of Komsomol members at the design institute, and I, as a member, was involved in cultural work among the masses. This was back in 1969 or 1970. I decided to go to East Germany as a tourist through "Sputnik," which organized travel for youth. I filled out the necessary documents and application. There were several stages to this. The Komsomol committee had to approve the application, then a higher committee, then the party committee, then it was sent to your workplace, and finally to the neighborhood party committee. Because I was involved in cultural work among the masses they knew me in the neighborhood Komsomol committee. I had reached this stage in the process and received a recommendation from it. But when I turned in the recommendation and documents to the party organization at my institute, that very same organization, which also knew me, because its members organized parties, celebrations, and events with us Komsomolites, they said: "They all seem to be active, conscious Komsomol members, but if they go there, they'll gape at everything, and come back screwed up." There was the Iron Curtain, do you understand? Back then we really did feel it. My heavens, how I suffered! Precisely because I had put all my heart into Komsomol work, and then suddenly this distrust. And cynical distrust at that. I thought, damn all this Komsomol work. It was as if they had slapped my hands. Back then, when you're eighteen or nineteen, such youthful maximalism still exists. And when they spit in your face like this! Moreover, I had the sensation one has when they say one thing and do another. How could this be? Help me find a word for this, when they say that the youth is our vanguard blah, blah, blah, but in fact, they treat you like dirt. I didn't take this personally, but understood it as a cynical attitude toward young people. Not like toward a younger brother, but like toward a servant who, as they say, does what he's charged with doing, but has no respect. This episode undoubtedly shaped my worldview. Nevertheless, I believed in everything that was going on in our country. It seemed to me that probably that's how it should be.

While you were away the dissident movement got underway and there was a lot of commotion over human rights. Samizdat circulated. There was also an improvement in relations with the West, détente, which turned sour at the end of the decade. Did any of this affect you?

You know, that was all too far removed from me. We're far away from Moscow. There undoubtedly were people interested in this or people who knew things. Perhaps among those who had been repressed, and perhaps among their children. By the way, I even remember some like this. There was a woman who worked in the construction organization, who had been in camp for twenty-seven years. Maybe I have the number of years wrong, but it was either seventeen or twenty-seven, that is, it was for a long time. She wasn't altogether normal. Probably samizdat circulated among them, but I never encountered it here.

What factors shaped your identity? Have you felt that your gender has limited you in any way?

I've never felt that. I've always been very much a woman and very much a man at the same time. That is, I've never differentiated between what might be called men's or women's work. If I have the physical strength and ability to do something, I do it. Moreover, my relationship with my husband has turned out such that if I feel I can help him, I do. Thus, I've never felt restricted. At the same time, I don't have any feminist feelings of any kind. Absolutely none! I know that I'm very much a Russian woman, the kind about whom Nekrasov wrote, who can bring a horse to a gallop and charge into a burning hut [laughing].[20] That is, when I sense that I'm defending my family. . . . I don't know what this would be like on the level, of say, a country. But if the situation arose that I'd have to defend my family, I'd not hesitate for a moment.

How has your husband influenced you, or you him?

Well, he must have influenced me somehow, and I him. We're really close friends, because of our life together and of being married. But also because we do a lot of things together. Typically, men go hunting after which the women pluck the bird and cook it. But we went hunting together. Many of his friends' wives would say, "Why does that one take his wife hunting with him, and you don't?" They'd reply, "You just try to do what she does. She's not

---

20. One of Russia's most famous poets, Nikolai Alekseevich Nekrasov (1821–1878) is especially appreciated for his "Russian Women" (1872), which paid homage to the wives of the so-called Decembrists, who followed their husbands into Siberian exile when they tried to provoke the introduction of political reform in Russia in 1825.

our cook, but one of us." There wasn't anything I couldn't handle. We all endured the same difficulties. Because we were so close, I had the feeling that we were two halves of the same person. I still think that's the case.

Marxist teachings emphasize the importance of economic development. I recall that when I was doing research for my dissertation at Moscow University in the mid-1970s, and was told that I couldn't visit Saratov because it was a closed city, a student from Saratov whom I had met in the dorm said, "Of course it's closed: there's no meat." He was kidding, of course, yet I also heard stories about people coming from Saratov, an agricultural region, to Moscow to buy food and goods. How did you understand this back then?

Well, probably as some sort of lie. Yes, there's something to this. Because my circle of friends had full refrigerators. We didn't stand in any lines. That is, you understand, in principle there was enough, but one part of society made it possible for another part of society to earn money because of these shortages. To be honest, I had an acquaintance who worked in the sausage shop across the street. I'd go to her and ask, without humiliating myself too much, if she'd sell me a piece of sausage. It would all depend upon her mood. Sometimes she'd say no. I wouldn't go through the front door of the store, but around the back. I felt humiliated doing this. Later, when everything appeared in the stores, it seemed like there wasn't enough money to buy things with. But for me this was a bit, I wouldn't say better, but a bit more equitable than things were before. You know, many arguments take place over this today. Elderly people say that, despite the fact that there might not have been sausage back then, things were better because they had some in their refrigerator. That's a worldview for you, huh? To obtain a hunk of sausage by humiliating myself was less appealing to me. I never felt a sense of satisfaction in "obtaining" rather than buying something. I now feel a lot freer. Of course, I can't afford to buy expensive things every day, but I can, at long last, and I have an incentive to do so. I can save up. I often have this discussion with my daughter because when you're young you want everything right away and if you don't get it, then someone's to blame. But I believe that if I can't afford something then I myself am to blame. I feel I have more dignity in this situation than in the old one.

Did you travel to Moscow to buy food?

Why of course! I sometimes did. For instance, I worked in a construction company and did so through our trade union, which paid for half the cost of the trip. It came to about twenty or thirty rubles.

We'd travel to Moscow on Fridays after work. A large group would gather at work, whoever wanted to go. We'd hop on the train after work on Friday and arrive in Moscow the next morning. We'd spend all Saturday buying things, and would leave Moscow for home on Saturday evening, returning to Saratov on Sunday morning.

How often did you make such trips, once a quarter?

No, you see, you nevertheless were at a complete disadvantage in making such a trip. And since it was the trade union that paid for half the ticket, it didn't occur all that often. That said, people had to do it, for example, before a holiday or special occasion. Yet people were thankful that an organization helped to make such a trip possible. Yes, there were such trains. Some went to buy new boots, others to buy meat, still others for something else.

Did your husband also go?

No, he didn't.

During the Gorbachev period they began referring to the Brezhnev era as one of stagnation. What did you think of Brezhnev, and did your opinion of him change over time? I ask because when I first visited the USSR in 1971, people seemed to like him. However, this clearly had changed by the end of the decade. Did it seem to you that you were living in a period of stagnation?

You know, there was a great deal of hypocrisy. Many jokes circulated that basically reflected how things really were. I remember one anecdote from the period when everyone is traveling by train and the tracks come to an end. Shake the train, people said, and let them think that we're still moving. This circulated during the Brezhnev years. I don't know if anyone got into trouble for telling them, but what I want to say is that there aren't such jokes circulating now as there were back then. People told the jokes freely and weren't particularly afraid of anything, even though the jokes were at the expense of a specific individual and of real situations. Therefore, it wasn't that people felt all that constrained. Everyone probably felt that not everything was in order. Moreover, we're normal people, after all, and could see what was going on with the corrupt elite. For all that, we traveled to Moscow to buy sausage that was produced at a Saratov meat-packing plant. Some people thought that the meat was taken there because Moscow, after all, is the capital, and who, after all, comes to Saratov? No one. Everyone needs to see how wonderful things are in the capital. Therefore it's best to give everything to Moscow. That is, it was a crude form of window dressing. There were lots of things done for show. But for some reason we were tolerant of this window dressing. I'm not sure if it's part of our upbringing, but it probably does stem from this, that once something is done in such a way people believe that's how it should be.

I forgot to ask whether you or your husband joined the Communist Party.

I didn't. As for my husband, well, you need to understand that if you wanted to get ahead at work you needed to be a party member. And in order to join the party you needed to be a worker. Workers were given priority in joining. It was an absurd situation. He couldn't join the party when he taught, because at that time the neighborhood committee needed to enroll eight workers and one member of the intelligentsia. He tried to join the party here in Saratov, already as the head of a construction operation. It turned out that the time was ripe for him to join. An accident took place at work, and it was necessary to punish someone who was a party member. But he wasn't a party member, so they quickly had to enroll him in the party so that they could issue him a reprimand. This was in 1981 or 1982, I'm not exactly sure.

Why do you think perestroika took place?

You know, perestroika came from the top, from the top. I say that because if Gorbachev hadn't set things in motion, they would have continued as before. That is, there was no unrest or resentment among the people. Do you understand why people took such a strong liking to Gorbachev at first? First, Brezhnev was dying for years. It had become the reign of a decrepit old man. This was all too clear by how awfully he spoke, yet refused to give up power. As in any work environment, when you see that someone can no longer perform at all, but continues to occupy a post, you become irritated. Ever the more so because he implemented the policies of the Central Committee, and the Central Committee kept him in place. Will they give him yet another medal? For the most part there was considerable irritation in society. And after Brezhnev, as you know, we had what we called the "five-year plan of lavish funerals." Right after Brezhnev a state functionary came to power, Chernenko, I think. Right?

First there was Iurii Andropov, then Chernenko.

Right, first Andropov, then Chernenko. They took office when they were sick and died shortly thereafter. They were so old, to boot, and they all came from the same generation. You know, they'd say, well, he doesn't have a pension so where can he go? When Gorbachev came to power he was basically a young man. Besides, he had a charming appearance. And when he began to speak so clearly you wanted to listen. That was at a time in our life when my husband and I had a second calling and returned once again up north. We left Saratov already when things had become so sickening, this routine, the same old thing. That was in 1984. We spent seven years there.

Back in Susuman?

No, we returned to Magadan oblast, but this time to Chukhotka, to the town of Pevek on the Chukhotka peninsula.[21] Our friends also left, those who had formerly been in Dikson whom we had befriended in Saratov. Two families left for Pevek and we followed. Our daughter went with us. She started third grade there. It was there that we welcomed Gorbachev to power and experienced perestroika and all that was connected to it.

How was Gorbachev's program received there? Differently than it would have been here, or is that hard to say?

You know, I don't think so. We welcomed his program with open minds, like something we had longed for. You know, it's one thing to discuss things in the kitchen, but another altogether to begin to say openly that it's impossible to live like this any longer. The films, the literature that appeared at the time, there was so much of it! The journals published everything. Even Nabokov, whom I hadn't read before this time. If before it was popular to have a home library, the selection of books was, well, it was next to impossible to obtain what you wanted. But now everything was available. Before you could have purchased a poster of a home library and hung it up, because every family had the same selection of books: Chekhov, Gorky, Tolstoy, Jules Verne, Walter Scott, thirty volumes of Dickens, etc. Basically everyone had the same, because a subscription for a series was being taken at the neighborhood party committee, which chose this but not that title. People bought the books and resold them, but people nonetheless somehow managed to build a library. I remember standing in an amazingly long line at the store that took subscriptions. They handed out cards with numbers on them, tossed the numbers into a barrel, spun it, and in this manner selected who could sign up. Therefore, you must understand, that when so much literature was made available, I was thankful to Gorbachev

---

21. A small urban settlement designated by romantics and writers in 1967 as the first "city" located within the Arctic Circle.

and Yeltsin. Besides, I like Gorbachev as a man. I like Gorbachev a great deal. I know for a fact, no matter what they accused him of later, that it's his colossal achievement to have said that we can't go on living like this any longer. Everything that followed—I like Yeltsin too, because for the most part I think that a lot was gained during this period—but nevertheless, Gorbachev started it all. And the fact that he wasn't able to manage things, well, you have to keep in mind that there was no fail-proof program. Nonetheless, things changed. By the way, although I don't know much about American history, I think that the United States, too, at one time got things done by trial and error. They wanted things to be better, but they turned out like always.[22] There were a great many good intentions in his actions. They do say that the road to hell is paved with good intentions [laughing].

How has your life changed since the collapse of the Soviet Union?

To be honest, a lot of problems appeared. Before we lived in a single country, and keep in mind that my husband is from Ukraine. During those years before strict customs were set up we could still manage to visit. When his mother died two years ago the telegram served as our so-called visa to let us enter. Nevertheless, a lot of extortion goes on. They stamp your documents in the wrong place and you have to bribe. Then there's Ukraine itself. Before my mother-in-law left us we visited her several times a year. Let me make a short digression. My father-in-law was a real Communist, an inflexible, orthodox one, and all his life held a rather privileged administrative post. Yet he'd always say, "If only Ukraine didn't have to pull up Russia, we'd be so better off! Like Canada with its Ukrainians!" We always had the same old conversation that Ukraine was so wonderful, that if Moscow wasn't always taking things from Ukraine, it would be such a wonderfully rich country. And when the collapse of the Soviet Union occurred and we crossed what in our mind's eye was the border with Russia, which also was not in the best of situations, well, it was a shocking site. City streets were illuminated only by the light that came from the windows of homes and apartments. The streets of decent, rich mining towns! Miners were without work, mines were shutting down, and there were food shortages. There was no work anywhere. These borders now divided people. By the

---

22. Here Belovolova is repeating an aphorism made famous by Boris Yeltsin's often inarticulate prime minister, Viktor Chernomyrdin.

way, I can also give you an example when there was still a Soviet Union and people from Ukraine went to Russia to work or we went to Siberia. You reserved your apartment, say, in Ukraine. We didn't own our own place, because there was no privatization yet back then. The government would give you some facilities up north and would reserve yours until you returned. People regularly did this. They'd work here, in Russia, but return to Ukraine to receive the pension that they had earned working up north in Russia. There was no discrimination where you earned your pension. In 1991, when we returned from our second stay in Siberia, we could still fill a container with our belongings, load it on a boat, and have the government pay to ship it as part of our contract. But those who came along later lost out. They earned a pension here, but there, in Ukraine, they no longer reserved apartments. In regard to pensions, the situation is beginning to clear up a bit, but back then things weren't certain at all. People severed ties with their homes, because there was nothing good to look forward to upon their return. They'd arrive only to find that there was no work. Nothing. It turns out that there's enough bread in Ukraine, but there's no electricity, gasoline, or anything else. And as a result of this a certain animosity toward individuals or toward other nationalities emerged. It turned out that we Russians live better than Ukrainians. This means that we must be taking something of theirs. Things shouldn't be this way. I have to agree with Yeltsin that we should take only as much freedom as we're capable of handling. They overstrained themselves a bit. Today's politics are a consequence of what happened back then. But man, after all, descended from the apes, right? He can't learn from others' mistakes, and must experience everything himself. That's what all the fuss is about. The situation is not much better even now. My husband's sister is in difficult straits there and is hospitalized. She had been in an accident and they need to operate on her but there's no money. Send some. Even my husband sent money from here. It's all gotten so complicated! There aren't enough qualified doctors there. They've left either for Israel, Canada, or America. She needs an operation, so we need to bring her here. But all those customs and passport and visa controls have separated people. Before we could travel anywhere within the USSR, but now . . .

How are things at work for you?

I'm not working now. Stays up north allow you to retire early. But as a matter of fact, it's not that so much as it is how my life's unfolded. I'm raising my grandson, we're raising him. The older generation raises the younger. My daughter got married again and has a young infant. That's not the only reason. Things turned out that way. I'm not working, but in order to bring up our grandson, my husband has to continue working.

How can your life story help me understand what became of the Soviet Union?

Well, I felt that I'm a small part of my country. It seemed to me that I was working and contributing something. I was laying a few bricks in our country's foundation. I felt as if I were doing something useful. Then there came the period when I had the feeling that perhaps I hadn't done anything useful. I, like the majority of the population, worked. There had to be something useful in this, and there were so many of us workers. But our productivity! I realize the level was low. And the wages that we earned were commensurate with what we did. Yet there was pride in what we did, meaning in what we did. After all, we had to attend meetings, at which we felt that we were part of a collective and not an outsider. You experienced the same high, the same enthusiasm as all the others. For the most part, all this was the case, do you understand? We looked to the future with optimism. Well, I'm simply not one of those individuals who looks for nothing but mistakes in the actions of others, because I don't see anything positive in this. I'm also very patient about such mistakes. That's because, in principle, even if you're some important boss or the president himself, you nonetheless weren't born that way. You're not extraterrestrial. Moreover, there was no experience of this sort, ever the more so because the situation in the world is forever changing. As a result, it's difficult to do only what's right. Once again, what is seen as something positive today turns out, when you have some perspective on it, to be not so good. It's very hard. I'm very patient in regard to what we're living through today. But, at the same time, I'm not laboring under any delusions either. When Gorbachev came to power and they held that first congress or conference . . .

The Nineteenth Party Conference?[23]

Yes. Well, we were living in Pevek. You can't imagine it! We watched it as if it were some sort of gripping political romance. My husband and I couldn't believe what we were hearing. How could he

---

23. The Nineteenth Special Party Conference, held in June 1988 and televised, offered the most open political debate in Russia since the 1920s.

say that! Listen to what he's saying! There was real euphoria. Now it's gone, do you understand? We also lived through that period. Our life is like this, it's in distinct blocks. We arrived in Pevek in 1984. I'll backtrack a bit. It was 1984 and a small clan was formed there. It turned out that the head of the construction industry for the city of Saratov, the main engineer of the industry, and my husband, the deputy director of the construction industry, also from Saratov, were all friends. A clan was formed. Now it's normal to use that word, but back then we were a team, for clan would have been understood as something negative. And the prestige of the construction organization was considerable. It was a small town with a population of 12,000, but it's the largest trading center of the navy that far north, and the construction organization belonged to the Naval Ministry as well. Some kind of advanced construction methods were used there on large projects. It somehow turned out that the prestige of these people created competition for the regional party committee. It sounds funny to admit that today, but it's true. They began to squabble and a game of musical chairs began. Someone got removed, someone got promoted, someone else held on to his position. Then someone felt infringed upon. Maybe there was something personal in this, but for the most part it was done in order to reorganize things. All sorts of denunciations got underway. They began to concoct a story. But back then how could you get rid of someone at work if he got things done? Well, they began to search for a criminal. But what kind of criminal? Since no one had been murdered they began to look for someone who used his position for personal gain. They came up with such a scenario and its initiator was the secretary of the regional party committee, which began to press down hard on the clan. But for some reason the chairman of the executive committee was on their side. They created a situation in which even he . . . well, they expelled my husband from the party and fired him. The head of the administration, just before the party bureau was to make its decision, was in Moscow where he reached an agreement with the Naval Ministry. He, how shall I put it, kept his party card in his pocket, while my husband had to turn his in. And this is a small town of 12,000. My daughter went to school there as did the daughter of the first secretary, and the son of another. We tried with all the means available to us to convince our daughter that her father was not the scoundrel and criminal they said, and that she didn't see or know what was really going on. Then Gorbachev came to power. When my father-in-law found out about the situation, well, imagine, he, after all, had raised this son and suddenly either the son's a scoundrel or else something's going on. He wrote to the Central Committee. My husband also appealed to the Central Committee. But this was such a vicious circle, when everything depends upon your own kind. He wrote to the higher organs only to have them turn to the lower organizations to resolve things. That is, it was a veritable dead end. Things even got to the point that the regional party committee threatened others not to hire him. We were practically driven out of the region. And then the head of the port authorities there, a decorated worker, who since has become a close friend, well, he hired my husband as a dock worker, despite the fact that the first party secretary had pointed a finger at him. Then Gorbachev came to power and my husband wrote an appeal to the Twenty-sixth Party Congress. True, not much came of this. But then he saw an old friend on television. He wrote to him and through him, well, his friend was close to those that ran the country. To Ligachev, for instance.[24] He could pick up the phone and call him. And things turned out as they should have all along. That is, this resulted in a reexamination of the case. Within a half-year they reinstated my husband into the party and gave him his job back. But then the party fell apart. And he, departing Chukhotka and not knowing what to expect in 1991, went to pay his party dues in advance for the year [laughing]. The party no longer existed, but he had his membership card and had paid his dues. By the way, he still has the membership card, although I can't say that he remains a follower of the Communist Party. He's a realist. See what we had to put up with in our lives? When you're deprived of your party card you become an outcast, simply put. We, our family and our daughter, really supported him back then morally and spiritually. By the way, our daughter back then excitedly watched the congress and party conference on television with us. At home we read all the literature that appeared and since we were close we discussed it. And she grew up into a fine person with a strong core. Therefore, I'd like to say that my life was not lived on a village bench somewhere, where I didn't see beyond the village fence. I saw the life of my country and thereby my own, from a variety of perspectives. I even eventually made it abroad as a tourist.

---

24. Born in 1920, Egor Ligachev was a conservative hard-liner who was opposed to many of Gorbachev's reforms and who clashed frequently with Politburo member Boris Yeltsin.

When was this? Under Gorbachev?

It was under Yeltsin. I haven't been to Europe, apart from Bulgaria. But I've been to Egypt, to Turkey, and to the Emirates. These were tourist excursions that were affordable. I can't afford, say, a trip to Canada. But I allowed myself what I could. I didn't have the sense there, well, that we're worse off. We're simply different, do you understand? The generation that I belong to is the product of the country's entire history. Those values that I hold dear have not undergone serious change. I know that it's wrong to steal. I felt that way before, and I feel that way now. In any case, I don't infringe upon others. Yet where do the oligarchs in Russia today come from? Where do people with such amazing wealth come from? We all earned roughly the same pay from the state budget! Why does the country's wealth end up in the hands of a few? True, many people were duped by various financial scams, but that's nothing in comparison with what these rich people have done. They didn't build a factory with money they had saved in a jar under their mattress. They exploit this factory, which they probably somehow managed to buy. This didn't occur under Gorbachev. Things were not thought through, and some took advantage of the situation, which others failed to catch. I don't think this is right. But I also think there's no going back. . . . I'm not a supporter of this, but since it happened, and given the country's history. . . . Perhaps in time a different political climate will arise. I like what our president is doing now. I like the respect he shows to those who preceded him. Back when Khrushchev exposed the personality cult, we applauded. Putin is exposing nothing, and we once again are applauding. That is, as a nation we're something of a paradox. We're a very patient people. Back then, when I was young, it seemed that we were on the right path and . . . we didn't worry about our future. However, I now worry about raising our grandson. It's not that I'm an alarmist, but I hope very much that nothing bad will happen, that everything will get better. Whereas before I knew that he'd enroll in college, now I don't understand how this can happen. We don't have enough money to educate him. We have our pension, yet that guarantees nothing. It's not a pension system that has a future. Therefore, I don't know whether my grandson will receive an education or not. Of course, I understand that he has parents, too, but all the same I'm the one who is responsible for him and I'm concerned. That's what makes me anxious. Still, I want to believe that the future will be better.

6. "It's very hard to be a woman in our country" | Olga Vladimirovna Kamaiurova

June 12, 2003, Saratov

A. A. Konstantinov (see chapter 1) urged me to give top priority to finding and interviewing Olga Vladimirovna Kamaiurova, who also belonged to the B group of the class of '67. Although he had not seen her since leaving Saratov in 1967 to attend Moscow University, he assured me that I undoubtedly would find her as he remembered her: intelligent, introspective, engaging, and disarmingly honest.

Konstantinov was right. I interviewed Olga Vladimirovna in the apartment I had rented in Saratov. After providing her with a fuller explanation of my research objective, we examined old photographs that she had brought along to show me (and which she kindly let me copy). The "how to" literature on oral history emphasizes the wide range of factors that shape any interview situation, in this case possibly complicated by cross-cultural considerations that need to be factored into the equation. By the time I had poured tea and slipped the first cassette into my tape recorder I knew that we had clicked on a personal level. I did not sense that Olga Vladimirovna cast her life through a special cultural lens for foreign consumption. I also found much about her a bit out of the ordinary, and therefore very appealing.

One palpable refrain in many of the interviews I had already conducted among members of the B group was how special the group was. Most of its members get together for annual reunions or to see classmates visiting Saratov who now live in Moscow or Western Europe. Although deep personal friendships cut across and complicate the larger group dynamic, they also add to its cohesiveness. Moreover, the majority of those whom I interviewed cast their childhood as an incredibly happy one. Yet adolescence, Soviet or otherwise, remains a difficult period in the lifecycle to negotiate. Therefore, I appreciated Olga Vladimirovna's willingness to talk about the "other side" of growing up.

She, too, finds it pleasurable to link up with her former classmates to reminisce, but, unlike many of them, she recalls her school years as a difficult period. Not receiving a silver medal represented a profound disappointment to her at the time. She suspects this had something to do with a conflict she had with a counselor while at summer camp, yet acknowledges that her understanding of this important moment may be colored by her frustration over seeing the medal go to someone else. Her appreciation of opposing points of view resonates throughout her interview, revealing an enormous capacity for self-reflection.

Olga Vladimirovna spoke frankly about her family dynamic and about how it impacted her professional life. We learn about her complicated relationship with her mother, about how and why she became estranged from her husband, and about her interactions with her adult son and daughter. We learn about the vicissitudes of Soviet career trajectories, about her unusual profession, that of pathologist, about the difficulties she encountered in trying to balance the double burden of holding down a full-time job and bearing responsibility for family life, and about temporarily living abroad in a Soviet-bloc country. We also encounter a tale of self-discovery, independence, and spirituality both constrained and enabled by the many ways that perestroika and glasnost affected the Soviet Union and Russia today. Yet her interview also made me realize—as someone who is the same age—that many of her concerns had at least something to do with the stage of life she was in at any given time. There was something very Russian about her story, but also something that was all too familiar.

Why is it hard to be a woman in Russia? How does Olga Vladimirovna's account help us to understand everyday life in provincial Russia during the Brezhnev years? What does she regret and why? What experiences shaped her professional development? How can we evaluate the consequences of perestroika when viewed through the prism of her personal narrative?

My father, Vladimir Aleksandrovich Kamaiurov, was born in 1911. He was a college graduate who worked as an engineer, as the main technical specialist at an academic research institute called Giproniigas in Saratov. He died in 1974 from heart disease. My mother is still alive. She's a physician who worked all her life at an institute devoted to the study of cholera, called Microbe, as head of a laboratory. She wrote a candidate's dissertation and was prepared to defend her doctoral dissertation on preventive measures against cholera.[1] She has many inventions and scientific discoveries, and has been the recipient of numerous awards; however, for some reason she was not allowed to defend her doctoral dissertation. I don't know why for sure, but apparently this was still back when the party elite was in charge and, when she turned fifty-five, they dismissed her from the institute on some plausible pretext.

What year was that?

Good heavens! She was born in 1924, so it must have been in 1979. We're now using her doctoral dissertation to light our stove at the dacha.[2] The fruit of her life's labors! This, of course, was a terrible blow to her, which literally drained the life out of her. She had been full of vim, vigor, and ideas. On the whole, she's a very smart woman. But now she's failing. I had a brother who was ten years younger than me. He died at age twenty-seven. What can I tell you about my parents' parents? My grandfather on my mother's side was repressed in 1937.[3] He had been an accountant at some sort of enterprise. I don't know the details, of course, because my mother was thirteen years old at the time. A version circulated within the family [laughing] that they withheld paychecks from workers and that the workers got upset and demanded money from him and wanted to know why he had held up their pay. He said that it wasn't he who was holding up their pay, but the state bank. And for something like

---

1. The Soviet (and Russian) system of graduate education differs from that of the United States and Great Britain. It does not confer a master's degree, followed by a (final) doctoral degree, but a candidate's degree, which is often described as the equivalent of an American Ph.D. However, one normally spends only three years in graduate studies obtaining a candidate's degree. Some senior scholars write a second or doctoral dissertation much later in their careers.

2. A cottage or country house. For a history of the phenomenon, see Stephen Lovell's *Summerfolk: A History of the Dacha, 1710–2000* (Ithaca: Cornell University Press, 2003).

3. A euphemism used to describe those arrested during the Stalin period, when many were imprisoned, sent to labor camps, and/or executed. The term itself is an artifact of the de-Stalinization campaign of the 1950s.

this they put him away and he died locked up. The relatives of my maternal grandmother, Liudmila Gustavovna, came from Czechoslovakia. She died from hypertension at age fifty-three. My paternal grandmother lived long and died at the age of ninety-two. She was a housewife, a very attractive woman, you know, a real lady, with a real lady's manners. She was smart, attractive, happy, and loved to sing. I never knew my paternal grandfather, who died long before I was born. He was a Don Cossack.[4] I have an unusual surname, one that I've not encountered elsewhere. I'm not really sure why I have such an unusual surname, but they say that the family's from Yugoslavia. My childhood, for the most part, was probably typical. However, perhaps, my family was a bit better off than those of most other children of my generation. My mother earned a good salary, and my father, too. We had our own apartment, no, that's not right, we lived in a communal flat until I was thirteen. Do you know what that is? We shared a kitchen with two other families. It was located on the same street where my mother is living out her days, but in a slightly different neighborhood. When I was thirteen we moved into that apartment on Michurin Street where my mother still lives. That was back in 1963. The apartment was considered luxurious. It had three rooms and was located in a brick building with all amenities.[5] My mother's salary allowed her to hire a housekeeper. My mother was very busy at work, and we had a housekeeper-nanny who, for all practical purposes, was a member of the family. I was raised by my paternal grandmother, God bless her soul, and by our nanny. She was an altogether humble and charming woman. She was as unselfish as they come. She became a member of my family and she brought up not only my brother and me, but also my daughter, who is already thirty years old, and she even began to raise my son, who is now twenty-three. She died from old age. What else can I tell you? Well, my parents sent me to the special English-language school in the third, that's not right, the second grade. The school was located on Michurin Street, not far from my home, and in third

---

4. A branch of the Cossacks inhabiting the Don River region. Probably a Turkic word, "Cossack" denoted freebooters of various Slavic and non-Slavic origins who inhabited Russia's borderlands and fiercely guarded their independence. By the end of the eighteenth century, however, they had been incorporated into the Russian empire, whose borderlands they now defended. Be that as it may, popular usage of the term often implies a certain free-spirited nature or even someone slightly alien.

5. By "all amenities" Kamaiurova has in mind indoor plumbing, hot water, and perhaps an elevator and telephone.

grade we moved into the new school building.[6] Basically, our class, as I now appreciate but didn't at all realize at the time, was made up almost exclusively of children of the intelligentsia. There might have been two or three from working-class families. But we absolutely, I at least, I'm not sure about the others, I didn't give any thought to this whatsoever. It didn't interest me. I'm becoming aware of such things only now. For me it's a revelation. I was a very good student in school, receiving all A's, and was vying for a silver medal. They intended for me to enroll in the physics/mathematics department at the university or in a language college but, like my mother, I became a doctor. We graduated from school in 1967, after which I enrolled at the Saratov Medical Institute. With that my childhood came to an end. What else would you like to know?

Who among the adults influenced you most while you were growing up?

You know, it's hard to say. Perhaps my paternal grandmother, since she spent the most time with me. But also my parents. The company my mother kept was made up of all doctors, researchers at the same institute where she worked. Sasha Konstantinov's mother, for instance, is a very interesting, brilliant woman.[7] I remember well the Bakhrakhov family, also academic researchers, well known among the Saratov intelligentsia. By and large, the company my parents kept was composed of members of the intelligentsia. These were interesting, unaffected, deeply erudite people, and perhaps for this reason I somehow was drawn to medicine. Well, no, I can't really say that, that I chose this profession because of them. It's more likely that I was interested in many things and that somehow, by process of elimination, chose the Medical Institute. I wanted to help sick children, and for this reason I opted for the pediatrics department. But I worked as a pediatrician after completing the institute for only two years, after which I moved on to a more exotic specialization.

Why did your parents decide to send you to School No. 42?

Well, probably because they wanted to give me a good education, and School No. 42 provided just that, of course. In all likelihood its teachers were hand picked according to their professional qualifications. And the environment, the milieu in which a child

---

6. They actually moved into the new school building when they were in fifth grade.

7. See Aleksandr Aleksandrovich Konstantinov's interview in chapter 1.

May Day celebration, probably 1965. Olga Vladimirovna
Kamaiurova is second on the right (first full profile). *Courtesy
A. A. Konstantinov.*

grows up in school, is an important consideration. I wouldn't want
my children or my granddaughter to attend an ordinary school
even today. I sent my daughter to the special French school, from
which she graduated. The parents of the children in her class were
also mostly from the intelligentsia. My son attended a school with
a mathematics emphasis. It later became a special high school. He
graduated with honors. What else?

*Please tell me about your favorite teachers, about your favorite subjects,
and about your best friends at school.*

I had two close girl friends at school. I'm not sure if it's at all
interesting for the purposes of this interview, but I now am able
to evaluate myself in a way that I couldn't back then. I was a bit
aloof. And for many years after graduation, I didn't meet with my
classmates. But perhaps owing to some sort of nostalgia that comes
with age, for the past, well since 1980 or so, that is for some twenty
years or so, since the time I reached my thirties, I've been drawn
to my childhood. But before then I lived in the present and had no
interest in revisiting my past. Is this some quirk on my part? All
my classmates got together each year, beginning the year after we
graduated. They sang songs they all knew, they reminisced, they
recalled old teachers. Even now, when I listen to what they have

to say, I don't have any nostalgia at all for my school days. I can't say, as they do, that our "school years were wonderful." At our last—by the way I hope [laughing] that you will be the only one to hear these words—at our last get-together, when everyone began simultaneously to reminisce about our teachers and about certain events, one of our former classmates—whose name, of course, I'll not reveal—leaned over to me and said: "I remember it all as a nightmare." And I agreed with him. That's right. I can't say that I have happy, joyous memories. I simply lived in the present back then and live in the present now. I'm happy that I live in the present. I don't have any regrets or memories about the past that I'd like to relive. None whatsoever. You asked about my closest friends. Well, I had two fairly close friends. I shared the same desk with one of them, Nelia Egorova, who now lives in Germany. She was a sweet, gentle girl, intelligent by nature. I'm not even sure who her parents were. It's even possible that they weren't members of the intelligentsia. She and I skipped school, strange as it seems. Well, as they say, still waters run deep. We hid our school bags in her attic among the potatoes and then took off for the outskirts of Saratov, where we hung out. Later I lied and said that I had been sick. I simply couldn't stand attending school for six days in a row each week.[8] Once a week she and I cut classes. And my other close girlfriend was Olga Martynkina. She left our school after the eighth grade. She's a musician. But Nelia Egorova was closer, although after graduation we fell out of touch. Our lives went separate ways, that's all. It was nothing more than a childhood friendship.

You asked about my favorite teachers, right? Well, I liked our math teacher. She was an intelligent, interesting woman. Besides, I did well in math, and I enjoyed her class. I liked our chemistry teacher, Rosa Iakovlevna, also, undoubtedly, because I knew chemistry well. Then there was our literature teacher. I often think of her. Perhaps she treated us appropriately, but she was crude. I never found that to be pleasant—being crude and without ceremony. That's how I see her now. Yet all my other classmates, well, perhaps not all, but the overwhelming majority, remember her as being pleasant. However, I never went to see her after school and I didn't harbor any good feelings toward her. I was indifferent. She

---

8. At this time, Soviet schoolchildren attended schools on Saturdays as well as on weekdays.

was also favorably disposed toward me. Generally, I was a good student in all subjects. I really can't say that I remember any least favorite teachers.

How politicized was instruction at the school?

I don't recall. Our entire life was politicized. It would be hard to say that this somehow stood out at school.

How important was it that you learned English as a child. Did it play a role in your life?

You know, all my life I've regretted—and I regret now—that English remained a dead language for me. You understand what I'm getting at. I have a real yearning for, and would like very much to be able to speak, the language. After all, I had a real solid base. But, after becoming a doctor, this knowledge gradually slipped away. It's very important to have active command of a language, to have real practice. I think I'd have a good command of the language if I had the opportunity to speak with others. I liked coming into contact with English literature and the fact that I knew London's attractions, at least through pictures.

Do you remember when delegations from Bristol visited school?[9]

No.

Was there a difference between the A and B groups at school? Someone told me that the kids in the A group were the children of the party elite, whereas the kids in the B group were the children of the intelligentsia.

Perhaps that's the case. I simply didn't know. Once again, I was uninformed, or perhaps that simply didn't interest me. But by and large there was some sort of difference. Those in the A group seemed more elite. It seems to me, both now and back then, that they were a bit stuck up and that we were more down to earth. That perhaps is all that I can say on the subject.

I forgot to ask about religion. Did it play a role in your childhood?

You know, as Communists, my parents were atheists. My grandmother secretly had me baptized in church, probably when I was about three years old. But afterward, very likely until I reached adulthood, I wasn't at all interested in religion.

Olga Vladimirovna, what did you do in your free time back when you attended school?

---

9. Until Saratov closed to all Western contact, at least one delegation of teachers from Bristol, England, visited School No. 42 while the class of '67 was enrolled. Some of my informants have vivid memories of the British visitors, while others, such as Kamaiurova, do not recall these contacts at all, or else remember only hearing about the guests.

Group B girls marching in a May Day celebration, probably 1965.
Olga Vladimirovna Kamaiurova is on the far right. *Courtesy
A. A. Konstantinov.*

When I attended school? Well, I read a great deal. I liked music
when there was a variety show. I can't say that I ever especially
liked classical music, even though my parents doggedly sought to
educate me in this regard by introducing me to opera and ballet. I
loved ballet, but not opera. I didn't understand it. For ten years I
took piano lessons both at a music school and at home, but these ten
years didn't elicit anything in me other than an aversion [laughing].
After I left home I never once sat down at the piano bench. Now
everything's changed. Radically so. But you're speaking about my
school years, right? I read, I enjoyed music, and I played with kids
my age in our courtyard. Then there was the beach. And trips to the
country. That meant a lot. There were different diversions in winter
and summer. In winter there was the skating rink, which we went
to each day. It was like a narcotic. I couldn't get by without a fix. In
summer it was the beach and swimming.

What about summer camps?

I never attended camp. Not once. Each year my parents took
me to the sea. Back then this was simple and easy. I never went to

Olga Vladimirovna Ka-
maiurova (*left*) with two
of her classmates at a
beach on the Volga, circa
1966. *Courtesy A. A.
Konstantinov.*

camp, neither to Pioneer Camp, nor to any sport camp. Well, that's
not quite right. I once went to sport camp, but that was when I was
already enrolled at the [Saratov] Medical Institute. I can't say that
my parents watched over and controlled me, and that I was attached
to home even though I was a bit of a homebody. I simply was not
drawn to that sort of thing. The only experience of this sort from
my school days that sticks in my mind was a very interesting trip in
which we traced the tracks of Briansk partisans.[10] There were five
of us from our class: Sasha Konstantinov, whom you know, and his
future wife, Tania Okuneva. Then there was me, Maimistov,[11] who
practically no longer socializes with us today, and Kolia Khabarov.[12]
A representative of the adult generation, our Pioneer leader, was

---

10. During World War II countless Soviet citizens joined partisan groups that fought
against the Nazi occupiers. Briansk oblast lies in western Russia and borders Belorussia
as well as Smolensk, Kursk, Orel, and Kaluga oblasts.

11. Aleksandr Vladimirovich Maimistov belonged to the B group and also graduated in 1967.

12. Nikolai Aleksandrovich Khabarov belonged to the B group and also graduated
in 1967. I interviewed him during the summer of 2003.

with us. She was quite unpleasant. She simply wasn't very smart. And there were a few other Pioneers. It turned out to be a joint group of five Komsomolites and several Pioneers.[13] I can't recall how many or who they were. We traveled to Briansk oblast and interviewed partisans who had operated in nearby forests. Then we visited the forests and they showed us the dugouts in which they had lived. We slept in a tent. It was an interesting trip that sticks in my mind. I can't recall the specifics, but we had some sort of confrontation with the Pioneer leader, which, I have to say, really hurt me. It was back when we were in the tenth grade, that is, our last year. Ever since then, I've been under the impression that this ruined my chances for a medal, because I received one B too many. I graduated without a medal. For the most part I had worked hard for one, and everyone was sure I'd get a silver medal. But this is my impression today and perhaps I'm mistaken. Perhaps the person who got the medal was more deserving than I was. The number of medals was allocated and if it wasn't me, then someone else got it. I don't recall who. Perhaps this person really was more deserving.

How many medalists were there?

It was probably a fixed number in each class. But, generally, I think, that was determined from above, from higher organizations, that a certain class would receive a certain number of medals. I'm not sure, but I think five people received medals. You know, all that's forgotten now, it was so long ago that I simply don't recall, but there were about five. Insofar as I didn't get one, it must have gone to someone more worthy. I can accept this today, but I was really hurt by it back then, because it denied me the right to enroll in college with just one exam. I had to take three of them, that is, I had to prepare really hard and I could have failed and not been admitted. This was a tragedy for me back then, but no longer. It now seems so petty.

Did the fact that your grandfather was repressed play a role in your life at all?

---

13. Soviet school children at age ten joined the Pioneers. Pioneers were instructed to study hard, to be honest, and to learn how to live happily with others. Senior to the Pioneer organization was the Komsomol (All-Union Leninist Communist Youth League), which catered to young people between the ages of fourteen and twenty-eight. Membership in the Komsomol, an auxiliary of the Communist Party and training ground for party membership, was far from universal, but a high percentage of school-age children who had aspirations to enroll at a university joined the organization.

No, they kept this secret from me. I learned about it around the time I was in med school.

What did you think of Lenin when you were a schoolgirl?

Lenin, as we sang in a song that now seems like gibberish: "Lenin is always alive, Lenin is always with you. Lenin is in your spring, in each happy day."

What about Khrushchev?

You know, honestly speaking, I was apolitical. Yet now I think, my God, there were people after all who already back then understood everything. Take for example the invasion of Czechoslovakia.[14] I didn't know anything about it and didn't understand a thing. Not a thing. There were no conversations at home on such themes, at least not in my presence. After all, my parents were Communists, and they were Communists who truly believed. They were honest people who devoted themselves to the good of the Motherland. That's how it was in our home. I now understand that I was simply immature perhaps. There were no dissidents, in the positive meaning of the word, among our acquaintances, no one who thought in an unorthodox manner, no one who thought at all. Perhaps there were those who thought about such things, but they kept silent. At least in front of us. And that's a shame.

Did you listen to foreign radio broadcasts at home?

No, we didn't have a receiver, and when we acquired one they thoroughly jammed the broadcasts. The interference was so great that it was impossible to listen to the broadcasts. And even when someone said to me that he or she heard something on the radio, I didn't believe it. When they broadcast things that deviated from our radio broadcasts I didn't believe it. It seemed to me that they were slandering us, that's what they pounded into our heads. They were slandering us. Yes, I was quite naïve. Probably even now, but I was a typical child of the time. Typical.

That's to be expected. But how does your generation differ from that of your parents?

You know, I can't speak for my generation, I can speak only for myself. My parents had an anchor, which was their belief in the just cause of communism. But I don't have that. When perestroika began we were flooded with information, banned novels, and the

---

14. Determined to put an end to the reform movement in Czechoslovakia that promised to create a form of socialism with a human face, the USSR invaded the country in 1968.

like. You know, I was happy that my father hadn't lived to see this. I don't know how he would have reacted. He was a dedicated Communist. He wasn't a fanatic, but he believed that he lived the right way. I don't know how he would have endured having all his ideals destroyed. It was a tearing down of idols. It's a terrible thing. I can't speak for my entire generation, but we simply lost our anchor. We are like a balloon that's lost its air. Of course we began to think differently, but I recall the ancient Chinese saying: "May you never live in interesting times." It really is an awful thing to live in an epoch of extraordinary changes, of changes in one's worldview. I'm not even speaking of all sorts of material hardships, but of psychological changes, of the collapse of one's belief system. It turned out that everything we believed in, everything that we considered sacred and holy, in actual fact turned out to be not only unholy, but even the handiwork of the devil. That's terrible. Our children's generation is perhaps even worse off in this regard. There's nothing for them to believe in. Perhaps our parents were actually happier than our children. They, after all, had something to believe in; blind faith, generally, is not a bad thing. Our children believe only in themselves. However, it's necessary to give people something to believe in. Perhaps I'm wrong about this. This is purely my point of view, and I can't speak for my entire generation. Perhaps I differ a lot from them. Perhaps I was and remain more naïve than my contemporaries. Now, however, a new object of belief has arisen for young people—religion. Religion is on the rise now, and for me, too. I'm a deeply religious person, but don't belong to any church. Essentially, I don't understand how someone who truly believes in some kind of God can belong. No, I simply believe that everything is created by God, and that a part of him is truly in each of us. But perhaps that's not pertinent.

Are your children religious?

Both of my children believe in God. My daughter goes to church. She's Christian. As for my son, I can't exactly say. He's still a boy. I think men and women are altogether different, as they say, animals [laughing]. He doesn't socialize with me much. However, I know that he believes in God, probably in the way that I do. He's interested in the Orient, in Eastern religions. He believes in man, in the possibilities of the individual. He's interested in mystical teachings. Very interested.

In the first part of the interview, I asked about family, school, and your friends in order to understand what shaped your worldview. What did I for-

get to ask you about that would help me understand this? What else shaped your worldview?

Perhaps that's all. One's entire surroundings shape one's worldview. I was perhaps shaped by the milieu in which my parents operated. My contemporaries with whom I associated were as ordinary as I was. That's about it. But there's also education, particularly the natural sciences. They help to unite us and to keep us grounded.

Who among adults influenced you most?

Among adults? It probably was my mother, although we repel each other like two equally charged poles of a magnet [laughing]. Our relationship wasn't a particularly close one, although I understood her, most likely all too well, to feel love for her. And she, I feel, understood me. She respected me as a person, but probably didn't love me that much. She loved her son more. Consequently, the death of my brother also drained a great deal of life out of her—the loss of her beloved work, and of her favorite child. Her life really ended with this, but life is not supposed to just stop.

How did she understand the misfortune that befell her at work? After all, she belonged to the Communist Party.

Yes, she did. Well, apparently, she understood it as, well, that her place was needed by . . . by someone more important than she was, perhaps the relative of someone from the party organs. Yes, that's how she saw things back then. But gradually, from bits and pieces she said to me, I sized up that she had gotten into a confrontation with the institute's leadership. Not in a political way, but simply, well, you understand, in each large organization there are those who oppose how things are run. Perhaps those in charge held different views than the ones she supported. She and several others reminisce about it. Whenever I see them, they readily recall how she of course "paid dearly." That is, people realize she suffered, that she was indeed removed at the very peak of her professional life. She could still have contributed a great deal more, in all honesty, to society.

You said that it was a good thing that your father didn't live to experience the flood of information under Gorbachev. What about your mother? How did she react to it?

The same way I did. It astounded her. We simply couldn't believe it when we read *Ogonek*.[15] It became so interesting; there was so

---

15. A popular Soviet weekly magazine that became especially known for featuring the new journalism of glasnost during the Gorbachev era.

much information that simply had been off limits to us before. Then there were the novels of Aitmatov,[16] and the movies. For many years I belonged to a film club that watched movies, which, as they say, had sat on the censors' shelves for years. We were so overwhelmed by information that it was easy for me to accept the truth. I don't know about my mother because we didn't discuss it, but I know that she read everything with great interest. That is, unlike some, she didn't dismiss it as a bunch of lies. Not at all. She believed that in reality all of it was a long-term deception. They tried to force us to believe in those false idols.

After graduating in 1967 you enrolled at the Saratov Medical Institute, right?

Yes, and I graduated in 1973.

When did you meet your future husband?

We met when I was nineteen, and applied to get married when I was twenty. We got married the day after I turned twenty-one. My daughter was born when I was twenty-two.

Did you meet in med school?

No, he was from an altogether different crowd. The son of one of my mother's acquaintances had his friends over and we socialized for a long time. Ira Tsurkan and three guys from the Polytechnic Institute belonged to our crowd.[17] Well, some friends of the son of my mother's acquaintance showed up and among them was my future husband.

How did your husband influence you?

Perhaps not at all. Not at all. We lived together for twenty-four years and then divorced. Life drove a wedge between us. More precisely, perestroika did. As you know, when these difficulties started up factories began to shut down and people stopped getting paid.[18] That's very difficult for a family to live through. Basically, I was not only our main breadwinner, but also assumed the Soviet woman's double burden at home. You're probably unable to imagine how

---

16. Born in 1928, Chingiz Aitmatov is a Soviet author from Kyrgyzstan who boasts an international reputation. It is not clear to which of his works Kamaiurova is referring. It is possible that Kamaiurova is confusing him with persecuted writer Varlam Shalamov, author of haunting stories about the forced labor camps entitled *Kolyma Tales*.

17. Irina Semenovna Tsurkan graduated in 1967 from School No. 42 and also enrolled in the Saratov Medical Institute.

18. Many Saratov factories involved in the defense industry had a difficult time retooling after the end of the Communist period. Some cut back production and laid off workers or even ceased manufacturing.

hard that is. It's tough now, but it was even harder back then. In any event, such changes don't facilitate, rather, they perhaps do facilitate an improvement in family relations if everything else is going well and people are on good terms, but when things aren't so good, such changes draw people apart. The split grows wider and wider. But we nonetheless remain on good terms.

Olga Vladimirovna, I'd like to return to something you said earlier about the invasion of Czechoslovakia.

I only heard official information and interpreted it as the correct course of action for our country.

What about samizdat literature and the spread of the dissident movement in the 1970s?

It all passed me by. The word dissident was understood as some sort of swear word. It's terrible, simply terrible. How I regret that, back then, I was so far removed from people who understood everything. There were people who understood things already back then. It's a shame that I wasn't one of them.

What shaped the formation of your sense of self, of what today is called one's identity? You already explained that as a woman you had to endure a double burden. What else affected you? The word gender is popular today. How did the fact that you are a woman shape your life?

It's hard, very hard to be a woman. At least in our country. I recall my married years—I say this in all honesty—as a nightmare. Two children, all the household chores, and work. I couldn't afford to work only one shift, and was always moonlighting somewhere. Books and good movies saved me. I'm happy that I have a close girlfriend who has been my friend for thirty-four years. She also went to med school, but we studied in different departments. I can't speak for how she feels, but contact with her enriched me. And even now she and I are traveling the same path of spirituality. I thank fate, for there aren't many people who experience such happiness. Some people perhaps are blessed with meeting the love of their life, but for me it turned out to be a close friendship. Well, what can I say? Generally, I began to develop spiritually when my children started to grow up and I had a little time to breathe again. I began to read more, and I began to find God. I stopped feeling like a workhorse and like a household slave. Ever since then I've been on my own—well, I've not been alone, for I of course had, as you say, boyfriends. But I am not dependent upon anyone and no one can demand that I clean or put dinner on the table. You can't believe how much that frees you on a spiritual level. I now breathe freely and pity those [laughing] who haven't experienced this in their lives. It's perhaps strange for you to hear this from a woman. But I'm not altogether normal. A woman, after all, is supposed to appreciate the family and the home. But not me, I'm like a lonely wolf. I like being alone. I, of course, have my beloved children, my beloved granddaughter. In the end, these same household obligations remain. But I'm not dependent on anyone. This independence has probably become the defining feature of my life. Why did I choose an unusual specialty within medicine? I'm a pathologist. It was an American writer, Arthur Hailey, right, who wrote the book *The Final Diagnosis*?[19] Well that's my specialization, as a matter of fact, it's like checking up on the work of doctors. Life probably somehow brought me to this specialization. My thirst for independence, the fact that no one's supervising me, that we don't need anyone else, there's just the examination. In other fields of medicine you have other doctors and teaching faculty, but we're all alone. There are few of us in Saratov, only one or two in each hospital. You can imagine how few of us there are; we're a small but important group. You see, that's probably why things turned out like this for me.

Tell me about your first job after completing med school.

For the first two years I worked in a regional hospital in the town of Marx.[20] I wasn't assigned to Marx, but my husband was. I was a pediatrician there. However strange it may seem, I was very conscientious from the start. I had common sense and always got my work done. Our main doctor there appreciated me, even though I was still inexperienced. She tried to convince me to stay on when my husband and I decided to leave after two years. But our living conditions there were simply [laughing] quite out of the ordinary. We lived on the fourth floor of a large building without water, without heat, without indoor plumbing, but that's something you can't even imagine. We walked about inside in our winter clothes and hats. We slept in a miserable little room. . . . But it's hard for Americans to imagine our life, don't you agree? How can people live like that at the end of the twentieth century? It's probably hard for you to imag-

---

19. Born in Britain, novelist Arthur Hailey (1920–2004) lived and worked in Canada, the United States, and the Bahamas. *The Final Diagnosis* first appeared in 1959.

20. The town of Marx, formerly Katerinenstadt, is located about sixty kilometers from Saratov. One of the district centers of the former Volga German autonomous oblast, its population today is largely of German descent, since many Germans returned to their historical homeland following their rehabilitation.

ine my current dacha, too. It's so remote. To get to it [laughing], you have to make your way along paths, carrying in your knapsack all sorts of provisions, plus the cat under your arm. I've lived this way all my life, in such extreme conditions. Well, anyway, we returned to Saratov in 1975. By then I had already chosen this profession out of which I'd make my career: that of a pathologist. I worked in a hospital as a practicing pathologist, then they invited me to teach pathology at the Saratov Medical Institute. I taught for two years, and taught well, too. They appreciated me and intended for me to stay on. My mother was especially pleased, because she taught her entire life. She believed that there's nothing more interesting than a life of teaching and research. However, I, on the contrary, liked applied work. Just then they offered my husband an assignment in Romania as the trade representative for gas equipment. That was at the beginning of 1979. We spent 1979 and 1980 there.

Where did you live?

We lived in a small town in the Carpathian Mountains. A factory that made gas equipment was located there. We didn't live in a Russian colony, but among Romanians. We made some Romanian friends. There also were four families of our military-trade representatives. That is, there was a small community of Russians. We celebrated all holidays together, as if we were on a space ship together. You know the problems of compatibility. We had no other choice, no other possibilities. It was inevitable that we would spend our days off and holidays with them. It was all right. We got along. But when they asked my husband to stay on, I refused.

Did you work in Romania?

No, I didn't work there. I didn't have permission to work in Romanian hospitals, and there was no Russian organization in that town. I gave birth to our son there, and returned to the Soviet Union with a year-and-a-half-old child. That was when there was still a Soviet Union. I got comfortably settled in to work, although I once again was invited to teach. But I returned to applied medicine, and ever since have remained in the field.

How did the two-year stay in Romania affect you?

Well, there were far more opportunities to listen to foreign radio broadcasts there and we were there when they elected Bush. No, Reagan, right?

Yes, Reagan.

That's right, there were two candidates; Bush ran for vice president. We listened to Voice of America there quite openly. There was no interference. And one of the things people said was that if Reagan wins, there will be disarmament, even for the Soviet Union. But if Carter wins, there will be war. Perhaps I'm getting this mixed up? I do remember the alternative, that there will be war if one candidate wins, and peaceful development and an improvement in relations if the other does. I was in a panic. That is, I never got so upset during elections in our country as I did for the American presidential elections that year. Who will be elected? When, alas, they elected the more peace-loving candidate, it was simply, well, we celebrated.

Although it was Reagan who coined the expression "evil empire" and the like.

Nevertheless, that was the propaganda that we heard on Western radio broadcasts. We were really homesick and longed to return home. We had already forgotten all that was bad about it. After all, Romania is a foreign culture. That Latin culture—Italian, Romanian—it's not quite Western and it's not Russian. It's different from the others. We suffered during those two years when I raised our child.

What about the standard of living there?

Back then it was a lot higher than ours, and that's why I basically decided to give birth there. I thought, why should I sit there for two years in vain? And everything was in abundance in the stores there. Here, well, I don't think I'm revealing anything terrible [laughing], but here the stores were empty. Completely.

[Laughing] That's no secret.

Right, it's no secret. It was real torment. I remember when we saw sausage. My God, this probably is both funny and awful to hear. My father was a war invalid who fought through the whole ordeal. He got things through coupons, which he traded in once a month. Traded in! They gave him a pound of cooked sausage, a pound of smoked sausage, buckwheat groats, and tea. There was even a shortage of tea, which you didn't see in the stores. And this, while party officials got everything in abundance for mere pennies. Take the word "banana." I swear that I tried one for the first time when I was in Romania. Although I do recall that during my early childhood, when I was say five, six, and seven years old, I ate a jar of black caviar each day.[21] My parents could afford it. I remember how well stocked the stores were up until the beginning of the 1960s. We

---

21. During her childhood, caviar was indeed plentiful, particularly along the Volga.

had lots of things. Oh, the smells in the sausage shops! It was a gastronomical bacchanalia. How quickly it all changed and everything disappeared at the time of our departure for Romania. It was there that I recalled these childhood memories. In any event, I thought that it would be a sin to spend time sitting idly. It was probably most likely fate that gave me these years to care for my infant.

That is, here throughout the 1970s the food situation worsened?

It got worse. It's not true that this didn't happen.

Were there ups and downs or did things simply abruptly worsen?

It was all gradual. But I can't recall exactly when it all began. I remember when there was nothing in the stores, but everything was available at the farmers markets.[22] I had already started to work and was earning a living. You can't imagine how little Soviet doctors earned, the more so, because by then we had already purchased the cooperative apartment where I now live. For fifteen years, half my salary went to pay off the apartment. However, that's probably not unusual for apartments according to your criteria. Is housing also expensive in America?

Yes, very much so.

Yet at least I now have my own apartment. But those who received apartments free from the state also own their own apartments today. That is, things turned out the same. Yet we never had a chance in hell to receive one from the state. My mother's apartment was also paid for with her own money. My mother provided the down payment for us, after which I paid from my salary for fifteen years. I recall that there was nothing here. And when I saw such an abundance of stores in Romania, smelled the smells of my childhood, and saw chocolate, instant coffee, and, yes, toilet paper, well, you simply can't imagine how we used to live. Now it's different. At least the fear of going hungry is gone. Then we returned home from Romania. By the way, during our two years there the situation gradually became like it was here. In any event, we returned to coupons, and to lines thousands of people long in order to trade the coupons in, to rations once again. Frankly, it's terrible to recall this. I

---

22. Soviet peasants maintained small private plots on which they produced a substantial proportion of the country's food supply, selling their surpluses in farmers markets in urban centers. The quality of goods tended to be significantly higher than that of products found in state stores (if they were available at all), and were priced accordingly. Given the neighborhood in which they lived and their places of employment, the Kamaiurovs most likely frequented the central market near the university or the covered market on Kirov Prospect.

don't understand how some people remember the era of stagnation with fondness. I can't.[23]

It seems to me that those who remember the period fondly were those for whom it was easy to get things.

That's right, it's the commercial and party elite. Those who could, took advantage of it. Artists, too. Artists are talented people who went cap in hand to the dealers. And from the back door they gave them an entire sausage for a free pass to a popular show. But we lacked this possibility.

You were in Romania when the Solidarity movement in Poland started up.

However, I don't recall any information about it. I don't know Romanian, and I don't remember if we heard anything about it from Russia.

Did you travel around a bit while you were there? Did you visit Bucharest?

We often traveled to Bucharest to receive our pay. Once a month. We traveled to the Carpathians, but not to ski, since materially speaking it was not accessible to us there either. We simply went to see what we could. But not that often. I was still breast-feeding my infant son.

How did Romanians treat you?

Fine in the town where we lived. When we went to the capital it was a bit different. When we went shopping we experienced a certain arrogant attitude toward us. That's because as soon as we began to interact with them, it was clear that we were foreigners and also that we were from the Soviet Union. When they understood who we were we experienced a small amount of, well, contempt, a certain haughtiness. But ordinary people treated us kindly—and it was ordinary people that we mostly associated with. There was a doctor among our acquaintances, and workers from the factory where my husband worked.

You told me that once your children got a bit older you were able to find some time to read and to go to the movies. What are your favorite books and films?

You know, I can't say that I have favorites. I like the films they used to show at film clubs, that is, complicated, sophisticated films not for ordinary viewers. They showed us lots of such films, includ-

---

23. A reference to the Brezhnev years, 1964–82.

ing, my heavens, Fellini and Antonioni. It was like food for us movie lovers. There was a short lecture before each film. They chewed it for us, placed it in our mouths, and we only had to swallow. In general, I acquired a taste for good, sophisticated, intelligent, unusual movies. But I can't recall the names of specific films right now. There were so many of these clubhouse films. I didn't even go to the movie theaters to see them. Sometimes, when they picked some sensational film, I would think, my heavens, this is so extraordinary. That taste for good movies has remained.

As for books, I read a great deal of them. My parents had an excellent library of all the Soviet classics. I read a lot. I can't recall them all. Well, in particular, there's Harper Lee's *To Kill a Mockingbird.* I really love that book. Then there's the British writer, Evelyn Waugh. There are so many of them, but not bestsellers. More recently [laughing], well, one of my mother's acquaintances, a very smart woman who now lives in Israel, a professor with a doctorate, said, "It's shameful to admit, but I love detective stories." I'm also ashamed to say, but I came to like them too. And also fantasy. That is, that which doesn't weigh down the mind, however strange that seems.

Now, if they come my way, I read good detective stories, fantasy, and historical literature, especially mysticism. I read Castaneda, Rampa.[24] Recently I read only Osho. Bhagwan Shree Rajneesh, or Osho, an Indian mystic.[25] He's so extraordinarily intelligent; his mind is all embracing. I began with one of his books that I came across by chance. I had a sort of, well, when we returned from Romania, no, actually later, at the beginning of the 1990s. Perestroika had begun and I grew estranged from my husband. The situation at home was strained and we were in awful economic straits. I was depressed. I searched for a way to overcome it. Now I understand that it began with this [laughing]. Don't think that I'm strange. I'm absolutely normal. After all, people find God differently. For me, it was probably that my life got as bad as it could possibly get, and I found myself attending some classes. A Chinese—a real Chinese—from some university came to Saratov. He taught Tsigun, one of the movements of Tsigun, or energizing meditation. I ended up

24. Tuesday Lobsang Rampa is a Tibetan monk who writes about the Tibetan Lamaism tradition.
25. Bhagwan Shree Rajneesh (1931–1990) was born Rajneesh Chandra Mohan in central India.

at these classes for the first time. It was very expensive, but a male acquaintance of mine loaned me the money. It cost several months' salary. It was beyond my means, but I wanted it so badly, and when a person wants something so badly it's sent to them. This money was given to me unexpectedly and I ended up at the lessons. It all began with small things. I was given some sort of booklet, a purely informational one about Buddhist monks. And it gradually drew me into this world of the East. You know, it's unusual. These Eastern religions are all quite different—Daoism, Confucianism—yet they're so unlike our religion. They're so radiant and joyful. Regarding Osho, he wrote so many books that if you go into one of our book stores it will seem to you that half the shelves are filled with his works. Osho is his pseudonym. His personality, well, you know, his portraits reveal his radiant face. He's unusual. His eyes shine. He has the face of a subtly intelligent, unusual person. He's now dead. During his last years he had an ashram in America. He was persecuted for some reason, but I don't recall why.[26] I first came across his book, *Meditation: The Art of Ecstasy,* which somehow didn't interest me. At that time this was too far removed from my everyday life. But gradually I became drawn to him.

In 1990, I ended up in an advanced medical training course in Erevan.[27] I was also in advanced training courses in Tashkent.[28] I simply got lucky and got to go for lengthy periods. I lived in Tashkent for a month. It's an entirely different culture, and of course it's an unusual, interesting city. Then I was in Erevan, and twice in Leningrad. That's the love of my life. I always dreamed of living there. Well, anyway, I was in Erevan right after the terrible earthquake,[29] and your fellow countrymen, Americans, arrived to teach the Armenians meditation as a form of humanitarian aid. What's it called? Transcendental meditation. Actually it now interests me little, but at the time that was also a breakthrough to the East. The Americans instructed us in English through a translator. Of course, much, the very charm of this language, was lost as a result. But we attended the sessions with pleasure. We lucked out, because they were free

---

26. In 1981, Osho moved his ashram community to Antelope, Oregon, where it soon sparked enormous controversy. The ashram's unusual lifestyle and reports of all sorts of abuses resulted in Osho's arrest and deportation on charges of immigration fraud.

27. Then the capital of Soviet Armenia.

28. The capital of Soviet Uzbekistan.

29. The earthquake occurred in 1988.

since they were a form of humanitarian aid. It was hard to get in, but the classes were conducted at our institute for the advanced training of doctors. From that moment on, well, from there I ended up with the Chinese. And then I gradually got drawn more and more to the East. In the first book I read of Osho's, I came across his understanding of Orthodoxy, of Christianity. It's so odd that Christianity doesn't appeal to me. After all, we live in a Christian country and I should be drawn to that religion, but they altered it basically for the needs of the priests. It frightens people, it weighs heavily on them. It's such a strict religion—standing in churches for hours during a service, while they threaten you with hell and terrible punishments. Osho interprets Christianity not as something radiantly joyous but as something that's been radically changed by the clergy. This attracted me so much that I later began to read his books, where he explains all the world's religions. Except, perhaps, I haven't yet read what he has to say about Islam. He explains Daoism, Confucianism, and other Eastern religions. It's all so interesting. You get so absorbed in these books that for many years I didn't read any world literature, but only those books about mysticism. I simply lived them.

Now I'm once again beginning to read world literature a bit, and detective stories. In particular it's my son who pushed me in this direction. He reads while he's eating. I look and he's reading John Fowles's *The Collector*.[30] If I'm not mistaken, they've even made movies of his books. I read him for the first time. I came across his first novel. It wasn't bad. Well, now I want to read and to watch things that don't burden my consciousness, because such books drain you spiritually and emotionally. That's why I want to read foreign literature that's on the light side. The same is true of movies. As for the film clubs, I don't think they exist any longer. Perhaps they do, but I haven't heard of them.

I sensed that you had fallen under the influence of Eastern ideas when you told me that you don't live in the past or in the future, but only in the present.

You know, that's not the influence of these religions. I have the feeling that I was that way since childhood. I never regret the past and don't recall things with nostalgia. Perhaps that's why I'm not drawn to meet with my classmates. All that's in the past. That stage

---

30. Born in 1926, English author John Fowles published his first novel, *The Collector*, in 1963. This cerebral novel is a mix of thriller and analysis of class conflict.

in life is over. It's completed, that's all. I'm drawn to them in the same way I am to my relatives. You know, I look at them and I think, my heavens, we know each other for almost fifty years. They're all my brothers and sisters. Irina[31] and I also studied together at medical school, but then I have to say that our paths parted. And for a while we, well, we weren't exactly enemies, but our relationship grew strained, to put it mildly. But now I also look upon her as a relative. And the boys in our class, they've grown bald and have put on weight. You've seen Virich.[32] He's a real Karl Marx [laughing]. He always was. Or did you see him after he cut his hair?

I met him last year after he cut his hair.

He had a real head of hair; he looked like Karl Marx. He had a full beard, a bushy moustache. It's now all turned gray. He's had a stroke. My heavens, I look at him, and, well, we've all changed a great deal, of course.

Olga Vladimirovna, I'd like to return to a point we discussed earlier. Things got worse in a material sense in the 1970s in regard to what was available in the grocery stores. But what about at work? Did things get worse there, too, materially speaking? Or wasn't that felt as much? That is, could you carry out your work under normal conditions?

Well, when I returned from Romania with my son things were okay at first, for the first seven years, that is, up until the start of perestroika. As a matter of fact, I happened to ask my son today, "Zhenia, when was the last time that the two of us went to the Black Sea, was it in 1986?" Since 1986 I haven't been able to afford any vacations. They've become off limits for me. They're possible, everything's now possible, but only if you have the money. My income doesn't allow me much of anything. That is, since the beginning of perestroika our material situation has worsened.

But what about at work before perestroika? What was the situation in regard to equipment and medicines. Did things worsen?

Yes. That was during the years just before perestroika. Yet everything was free back then. If someone got sick, I could ask for, and they gave me, the necessary medications. But in recent years everything's gotten so complicated and is based on money.

Was it hard for you to go back to work when you returned from Romania? Did you get your old job back or did you have to hunt for a new job?

---

31. A reference to Irina Semenovna Tsurkan, mentioned earlier.
32. Aleksandr Grigorievich Virich, whom I interviewed in the summer of 2002.

Three young men from group B at a May Day or November 7 (anniversary of the Russian Revolution) celebration, most likely in 1966. Aleksandr Kutin, on the right, was one of the first to learn to play the guitar. *Courtesy A. A. Konstantinov.*

No, we knew the situation in Saratov like the back of our hand. I knew where there were vacancies. I showed up and they took me back where I had worked before, where I had started to work within my specialty, in that collective.

As an adult, what was your attitude toward China, let's say before perestroika?

You know, we used to make fun of them.

You weren't afraid of them?

No, I never was afraid. That's how official propaganda represented China to us, and that's how we regarded the place.

What about Cuba?

Regarding Cuba, well the Caribbean crisis was terrible, of course. With the benefit of hindsight we now know how terrible it really was; after all, we were on the brink of nuclear war. But we didn't know the whole truth back then, and Cuba was so far away that we, well, I'm speaking for myself now, I honestly was afraid of America. And you were probably afraid of us. We were like monkeys with grenades, as they say. Primitive man with an atomic bomb in his hands. Of course, our country is an altogether crazy one that's driven its intelligentsia to such dire straits: doctors, engineers, and the creative elite—actors, artists, those who work in our museums. We're practically destitute. Few could endure what we put up with. Businessmen are an altogether different breed, of course. Basically it's very hard. I can't adjust to the new life, and for that reason I'm destitute. I probably adapt to new situations poorly. There are people who readily adapt to change and quickly find for themselves a so-called ecological niche. I haven't. Therefore, I continue to work as before and the circle . . . of my interests, of my possibilities, grows smaller. But my needs remain as before. I'd love to be able to travel. Especially with age. More and more, I want to see things I haven't seen, but I'm able to do so less and less.

Were you in other countries apart from Romania?

I was in East Germany as a tourist in 1976 before I went to Romania.

How did that trip affect you? The living standard was much higher.

I was astounded, of course. But at the same time I understood that they deserved their standard of living. We deserved what we had, and they deserved what they had.

Is that how you saw things at the time?

Yes, yes. They're hard working and they love their little country. I think that our country is probably too large. And we're too, well, it's so big that we allow ourselves to deforest it and to pollute our rivers. There are always more forests and more rivers left. But, when a country's smaller, people simply take better care of it. Or perhaps it's just our Russian way of thinking. For the most part we're careless. If each of us, well, if you've read Bulgakov's *Heart of a Dog* you'd remember the line that decline sets in once people begin to relieve themselves on the floor alongside the toilet.[33] And that's literally what happened. People literally, not figuratively, relieved themselves wherever they wished, in any entranceway. My best friend lived in an old merchant-style house built before the Revolution. First they raised the height of it and made it five stories. It had brass doorknobs and very pretty awnings above the entrances with grates made of iron. The metal stairway was also lovely and had

---

33. Mikhail Bulgakov (1891–1940) was a distinguished Soviet author who did not emigrate. By 1930 his works were barred from publication. *Heart of a Dog* satirizes attempts to make the new Soviet man and woman.

interlacing steps and wrought iron balusters that held up the banisters. And there were flowers at the entrance. That is, people loved their apartments and took care of what was outside them. Nowadays things are probably really nice inside people's apartments, but people don't give a damn about anything outside it. In any event, people made off with the brass doorknobs and everything else. It's all been vandalized. Everything's broken and falling apart. Such is our country. It simply can't climb out of this ruin. As people used to say, the most powerful cannon in the world was the one on the Battleship *Aurora*.[34] It fired one blank shot, and then rotted away for decades [laughing].

Like the Tsar-Kolokol [laughing].[35]

Yes, like the Tsar-Kolokol.

In all societies myths help to unite people. Can you tell me about the myths in Soviet society? That is, as a child you believed in the system. Did this faith in the system continue or did it weaken over the years?

Do you mean faith in the ideals of communism? It collapsed, not gradually, but it came crashing down with the advent of information.

What about before then? That is, during the Gorbachev era they began referring to the Brezhnev years as a period of stagnation. Did you begin to lose faith in the system already back then?

No, although by the time we had become adults the slogans found on buildings seemed silly to us: "Communism is our goal." "Communism is the radiant future." But I especially remember reading something by one of our Soviet authors, *The Island of Crimea*, by, my goodness . . .

By Aksenov.[36]

Yes, by Aksenov. I remembered that his name began with an A. Overall, I've begun to forget lots of things, and I had read this so long ago. In any event, he describes his route from the airport to

---

34. This is a reference to the October Revolution of 1917. Anchored in Petrograd's Neva River with its guns fixed on the Winter Palace, the Battleship *Aurora* fired a blank round from its bow to intimidate the forces inside the palace defending the Provisional Government. The *Aurora* later served as a sort of shrine to the Revolution.

35. Tsar-Kolokol, or Tsar Bell, was cast in 1735. It cracked soon afterward and has never been rung. Weighing some 223 tons, the bell is on display on the grounds of the Kremlin.

36. Born in 1932 and exiled from the Soviet Union in 1980, Vasilii Aksenov got his start in the USSR by publishing stories of disaffected youth. He taught at George Mason University in Virginia until his recent retirement.

the city and all the slogans he passes. My God, it seemed to me, all those slogans were a bunch of gibberish. However, we had grown accustomed to seeing them. Even now on the building where I live there is written in brick relief "Peace to the World." What does this mean? But that's how it was. On the neighboring building in meter-high letters was written "Communism is our goal." We grew accustomed to it; it was part of our everyday prosaic existence. We didn't even notice. The hammer and sickle were everywhere. Perhaps it even seemed a bit funny. But then, with the advent of information, it all caved in and I saw the light. Good heavens, where had I been earlier? Where were my eyes, my ears, my brain? How could we fall for all this nonsense?

Did your husband also have a change of heart back then?

He was always a Communist. He joined the party because he served in the army. He had to join. That was the situation back then. However, I never, they never asked me, rather, they invited me to join when I began working. I can't really explain it, but . . . the very idea was unpleasant to me. I didn't need it and, if they had begun to pressure me, I would have categorically, I would have found some way to worm my way out of it. However, my husband joined and I respected him a good deal when we became acquainted. He was five years older than me; he was a grown up, a Communist. And I was especially smitten [laughing] by the fact that he was a Communist. I really wasn't in love with him. I simply respected him. Later I understood that he was the same as I was. He was also in a state of stupor. He too had been deceived. Well, yes, we came to see the light together, but perhaps it wasn't so painful for him. It's simply that women are more emotional, and, you know, I took the recovery of my sight hard. I was so ashamed that I hadn't seen the obvious, that I hadn't understood what was going on.

How did you react to the invasion of Afghanistan at the end of the 1970s?

I accepted the official version that they put out. I now understand that it was just like the Americans in Vietnam. But the main thing for me, what year was that in?

In 1979–80.

That was exactly when my son was born. And for some reason I lived in such fear during those years that I actually was sick over the fact that our boys were dying there. They sent our eighteen-year-old boys over there and they were dying by the hundreds. Many were maimed. It was terrible. I simply didn't understand that our country was guilty. However, the fact that we lived peacefully here, with the sun shining over our heads, made me anxious. Basically I've always feared war, because I was born in 1950 and there were so many films and books about World War II. I can't even begin to convey to you how much I feared war. Consequently, I couldn't imagine, since we lived under a clear blue sky, that there was war going on somewhere else, that people were suffering, that people were dying, dying with children in their arms. This terrified me. However, back then I didn't understand that we had started the war, that we had invaded another country. It was terrible. And all those years I feared new wars, namely as a mother who is raising a future soldier. I was in a panic. Fortunately, he came down with an illness that gave him a military deferment. But when his deferment ends? All that time I thought that things would change in eighteen years, that they'd set up a volunteer army, that there wouldn't be any more wars. Twenty years is a long time, and nothing's changed. New wars have flared up, even within the country, civil wars. And they're as terrifying, since our boys are cannon fodder.

Why do you believe perestroika occurred?

It was time. Yes, just as the time had come for a Khrushchev, the time had come for a Gorbachev. Everyone says Gorby, Gorby, he got things moving. But it wasn't he. He was simply a pawn in the hands of higher forces. When the need came for such a man, he surfaced. If it hadn't been he, someone else would have emerged on the scene and would have gotten things moving. Someone always appears at the right time. Personality is not important. He simply showed up at the right place at the right time.

You've already told me a bit about how your life has changed during the past twelve years or so. How has your life changed since the onslaught of perestroika? For better or for worse, materially speaking, and also in a spiritual sense? How do you evaluate the changes? What did perestroika give Russia?

I can't say what perestroika gave Russia, but I know what it gave me. At least we're no longer the brainless, blind robots we were. I at least have become informed. I can draw some conclusions on my own, and I've become psychologically free. Do you understand? Perhaps I don't get enough information—honestly speaking, I generally avoid the news. That is, I now, well, there's been so much negative information that . . . I, well, it turns out that I, of course, watch the news from time to time and hear something unpleasant.

On the whole I have a good understanding of what's going on, and that's a good feeling. I believe that perestroika changed my personal life for the better. Well, even if it's materially worse, perhaps that's actually better, for if things had been better materially, I would not have made progress in the spiritual realm. You know, the material and the spiritual, by rule, conserve energy. When one grows smaller, the other grows larger. The better the material side of things, the less need there is for the spiritual. The fact that we're limited materially, well, that probably also made us advance spiritually. And that's probably not a bad thing for Russia, because I know that today many people are in quest of the spiritual, of God. And the goal of anyone's life is to find God. Along different paths. Each chooses for himself an acceptable one.

To what extent do your children share your assessment of perestroika? That is, you at least weren't in the know. But how did they make sense of all that happened, of the collapse of the Soviet Union?

You know, I haven't discussed these things with them. But my son's a smart lad. Very smart. He's altogether without hang-ups, or so it seems to me. He's free. And this life is fine for him. He probably would have had a rough time back in the Soviet Union. We were kept harnessed. Things are hard for him right now financially; he's making his own way in life. My daughter gave birth, and she's more materially minded. Although she believes in God, she's utilitarian minded enough. She's consumed by daily life. But my son's free and it seems to me that our young people today are far better off than we were.

How would your answers to these questions have differed had I asked them before perestroika?

I'm not sure, but, you know, there was fear in our family, probably a leftover of Stalin's personality cult, and I probably would have been somewhat afraid. I'm generally afraid. I'm afraid of physical assault, I'm afraid of prison, I'm afraid of all sorts of deprivations. And perhaps this fear would have partially scared me. There would have been some things that I probably would have been apprehensive about saying.

I'd like to change the subject. One historian has argued that the enormous flood of people from the villages into the cities during the first five-year plan turned the cities into big villages. Would you agree with this?

Yes, in part. And who remained in the cities? They killed the majority, the greater part at least of the better-educated people. The gene pool's been depleted. Who is giving birth today? The descendants of Bulgakov's Sharikovs.[37] The elite, the intelligentsia, those who could, they left. Those who couldn't leave rotted away in the camps. As a result, the composition of our people has changed. And they learned how to adapt themselves well. Especially those from the villages, for, you know, they're so tenacious. I mean that they adapt in a material sense. They know how to establish themselves and their children. But we probably shun the masses a bit. Saratov is out and out Americanizing? Why do we need all those signs everywhere in English? Those ads everywhere? That's not us. It's all alien. It's not our culture. The Iron Curtain has fallen, and now we . . .

I can't imagine how things could have turned out any other way. And take the younger generation for whom all this is familiar. If the young turn on TV and see these things, they grow accustomed to them.

Yes, it usually does evolve around daily life.

I wanted to ask how your life story can help me understand the fate of the Soviet Union.

I don't know, concretely, for I'm probably not typical. Well, actually, that's not the case. [I'm representative] of the intelligentsia that has a hard time adapting itself to changes, to circumstances, and finds itself in spirituality, in the search for God. But that's probably not true of everyone in my generation. It's true of individuals, like me. You've met with others. I'm probably a bit different, right? Have you noticed that or not?

You know, I think everyone feels that way. Maybe it has something to do with our age. I feel the same way myself.

I feel as if we belong to a somewhat lost generation. We're at the turn of an epoch. We've left one, but it's hard for us to enter the new one because our conditioning took place during the old one. It's hard to change one's way of thinking. One's way of thinking is basically formed during childhood, during one's youth. Our stereotypes have been destroyed, but it's very hard to create new ones. It's hard to adapt oneself to changing circumstances. But, nevertheless, we go on.

Have I asked you about everything that you would like to tell me? What have I forgotten?

Perhaps nothing. What else can I tell you? Nothing. We've

---

37. Sharikov was the crude "new" Soviet man in Bulgakov's satirical novella *Heart of a Dog,* in whom a dog's heart beat.

touched upon all the basic milestones in my life. There was much about my life that was hard. There are people who had a happier fate, and those who had a harder one than me. That is, statistically speaking, I've had an average life. True, there have been many deaths among those close to me, both relatives and friends. In this regard, I've had a great deal of personal grief to endure. But that's all right. If you reflect upon it, I'm a happy person. I have children, my granddaughter is growing up, my mother is still alive. As long as my mother is alive it's as if I'm still a child. I'm not yet an orphan, right?

7. "I came to understand things, but only gradually" | Aleksandr Vladimirovich Trubnikov

August 10, 2003, by telephone

Like A. A. Konstantinov, whose interview opens this volume and who graduated at the top of his class in group B, Aleksandr Vladimirovich Trubnikov received a gold medal for the most distinguished academic record among those in group A. His classmates spoke fondly of him, insisting that he would be an informative and engaging interviewee. From them I learned that he not only was a brilliant student, but also a skilled athlete, and a hit with the girls in his class. It ultimately did not prove difficult to track him down, but what I learned about his whereabouts posed logistical problems for me: Aleksandr Vladimirovich had emigrated and now resides in the Israeli city of Petakh Tikva, where he works for a foreign firm, Bordeaux Digital Printink. Five of the fifty-eight members of the class of 1967 now live abroad. Trubnikov is the only male in the group to have left Russia, and the only one to have immigrated to Israel. When I established contact with him via e-mail, he readily agreed to the idea of my interviewing him over the phone. Beforehand, I called him to become better acquainted. I conducted the interview from my home in Chapel Hill, North Carolina.

Although I initially felt the obvious drawbacks of not interviewing him in person and fumbled with the controls on my tape recorder to achieve an appropriate volume level, we nonetheless established a real rapport. In this regard the interview did not seem much different from many others I had conducted. Following the interview, Aleksandr Vladimirovich good-naturedly responded in writing to several additional questions that came to mind when I studied the text version of our conversation. He also scanned several photographs for me.

Unlike most of the pupils enrolled in School No. 42, Aleksandr Trubnikov ended up there somewhat by chance and not as the result of his parents' intervention. After graduating in 1967, he enrolled in the physics department at Saratov University, took his undergraduate and graduate degrees there, and went on to work as a research scholar at his home university until his emigration. A quick, insightful, and witty respondent, Trubnikov recounts how effective the Soviet system and the values instilled in him by his family were in turning him into a true believer. Yet all of this would change, and it is his journey of self-discovery that becomes the defining frame of his interview.

In what ways does Trubnikov's life story help us understand both the successes and failures of the Soviet system? What caused him to question his beliefs and eventually to become critical of the system in which he lived? Why did he decide to leave Russia for Israel? How might his decision to leave Russia have colored his memory of his life there? Is it possible to live without an ideology?

I was born in Saratov into a military family. My father served in the military as an engineer. Let's put it like that. He worked at a factory in Saratov. Saratov was not the first city my parents lived in. People in the military moved around a lot. But, after the war, he arrived in Saratov, began to work, and in 1950 had a son. That's me. I also have a sister who is five years older than I am. Thus the entire family lived in Saratov. Up until the age of seven I had an ordinary childhood. It would be hard to say that anything distinguished my childhood from all the rest, because so much time has elapsed since then, but my memories are good ones. Ours was a close-knit family and our parents loved us and took care of us. And I turned out to be normal and happy.

Was your father from Saratov? Was he born there?

No. My parents were born in Rostov-on-the-Don.[1] My father often ended up in the environs of Rostov and it was there that he

---

1. The city of Rostov, with a population of roughly one million, is the eleventh-largest city in Russia today. Founded in 1780, it is situated on the Don River some forty kilometers from where it empties into the Sea of Azov. Rostov is an important industrial and railroad center and also a critical river port. During World War II, the Nazis seized and occupied the city (1942–43).

Aleksandr Vladimirovich
Trubnikov at the time
of the interview, August
2003. *Courtesy A. V.
Trubnikov.*

met my mother. They got married, but then the war began, and he
was drafted. After being reunited with my mother, they were sent
to live in various cities throughout the country. Then they moved to
Saratov. For them, Saratov was but one of the cities they had lived
in, but for me it's my hometown.

*Who among the adults in your life influenced you most when you were
growing up?*

That's a tough question, but it probably was my mother. It seems
to me books and music also. . . . We had an international family.
My mother was a Jew and my father a Russian. As I now understand things, that also affected our life, but back then this wasn't so
obvious, because in the Soviet Union the nationality question out-
wardly didn't exist. But in reality it did. However, since my father
was Russian and my surname was not Jewish, everyone took me
for a Russian. I didn't experience what many others did who had
Jewish surnames. There was a big difference. The most interesting
thing is that, here in Israel, I'm a Jew because my mother is Jewish.
Nationality comes from your mother's side; therefore I'm a Jew here.
But in Russia everyone considered me a Russian, and that's what's
written in my passport. That's probably why I never experienced any
consequences of my being half-Jewish. However, my Israeli passport
indicates that I'm a Jew.

Did your mother experience any discrimination?

Well, for one thing, let's begin with the fact that she experienced not only discrimination, but when war broke out, well, as you know, the Germans were in Rostov. She was evacuated from Rostov. She left on foot. Her family lost all its property. Her father was in the army. They saw their share of suffering because of their nationality. But, no, I wouldn't say that she experienced any discrimination. She worked in her field. She had a college education. She graduated from an institute in Novocherkassk, not far from Rostov. She and my father studied there and met there. No, I don't think it was discrimination back then. In general, this is a complicated question. Besides, she was a woman. She didn't need to hold any top positions. She didn't need to join the party. It was the men who in fact experienced discrimination. She held a not very high position and worked as an electrician and therefore there was no discrimination to be experienced. She didn't aspire to hold an important post. Moreover, her husband was Russian.

Did your mother stay home to take care of you when you were very young or did she work?

She worked. Back then women didn't stay home with their kids. I went to a nursery school, like most children. I had grandmothers, but since we lived far away from them they didn't sit with us. They visited, and I went to a nursery. Back then they had round-the-clock nurseries where parents could leave their kids during the week. People believed that the most important thing was work, and that children needed to grow up as part of the collective. I went to nursery school each day, too, but I didn't spend the nights there, because my parents didn't work shifts. I grew up like all children.

When you were a child did you also travel to visit your grandmothers? Did they both live in Rostov?

We visited them, and they came to see us. My maternal grandmother lived in Rostov, but my paternal grandmother lived in Stavropol.[2] She lived with my father's sister, and my maternal grandmother lived with my mother's sister. My mother came from a large family of three children. Her brother, my uncle, now lives near New York, and my mother's sister lived in New York until her death two years ago. I used to stay with him when I visited [Rostov]. But that

---

2. Today the city of Stavropol has a population of roughly 330,000 and is the administrative center of Stavropol region, situated on the northern range of the Caucasus Mountains. Rostov oblast borders Stavropol in the north.

was long ago. By the way, my aunt moved to New York with her husband in 1995 or 1996, following her daughter who, in turn, moved there with her son. She had lived all her life in Rostov-on-the-Don, in the building where my mother was born. She was an epidemiologist, a doctor of medical sciences, a very intelligent and accomplished woman.

What were you interested in as a child?

Apart from all sorts of games, I loved to read. I learned how to read when I was five and I have loved to read ever since. I'm a fast reader, and I can read twenty pages an hour in Russian. I read slower in English. I've read an awful lot of books in my life, beginning with the ABC's. Besides the games kids play, I also was interested in sports. It was nothing special.

Where did you live in Saratov back then?

We lived near the Volga, on Lenin Prospect, which is now called Moscow Street, in a building that housed the Saratov city library. It's a well-known building that back then belonged to the factory where my father worked. At first there were communal flats there. They're an amazing thing. A creation of the Soviet system. I don't believe they exist anywhere else in the world. There were large apartments comprising several rooms in that building. Our family was given a single room at first. We had three families for neighbors. Then living conditions gradually began to get better and eventually we lived in our own flat. That's a major lifetime event for a Soviet family to live in a communal flat and then receive its own apartment. It was cause for real celebration. People fought to get this, and some died still living in communal apartments, of course.

Many interviewees told me about all the time they spent in the courtyard of the building where they grew up.

Of course. Where else could we play? It certainly had its own rules. Why? Because the building was packed with people. Several families inhabited each apartment, and all of them had lots of children; therefore the courtyard was packed with kids. The children grouped together by age. We played with each other, and fought with each other, all according to rules of the street. There were young criminals there who smoked what today is called marijuana. But back then we called it anash, or hash. The words have the same root. Hemp grows everywhere. It's probably the same in America. It's very widespread, a weed that you can pick anywhere. They used to sell it for pennies, which meant that anyone could try it.

How old were you when you first smoked it?

I was probably around eight—not that old! For the most part, I truly disliked it. The problem was that it was of really poor quality. Perhaps if it had been of better quality, my life would have turned out differently [laughing]!

Did it seem to you that the phenomenon was widespread or was it the exception, something peculiar to where you lived?

Well, our courtyard was not all that far from what was considered the center of Saratov's criminal world, Glebuchev Ravine.[3] And all sorts of people lived there, not exactly the dregs of society, but. . . . Therefore, the influence came from there. I can't say what it was like in other parts of the city, but I rubbed shoulders with those who came from there, almost all of whom ended up in jail. They're probably no longer alive. The living standard was altogether different there. We lived modestly, but our building was nonetheless better, because the factory supported us. The factory paid our wages. By the way, it made refrigerators, "Saratov."

How old were you when your parents received a separate apartment?

I don't know for certain. I was about thirty. I already lived on my own. It was sometime around 1980. My parents were already spent. They were sixty-five years old, but they nonetheless received their own apartment [laughing]. Even now there are lots of communal flats in Saratov.

Why did your parents select School No. 42 for you?

It wasn't a matter of their selecting it. I ended up there completely by chance, unlike the majority of those who were in class with me and in the parallel class. I went to school when I was eight years old, to a regular, ordinary neighborhood school, which was located in the courtyard of the building we lived in, and where, of course, the kids in our yard went. My older sister graduated from there. I went there for first grade, and I was a good student, I recall, a straight-A student. When I finished the first grade, I have to say in all honesty, I didn't know anything about School No. 42. It was far away from where we lived and I had never heard of it. My parents knew of it, but in a very roundabout way. We didn't know anyone who went there. But when we finished first grade our teacher from the elementary school, who was very good, received an offer to teach at School No 42. And she, well they allowed her to pick two students from her class to take with her, and she picked a girl and me. She discussed this with my parents. Frankly, they at first weren't

---

3. Historically, the Glebuchev Ravine district has been one of the poorest, least developed, and most dangerous neighborhoods in Saratov.

keen on the idea, because they would have to take me to school. The school was far away. It was a magnet school for the entire city. Then there was the problem of work shifts. However, my mother insisted that I be given a chance in life. That's how I ended up there. As for how the others got there, I can't say [laughing]. I suspect that it wasn't easy. Yes, the other pupil—Rozanova—and I ended up there by chance. And frankly, at first we didn't like it all that much. For one thing, I had friends at the other school and already belonged to the collective. Everyone who lived in our building went there. And to all of a sudden wind up in an altogether different environment . . . Then, too, I had to travel far to get there and I didn't like the other kids. But then I got used to the place.

How would you describe the school and the class and national composition of its pupils?

From the very start it was clear that the school was indeed a special one. As far as I understand, those who went there did so because of who their parents were. Moreover, the situation is the same today. After all, nothing ever changes in Russia. My daughter went there. Probably the kids who go there now do so not so much because of who their parents are but because of how much money they make. Yes, that's absolutely right. The teachers, as I now understand but didn't back then, well, I now understand that the teachers behaved accordingly, let's put it like this. And the children were different. Yet you have to give Soviet power credit. It prohibited having children driven to school. This was simply not acceptable. Well, there were two times when kids were brought in fancy cars that one wouldn't even see in America. However, back then there was equality and brotherhood [laughing]. Well, at least they kept up the appearance. Of course, I came to understand this only later. But back then, well, children are children. It was hard to grasp the particulars. For the most part, we took an active interest in things and all marched on Red Square, so to speak. Didn't we? Only a small percentage of people [felt otherwise], and this didn't concern me in the least. You have to give credit to propaganda. I, for example, and many of my friends, too, even believed in socialism, further still, in communism, which was even more special. I even remember arguing with my friend, Nemchenko,[4] whom you've interviewed, whether we'd each have a personal helicopter in 1980, by which time we'd have built

---

4. Vladimir Ivanovich Nemchenko made a fortune, and lost it, following the collapse of the USSR.

Aleksandr Vladimirovich Trubnikov and Vladimir Nikolaevich Kirsanov in their school uniforms preparing to clean their classroom, probably in 1962. *Courtesy A. V. Trubnikov.*

communism, as Nikita Sergeevich Khrushchev promised. I still remember this. I remember very well how natural this seemed back then. I now see that our childhood minds were so tainted that we believed that we'd have a bright future. It's great that at least now I understand that they duped a huge part of the population. You need to have real talent to do so. And the propaganda organs especially affected young people. As far as I know, there was no one in our class or in the parallel class who was in fact able to see things for what they were. Those who vote for the Communists [today], and that's a quarter of the population of Russia [laughing], are like I was back in the tenth grade. When I read Lenin's own writings, I remember how, during exams, I'd say that each cook must learn how to run the government.[5] We were all at an impressionable age.

---

5. During the Revolution, Lenin made what would become an oft-cited remark that "any cook should be able to run the country."

Please tell me about your favorite teachers and subjects, and about your friends.

All right. I always liked our physics teacher. I think his name was Mikhail Dmitrievich. He was loud mouthed and very lively. He taught physics well. It probably was because of him that I studied physics in college. I think everyone has favorite teachers, and I remember him well. I even remember his name, which for me is something since I have trouble remembering other things. Of course, we had a homeroom teacher who taught us English, Rappoport, who was very intense. I remember her well because we had English so often and because she was our homeroom teacher. We kept in touch with her until recently. As for friends, well, as in all classes, people were divided into, well, it's hard to say why this is the case, but you know that it's hard to explain why someone becomes your friend and why someone else doesn't. It's like marriages made in heaven. And therefore, my friends, well, perhaps we simply lived near each other. There was Nemchenko, and also Bobrov, Valentin Evgenievich.[6] We were close because they lived nearby. That was especially true of Nemchenko. We went to school together. There was another group comprised of Kirsanov and a few other guys.[7] But for the most part, I don't think that there was anything special about life at school that merits attention. That is, probably everyone had favorite teachers and friends, everyone had a life. However, one thing that we had that other schools didn't was that during the summer we vacationed together on the Volga with our friends. With Zhenia Meier, whose name is now Podolskii.[8] We're close friends, even now. Probably he's the only one from my class with whom I've remained close. And Zhenia and I along with the others vacationed on the Volga. No other school in Saratov had anything like this. It wasn't because we were a special English-language school, but because we lucked out with our physical education teacher. The memories I have of this are wonderful ones. I often recall how we kids camped together, for a month on end, on an island in the

----

6. Vladimir Ivanovich Nemchenko. Both Nemchenko and Bobrov graduated with Trubnikov in 1967.

7. Vladimir Nikolaevich Kirsanov received a silver medal in 1967 and enrolled in the Saratov Medical Institute. I interviewed him in 2002.

8. Evgenii Mikhailovich Meier belonged to group A as well. When it was time to issue him an adult passport, his parents decided he should take his mother's maiden name, because it would not identify him as being Jewish. Today Evgenii Mikhailovich is a successful businessman in Moscow.

Volga. The water was so clean that you could drink it, imagine that! I drank right out of the river. I drank and swam on. You'd swim, take a sip, and swim further. I don't know if you have any rivers like this in America today. Yet back then this was normal. It was so clean! These memories are probably the happiest that remain from my school years. I'm not sure about the others. Not everyone went there, but I loved the Volga. I still do. And I remember all the kids, my friends, who were with me. And all the teachers.

Did members of the A and B groups vacation together on the Volga?

Yes, of course. We vacationed there not by class, but by age. That is, when we reached thirteen or fourteen we went there for the first time, and afterward went each year until we finished school. We had our own motorboats and tents. It was really a great summer camp. The teachers who went there with us included my physics teacher and the physical education teacher. There were lots and lots of people there. Everyone visited. I think this is what I enjoyed most about my school days. We impatiently waited for summer to begin. As I recall it today, this was real happiness, when you're young, when you don't yet work, and when you're on the Volga. It was simply wonderful. Yes, that's what I remember.

Many others have also told me what fond memories they have of summers on the Volga. But some didn't participate in this and told me that they generally went down south to the sea with their parents. I understood that these were children of really prominent people, right?

Well, yes, of course not everyone went to the sea with their parents. It's true that few could afford that. It was expensive, even for Soviet times. Even for some who went to our school. I went several times. But the Volga, well, yes, it was affordable. Affordable and beautiful. Of course, the majority from our class did not go to camp. And that's not only because they went on vacation with their parents, but also because not everyone liked living in a tent and roughing it. People probably had different desires and different understandings of what constituted rest and leisure, even when we were young. But for the most part, of course, you're right. We did feel the distinction. Because the people, the children who ended up in the school by chance, such as me and Rozanova, and a few others, and those who, how shall I say, ended up there by right, well, their parents could permit themselves altogether different [luxuries]. . . . That's understandable, but frankly the difference is even greater today. Yet this probably didn't affect my relationship with the other kids. However, I know that it did affect others. People ar-

Summer camp on the Volga, circa 1965. Students took turns washing pots and pans. Their jerry-rigged table is on the left. *Courtesy A. A. Konstantinov.*

rived at the camp and did what they pleased. But back in Saratov, I thought about other things, that soon we'd achieve the bright future and everyone would be equal.

What did you do during your free time when you went to school?

I played sports. I played volleyball and I read books.

Did you join any school clubs?

I'm not sure if there were any at school. I can't recall that we had any special clubs. I was more interested in sports, and we had all sorts of evening coaching sessions. We'd go to school to train. That we did. They held such evenings at school.

How would you assess the instruction at School No. 42?

It depends upon the subject, because they taught English there very well. I now understand that. Not only well, but they taught those who wanted to learn. When I moved to Israel I found work within two months. My first boss was from America, and that, of course, was a direct result of the fact that I had studied English and still kept up my skills. Moreover, the teaching methods were very good, the teachers were good, and they demanded a great deal from us. That is, English was taught on a very high level there. But all the other subjects in my view were the same as you'd find at a neighbor-hood school. Back then we also had special schools for physics and mathematics. I hung out with their graduates. There, physics and mathematics were taught on a higher level. Yes, all the other sub-jects at our school were accessible. It was another matter altogether that the building itself was much nicer, and much cleaner, than, say, my neighborhood school. Selectivity is selectivity. Let's just say that we didn't have anyone who became criminals in the eighth or ninth grades. That's for sure. And in regard to overall level, I'd have to say that a lot had to do with the language.

In your view, how politicized was the instruction from today's perspec-tive?

I think that [laughing] as in all schools it was the social sci-ences. Our principal was a Communist. Instruction was not only politicized, but super-politicized. It's only natural that, as a result of this, at age sixteen I sincerely believed that I would have my own helicopter under communism. I had no doubts whatsoever that everything that was taking place in our country was right and was good. It was another matter, perhaps, that I was unlucky and that no one explained how things really were to me. I didn't talk about such things with my parents. In this regard they brainwashed us very well. This, indeed, was a great social experiment. It's only now that I understand, in general, what they did to us. It's a real nightmare. But for a young man it was simple. Imagine a young man who un-derstands nothing, who doesn't have the opportunity to hear other opinions, who doesn't have the opportunity to travel anywhere, and who doesn't even have the opportunity to listen to the radio, for the Voice of America was very difficult to listen to.

Because they jammed it?

Yes, it was simply impossible. You had to exert tremendous ef-fort, which, well, who needed this? You literally had to sit for hours in front of the receiver to catch [it]. . . . So that your parents didn't hear you, for heaven's sake. The propaganda really was effective. I can't say how it affected others, but I can only share my own views. Let's just say that up until the time I graduated from the university I fully backed the party line. I can say that, in my case, they were very successful.

Many turning points in the history of the country took place during your childhood, Aleksander Vladimirovich. Did your parents discuss in front of you such things as the Twentieth Party Congress and Khrushchev's denun-ciation of the Stalin cult?

Not with us. My father belonged to the party and attended all party meetings, but never discussed any of these things with me. Perhaps they thought it was better not to. That's probably the case. They never did. Oh, no, that's not quite right. When I had grown up my father, well, we argued about this, when I already began to put two and two together. It was late, unfortunately, but he'd argue with me and make much of the fact that he was the son of a cook. His father was an alcoholic who got crushed by a train, and his mother was a hospital cook. My father was born in 1914, and they survived only because she worked in a hospital and was the cook. There was food. And this son of a cook received a college education. He obtained a decent military rank and lived normally. That is, he worked as an engineer. He used to always say to me that under capitalism he never would have achieved so much in life. He sincerely believed in Soviet power. He'd argue that "many of my friends who began to drink, well, they got derailed, but socialism and Soviet power gave upward mobility to all of us." There's probably something in this. It's true that Soviet power raised people up and gave them an education. It's another matter altogether what price they had to pay for this. They really duped us. For half our lives [laughing]. I'm not sure about the others. It's only when you're much older that you understand what sort of country you live in. That's sad, of course. Very sad. How we might have lived if the country had been normal! I don't think we would have been inferior to the United States.

What did you think of Lenin back then?

Of Lenin? When we went to school, to be honest, I didn't think about him because I had other interests. Well, they taught us about the Great Lenin, the founder, the leader. It was all, well, I'm not sure how to express this, but all this began at such an early age, as if it were imparted in us through our mother's milk. The propaganda system was so comprehensive, so all-encompassing that, well, it was hard to think something other than that Lenin was a genius who showed us the bright path. I, for one, didn't think otherwise until I attended the university.

I certainly understand. What about Stalin? What did you think about him?

Stalin, of course, is a complicated matter, because I suspected that they were hiding something from us. I suspected this because everything was so confusing. When I was really young, Nikita Sergeevich [Khrushchev] denounced the Stalin cult. And when we finally began to understand things, this cult gradually began to return once again. I remember that, already in 1963–64, no one had anything negative to say about Stalin anymore. As soon as they removed Khrushchev, I remember how they quietly [ended any public criticism of him]. . . . Our poor history teachers simply didn't know what to tell us! It was as if he had made mistakes and had some shortcomings, but, on the other hand, he won the war. That was the most important thing in fact, the war. There's a proverb, "War justifies everything." Now I understand that their aim was not to focus attention on what Stalin did, but instead to tell us what a genius Lenin was, who showed us the way to the present. In any event, this is what I recall. Those at the top clearly didn't know what to say. It was hard for them to answer.

What did you think of Khrushchev?

Oh, you know [laughing], there was a great kid in our group, who, unfortunately, refused to let you interview him, Arkasha Korchmar.[9] He was unlike the rest of us in that he could really draw. He drew caricatures, batches of them, of Khrushchev's adventures in Africa and elsewhere. They were like comics, like what you see in cartoons. They were real comics, although we didn't use the word back then. He was a talented artist, and my perception of Khrushchev came from his drawings and remains today. He apparently understood things far better than I did at the time. He knew. That's what I now think. I looked at all this and, well, we simply didn't see Khrushchev as the equal to Lenin, let's put it like that. I remember these drawings even today.

And what about Brezhnev?

Oh! At first he made a positive impression on all of us. Especially if you consider the stage we were at back then. It was during a primordial approval of communism and of Soviet power. And against this background appears a man who speaks sensibly and doesn't bang his shoe at the UN [like Khrushchev]. For the most part, he made a normal impression. But, in all honesty, I don't think that at that age any of us thought much about politics. I, for one, certainly didn't. I somehow took in all that was happening as if it were going on without me. When you're a kid you have different interests for the most part. And when you don't have to run up against flagrant inequality.

---

9. Arkadii Efimovich Korchmar teaches chess in a children's club in Saratov. Suspicious of my intentions, he refused to let me interview him.

Yes, but you grew up during the Cold War. What were your attitudes toward the West back then?

That's also complicated, of course, because my feelings were ambivalent. On the one hand, there was the influence, once again, of everything that I read and heard in school and over the radio and on television. On the other hand, it always seemed strange to me that, if they were all such terrible capitalists, then why do they have such a high level of science and technology, and such a high standard of living? I have to say that it was impossible for them to hide this from us. Even Soviet propaganda was incapable of doing so. I remember that when I mulled this over it didn't make sense. There's such a terrible class war going on in the West with strikes and the like and, as they taught us, the working class would soon seize power because it's brutally exploited. It's growing poorer, it's growing poorer all the time, something's always happening to it. At first it was a comparative impoverishment of the working class, and then it was its absolute impoverishment. It seemed to me that it was time for the working class to be totally spent already! After all, how much could it take? It grew poorer and poorer each year. But then, all of a sudden, there were such things as the American exhibit in Moscow in 1957.[10] I, of course, didn't see it; I was very young, but acquaintances of my parents visited and they told us about the altogether amazing displays that were there, and about other things. This struck me as being strange. However, they would explain to me that the capitalists had squeezed the last drop of blood from the poor workers. And that the workers had reached their last breath. I remembered it roughly like this. That soon they'd stop putting up with this. They really had become impoverished. Then, too, there were also countries, they taught us, which embarked upon a socialist road of development. I recall quite well that, at the time, they taught us that Africa had so awoken that the dark continent had thrown off the colonial yoke and in a flash had become socialist, and the like. Back then I considered this real history. For the most part it's

---

10. The exhibit actually opened in Moscow's Sokolniki Park in the summer of 1959. At the same time the Soviet Union launched an exhibit in New York. In the American exhibit's seventy-eight-foot-high geodesic dome, a huge screen flashed alluring slides of American life that conveyed a real sense of technological superiority, thereby undermining Soviet propaganda. At this exhibit, Vice President Richard M. Nixon and Khrushchev angrily debated the virtues of their respective countries. This episode is often called the "kitchen debate" because it took place against the backdrop of an American dream kitchen in a model ranch house.

actually an amazing thing to deceive your people so much that they believe whatever they're told. How could I not believe this? After all, I, for example, didn't know who Patrice Lumumba in the Congo really was. I read papers and thought that that's how things were, that colonialism was a terrible thing, and that Africa had become free and that everything there was all of a sudden fine. Besides, they told us that the number of socialist countries would soon surpass the number of capitalist countries. And that it was possible to make the change over from capitalism to socialism peacefully, without revolution. Seriously, I really believed this back then.

Of course you did! And besides Africa, there was the revolution in Cuba. What did you think of Castro, by the way?

Well, once again, we used to sing such wonderful songs, I can't recall them today, but we basically loved him. He was a national hero. Simply a national hero who, on a tiny little island, challenged terrible bourgeois America. He became our friend and he began to build communism. And we were even fonder of Che Guevara. He was, as they now say in Russia, even cooler than Castro. He set out to make revolution, to make world revolution. But we were too late, we were too late. Somehow I couldn't understand why they live so poorly over there. This, too, seemed strange to me. They taught us that the transition from capitalism to socialism is always difficult, and that the bright future is already approaching. You had to believe this. They raised young people like me, for instance, so that I didn't have a single doubt. Everything in life was planned beforehand. We harbored no doubts that we lived in the greatest country in the world, that we had fine futures ahead of us, that "here the young always have a clear roadway, and the old are always shown respect,"[11] and that life was steadily improving. Well, as Stalin used to say, "Life has gotten better, comrades, life has become more joyous." That's how it was all the time. And I really believed this and no one tried to convince me otherwise. I don't know about the others; perhaps their parents told them the truth late at night in the kitchen. But no one said a thing to me and I viewed this world with optimism. Everything was getting better and better. Then, all of a sudden, there was no bread. Things got so good that we were without bread in

---

11. These are words from "Song of the Motherland," an extremely popular patriotic song written by V. Lebedev-Kumach and I. Dunaevskii in 1935, for the movie *Circus*, starring Liubov Orlova. The compelling melody became the broadcast signal for Radio Moscow during the 1930s.

1962 [laughter]. But they once again explained things away, that Nikita Sergeevich ran things poorly, that he was at fault.

I heard that there were long lines back then and that they handed out a roll to each of the children at school.

Yes, a white roll, because it was impossible to buy white bread. I remember those rolls well. Once again, if only someone had suggested that it was possible to live differently. But when you see nothing other than this life it seems that that's how things ought to be. Especially when they tell you twenty-four hours a day that this is the right life, that this is how things ought to be. We live better than anyone in the world and soon we'll start living fabulously. That's how we lived, in any event. Perhaps there were those who felt otherwise, like Shcharanskii.[12] He often tells how he demonstrated on Red Square in 1968 to protest our invasion of Czechoslovakia, while I, for one, believed that we had done the right thing. I was a college freshman at the time and was convinced that we had to nip things in the bud. True, Shcharanskii's a bit older, and perhaps things were different in Moscow. You have to bear in mind that in Saratov, well, I saw a foreigner for the first time when I was probably around thirty. This, too, is a very important point. It was a closed city and there was simply no one we could have learned things from or compared things with. No one. Of course, life was probably different in Moscow. But we stewed in our own juices and couldn't listen to the radio or see things on television, or talk to foreigners. The most important thing is that, I don't know, perhaps someone needed this, but when you're young I was more interested in money. Therefore, well, you understand [laughing], it's not always about politics. Soviet power was really very stable. And it got things done.

Several people mentioned to me that there were some contacts between School No. 42 and the city of Bristol, that delegations from England visited. But others don't recall this at all. Do you know? Perhaps the delegations met only with teachers and not with students?

No, there were delegations, but that was before our time as far as I understand. That is, Saratov didn't become closed all of a sudden.

---

12. Anatolii (Natan) Shcharanskii (b. 1948) is one of the founding members of the Helsinki Group, the oldest human rights organization in the Soviet Union, founded in 1976. As a prominent Jewish dissident, Shcharanskii applied to emigrate and was arrested and sentenced to fourteen years of prison in March 1977. Released in February 1986, he emigrated to Israel, where he founded the Yisrael B'Aliyah Party. He has also held several ministerial positions in the government.

During the 1950s, when I was in school, Bristol was a sister city. But then they closed Saratov.

Because of the military factories?

Yes, because of them, including the one where my father worked. That was the end of it. We lived in a vacuum, in a real vacuum. I can't honestly say that that was a bad thing, but it nonetheless affected our lives.

Please tell me about Western music. Were you interested in it, particularly in the upper grades?

Yes, we all were. But, simply put, it was really hard to listen to it. Once again, this wasn't Moscow. That is, they didn't jam it, but the quality was practically, well, it was often the tenth copy of a tape recording. I also remember how they used to rail at the Beatles. It was, as Galich sang, "the pernicious influence of the West," the Beatles performing with toilet seats around their necks.[13] Yet we were all carried away by this. Moreover, I even understood what they were singing about, unlike those [laughing] who didn't go to the English-language school. I really liked them. And everything else that we were able to get our hands on. But the extent of this, well, all of this was to all intents and purposes banned. I don't know about elsewhere, but in Saratov it was practically forbidden. If they had caught us with a copy of a tape, say, of the Beatles at a school party, we would have been in deep trouble.

What about relations between boys and girls at school? Were there any school romances?

In this regard I don't think our school differed from any of the others. We reached the age, and romances began. Even Soviet power couldn't do anything about this [laughing]. Basic instinct was at work. In this regard I think everything was more or less normal.

You can pass on this question if you like. Were the students who attended your school sexually active by the time they graduated?

It seems to me that this depended on the neighborhood you lived in. Since the school was a magnet school for the city, the children who went there were not necessarily from the area. My neighborhood bordered on Glebuchev Ravine, where there were always loose morals. Many of my neighborhood friends were older and more experienced than me. They taught us everything and in-

---

13. Aleksandr Galich (1919–77, exiled 1974) was a famous bard-poet, whose popular, tape-recorded ballads troubled Soviet authorities.

troduced us to the right people. But at school, as far as I remember, there was no particular activity observed.

Did the young men ever drink while attending school?

Why, of course! Of course, we drank, and smoked. These were far less serious sins than listening to Western music. They were simply incomparable, simply incomparable. But this was always considered normal in Russia.

How does your generation differ from that of your parents?

Well, I think it differs only in that our generation was luckier and we got to experience real life. Many of my friends' and acquaintances' parents died before they understood or saw anything. But we really are lucky. It's another thing in regard to who is poor and who is rich, but I think this is secondary, because life is life. Not everyone can be rich. After all, now in Russia there are gangsters and just about everything else. Society is dividing into rich and poor like nowhere else in the world. Nevertheless, I still think we were really lucky. After all, we're a generation that for the most part had already lived through a lot, and the fact that I now understand in what kind of world I live and experience freedom is wonderful. We never could have imagined this, say, back in 1982 or 1983, when we already thought we were so wise, we could never have imagined that things would turn out the way they did. Of course, there's a Chinese proverb: "May you never live in interesting times." It's quite appropriate. We lived through precisely this kind of period. Many were broken by it, including some from my class. They simply lost everything. As Leonid Ilich Brezhnev used to say, they lost confidence in tomorrow. But, as a matter of fact, even they understood that we're now living in the real world. And this, in my view, is simply invaluable. I can speak only for myself, but before they duped us so much that we lived in an artificial world. Now I live in the real one. Sometimes the going gets tough, but I live in the real world. This is probably the biggest difference between the generations. For example, my father never understood what happened. He was old. He believed that the democrats sold Russia, let's put it like that. That Soviet power was better. However, he wasn't in a position to evaluate things. We, well, we're not exactly young, but we had time to do so. And our children, may God bless them. Then, of course, nothing in Russia is guaranteed [laughing]. Yet I think there's no returning to the past. I think that, well, it might become like Colombia, but it won't be like it was in the Soviet Union. We argue with our friends over this a lot, but I nonetheless think that it would be better. Everything that's taking place is better than it was before. And it's mainly in this regard that we differ from our parents' generation.

I understand. You said that several of your schoolmates fell apart. How do you explain this?

Well, I don't want to mention any names, but, to put it bluntly, they couldn't cope with this new life and they became inveterate drunkards who don't work. Let's put it like that. It's all very sad, and I can name one of them, because he's dead for this very reason. The situation was complicated. But what can one do? What happened is not surprising.

Perhaps what happened to them had nothing to do with the changes that occurred. That is . . .

Perhaps, perhaps. But the changes made it even harder to survive.

With these questions I've tried to understand not only your childhood but also the formation of your worldview. What else do I need to ask you in order to understand this?

Well, for the most part, in regard to worldview [laughing], it's not so simple because those of us who lived in the Soviet Union found ourselves in a unique social experiment that the world had never seen before. For seventy years they made fools of generation after generation, and I can honestly say, I admit, that in my case they succeeded while I was young. I was duped 100 percent. I sincerely believed. But very gradually and slowly my worldview changed, after I began to associate more, and now, I hope, I greatly hope, that my worldview is normal. That is, I'm not speaking about the fact that some people understand things better than others. Or that someone is better educated. In my view, it's simply like leaving a mad house for the real world. Do you understand what I'm saying? That was the most important thing in my life. The fact that I couldn't stand up against this machinery of state makes me like the majority of others. And those who say otherwise are, to put it mildly, deceiving themselves. It was the rare individual who was against the system from childhood, those whose parents were. That, too, is a tradition. The fact that I gradually could become a normal person, I think, speaks volumes about my worldview or about whatever you want to call it [laughing]. I think I'm lucky, like all those my age who had the misfortune of being born in the Soviet Union. We became normal people at an age in our lives when we could still accomplish something. That's really important.

Please tell me about your sister. How did she influence you?

You know, my sister and I haven't lived together for a very long time. After graduating from the university she left for the Moscow area, and I rarely see her. And when we were in school there was a five-year age difference between us. To be frank, she didn't influence me at all. She was nothing but a girl back then.

Where did you study after graduating from School No. 42?

I enrolled in the physics department at Saratov University.

Since you were a gold medalist you didn't have to take entrance exams, right?

No, I had to take two of them. If you got an A on them you got admitted without taking any others, and I did.

Did others from your class enroll with you?

Yes, for example, Zhenia Meier and Volodia Nemchenko. We studied together in the same department. There were some girls, too. Olia Gorelik, for example. Several others from the parallel class did, too. There were quite a few of us.

How would you assess the education you received at the university? To what extent did your views change?

Well, it's only natural that little by little my views began to change, although you could feel the influence of ideology even more so than at school. We had quite a few required subjects such as the history of the Communist Party, an altogether wonderful subject. And scientific communism, and whatever you could imagine. I had a hard time trying to explain those countries that were not on a socialist or on a capitalist path of development. I found it all very interesting. They tried to brainwash us at the university, even more so than at school, but by then our contacts were different, and I already began to understand things a bit. At the university I already began to understand a bit what a wonderful country we lived in.

But how do you explain this?

For one thing, I came into contact with lots of people. I began to travel to other cities, to Leningrad and Moscow. I began to interact with others. I, in fact, began to listen to the radio, to Voice of America, and to BBC. I recall the program *The View from London*. It was a very fine program. And I really began to get interested in all this. It's only natural that I began to question things, but slowly.

What about samizdat?

No, I didn't read any. I didn't have the occasion to do so, otherwise I would have done so with pleasure. It was hard to come by. You had to search out samizdat. And I didn't have any friends who offered to show me any. I got access to it only many years later, let's say, but during the Soviet period. By then I had acquaintances who [offered it to me], but otherwise it was of course hard to get in Saratov. I did hear the chapters of *Gulag Archipelago* that were read over Voice of America. That was the only means, but with the jamming that too was hard. Very hard. Besides, to evaluate all this without having books. . . . And samizdat is mostly belletristic writing. You need to live under the present system in order to understand all this. Therefore, it was in fact very complicated for the average Joe who didn't search this out and who didn't have any connections. I didn't have any. The only thing available was conservations with other people and foreign radio broadcasts. But you had to listen to them in secret. You had to be careful when you listened. Heaven forbid that the neighbors hear!

During the years you studied at the university the so-called Romanov Affair took place in the history department. A group of students there formed a Marxist reading group, and they eventually got arrested. Did you know about this?

Just a bit, and about the way you put it. Later I had a friend in the mechanical-mathematics department who was tied to this affair. But the history department was far removed from us. We had nothing like that in our department.

You graduated from the university in 1972. Did you enroll in graduate school afterward?

Not right away. I first worked for a year. I enrolled in the same department and completed graduate school in chemical physics in 1977, after which I began working at the university. I didn't get assigned elsewhere, but simply remained there. They offered me a position there. I held various positions there until I left for Israel. I taught there and was a research associate. I was an associate professor when I left.

Did you meet your future spouse there?

Yes, and I got married in 1978. My wife worked in the police department. She's a chemist, an expert criminologist.

How did your wife influence you?

Oh, my [laughing]! Well, back then in the Soviet Union criminality was classified information. But owing to her work, she had access to it, and knew what was actually going on. Let's say that the truth that she had access to, that it, too, affected my worldview. I began to wonder why they kept this information from us. It was one more small thing that made me question.

How many children do you have?

My daughter is twenty-four and my son is sixteen.

What shaped the formation of what we today like to call your "identity"?

That's a very complicated question. I'm not sure I understand what the word identity means.

Let me rephrase the question. How would you describe what it meant to be Soviet in a cultural sense?

Oh, in that regard. Once again, I'd have to say that my views evolved. The evolution was very strong throughout my life, beginning with my real desire to become a Soviet patriot. Of course, I didn't want to leave for any virgin lands campaign.[14] But I can offer an example from the Vietnam War, when the Soviet Union helped the North Vietnamese fight against the Americans. I remember in all sincerity saying to my father, "Why don't all the people working in the Soviet Union give a portion of their wages to help battle against American imperialism?" Do you understand? That's what it meant in my view to be Soviet. That's a good example. I honestly said this in all sincerity. But then, well, it was very hard for things to have an effect on you in Saratov. For that reason, my transformation was a gradual one. However, I acquired information through experience, and from what I saw, and from what reached us, say, from abroad. Also, when I began conducting research the difference in the level of science became obvious. And this, despite the fact that the Soviet Union had so many scientists. I began to understand a little bit what was going on in Russia and what was going on in the West. Moreover, this somehow contradicted what they wrote in the papers and said, say, at party meetings at the university. Then people were allowed to emigrate to Israel. This too had a big impact on me, because one assistant professor working with me left. First his mother, an old woman, left. They called a party meeting and began to insist that he denounce his mother, that is, to say that she was a bad person who betrayed her homeland. He refused to do so. He got sacked from work and ended up following her. I remember how

---

14. A program launched by Khrushchev, which increased the sown area by some 35 million hectares between 1954 and 1956. Khrushchev's controversial plan comprised two interrelated parts: he sought to introduce and expand production of corn (maize) in order to increase livestock herds and consequently meat and dairy production and consumption. But so as not to do so at the expense of wheat production, dry-farming land (virgin land), mostly in Kazakhstan and Siberia, was brought under cultivation to grow wheat. Carried out at a feverish tempo, the campaign recruited Soviet youth through Komsomol organizations.

strongly this affected me. This was back in the 1970s. Several left in 1975 and 1976. I already began working at the university and saw and heard all this. I saw people foaming at the mouth denouncing him and saying that he too betrayed his country. This, too, made a big impression on me.

You emphasized how much you were a product of the Soviet system and how your views changed over time. Do you think that most of your colleagues and friends in the 1970s and 1980s shared your views? Can you recall a time by which people's attitudes had become more critical?

I can't say that many of my friends shared my views. At that time much depended upon nationality, and my Jewish friends were almost all quite critical. Moreover, it was dangerous to open up, even to a friend, because everyone knew that in each organization was someone recruited by the KGB. It's possible that I was simply more trusting than the rest and it was easier to deceive me. As regards dissatisfaction with the regime, in my view it began to appear at the beginning of the 1980s, when the economy began to decline and the shortages became unbearable.

Did you join the Communist Party?

Never. It actually was hard to join at the university. They admitted very few there, considering it necessary to enroll workers. They believed the intelligentsia was rotten and generally unworthy. Yet many at the university sought to become a Communist. There was a long line, and you needed to "show your worth," that is, you needed to find some acquaintances to back you or to suck up to someone. I really never had the desire to join the party. None whatsoever. They said it was necessary in order to move up the career ladder, but I was never a party member. The Lord spared me.

When was the first time you went abroad?

In 1995, when I was already forty-five years old. I visited my daughter who was studying at a boarding school in Israel that has a program for children from Russia.

Did your attitudes toward the West change as an adult?

They changed, but once again, only gradually. I can only repeat that a contradiction emerged between what I knew, what I believed, and what actually took place. Of course, this occurred for the most part when I began to conduct research, because before then I hadn't been anywhere. I had but seen Western automobiles. What else could I think? Nothing else. But when I began to read scholarly articles and began to figure out what's what and to understand what directions each was going in, at that point I seriously begin to think that society was somehow rotting but, as they said, smelled very good [laughing]. That's a well-known joke; however, it reflects reality.

I also wanted to ask you about your attitudes toward China, because the eternal friendship had given way to animosity. How did you understand this?

That took place while we were still in school. I remember it well. But, honestly speaking, even as a child, perhaps because my father said so, I never considered the Chinese to be our friends. Never. And that's how things actually turned out. There's something else that's interesting. China also shaped my worldview in that it was a kind of distorted mirror image of the Soviet Union. I somehow began to understand that all the features of Soviet power became more pronounced there when taken to their logical extreme and everyone was dressed in the same Mao jackets and ate the same hundred grams of rice a day. That was real socialism with a human face [laughing].[15] And that influenced me.

Many of those who went to school with you traveled to Eastern Europe in the 1970s. Did you go anywhere?

I couldn't, because of my work. It was connected to the [defense industry] and was secret. It was that simple. That, too, was another fine method [of controlling people], as I now understand. They tried to block the exit of as many people as possible, for any reason. I simply couldn't work otherwise, because in order to work I needed to visit various organizations and factories and they were all secretive. Therefore, if you wanted to work, you had to give up any right to travel. I simply had no other choice, and it wasn't easy, as I now see.

How important is it that you learned English as a child? Did it play a role in your professional life?

A very large one. It played a role in everything. There was Karl Marx, right? He coined a wonderful phrase, despite the fact that he was the founder of Marxism. The phrase goes that "a foreign language is a weapon in life's struggle." Ever since I heard it I've noticed that it's actually true. For me it was English. I consider myself lucky that my teacher took me with her [when she left for School No. 42]. Of course, I've kept up with it my entire life. I've lived in Israel now

---

15. Trubnikov is ironically referring here to Communist Party secretary Alexander Dubček's attempt during the 1960s to create in Czechoslovakia a more humane version of socialism, "socialism with a human face," which culminated in the so-called Prague Spring and ultimately the Soviet invasion of the country in 1968.

for four and a half years. I don't know Hebrew. Well, there's nothing else to say. English is really important for me.

Marxist teachings underscore the importance of economic development. How did you understand your standard of living back then? What did you think of the black market, of the need to have contacts in order to acquire things?

First of all, when we were very young there was far more equality. I remember that well. Back then, in fact, the black market was probably not that extensive. Once again, the Iron Curtain was heavier, the iron had not yet rusted, and everyone lived more or less the same. At least in the building where I was born and grew up. But then things began to change. Yet the black market was only one side of things. There was also a very good word, "blat,"[16] and it's altogether something different. The black market was where you could go and, for lots of money, buy things. They used to explain this to us, too, as the result of temporary difficulties. However, they grew. With each year we were told that things were getting better and better, but in ten years everything had disappeared.

Did you travel to Moscow to buy food? Many have told me about the so-called sausage-car trains and the like.

Well, it wasn't a matter of making special trips just to buy food. But when I was sent to Moscow on business it was really hard to do things. We simply had no choice but to buy as much as we could trundle back with us.

How did you understand the difference between Moscow and Saratov? That is, many have said to me that since Moscow was the capital they expected people to live better there.

I honestly didn't believe this. At first, I saw it as a big showcase. Foreigners had to see how good things were in the Soviet Union. They simply weren't allowed to visit Saratov. There was no problem. No one was interested in how people lived in Saratov. That's how I later saw things.

Did the living standard change at all in Saratov during the 1970s and early 1980s?

No, but that's the case throughout the country. By then socialism had already shown [laughing] its full potential. It actually began to decline. At the very start of the 1970s things weren't all that bad. But then it was real agony. Life began to get worse even in Moscow. The degree of difference [between the two cities] remained, but the

---

16. Blat translates as "valuable connections" or "pull"—in short, whom you know.

difference itself continued to spiral downward. It's only natural that this shaped my worldview too. Very much so when the oil money ended.[17]

In all societies myths help to unite people. Tell me about the myths that united Soviet society. After all, you told me that, as a child, you believed in things.

Myths? Well, the main myth was that Soviet power was the best and most just in the world. "Just" was the key word. We didn't have exploitation of man by man as you did under terrible capitalism. Everything we had belonged to the people. That was perhaps the main myth. And all the others flowed from this. We don't have private property, which is the source of all misfortune. That's also an important point. Private property entails [laughing] the "brutal bared teeth of capitalism." That's how it was. I honestly believed that it was a good thing that everything belonged to the people. Because it was mine, too. All the other myths stemmed from this. The Communist Party is our helmsman, but it's a temporary helmsman. There was the myth that with the development of communism the party would cease to exist. It would solve all the problems of the transition period and then would no longer be needed. Another myth is that everyone who works responsibly would have an abundance under communism. I remember that "material welfare is beginning to flow full stream." Do you see how they taught us? I'm quoting them. At the university I liked reading original sources, Engels, Lenin, and Marx, because I found the bulky books on party history tedious. I'd read the original and go take my exams. Those were the main myths. They really had an effect on me. Many really believed that communism was a good thing, and many still believe that today. When we'll have full equality, when everything will be in abundance, when there will be no poor, no hungry, and when everyone will be employed. Everyone worked in the Soviet Union. It's true that everyone worked [laughing], but what they did was another matter. That's an altogether different question. There was also the wonderful myth that was called "confidence in tomorrow." That myth is still around today. These are perhaps the main ones that they pounded into me.

-----

17. As a major oil-exporting country, the Soviet Union benefited enormously—but temporarily—when oil prices rose precipitously following the world oil crisis of 1973. Oil profits helped to keep the Soviet economy afloat and helped mask its declining performance.

Under Gorbachev they began calling the Brezhnev era one of stagna-
tion. Did it seem to you at the time that you were stagnating? What did you
think of Brezhnev?

Generally speaking, by that time we were already mature people.
Attitudes toward Brezhnev were expressed in jokes that circulated
about him. The number of anecdotes is enormous and there are
some marvelous ones among them. That is, he wasn't taken seriously. People didn't relate to him as a leader, Lord forbid, there was
nothing but jokes at his expense. Although, in regard to stagnation,
one might say that there was, as people like to say today, stability.
Under Brezhnev things weren't so bad in regard to "confidence in
tomorrow." No one was afraid of him. People told these jokes about
him and no one was imprisoned for doing so. At work you could
quietly tell jokes about Leonid Ilich and no one would inform on
you, no one would come after you, even though there was a system
of informants in the Soviet Union. In every organization there were
people who reported on the mood of others, on who said what.
Everyone was well aware of this.

Was it obvious who the informant was?

Not always, but we knew that they existed. That too is one of
the wonderful things about the Soviet Union. Even they calmly
listened to the jokes. Therefore, in certain respects, this is an excellent example.

There was a lot of commotion back then about the problem of human
rights. Was that a taboo topic, or did people discuss it, say, among friends
or at work?

Of course they did, once people understood that we lacked basic
rights, for example, freedom of movement. They even discussed
this at party meetings. They'd say that [in the Soviet Union] it was
[laughing] like in the joke "but at the same time [in America] they
lynch Negroes." That is, we have no unemployment and our medical
system is free. We have confidence in tomorrow. We have equality.
But there's a price that has to be paid for this. And we pay it. We
have our laws, and they're better than yours. Who needs this freedom of movement if everyone in the West is poor and exploited?
You know, many people in Russia are saying the same thing today.[18]
Now you can say what you please, but the majority of people lack

18. The situation in Russia has stabilized—and improved significantly—since Trubnikov left Saratov for Israel.

money even for food. They say, "Who needs this freedom of move-ment?" Life's not so simple for the most part. Yes, things are difficult in Russia and for this reason many are nostalgic about Brezhnev. Back then there was something positive after all.

You had told me that as a child when you would vacation on the Volga it was possible to drink the water right from the river. What about ecological problems? Did people discuss them? After all, within twenty years it was a fact that the Volga had become polluted.

Yes, of course. But again, it was all about what you saw. Every-thing was getting worse, but we read in the papers that everything was greatly improving. Everything was, how shall I say [laughing], the authorities controlled everything and they'd say that industry was developing.

Please tell me about your reaction to the invasion of Afghanistan.

I was very much against it. When the Soviet Union had invaded Czechoslovakia I didn't understand a thing and "voted" yes, so to speak. But when they invaded Afghanistan, well, by then, people even told me that I might get in trouble, because I so disliked what had happened. I understood that it was all too similar to the Americans in Vietnam, but in a worst-case scenario, and that no one needed this. People were perishing, our soldiers were getting killed. I knew people who perished there. It was terrible. By the way, I wasn't the only one who felt this way. This was an altogether different time. That is, society had matured and the basic mass of people opposed this.

Please tell me how you ended up in Israel and why you decided to emi-grate there. How did this come about?

There were many reasons, including personal ones. My daughter stayed here and we needed to help her. She was here alone. Then I began to intensely dislike Russia at that particular moment. It was during the crisis of 1998, as you recall.[19] Over a two-month period, the ruble fell six times. People began to receive altogether unimagin-ably low wages of about thirty dollars a month. And the outlook was not optimistic, especially for those at the university [laughing], for those who weren't in time for the distribution of property,[20] people

---

19. The ruble defaulted on the world market during the summer of 1998, resulting in an immediate but short-lived economic crisis.

20. A reference to the privatization of formerly state-owned industry, which took place in two waves under the presidency of Boris Yeltsin, resulting in some individuals accumulating enormous wealth. Popular opinion remains critical of the distribution of property, which gave insiders enormous and unfair advantages.

like me, for instance. Things became really awful for us, because in Russia at the time the labor of scholars and university professors was not appreciated. We were at the bottom of the food chain. The only people lower were schoolteachers, unfortunately. All this had an effect on me. In combination with my daughter's problems it was enough to make me decide to give it a try here. Hence, life demonstrates that this is all probably quite natural. For seventy years they oppressed people and turned the country into what it was, trampling all freedom. Then, when they opened the locks, everything poured out. And who ended up on top? You know what always rises to the surface, it's always the foam. That's what happened in this case [laughing]. Therefore it's only natural that I understood all this, these problems, not as the result of perestroika, but as the consequence of Soviet power. It's all understandable, but, unfortunately, we have but one life and I thought why wait until things become normal—it's already so hard. It's hard living during transitions.

What difficulties did you encounter when you decided to leave?

With none whatsoever. In this regard things have become normal in Russia, and I encountered no difficulties. I remain a Russian citizen. I have a Russian passport and I can return whenever I please. In this regard Russia's become a real country. A democratic one.

Aleksandr Vladimirovich, I'd like to clarify something. Did you first visit Israel because your daughter was studying there?

Yes.

What impressions did you have of this first visit?

Well, when you go as a tourist it's not at all like living in a country. It made a fabulous impression: an Eastern culture, Jerusalem, Christ's Tomb, Nazareth, the church on the site where Christ was born. And the Wailing Wall and the Jewish sacred places, they're all wonderful sights. There really is something to see here, isn't there?

But it's an altogether different matter when you live in a country, right?

[Laughing] When you live there you have to work.

How did you manage to land a job? What do you do in Israel? How are you living?

I work in my field, as a physicist. At first I found a position in a company whose boss just so happened to be an American. It was a high-tech start-up firm. I worked there a bit at first, but in my field. Then the company collapsed along with the fall of the high-tech business. I now work in another firm, also a start-up one, also in my field. I do practically the same thing I did in the other one, but it's well established, let's put it like that. It's okay. I'm doing what I did in Russia, but at a somewhat different salary [laughing]. It's been almost five years since I left Saratov and I haven't been back since. But I want to. Perhaps sometime this year.

What other obstacles did you face during your emigration?

Well, I wouldn't really call my move to Israel emigration, as I understand the word—torn from your roots, in a foreign country, hard to adjust, hostility from the native people, etc. It so turned out that, at the time of my arrival, almost all my close friends, with whom I had been connected for decades in Saratov, lived in Israel. Moreover, there's a tolerant attitude toward repatriates who don't know Hebrew. This is something specific to the country—its ideology is founded on the return of Jews to their historical homeland. I received citizenship and all rights immediately, along with my passport. In order to move here I had to prove my Jewish heritage at the Israeli embassy, that is, show my birth certificate and my mother's documents to get a visa. Afterward, they gave me a free ticket. I arrived in Israel, where my daughter and friends met me and within two months, with their help, I found work in my field and ever since then have not experienced any special problems. I get together with my friends more often than I did in Russia, even though we live in different cities. Therefore, I didn't lose the luxury of human contact, but just the opposite—and as far as I know that's one of the biggest problems, for example, for émigrés in America.

What do you think caused perestroika?

Well, it probably was simply already predetermined by fate, because everything simply gave out. The internal spring broke that kept socialism going, you can put it like that. Thank God that it all took place peacefully. Money came to an end, oil came to an end, as did everything else. Nevertheless, the people are succeeding in building a normal life. I think that even without Gorbachev, all this would have come to an end. It was already clear that people had become altogether different, they no longer could put up with all that. It was no longer possible to deceive people. It's another matter, of course, what will become of this.

How would your answers to my questions have differed had I asked them before perestroika?

First of all, let's begin with the fact that you wouldn't have been able to ask them. We simply wouldn't have met. I was not allowed to meet with foreigners. I signed a statement.

How does your generation differ from that of your children?

How do we differ? They altogether lack the stereotypes that we had. Nothing has been pounded into their head since childhood. I think they're simply normal people. We remain abnormal. And some [from my generation] will remain that way until the end, unfortunately. Probably about half or so. But our children are normal. They're simply people, citizens of the world, who live altogether differently. Let's say that they're normal in that they live without an ideology, unlike us.

Does your wife work?

Yes, and also in her field.

What about your relatives?

My mother is in Saratov and my sister in Moscow. My wife's parents are in Saratov. And we still have lots of friends there.

What did they think of your decision to leave?

They were fine about it. Life in Russia had undergone sweeping changes. No one said that we were betraying our homeland.

Would you ever consider moving back to Russia? What would it take to convince you to do so?

That's a really difficult question. Even the Lord is unable to predict what will happen in the future in Russia, in Israel, and in my family. I don't think there'll be a serene life anywhere—take the example of the World Trade Center as confirmation. By the way, I walked around near the towers about two weeks before September 11. It was a marvelous sight. At least the road back to Russia is not closed. I'm a Russian citizen.

May I ask about your attitude toward the Palestine question?

Honestly speaking, it's complicated for me because I lived here for, it seems, four years, but I haven't yet become part of this life. It's hard for me. It's all so complicated and mixed up. For the most part I'm more on the left. But I'm afraid to discuss this with my friends, because they're all on the right. I simply think that I've lived here for such a short time that I don't yet have the right to have an opinion.

How can your life story help me understand the fate of the Soviet Union? That is, in what ways does your life reflect larger processes?

That's a tough question. I think that my life, like anyone else's, actually does reflect them. It reflects the ideology that our leaders all those years tried to implement. The ideology with which they tried to create, in other words, a "new historical community, the Soviet people." That's how it seems to me. And the fact that they expended so much effort to turn me into a piece of this society, well, we'd have to say that they succeeded, at least while I was young. That is, this speaks to the point, it always seemed to me, that man is controllable. But they controlled people for several generations, unlike Hitler, who did so only for ten years. They duped us in Russia over the course of seventy years—I was born already toward the end of the trajectory, let's say, but nonetheless this machine was so powerful that it had me in gear, went into drive, and repeated this with tiresome monotony. In this regard it seems to me that this ideology was basically effective. Of course, I understand that this was a certain crime against the people, unlike any in world history. They seized a huge country and turned it into a concentration camp. And a refined one at that, in which people had to knowingly live, like in a concentration camp, and not only put on prison uniforms with numbers on them.

Is there anything you regret in life?

Regret? Naturally, the same, the same. I regret that when I was young I was unable to live a normal life, that is, like my children do now. I think my life would have turned out differently. But, of course, we don't pick our parents and we don't pick our country. And we don't pick the time in which we live. However, we nonetheless can regret such things. Now I live like a normal person. Yet I could have done so thirty years ago, too. Not under the weight of ideology and the like. Perhaps I would have been worse off, yet for some reason I think I would have been better. Many believe that lots of people perished during the struggle for existence under capitalism, but I don't think it was that way at all.

8. "People have lost a great deal in terms of their confidence in tomorrow" | Gennadii Viktorovich Ivanov

July 6, 2004, Saratov

I interviewed Gennadii Viktorovich Ivanov in an apartment I rented that summer in downtown Saratov. I was eager to meet him, because I knew that he had been in Afghanistan at some point following the Soviet invasion of that country in December 1979. Moreover, his classmates had described him as an avid sportsman in his youth, someone who was both fearless and perhaps even a bit reckless. This appealed to me, perhaps because I'm neither. Yet I was also apprehensive about our prospective encounter, especially since someone had led me to believe that Gennadii Viktorovich served in the security police (the former KGB). I had spoken with him over the phone when I was in Saratov in 2002, and again in 2003. Both times he questioned me about where I lived and about the purpose of my visit, but did not call back to set up an interview. This behavior made me wary. However, when we finally met in June 2004 I soon realized that my suspicion had been unfounded. Until his retirement, Gennadii Ivanov had worked as an investigator and operative for the criminal police. He had not met with me earlier, because, after retiring from the police force, he took a security job with a firm located in Saratov's suburbs and rarely came to the center of town, where I lived.

Gennadii Viktorovich appeared to enjoy answering my questions, and he did so with a slight irreverence and playfulness that revealed strong attitudes about all sorts of issues. His unpredictable replies to my queries made the time fly quickly, except for the fact that he smoked incessantly, like so many other of his male classmates, some of whom suffered from a variety of health problems as a result. A police operative and investigator, Ivanov brought a unique perspective to the interview. However, I realized that normally he was the one asking, not answering, the questions. He weighed his words carefully. Sometimes I felt as if he formulated answers specifically for me, as a cultural outsider, and as an American. Yet this did not prevent him from assessing his own surroundings with a critical eye. He had interesting things to say about a variety of topics, from gangs in Saratov to nationality, police practices, the war in Afghanistan, and the outside world. He seemed to regret that he didn't have time after the interview to stick around for a cup of coffee.

What is Gennadii Viktorovich's take on some of the more controversial chapters in Soviet history discussed in the interview? What role did nationality play in his life and in that of his family? How does he understand and assess the Soviet involvement in Afghanistan? Do his views differ from those of his classmates also interviewed here? How does his generation differ from that of his parents and from that of his own children? Are there any topics that he seemed reluctant to discuss?

I doubt I can give you the details about where my parents met. They're both physicians, university graduates, who knew what war is. Mother was a medical researcher. At the end of the war, Father found himself in military hospitals in the Stalingrad region. Mother did not participate directly in the war, but was a student at the time. I don't know where exactly they met, but it was in Saratov. Mother was from the Volga German Republic.[1] She's German. After the war my father served for several years as a medic in the Soviet Army. He finished serving at the rank of captain in the medical corps. Afterward, he worked at a variety of medical facilities in Saratov. He retired to the city of Khvalynsk in Saratov oblast,[2] where he currently

---

G. V. Ivanov requested that I not use his complete interview. What is printed here is an excerpt.

1. In the 1760s approximately 25,000–27,000 Germans resettled in Russia's Volga region, mostly in Saratov and neighboring Samara provinces, where they engaged in agriculture and related endeavors. The Soviet government established the Volga German Autonomous Republic in 1924 and abolished it on August 28, 1941, following the Nazi invasion of the Soviet Union, at which time the Kremlin deported the German minority to Kazakhstan and Siberia.

2. Khvalynsk is a district center located on the Volga River in the northern part of Saratov oblast.

resides. He's chief physician in the regional hospital. My mother is dead. For many years she worked at the Saratov Medical Institute. She received her candidate's degree, then her doctoral degree, and worked as an associate professor and professor. Later, she lived in Aktiubinsk, now in Kazakhstan, renamed Aktobe today.[3] She died there. I brought her ashes back here and buried them.

What about your grandparents?

My maternal grandfather died soon after I was born, and we lived with my grandmother until I was almost in ninth grade. She lived with us in Saratov until she died. She was also in medicine, in gynecology, but she retired in order to take care of me so that my mother could work and conduct research. I knew my paternal grandfather and grandmother well, and my father's eight or nine brothers and sisters. Several of them are still alive. One brother also lives in Khvalynsk. He spent his life on Sakhalin [Island]. He's also a physician, a radiologist. Most of my relatives live in Volsk.[4]

Tell me about your childhood interests.

It's hard to say. Probably like all boys, I wanted to be a sailor. What didn't I want to be? What was I interested in? I read a lot and played sports.

Why did your parents decide to send you to School No. 42?

Well, I wasn't exactly drawn to technical subjects. They apparently wanted to give me something that would become useful later in life, if not in some technical sense, then in the humanities. School 42 was quite renowned in the city. And indeed they taught us well there.

Who went there? That is, who were your classmates' parents?

We weren't very interested in such things back then, but I think we came from all strata of society, but mostly from the intelligentsia. There were a few from the working class. There were engineers, teachers, physicians, perhaps some factory directors, basically everyone. I wouldn't say that there were children of party and Soviet officials.

But I understand there were more of them in the A group than in your B group.

Well, you know, if there were children whose parents belonged

---

3. Founded in 1869, Aktobe is located on the Ilek River in western Kazakhstan and has a population of 267,000 today.

4. Another district center of Saratov oblast, located on the Volga River between Khvalynsk and Saratov.

to the party organs, they were not on the level of, say, a first or second secretary. I do remember that the mother of one student was a secretary, but of a neighborhood executive committee. At any rate, we weren't interested in such things; therefore I can't give you any reliable information. Then, too, judging by my own experience, parents in their thirties were too young to have been high-ranking party members. If we're speaking about a second child, then perhaps the parents had achieved something by that time. But someone, say, around twenty-eight or so, would not have.

You mentioned that you're half-German.

Oh, I'm a mixture of many nationalities. Let's see, on my father's side they're all Russian, and on the other they're also Polish and Jewish, and whatever you like all mixed up. Yes, we were all mixed. There was even someone in class of Gypsy origin. But, again, we weren't interested in this.

What about your favorite teachers?

On the whole, I was really lucky with my teachers. At School No. 42, I first had Aleksandra Sergeevna, whose surname I've forgotten. She, too, was very good. For the most part the teachers were not bad at all. But among my favorites there was a physics teacher, a former naval infantryman, in good health, with a full beard. I think he's still alive. I especially am fond of my first teachers. As for the rest, well, they were all good people. Albina Ivanovna was our homeroom teacher. I have nothing but good to say about her. And many of them, well, were ruined by perestroika.

Tell me about what you did in your free time.

Well there was very little of it. If in the later grades it was wrestling, then when we were younger it was basketball. If we're speaking about the courtyard where we lived, well, I had limited experience, but there's a game in Russia called "King of the Mountain." I wasn't that interested in technology, but many of the guys were. I also took piano lessons, but I can't really say that it became a goal of mine or something that I continued with later. I mostly spent my free time playing sports.

What about young people's music. What type of music did you enjoy back then?

Naturally, I listened to the Beatles. I love to listen to music, but I'm not the sort to chase after groups. Yet I like listening to music from, let's say, those years when I was in eighth or ninth grade. I can be more critical of it now [laughing], but, with age, we all probably remember these as the best years of our lives. They're more exciting

Group B, probably in the spring of 1965 (eighth grade). Gennadii
Viktorovich Ivanov is in the back row on the far right. *Courtesy of
A. A. Konstantinov.*

and full of optimism. But for the most part I'm fonder of the years
I spent in college. At school we were expected to be specialists at
everything, whereas in college you know what you like and what
disciplines aren't useful to you.

Did you listen to foreign radio broadcasts?

Of course I did. Probably no one could escape this. We sometimes listened but in what was a limited way. For the most part it
wasn't seriously banned backed then. My parents of course knew,
and if we caught a signal, we'd listen. So what?

What about religion? Did it play a role in your childhood?

In general, I'm an atheist, although not a militant one, and I
don't believe in God. I believe in fate, that man is dealt a certain
deck of cards, and that much depends upon how he plays them. I
believe that the age we'll live to is, how shall I put it, programmed.
And, as a matter of fact, science is reaching the same conclusion that
a great deal has to do with genes. [Insofar as I work in the police]
I see this from a specific vantage point. They criticized me severely
for the high levels of juvenile delinquency, but now they say that

much of this has to do with one's nature. Although we sense that one's upbringing and environment are important, even enormously so, a great deal also depends upon one's genetic makeup and how we're programmed at birth.

How does your generation differ from that of your parents?

We'll, we're probably closer to the generation of our parents than [our children are to us]. I was born on July 18, 1950. If you take those born in 1950, it's one thing, but if you broaden your definition and include those born after 1945 there's another rupture. If you take us, that is, those who grew up in the 1950s, we're much like our parents in regard to our views and other things.

Many momentous events in the country's history took place during your childhood. Do you recall how your parents reacted to such things as the denunciation of the Stalin cult or Khrushchev's ouster in 1964?

You know, I don't have any clear recollections of this, of, let's say, attacks on the cult of personality. Nevertheless, Stalin was still alive when I was born. People say they were afraid. But I never experienced this fear. Apparently, no one had been repressed in our family or among our circle of acquaintances. Nor can I say that we were afraid to speak or to tell a joke, that we were afraid they were listening in. People told jokes at mealtime and whenever you like. At the same time, I can't say that I recall people mourning over Stalin's passing, although, of course, this was in 1953, when I was three years old, and it may not have made an impression on me. However, [under] Khrushchev people began to pay more attention to the Stalin cult, but then bread suddenly disappeared.[5] Well, we now know that all that was a provocation. People managed to make fun of him, well, when he pounded his shoe [at the United Nations]. Then there was corn and jokes about it and other things.[6] But they weren't malicious, and were more like statements of fact, since we all have our weaknesses.

Under Khrushchev, the party issued a new party program that spelled out the date by which communism would be constructed in the USSR—1980. How did you react to all the slogans connected with this when you were a kid?

You know, for the most part we really did try to build communism. There's nothing wrong with this. There was tremendous

---

5. Many respondents vividly remember this episode, which probably occurred in 1962, when they were thirteen or so.

6. See chapter 7, note 14.

construction at the time. So, what of it? They tried to build communism.

I'd like to ask about how you spent your summer back then. Many of your classmates went to camp on the Volga. Did you?

I didn't go to camp often, since I really didn't like it. During my school years I never went. Later I went once or twice, but it really didn't interest me. For the most part we tried to vacation as a family and, as a matter of fact, we still try to do so. To be honest, we went down south [to the sea]. Yes, it was possible to permit oneself this, and my wife and I did so until, how shall I put it, we were no longer of vacation resort age, ever the more so, because our children were practically living with their own families. But we tried to take them along with us, despite the fact that we weren't exactly all that well paid. That's how things were.

Where you afraid of the West when you went to school? After all, we're veterans of the Cold War.

You know, my views of the West are, as a matter of fact, roughly the same back then as they are now. No one wishes us well and no one will do anything that's really in our interests. It's up to us to resolve our own problems. Regarding how enemies were perceived, well, if you exclude Germany, it's a complicated question. With all other countries, well, people are the same everywhere. No one antagonized us. What does your ordinary American really care about what goes on in Russia? That was the case back then and probably now, too. What's it to him? And the arms race? Well, you have two great powers. It's going on now for the most part, too. No one is simply going to hand something over to the other. Just the opposite. They're trying to lay their hands on more.

What were your attitudes toward China back then? I ask because the great friendship between the two Communist powers turned into enmity.

Well, I reacted with amazement to the Damansky Island crisis.[7] We had friendly relations with China. It was something real that we experienced both between individuals and nations. Then there was a feeling of amazement and of bewilderment in regard to why all these events took place. Where did [their cultural revolution] come from and who needs it? Then the Damansky Island episode occurred.

What about Cuba? What was your attitude toward it?

---

7. In 1969, Damansky Island, a small, uninhabited island located in the Ussuri River marking the border between northeastern China and the USSR's Far East, became the center of serious border clashes between Communist China and the Soviet Union.

I'm very favorably disposed toward Cuba both now and back then. I have deep admiration for these people, who, despite their small numbers, solved such large problems. Once again, I think you need to be there to know what's actually going on. But I think that any country would find itself in difficult economic straits if it were under what, in effect, is a blockade for so many years, close to more powerful countries that constantly pose a threat to it. It would be hard for any country to develop economically.

What else do I need to ask you in order to understand what shaped your worldview as you grew up?

Well, I'd ask about books, probably, and about movies, apart from the family, school, the general ideological climate, and, one might say, the mood of society and the like. Yes, probably books. Mostly books, but movies, too. I have a bad memory for the names of film stars. But, for the most part, the generation of actors that is dying out is my favorite. There were lots of serials from the classics, take Ostrovskii,[8] for example. Not serials, but televised performances. There were also a large number of movies. If you exclude, say, your basic detective story, which everyone likes, then I'd have to single out historical films. Beginning with *Aleksandr Nevskii* and the like.[9] Also films about daily life. I'm basically a movie buff. As for books, well, for the most part it was Jack London, Mark Twain, and Guy de Maupassant. We had a good library. I read almost everything in it.

I forgot to ask whether your parents joined the Communist Party and if you were in the Komsomol.

My father did, but my mother didn't. As for the Komsomol, I joined it, like most, when I was about fourteen, perhaps not among the first to be invited to join, but when the time came.

Can you tell me what you thought of Lenin and Stalin back then? Was there a difference?

You know, regarding Lenin, I probably can't say. As for Stalin, well, there was so much said about him that was positive, and then

---

8. Aleksandr Nikolaevich Ostrovskii (1823–86) was a major Russian playwright who wrote or coauthored some fifty plays. Writing in a realistic style, Ostrovskii made the true-to-life situations in which his protagonists found themselves accessible to readers and viewers.

9. One of the six films completed by the great Soviet filmmaker Sergei Eisenstein. Released in 1938, the film features a highly memorable "Battle on the Ice" between Russian prince Aleksandr Nevskii and Teutonic invaders, a self-conscious moral lesson to would-be invaders of the Soviet Union.

so much that was negative. I think it's clear if you sum things up that he was a great historical figure. I'm not sure it was possible in such circumstances to have done things otherwise. Why? Well, the country was in ruins. How could you in so-called democratic ways [restore it] if at any moment war might break out? To be prepared you needed to industrialize. Then, too, in party documents issued during the Stalin years all the negative things were censored. Take the "Dizzy with Success" speech,[10] when they took collectivization too far. Inertia plays a very large role in our country. As Chernomyr-din put it today, we wanted things to be better, but they turned out as always.[11] Yes, I think there was a lot of bungling back then, too. Local party bosses wanted to rise above those from other oblasts and distinguish themselves by completing collectivization and setting up more collective farms and state farms than in other locales. From the perspective of why so many people were driven behind barbed wire, I don't understand Stalin. I don't understand why he thought that was necessary. Perhaps it was the result of his being ill; after all, everyone's life goes through stages.

I wanted to ask you about relations between boys and girls when you were in school, say in the ninth and tenth grades. Were there romances?

Of course there were. It's normal. Just about everyone had a first love when we attended school. It's altogether rare, however, that someone had a first love that lasted all his life, although there are a few exceptions. I know a fellow in the class a year younger than mine, for instance, who fell in love already at school. I've been friends with them ever since. There's no longer any passion-ate romance in the relationship, but they're still married and have raised their kids. They're not planning to go their separate ways and divorce.

One of the people I interviewed told me about gangs in Saratov and also that their presence was even felt a bit at school. I'm sure the girls were far removed from this, but do you recall this?

I'm a well-known specialist regarding gangs, since I've worked in the police all my life. Therefore, I recall that there were gangs in Saratov. For example, there was the Glebovrag gang made up mostly

---

10. Stalin delivered his "Dizzy with Success" speech on March 2, 1930, in which he criticized overzealous local party officials for exceeding the targeted goals for collectiv-izing agriculture.

11. An aphorism made famous by Boris Yeltsin's often-inarticulate prime minister, Viktor Chernomyrdin.

of Tatars.[12] But there were no hooligan groups in our school. Well, sometimes the delinquents would go from school to school and cause trouble. This happened two or three years before my time. Things were simpler at our school, because we came from different neighborhoods of the city and, if they came to pester us, we could enlist the help of those from our neighborhoods, in which case no one could equal us. First they came from Glebovrag, then there were the so-called "Industrialists." They each had their own social origins. The Gagarin Industrial Technical School later fell under my jurisdiction. Things were organized there along paramilitary lines. They were divided into platoons, regiments, and so on, devoting a lot of time to drills. They lived in a dormitory at the technical school, but it didn't have separate rooms and was more like a barracks. Therefore, it was very easy to assemble them, and no one could worm his way out of it, even if he didn't want to join in. They'd go off somewhere. At a moment's notice they'd get into small platoon and regiment formations. Then they'd go to beat up the offenders. The Glebovrag gang later disappeared for a long time, but then reappeared in, let's see, what year was it? Sometime in the 1970s. Yes, it was in the 1970s that they somehow resurfaced. But, as for today, I haven't heard of any gangs, of any second offenders such as those in Samara. There they allowed things to go too far. Entire bands have formed there. We didn't tolerate this. In the industrial technical school they built a regular dormitory with rooms; therefore, if someone didn't want to join in, he didn't have to. They'd knock on the door, but you didn't have to answer. In this way the Industrialists disbanded. They gradually adapted them to a more civilian lifestyle. The Glebovragers, well, they probably assimilated more, although not to a large extent, but I haven't heard about them, although they were active at one time.

You graduated from school in 1967 and then enrolled at . . .

The Law Institute. As far as I recall, I was the only one from my class to go there. It was complicated [getting admitted]. You had to gather character references. If you were a member of the Komsomol, then from the neighborhood committee or city committee. I had one from the city committee because I belonged to an operational squad at school.

---

12. Named after the Glebuchev Ravine neighborhood in Saratov, one of the city's poorest.

Graduation night, 1967. Aleksandr Konstantinov is in the first
row on the far left. Olga Kamaiurova is in the second row from
the bottom, second from the right. Wearing a white shirt, Gennadii
Ivanov is second from the left in the next-to-last row. Arkadii
Darchenko is on the far right, third row from the bottom. *Courtesy
A. A. Konstantinov.*

*Why did you enroll there? After all, you come from a family of physi-
cians. Did your parents want you to follow in their footsteps?*

I'm not sure why. My parents didn't insist that I study medicine.
Law seemed more interesting to me. For one thing, the subjects
taught interested me enough. I also liked the freer lifestyle. By that
time my parents had divorced. I found it more interesting there than
at school, and you could study what you liked. That is, there was
no more mathematics, physics, and chemistry. The workload was
perhaps greater, but legal questions were always more fascinating
to me. I wanted to work in law enforcement, yet back then I didn't
understand the difference all that well between an investigator and
an operative. Later, I realized that I liked the work of an operative
more, and it turned out that that's exactly what I became.

You enrolled in 1967 and the next year the Soviet Union invaded Czecho-

slovakia. How did you react to this and how did the students at the Law Institute respond?

You know, there had been a dissident group at the institute among the older students and they were locked up for two years. This took place about the same time as the invasion. They raised questions that were not acceptable back then, although common sense would dictate that they had the right to ask them. Back then this was considered an anti-Soviet group, but I don't think it was. As for the invasion, well, this too astonished me. What were the people there lacking? They lived well. One of my classmates took part in the invasion of Czechoslovakia and told us a few things about it.

Did you graduate in 1972?

No, in 1971. Back then it took four years to complete the institute, but now it's five years. After I graduated I was assigned to work in the police. We had just gotten married, and at first they sent us to Saransk.[13] We were students together in the same class. Well, when we arrived in Saransk, in Mordovia, we faced the matter of my having to serve in the army, but my wife was pregnant. They weren't about to give us our own apartment right off, and she would leave when the time came to give birth anyway. Therefore, the two organizations decided things between themselves. They released her from her work assignment in Saransk, and they found a job for me with the police in Saratov. I worked there for a couple of months and then was drafted into the army for a year. That was in 1971. She gave birth at her parents' place in Tambov, and, in 1972, I returned from the army and brought her back to Saratov. I returned to work where I had been before. After a while she found a job as a lawyer for the railroads and has worked there ever since.

How has your wife influenced you?

Women always have a calming effect on men, because they are, how shall I put it, both more assertive and show greater initiative, even though it's sometimes misplaced. We lived all these years in opposition both at war and peace [laughing]. It's hard to say who influenced whom, of course, because this changed at different times. We probably both influenced each other without being aware of it. We have two children. The first was born in Tambov, and the second one ten years later, that is, in 1981.

---

13. Saransk is the capital of the Republic of Mordovia located in the European part of Russia in the Volga basin, north of Saratov. It borders Nizhnii Novgorod, Ulianovsk, Penza, Riazan, and the Chuvash Republic.

Did you work in the same place all your life?

I worked in different departments of the police at different times, with different ranks and responsibilities. But I basically spent my entire career there, except for the period I spent in Afghanistan.

How would you evaluate the changes that came to your country over the years from the vantage point of your work in the police?

In what sense? Through the prism of my work? I worked in the criminal police all my life, and not in the political police. Therefore, I can only evaluate things from the point of view of criminality. That it grew during these years is beyond controversy. The measures that are very often being taken today, I would in no way support. . . . Of course, some things are better and some things are worse.

How important is it that you learned English already in school? Did it play a role in your life?

It played a role at an everyday level. I understand most of what's being said on television, say on the "European News." I understand practically everything in the captions, but sometimes I simply am unable to read them fast enough. If I could, I'd probably understand them. Knowledge of English helped a bit when I was in Afghanistan, and a bit today at work. We took some trips to Holland, where we communicated with the Dutch in English. We communicated fine. In all honesty, it's easier to communicate with the Dutch in English than it is with the Americans. I think American English differs a great deal from British English [laughing]. I know some Americans who have a hard time understanding each other. One of my classmate's daughters married an American. We have a hard time understanding each other. American and British English, of course, are different languages. Well, again, at an everyday level, I've had use of it. I was in Turkey, where I was able to communicate a bit in English, and also, as I said, in Holland.

When did you go abroad for the first time?

Well, when I ended up in Afghanistan, if you count that [laughing], in 1987–88.

Was that after Soviet troops were withdrawn?

No, we practically were withdrawn together. Well, what's there to say? It was an interesting period, of course. I was there as an advisor on criminal investigations. I mostly worked as an investigator. We had to deal with all sorts of contraband. By the way, I think that going in was the right thing to do. If we hadn't done so, someone else would have. From a legal point of view, there was a mutual aid agreement, so our actions were 99 percent correct. They asked us to go in. In any event, it was far more legal than America's going into Iraq [laughing]. America felt it had to, so it invaded, although there were absolutely no grounds for doing so, ever the more so because Iraq is far away and the weapons of mass destruction there turned out to be mythical. Why did America have to decide the fate of the president of Iraq? But in Afghanistan there were some wrong steps, and they did overthrow the [legitimate] ruler. We invaded on legal grounds, yet then got drawn in deeper for nothing. We should have given them more of an opportunity to do what they needed to do. Ever the more so because we already had the American experience in Vietnam to go on. In today's world nothing gets decided by the use of force. We needed to go in so that someone else didn't, so that we'd have a base there. After all, from the mountains all of Central Asia is visible. I mean with radar and the like. It's our weak underbelly. Thus we went in, perhaps rightly so, so that someone else didn't. We learned the particulars only afterward. For a hundred years, even during the tsars, we had friendly relations. Why did we get drawn in? They tried to create socialism there when it was too early to do so. I think that Russia itself came off second best, let's put it like that, because we tried to build socialism too early as well. We probably should have extended the period of the New Economic Policy longer.[14] I think it's the Swedes who say that they have a capitalist system of production, but a socialist system of distribution. I believe that this is a far superior model to that in Russia. I think that the revolution in Russia scared the world so much that everywhere else they tried to construct socialism in a peaceful manner. In other words, they built socialism there, not here.

How long were you in Afghanistan?

For about one and a half years. From a military perspective everything was okay, but there were separate wandering bands. These were exclusively police functions that needed to be carried out. There was no serious military threat. What's it called? The People's Democratic Party of Afghanistan.[15] Like with us, they were

---

14. Introduced in March 1921 as the Russian Civil War drew to a close, the New Economic Policy amounted to what party stalwarts called a "pact with the devil," because they feared that the policy would strengthen forces inimical to the goal of building socialism. Although the state continued to own large-scale industry, it allowed small-scale private economic activity and also put an end to the unpopular requisitioning of grain from the peasants, replaced under the NEP with a tax in kind. The party saw the NEP as a temporary measure, but Lenin soon concluded that it probably needed to be extended so that the organic preconditions for socialism could develop more fully.

15. The People's Democratic Party of Afghanistan overthrew the regime of Mohammad Daoud in 1978.

split into Bolsheviks and Mensheviks.[16] There were the Khalq and the Khalquists, and the people knew their banner. It's not important. There were two wings, one was more bourgeois, the other more radical. The Khalquists were the more radical ones.

It must have been terribly difficult working there.

Well, actually, it was all quite interesting. The Afghans are good, decent people. But more than five million of them went to neighboring countries. If you're familiar with their history, you'll know that it's impossible to maintain the border because the British at one time divided the territory with Pakistan in such a way that if you're in the stock-breeding business there's no way of keeping a border. People come and go. There are eight million Pashtuns here and approximately fifteen million there.[17] How can you divide them? To fix the border you'd have to build a great wall as in China.

Quite a bit has been written, and even some films were made during perestroika, about the young soldiers who served there and about how they fell under the influence of narcotics.

Yes, we saw everything. They sent young men there. Of course, the time has come for a professional army, and for providing everyone else with basic military training for two or three months. That was already true back then. Besides heroism, it gave us nothing but cripples and drug addicts. I would estimate that about 40,000 people died each year in the former Soviet Union in automobile accidents. In Afghanistan over a ten-year period some 14,000 of our soldiers died. I wouldn't say that those are big losses for a ten-year period, although, of course, we feel sorry for those who perished. But they could have gotten run over here. They could have gotten hooked on drugs here. It was the same thing there. Not everyone who went there got shot among the 14,000. A truck turns over somewhere and people die, although for the most part we'd say the death was caused by combat. The five million who remained in Afghanistan have only one possible way of making a living, and that's to buy up land mines and go and plant them so that people can be blown up. It was that way everywhere. The Afghans got used to having foreigners there all the time.

During the Gorbachev era they called the Brezhnev period one of stagna-

---

16. Soon after the People's Democratic Party's founding in the 1960s, it split into two factions, the Khalq faction of Nur Mohammad Taraki, who became president after the overthrow of Daoud, and the Parcham faction of Babrak Karma.

17. The estimated 42 million Pashtuns inhabit Afghanistan, Pakistan, and India, and are often referred to as "ethnic" Afghans, since they compose the country's ethnic majority.

tion. Did it seem to you back then that a period of stagnation had set in? Or do you think the term is unfair?

No, the stagnation was of course real when he began to lose the reins of power and grew ill. Probably during the last ten years of his rule.

Marxism underscores the importance of economics. How did you react to the fact that Saratov was an agricultural region, yet there were shortages and people had to travel to Moscow to buy things?

I thought it was disgraceful, of course. All those trains to Moscow. But I nevertheless think it was due to lack of organization. Of course, I'm a sensible person and realize that, with the Soviet system, you could hardly achieve the level of abundance you have in the West. But, on the other hand, I question whether this is really necessary. All these sausages today lie there and go bad. Does it matter if there are two varieties of sausage or ten? Is that really the meaning of life? If they lie there, then this must be a good thing? No, I'm not sure. People have lost a great deal in terms of their confidence in tomorrow. Money now decides everything. I'd like to return to something you asked earlier. I think things improved a great deal here just before the start of the Gorbachev period. Auxiliary farms began operating in the Engels region.[18] As a result, we had fresh vegetables year round. I'm not saying that it was like things are in the West where you can go and buy what you want. But everything became available. Enormous poultry farms started up and chicken was available year round. Again, I'm not saying that it was on the same level as in the West, but things began to improve in the early 1980s. We had an intelligent first party secretary here, who I think came from Tambov. He later became a minister of industry. His name was Gusev. The improvements under him were real ones. When the Gorbachev collapse took place and cooperatives opened up all this was ruined. You know, we go bumbling along and then, "Bang!" Our leader has an idea. Someone gets the idea to grow corn. Perhaps it's a good idea, but Russia's always had its share of blockheads who go along with everything. And instead of other crops, let's plant corn, even though it would never grow there or we don't need that much of it. We lacked corn specialists. But since our leader said grow corn and that it was a good thing, that's all it took [laughing]. You might have seen the TV serial about Siberia where the chairman of the

---

18. The Engels region is located directly across the Volga from Saratov.

collective farm has to decide whether to sow rye or wheat. "Well, what's more important for the soldier at the front? To have a piece of white bread this size or a real piece of, whatcha call it, rye bread? Rye grows fine here. Why are they forcing us to plant wheat?" Yes, there were all sorts of extremes at the local level that, of course, had their origins somewhere at the top with our leaders. That was the case here.

Did you join the Communist Party?

Yes, I'm a party member. I joined, let's see, when was it? Sometime in 1986, I think. No, that can't be right. Let's see. I'm getting mixed up. It must have been earlier, in 1982 or 1983. I think it was before Gorbachev, in the early 1980s.

In any society myths unite people. Tell me about the myths that existed in the Soviet Union.

I can't say. It was one thing back then, and now another. It's hard for us to say where the truth lies. Take Chapaev.[19] He's depicted one way, then another. You need to look at the historical record to decide. There are many other cases like this. Take the "Young Guard."[20] They say that this organization actually didn't exist. It's a myth. They say that the Panfilovtsy turned out to be a myth.[21] It's hard to say, but there are such cases. But what's the difference if they were located in one place or scattered about? If they set fire to twenty tanks or some other number? Or if they all died or not? They say that some of them ended up in concentration camps and that a few managed to survive, that they watched out for them. What really changes because of this?

I have a question for you, since you're the first person I've interviewed who works for the police. The fact that you work as a criminal investigator means that you were aware of the crime rate. But back in the Soviet period, people didn't know how much crime actually existed in society. I recall that

---

19. Vasilii Ivanovich Chapaev (1887–1919) was a Civil War hero killed in action while contributing to the defeat of Alexander Kolchak's White forces. Chapaev might have been forgotten had it not been for the publication of Dmitrii Furmanov's proto-Socialist-Realist novel, *Chapaev,* in 1923, and the release in 1934 of a film by the same name, which became the biggest box-office hit of the decade.

20. A group of young guerrilla resisters to the German occupation during World War II, mythologized in a novel by Aleksandr Fadeev in 1945, for which he received a Stalin Prize, first class.

21. The legend of the twenty-eight "Panfilov men," a detachment of poorly armed Red Army soldiers who heroically held at bay attacks by German tanks, emerged during the Battle of Moscow in late 1941, when the Germans threatened to seize the Soviet capital.

when I was a graduate student back in the mid-1970s at Moscow University, there was a serial killer who strangled many women. But because the media didn't keep people informed, all sorts of wild rumors circulated that probably exaggerated the extent of the killer's activity. Can you explain to a foreigner why such information was kept secret?

You know, it wasn't that someone decided to make a secret of this. I'm not sure that all those headlines that we have today are necessary. The papers describe in detail how a crime was committed and who the victim was. Why? Who needs this? Then, excuse me, but there's a difference in the number of murders today and back then. It's about five times higher. Why tell people that there were a 100 and now there are more than 500? Will this affect the crime rate or not? Why frighten people so that they're afraid of every shadow they see? What's the sense of telling people that there's a murderer on the loose? Whenever there was a need to do so, we informed the public. That was usually the case when we were dealing with a maniac. Back then, there were even statistics on this that appeared approximately every five years. I remember a murderer named Khaiust, who was a student for a long time, a volunteer militiaman, therefore, to a certain degree, he was well versed in these things. They'd post more police, and nothing would happen. Or they'd remove them, and, bang, a woman gets killed. The longer a killer's at it, the more facts there are to investigate. So why is it necessary to frighten people? After all, we know that people steal, but why turn that into some kind of tragedy? They steal, but much of this gets uncovered. We had a crime detection rate of roughly 90 percent. Someone steals and gets caught and the police return what's stolen and imprison the thief. What of it? But now if some vagrant steals, you can't take a thing from him, not even his stolen Mercedes [laughing]. Or take the drug addict. Everything goes for his next fix. What can you take from him? In order to buy drugs, he needs a large sum each day, which he gets only by stealing. But what changes by broadcasting this? You can decide to behave like this or not. It doesn't affect you in the least. Therefore, I'd say it wasn't only that we had less crime back then. It played an altogether different role. Back then we talked about crime at meetings, and over the radio, that it was necessary to fight against crime, that it was an abnormal phenomenon that still takes place in our society. Speaking about myths, well, here's one for you, that we could eliminate crime in our society. That's a myth, of course. But they used to demand that we achieve a 100 percent detection rate, which cost them some good investigators. Is it his fault that crime goes up one year? And today? A policeman doesn't know what he can or cannot do. His pay is low and it's easier for him to work as a guard in some shop where they give him extra money, otherwise he can't feed his family. That's how it is.

Why do you think perestroika took place?

Well, because enormous resources were put into it. Nothing takes place without preparation. . . . Somewhere it got linked up with domestic resources, because they stole an awful lot during the last years. It had to unfold this way. They had to put their capital somewhere.

Are you saying that those who stole wanted to somehow legalize their fortunes?

Yes, so that they could go abroad and finally talk about this. That's on the one hand, but on the other hand, I think there also was help from abroad.

Was this apparent to you as a Communist Party member? Did party members discuss this?

It was a very chaotic time, for there was rapid change in government appointments. Russia would send the Ministry of Internal Affairs of Russia one thing, and the Ministry of Internal Affairs of the Soviet Union another. It was unclear who was subordinate to whom. Both were Communist Party members. No one at that time said, "Let's put an end to the USSR" [laughing]. A referendum had just taken place, which backed the further existence of the Soviet Union.[22]

You said you believe that resources came from abroad. What kind of resources, from where did they come, and how do you know this?

Well, money, of course, is always involved. I know that nothing takes place without it. It's sort of like with soccer games.[23] Well, let's say, for instance, that Gorbachev gives the order to withdraw troops from Germany and takes nothing from Germany. How does that affect the soldiers? How does that affect his own people? The soldiers

---

22. This is a reference to a March 1991 referendum that backed Gorbachev's plan for a new and looser union treaty for the Soviet republics. Ivanov's remark needs fine tuning: the Baltic republics, Moldavia, Georgia, and Armenia were actually determined to become independent. On August 18, a few days before the new treaty based on the referendum was to be signed, Gorbachev's conservative opponents within the leadership tried to overthrow him and to keep the new treaty from going into effect.

23. Here Ivanov is suggesting that soccer matches can be bought.

are also people; so are the officers. They're withdrawn from there and everyone is astonished that he gets no political or economic benefits from this. Then he gets a Nobel Prize and opens some sort of Gorbachev Fund. But where does the money for this come from? I think it's clear. Then there are credits, which vanish. Credits for what services?

That is, you believe that Gorbachev was not a devoted Communist and that he fell under Western influence?

I don't know whose influence he was under at any given time. But that's simply the way he was. Perhaps he believed in what he was doing. Have you heard the joke: "Do you think perestroika was launched by scholars or politicians? Of course by politicians. Scholars would have first experimented with dogs." I think they all should be in jail. We have a guard at work. If he didn't keep an eye on preventing things from getting stolen at work, they'd institute a criminal investigation against him for negligence. But these people, whatever their intentions, should nonetheless be charged with negligence.

Those who ripped things off during the Gorbachev years were party members, right?

No, well, there were party members too. During the period of stagnation it happened that the wrong people ended up in higher and middle-range party organs and Soviet organizations.

The wrong people? What about glasnost? How did you react to the flood of information unleashed under Gorbachev?

Well, there's a flood of information, now, too. What of it?

I have in mind the sorts of things published in the so-called thick journals that everyone was reading back then. Did this tend to confirm what you already knew or suspected, or was there new information?

Of course, there was new information. It's another matter altogether whether to believe it or not. Do you have in mind information of a more important nature, or of who stole what?

The former. At first, of course, a lot was written about politics, about the dark chapters of Stalinism.

Well, of course. But please understand correctly what I'm about to say. My mother was a Volga German, right? They forcibly resettled the entire Volga German Republic from here, right? That's a fact. But they let her stay in Saratov and didn't touch her. That's also a fact. Why? Well, they summoned them, everyone here says that they summoned all of them. Well, they summoned her and the committee members said, "Why do this to a young girl? Why ruin her life? What kind of threat does she pose to us?" And they let her stay. She was a girl of twenty. She was old enough to have signaled to the Germans so that they could attack the bridge over the Volga. After all, the Germans did bomb the railroad bridge. Yet they let them [his mother and others] go. Why? Your countrymen drove all Americans of Japanese descent into concentration camps after Pearl Harbor, yet no one today sees this as some sort of terrible crime. Here they resettled them. Of course, they were better off in Saratov than being resettled. It was worse in Kazakhstan. Yet the very same Soviet people lived there. That is, they didn't force them into concentration camps, but merely resettled them. I understand that this was done for the people, and that the countries concerned aren't guilty. However, in these circumstances the Americans opted for what they did, and they don't see themselves as criminals. Stalin opted for what he did, and he's seen as a criminal. Volgograd [then Stalingrad] is only 400 kilometers from here and the Germans were there. If we had left the Volga Germans here, it's unclear how things might have turned out. If they had dropped a landing party here, how many would have risen up with the German landing party? It's unclear. But on the other hand, I was chatting once with a former party secretary here, some 60 kilometers from Saratov—in Krasnoarmeisk. He was from the Volga German Republic. I spoke with him twenty or thirty years ago. He was already a very old man. He said that [back during the Civil War] various armed bands roamed about and drove away two Red Army detachments. One was a German Red Army detachment, the other a Russian one. He said they showed up in a German village and all was calm. But when the Germans came, shooting broke out among the Germans. Therefore, it's hard to say anything with confidence on the basis of nationality. What I know is that they decided things on an individual basis [when they resettled the Volga Germans]. Perhaps elsewhere some son of a bitch more quickly resettled, say, a thousand people. Perhaps they gave the order to surround a village and to allow only two hours for people to gather their things before they packed them off into train cars. It could have been like that. But we don't know what order Stalin or Beria gave.

Of course, these were difficult times. Afterward, we know all too well what kind of nationality policies there were. I myself, for instance, was never in Chechnia before all the trouble there started up, but some acquaintances of mine were. The Chechens are a very hospitable people, especially in the capital, Groznyi. They visited villages like tourists and everything was fine. That is, despite Stalinist policies toward the Chechens, things were okay. Even after the resettlement.[24] But the result of democratic policies is war. The extermination of the Chechen people is going on today over the past decade or so. There's so much stealing going on today that I think Stalin would have said: "Yes, I expelled too few back then." If I were in Stalin's place today, I'd expel even more with their Chubais boxes packed with $500,000.[25] The country doesn't know how to, watcha call it, pay pensions. Here they're preparing for elections and these people get caught with $500,000 in shoe boxes! What do you call this? And nothing comes of this. If they wanted to put a stop to all this, I suspect the reaction would be altogether different. But they don't want to. Take narcotics. Those countries that want to can increase criminal responsibility for narcotics. All those Thailands and the others. And America, I think, too. At least they're not decreasing it. Here, for some reason, you can have a certain number of fixes on you and not get punished. Is this a real desire to put an end to this or to limit it? I think it's an unwillingness to feed extra mouths in prison. They let them continue to steal and to recruit new drug addicts. Even if he's simply an addict, and even if it's a disease, they could at least isolate them by treating them at drug prevention centers. You understand? They didn't give people their due after the various defaults. Take [for instance] when my mother died. She had over 3,000 rubles in one savings account and either five or eight thousand in another. I no longer remember. When she died I tried to sell the apartment, and eventually did so for fifty or sixty thousand rubles. That's dirt cheap. But Russians began fleeing from there and the apartments were being vacated. The last time I was there I went to the savings banks, but they wouldn't let me withdraw the money. I think it was back in 1990. They led me on for awhile and then said that, as a result of all the economic turmoil, they could pay me fifteen kopecks for one savings account and thirty kopecks for the other. That's the sort of debt they owe the people of our countries. They pay their foreign debts, although, to be

---

24. Whereas the Soviet government resettled its Volga German population as a "prophylactic" measure in 1941, it forcibly resettled the Chechens in 1944 for purportedly collaborating with the Nazis. They were rehabilitated in 1956.

25. A reference to Russian politician Anatolii Chubais, who, during Boris Yeltsin's election campaign, was linked to a scandal involving $500,000 removed from the Kremlin in several large boxes. Chubais denied any links to the money, but was later caught in the lie.

honest, no other country in the world pays off its debts today. And those who lent the money are not interested in having it paid back. They're interested in the interest it earns. Why should we pay these debts off, when you'll need to settle up again? But the population gets nothing. And I'm giving you an example of what this actually means. Back then the money was enough to buy a car with. What they gave me, though, probably isn't even enough to buy a box of matches today. They owe the people a great deal.

How has your life changed during the past fifteen years or so, say, since the collapse of the Soviet Union? For one thing, crime rose, so you probably were busier at work.

The profile changed somewhat. About a year after my return from Afghanistan I became the deputy chief of the regional department against organized crime. If at my other job I had to deal with theft, murder, and everything else, I now dealt with organized crime in the Volga region, which comprises several oblasts. There was an enormous amount of it. It's not politics, but the result of politics. Mainly banditry.

You said you had gone abroad at this time, to Holland.

That was later, after I retired. I now work as the head of security at a transportation company that's a joint concern involving the Dutch. I traveled there to see what it's like. It seemed a bit boring there, at least in our terms, because at night everything comes to a standstill. That excludes Amsterdam. However, even there all the action is found in small restaurants lit up with candlelight. But the shops close around 6 PM. True, I was there in the winter, and perhaps that had something to do with it. I can't really say that they work longer or better than we do. They're getting poorer, and probably because they steal there, too.

How does your children's generation differ from yours? I guess we're speaking of two generations, since there's a ten-year difference between them.

That's a logical question. They grew up during a transition period. The older one, born in 1971, is more like us, whereas the other born in 1981 is more modern. The older one is more like us, but the other is altogether different, let's put it like that. Of course, if we measure things by the decade, then there's always lots of change. Now, when I come downtown, which is rarely because the firm I work in is in the suburbs, I don't know the city with all the new signs and advertisements. For me it's become a different city. But my younger one is like a fish in water here.

How can your life story help me to understand the fate of the Soviet Union? That is, to what extent does your life reflect larger, more global, tendencies?

Well, it's hard to say. There's always some major turning point in Russian history, so it's not only a matter of our generation. I think America is going to experience something similar. Especially with the current leadership, which is treading dangerously. In today's world nothing gets resolved through the use of force. If you seize hold of too much you won't be able to control it. If you take too much on yourself just to have it, that's a big responsibility. You can expect a blow from terrorists. If you back a dog into a corner, he'll bare his teeth and lunge at you. It's the same with terrorism. Terrorism is the result of something that can't be resolved any other way. It's actually quite simple. I'm not speaking of, say, real crazies, or of some kind of fanatics. It's impossible to solve things otherwise in Palestine, for instance, because no court would take action. They don't say who is right or wrong. As far as I know, it's a real mess there, even worse than Afghanistan. It's based on contradictions over religion, which they've added to their arsenals. I'm not saying that the religions there are bad, but that they're using them in what's become a clash between Christianity and Judaism with Islam. It's the same with Russia's involvement in Chechnia and America's involvement in Iraq. Why did you need this? Economically speaking, America could have gotten far more by having relations with Saddam Hussein. Now everyone's on the offensive. It's like our involvement in Chechnia. People have lost a father, a mother, an uncle, or someone else. How much hatred is there? We shouldn't be concentrating our efforts on large troop engagements. We need to capture and destroy. Or reach an agreement.

Why do you believe the first Chechen war broke out during the Yeltsin era?

Only so that Yeltsin could seize power, and the second war in Chechnia so that Putin could. There's no other reason.

What's your opinion in general of Russia's last three leaders, Gorbachev, Yeltsin, and Putin?

They're peas from the same pod. Under Putin they say one thing, and do another. Take, for example, the fact that practically not a single nongovernment television broadcast exists any longer. Yes, there's one, but they'll remove it, too. They claim there are some economic reasons for doing so, that they had an agreement with them and they didn't pay up. But the others didn't pay up either, and they're still on. It's absolutely illegal to victimize the oligarchs.[26] We need to introduce specific legislation and not just can them. Let them spend time, pay up, and release them. I believe that the laws should work. You need to build a government based on laws. Take for instance the oil business. What does it have to do with the government? They speak about this openly, that they're processing only the oilfields discovered in the USSR. No one is looking for new oilfields to tap. And what kind of selling is this? Let's increase the sale of oil abroad, and so on. What will be left for our grandchildren? Excuse me, but why is it that America is working only the Alaskan oilfields, while she's abandoning those strategic ones that are closer such as in Texas and elsewhere? They search for new oilfields and then shut them down, and import oil from the Near East. Why, because they're stupid people? No, they're not stupid. They'll become tomorrow's monopolists. And what will we leave for our children and grandchildren? Fuel is not the main thing. It's altogether possible that there'll be alternative sources of energy. But it's the raw material for industry. Excuse me, but tomorrow there'll be no wheels for cars, there'll be nothing to make them from. Maybe I'm wrong.

I forgot to ask whether you actually withdrew from the Communist Party during perestroika.

How can I put it? Not officially. There's a lot I don't like about how the Communist Party today conducts itself. But there's nothing else to replace it. For all intents and purposes, I withdrew when I stopped paying my dues and stopped attending meetings, but I didn't demonstrably quit.

How would you characterize your generation? Several of your classmates have called it a "lost generation," while others disagree.

I'd call it a typical one that inherited its share. How could it be otherwise? Isn't this true of all generations? The wartime generation? The postwar generation? The generation born before the war? The Civil War generation? It's not yet clear about the generation after ours. It's really hard for young people today. No one really looks after the young people today. They've launched some hesitant efforts to provide credit for them so that they can purchase apartments, but this is on such a small scale that they either become

---

26. Men of great wealth and power, such as oil baron Mikhail Khodorkovskii and media magnate Vladimir Gusinskii, who helped run the country until they became locked in a bitter power struggle with President Vladimir Putin.

gangsters, drug addicts, drunks, or thieves, or else get by with help from our generation. Without our generation it wouldn't be able to accomplish a thing. I'm certain of this. Somehow they're making their way in the world, but it's hard, because today money or being exceptionally talented determines everything.

You're a professional investigator. If you wanted to understand my life, what would you ask me that I haven't asked you? In other words, what have I forgotten to ask you about?

I'd ask what are the main goals in your life. I'd ask you that. What are your goals right now? A lost generation. In what ways is ours a lost one? Everyone inherited his share, and everyone of course feels wronged by something. If you'd have asked me this question, I would have answered that my goals are to help my children reach a certain social and material level, and put aside a bit for myself to live on. I'd say this because acquiring things no longer interests me. If I didn't have this outfit, I'd throw on something else. And no matter how much I eat, I don't need to fill up the refrigerator. I've also done my share of traveling. Perhaps I'd like to visit America, but I'm honestly not sure about this. For one thing, it's a long flight, and they're nonsmoking flights [laughing]. Well, we too are going too far with such things. We put cans of beer in a bag and sneak them on board. Or else underage kids can't visit certain places after a certain hour. Of course, there's some sense in this. In any event, I'd like to join a tourist group. Materially speaking, I could afford this. My wife could, too. But this year we'll probably once again go to a resort with mineral baths in order to calm our nerves. I'd like to travel to Europe again, but not to visit acquaintances, because I'm not fond of all those meetings, goodbyes, and the like. I'd simply like to go as part of a tourist group that visits the major cities and sees the main sites. It's not a dream of mine, but it's something I wouldn't mind doing. And why not? I have two sons, and they have their own apartments, and I have mine. They both have cars, and I have a car. They both work, but would like to get better jobs. One has a wife and daughter, and the other is getting married in August. That is, there's not a lot left for me. They'll both soon be married, but they couldn't have had a real wedding without our help. And nothing will get settled at work for them without our involvement. This also depends on acquiring some experience. The younger one, for instance, is straight out of college. Once he acquires some experience, the problem can be dealt with. We'll pay for the wedding and help him get settled at work. He already has an apartment. We'll die, they'll divvy up our apartment,

Group B reunion, February 2004. Olga Kamaiurova is on the far left; Gennadii Ivanov is third from the right. Arkadii Darchenko is next to him. Natalia P. is standing, second from the left. *Courtesy A. O. Darchenko.*

and will live even better. By and large there's not much left for us to do then. Well, my granddaughter will soon be on her own, and perhaps there'll be more for us to do. But what else do I need? I'd like to have my health back. But how can we be a lost generation if we're still able to do things for the next one? Other generations probably also strive to make things better for their children. Communism had the goal of making things better, not worse. I guess in that regard we're a lost generation to a certain extent. We set about building communism, but things turned out differently. Yet we did accomplish a few things.

The B group from your class still gets together each year. How do you account for this degree of cohesion, for the fact that people remain friends after all these years and keep in contact with one another?

Well, to answer that, you'd probably need to return to our childhood. We have a lot in common in that regard. My classmates don't know what it was like for us when we had children, but we now have our childhood to talk about, something to remember. I think this is only natural, although some aren't eager to take part in this, apparently, because they didn't get along with everyone. The last time we gathered more than twenty people showed up out of almost thirty in our class. Some weren't there because they're no longer in Russia. It appears that one's dead. Perhaps I've forgotten someone, but as for the others, not everyone shows up each time we meet. Sometimes circumstances prevent them from doing so. As for turning to each other in times of material need, well, I never did so. Several turned to me for help, I suppose, because my work enabled me to help them. Well, I guess every now and then I did turn to someone. Without connections it's hard to get anything done.

What do you regret in your life?

Well, of course, there are things I didn't have time for and other things that I'd perhaps have done a bit differently, but nothing fundamental. Let's say that having lived your life and seen how it turned out, you'd do things differently if you had a second chance. Why live the same life twice? I can't really say that my conscience gnaws away at me over anything. I always preferred to sleep peacefully at night [laughing], although they didn't allow me to do so at work. But I didn't do anything that hangs over my soul. There's nothing of the sort.

Have you told me everything you had hoped to say to me?

You know, there's a joke about a policeman who resembles me because, please excuse me, but 99 percent of the criminals tell me everything. I'm able to talk to people. Life taught me how. Well, this policeman dies, but his tongue continues wagging for three days. Well, a policeman, especially an operative, is about the same as an investigator, that is, as me. What's there to say? Well, I can tell you what I don't regret. I told you everything I wanted to say, and I can also listen with pleasure [laughing]. I don't expect anything for myself to come out of this, and I have nothing to be afraid of. That's how it is.

Selected Bibliography

Adelman, Deborah. *The "Children of Perestroika": Moscow Teenagers Talk about Their Lives and the Future.* Armonk, N.Y.: M.E. Sharpe, 1991.

Alekseeva, Liudmila. *U.S. Broadcasting to the Soviet Union.* New York: U.S. Helsinki Watch Committee, 1986.

Alexeyeva, Ludmilla, and Paul Goldberg. *The Thaw Generation: Coming of Age in the Post-Stalin Era.* Pittsburgh: University of Pittsburgh Press, 1990.

Alexievich, Svetlana. *Voices from Chernobyl.* Translated and with a preface by Keith Gessen. Normal, Ill.: Dalkey Archive Press, 2005.

Bacon, Edwin, and Mark Sandle, eds. *Brezhnev Reconsidered.* New York: Palgrave, 2002.

Ball, Alan M. *Imagining America: Influence and Images in Twentieth-Century Russia.* Lanham, Md.: Rowman and Littlefield, 2003.

Barker, Adele Marie, ed. *Consuming Russia: Popular Culture, Sex, and Society since Gorbachev.* Durham, N.C.: Duke University Press, 1999.

Baron, Samuel H. *Bloody Sunday in the Soviet Union: Novocherkassk, 1962.* Stanford: Stanford University Press, 2001.

Bertaux, Daniel, Paul Thompson, and Anna Rotkirch. *On Living Through Soviet Russia.* New York: Routledge, 2004.

Blekher, Feiga. *The Soviet Woman in the Family and Society: A Sociological Study.* New York: John Wiley, 1979.

Boym, Svetlana. *Common Places: Mythologies of Everyday Life in Russia.* Cambridge: Harvard University Press, 1994.

———. *The Future of Nostalgia.* New York: Basic Books, 2001.

Brady, Rose. *Kapitalizm: Russia's Struggle to Free Its Economy.* New Haven: Yale University Press, 1999.

Breslauer, George W. *Gorbachev and Yeltsin as Leaders.* New York: Cambridge University Press, 2002.

———. *Khrushchev and Brezhnev as Leaders: Building Authority in Soviet Politics.* London: Allen and Unwin, 1982.

Bronfenbrenner, Urie. *Two Worlds of Childhood: U.S. and U.S.S.R.* New York: Pocket Books, 1970.

Brown, Archie. *The Gorbachev Factor.* New York: Oxford University Press, 1997.

Brumberg, Abraham, ed. *Russia under Khrushchev: An Anthology from* Problems of Communism. New York: Praeger, 1962.

Byrnes, Robert F., ed. *After Brezhnev: Sources of Soviet Conduct in the 1980s.* Bloomington: Indiana University Press, 1983.

———. *Soviet-American Academic Exchanges, 1958–1975.* Bloomington: Indiana University Press, 1976.

Chumachenko, Tatiana A. *Church and State in Soviet Russia: Russian Orthodoxy from World War II to the Khrushchev Years.* Trans. and ed. Edward E. Roslof. Armonk, N.Y.: M. E. Sharpe, 2002.

Clements, Barbara E., Rebecca Friedman, and Dan Healy, eds. *Russian Masculinities in History and Culture.* New York: Palgrave, 2002.

Cohen, Stephen F., Alexander Rabinowitch, and Robert Sharlet. *The Soviet Union since Stalin.* Bloomington: Indiana University Press, 1980.

Dickson, Paul. *Sputnik: The Shock of the Century.* New York: Walker and Co., 2001.

Dornberg, John. *Brezhnev: The Masks of Power.* New York: Basic Books, 1974.

Engel, Barbara, and Anastasia Posadskaya-Vanderbeck. *A Revolution of Their Own: Voices of Women in Soviet History.* Trans. Sona Hoisington. Boulder, Colo.: Westview Press, 1998.

Evangelista, Matthew. *Unarmed Forces: The Transnational Movement to End the Cold War.* Ithaca: Cornell University Press, 1999.

Fisher, Wesley. *The Soviet Marriage Market: Mate Selection in Russia and the USSR.* New York: Praeger, 1980.

Geiger, Kent H. *The Family in Soviet Russia.* Cambridge: Harvard University Press, 1968.

Gorbachev, Mikhail. *Perestroika: New Thinking for Our Country and the World.* New York: Harper and Row, 1987.

Graham, Loren R. *Science and the Soviet Social Order.* Cambridge: Harvard University Press, 1990.

Grant, Nigel. *Soviet Education,* 4th ed. New York: Penguin, 1978.

Hanson, Philip. *The Rise and Fall of the Soviet Economy.* London: Longman, 2003.

Hendel, Samuel, and Randolph L. Braham, eds. *The U.S.S.R. after 50 Years: Promise and Reality.* New York: Alfred A. Knopf, 1967.

Hitchcock, William I. *The Struggle for Europe: The Turbulent History of a Divided Continent, 1945 to the Present.* New York: Random House, 2003.

Holmes, Larry E. "Part of History: The Oral Record and Moscow's Model School No. 25, 1931–1937." *Slavic Review* 56 (1997): 279–306.

———. *Stalin's School: Moscow's School No. 25, 1931–1937.* Pittsburgh: University of Pittsburgh Press, 1999.

Humphrey, Caroline. *The Unmaking of Soviet Life.* Ithaca: Cornell University Press, 2002.

Inkeles, Alex. *Public Opinion in Soviet Russia: A Study in Mass Persuasion.* Cambridge: Harvard University Press, 1951.

———. *Social Change in Soviet Russia.* Cambridge: Harvard University Press, 1968.

Inkeles, Alex, and Raymond A. Bauer with the assistance of David Gleischer and Irving Rosou. *The Soviet Citizen: Daily Life in a Totalitarian Society.* Cambridge: Harvard University Press, 1961.

Jacoby, Susan. *Inside Soviet Schools.* New York: Hill and Wang, 1974.

Keep, John. *Last of the Empires: A History of the Soviet Union, 1945–1991.* New York: Oxford University Press, 1995.

Kerblay, Basile. *Modern Soviet Society.* Trans. Rupert Swyer. New York: Pantheon Books, 1983.

Kon, Igor S. *The Sexual Revolution in Russia: From the Age of the Czars to Today.* Trans. James Riordan. New York: Free Press, 1995.

Kotkin, Stephen. *Armageddon Averted: The Soviet Collapse, 1970–2000.* New York: Oxford University Press, 2001.

Kozlov, Vladimir A. *Mass Uprisings in the USSR: Protest and Rebellion in the Post-Stalin Years.* Trans. and ed. Elaine McClarnand MacKinnon. Armonk, N.Y.: M. E. Sharpe, 2002.

Lapidus, Gail. *Women in Soviet Society.* Berkeley: University of California Press, 1978.

Lewin, Moshe. *The Gorbachev Phenomenon: A Historical Interpretation,* exp. ed. Berkeley: University of California Press, 1991.

Linz, Susan J., ed. *The Impact of World War II on the Soviet Union.* Totowa, N.J.: Rowman and Allanheld, 1985.

Lourie, Richard. *Russia Speaks: An Oral History from the Revolution to the Present.* New York: Edward Burlingame Books, 1991.

Madison, Bernice. *Social Welfare in the Soviet Union.* Stanford: Stanford University Press, 1968.

Matthews, Mervyn. *Education in the Soviet Union: Politics and Institutions since Stalin.* London: Allen and Unwin, 1982.

———. *Privilege in the Soviet Union: A Study of Elite Life-Styles under Communism.* London: Allen and Unwin, 1978.

Medvedev, Roy A. *Post-Soviet Russia: A Journey through the Yeltsin Era.* Trans. and ed. George Shriver. New York: Columbia University Press, 2000.

Medvedev, Roy A., and Zhores A. Medvedev. *Khrushchev: The Years in Power.* New York: W. W. Norton, 1978.

Millar, James R., ed. *Politics, Work, and Daily Life in the USSR: A Survey of Former Soviet Citizens.* New York: Cambridge University Press, 1987.

Morrison, John. *Boris Yeltsin: From Bolshevik to Democrat.* New York: Penguin, 1991.

Nove, Alec. *Glasnost in Action: Cultural Renaissance in Russia.* Boston: Unwin Hyman, 1989.

Paperno, Irina. "Personal Accounts of the Soviet Experience." *Kritika* 3, no. 4 (2002): 577–610.

Petro, Nicolai N. *The Rebirth of Russian Democracy: An Interpretation of Political Culture.* Cambridge: Harvard University Press, 1995.

Putin, Vladimir. *First Person: An Astonishingly Frank Self-Portrait by Russia's President.* With Nataliya Gevorkyan, Natalya Timakova, and Andrei Kolesnikov. Trans. Catherine A. Fitzpatrick. New York: Public Affairs, 2000.

Ransel, David L. *Village Mothers: Three Generations of Change in Russia and Tataria*. Bloomington: Indiana University Press, 2000.

Remnick, David. *Lenin's Tomb: The Last Days of the Soviet Empire*. New York: Random House, 1993.

———. *Resurrection: The Struggle for a New Russia*. New York: Random House, 1997.

Ries, Nancy. *Russian Talk: Culture and Conversation during Perestroika*. Ithaca: Cornell University Press, 1997.

Ritchie, Donald A. *Doing Oral History*. New York: Twayne Publishers, 1995.

Ruffley, David L. *Children of Victory: Young Specialists and the Evolution of Soviet Society*. Westport, Conn.: Praeger, 2003.

Shlapentokh, Vladimir. *Love, Marriage, and Friendship in the Soviet Union: Ideals and Practices*. New York: Praeger, 1984.

———. *A Normal Totalitarian Society: How the Soviet Union Functioned and How It Collapsed*. Armonk, N.Y.: M. E. Sharpe, 2001.

———. *Public and Private Life of the Soviet People: Changing Values in Post-Stalin Russia*. New York: Oxford University Press, 1989.

Siddiqi, Asif A. *Sputnik and the Soviet Space Challenge*. Gainesville: University of Florida Press, 2003.

Smith, Kathleen E. *Mythmaking in the New Russia: Politics and Memory during the Yeltsin Era*. Ithaca: Cornell University Press, 2002.

Stoner-Weiss, Kathryn. *Local Heroes: The Political Economy of Russian Regional Governance*. Princeton: Princeton University Press, 1997.

Taubman, William. *Khrushchev: The Man and His Era*. New York: Norton, 2003.

Thompson, Paul. *The Voice of the Past: Oral History*. New York: Oxford University Press, 1978.

Tonkin, Elizabeth. *Narrating Our Pasts: The Social Construction of Oral History*. New York: Cambridge University Press, 1994.

Vladimirov, Leonid. *The Russian Space Bluff: The Inside Story of the Soviet Drive to the Moon*. Trans. David Floyd. New York: Dial Press, 1973.

Von Bencke, Matthew J. *The Politics of Space: A History of U.S.-Soviet/Russian Competition and Cooperation in Space*. Boulder, Colo.: Westview Press, 1997.

Weiner, Amir. *Making Sense of War: The Second World War and the Fate of the Bolshevik Revolution*. Princeton: Princeton University Press, 2001.

Weiner, Douglas R. *A Little Corner of Freedom: Russian Nature Protection from Stalin to Gorbachev*. Berkeley: University of California Press, 1999.

Wertsch, James V. *Voices of Collective Remembering*. New York: Cambridge University Press, 2002.

White, Stephen. *After Gorbachev*. New York: Cambridge University Press, 1993.

———. *Russia's New Politics: The Management of a Postcommunist Society*. New York: Cambridge University Press, 2000.

Woll, Josephine. *Real Images: Soviet Cinema and the Thaw.* New York: I.B. Tauris, 2000.

Zajda, Joseph I. *Education in the USSR.* New York: Pergamon Press, 1980.

Zubkova, Elena. *Russia after the War: Hopes, Illusions, and Disappointments, 1945–1957.* Trans. and ed. Hugh Ragsdale. Armonk, N.Y.: M. E. Sharpe, 1998.

Index

Abakan (Siberia), 122
Academy of Sciences, USSR, 50
Afghanistan, 265, 266–67, 275, 276; invasion of, 21, 47, 109, 112, 145, 215, 248, 253; war in, 97, 254
Africa, 161, 233; and decolonization, 56, 234–35; students from, 43
Agitation brigade, 42, 44
Aitmatov, Chingiz, 201
Aksenov, Vasilii, 214
Aktobe (Aktiubinsk) (Kazakhstan), 255
Alcohol, 32, 76, 94. *See also* Drinking
Altukhova, Natalia Valentinovna, 55–57, 75n22, 87
America. *See* United States
American exhibition (Moscow, 1959), 35–36, 234
Americans, 99, 100, 115, 148, 209, 215, 242, 248, 249, 259, 273; caricatures of, 35; communication with, 265; competition with, 1; interaction with, 59, 60. *See also* Foreigners
Amnesty, 156, 165
Amsterdam (Netherlands), 275
Andropov, Iurii, 179
Anecdotes, 34, 247. *See also* Jokes
Angara (Siberia), 141
Antisemitism, 30, 156n1
Apartments. *See* Housing
Argumenty i fakty, 151
Armenia, 109; and Armenians, 80n26
Arms race, 259
Army, Red, 4, 164, 254, 273; and draft, 264; service in, 21, 107, 147, 215
Art, 52, 93, 109; exhibits of, 34n7
Artists, 34, 207
Atheism, 118, 257
Atheists, 74, 194
Atomic bomb, 4, 144n28, 213
Australia, 25, 52, 161

Baikal-Amur Magistral Railway (BAM), 48
Baikonur Cosmodrome, 1
Ballet, 91, 102, 103, 195
Bandera, Stepan, 124
Baptism, 125, 194
Basketball, 256
Beatles, 38, 65, 68, 69, 139, 166, 237, 256. *See also* Music, Western
Belgium, 150
Belief, 74, 75, 83, 85, 101, 114, 201, 221, 231; collapse of, 199; in communism, 17, 132, 198, 214, 226, 246; among Communists, 146; in Soviet system, 73, 232, 239; and youth, 234–35
Belovolova, Natalia Aleksandrovna (Ianichkina), 154, 158, 170
Beria, Lavrentii, 144, 273
Berlin, 148–49
Berlin Wall, 85
Beslan (Russia), 53
Black market, 18, 81, 245
Black Sea, 169, 211
Blat, 245
Blockade, 48, 260
Bolsheviks, 267. *See also* October Revolution
Books, 180, 208, 222, 230, 260. *See also* Library
Borders, 181, 267
Bratislava (Slovakia), 13
Brayne, Mark, 43
Breslauer, George, 17
Brezhnev, Leonid, 14, 17–18, 34, 54, 84, 128n12, 145, 179, 238, 248; attitudes toward, 46, 113, 233, 247
Brezhnev era, 15, 17, 54, 94, 178
Briansk (Russia), 131, 196, 197
Bristol (England), 161, 194, 236–37

British Broadcasting Corporation
(BBC), 19, 166, 240
Bucharest (Romania), 207
Bulgakov, Mikhail Afanasievich, 83,
83n31, 133, 213, 218
Bulgaria, 142, 186; and Bulgarians, 145
Bush, George, 54, 204

Camp: Pioneer, 196; sports, 142, 196;
summer, 16, 32, 33, 93, 94, 134, 135,
139, 147, 188, 195, 228–30, 259
Campaignism, 17
Canada, 150, 181, 182, 186
Capitalism, 153, 232, 234–35, 246, 252
Career, 21, 50, 140, 153, 188, 204; ad-
vancement of, 136; changes in, 55,
115, 116–17, 142–43; and Commu-
nist Party, 243. See also Employment;
Profession
Carter, Jimmy, 205
Castro, Fidel, 43, 235
Caucasus, 80, 162–63
Celebrations, 93–94, 212, 224
Central Asia, 155–56, 157, 266
Chapaev, Vasilii Ivanovich, 269
Chardym (Russia), 139, 142
Chechnia, 113, 115, 144, 273; war in,
53, 97, 145, 276; and Chechens,
80n26, 273, 274
Cheka, 74n21. See also NKVD
Chekhov, Anton, 180
Chernenko, Konstantin Ustinovich, 179
Chernomyrdin, Viktor, 181n22, 261
Childhood, 73, 80, 90, 96, 190–91,
192, 210, 251; happy, 16, 58, 187;
interests in, 28, 60–61, 124, 157,
224, 255; memories of, 92, 104, 123,
205–206, 221, 229, 279
Children, 39, 51, 91, 159, 183, 191,
199, 203, 219, 224, 242, 278, 279
China, 114, 128, 267; attitude toward,
42, 128–29, 143–44, 166, 212, 244,
259; and Chinese, 145, 208, 210,
244; relations with, 69–71; travel to,
150
Christianity, 210, 276
Christmas, 91n4, 95
Chubais, Anatolii, 274n25

Chukhotka (Siberia), 180, 185
Church, 17, 37, 108–109, 125, 199,
210; and rituals, 74; Russian Ortho-
dox, 91n4
Churchill, Winston, 109n18
Cinema. See Films
Civil War, 259, 273
Civilization, 144, 148
Clothing, 102–103, 152; school, 92 (see
also Uniforms); styles of, 93, 129,
130, 138, 149, 158, 166, 167. See also
Jeans
Clubs, 15, 93, 157, 230
Cold War, 1–2, 2n6, 5, 7, 234
Collectivization, 261
College, 19–20, 21, 159, 257; enroll-
ment in, 136–37. See also Exams, en-
trance; University
Colombia, 238
Colonialism, 56, 234–35
Communism, 5, 138, 198, 226, 231,
233, 246; achievement of, 17, 72–73;
building of, 132, 162, 226–27, 235,
258–59, 279; collapse of, 9, 22, 49,
83; goal of, 214, 215; and myths, see
Myths, Soviet. See also Socialism
Communist Party (CPSU), 17, 22,
48n28, 59n6, 95, 242, 246; Central
Committee of, 44, 72, 179, 185; children of, 8, 157; course on the history
of, 20, 65, 127, 138, 240; documents
of membership in, 184, 185, 261; ex-
pulsion from, 155, 184; membership
in, 15, 21, 27, 49, 57, 59–60, 72, 80,
125, 132, 136, 140, 146, 179, 200,
215, 232, 243, 260, 269, 271, 272,
277; Nineteenth Conference of, 183;
Twentieth Congress of (1956), 2, 33,
71–72, 102, 131, 231; Twenty-sixth
Congress of, 185
Communists, 89, 114, 118, 146–47,
181, 194, 198, 199, 215, 231, 272,
277; Chinese, 5
Concentration camps, 252, 269, 273.
See also Labor camps
Confidence in tomorrow, 246, 247, 268
Confucianism, 209, 210
Connections, 280. See also Blat

Conspiracy theory, 88, 100n10, 115
Construction brigades, 141–42
Consumerism, 47
Cooperatives, 268
Corn, 17, 258, 268
Cosmopolitanism, 154, 156
Cossacks, 118, 190
Counterculture, 15, 65n11
Courtyard, 15, 224, 225, 256
Crime rates, 269, 270–71, 275
Criminal code, 97
Criminality, 265
Criminals, 47, 224, 225, 231, 273
Cuba, 34, 42–43, 129, 150, 212, 259–60; revolution in, 235
Cuban Missile Crisis, 33, 34, 56, 76n23, 132
Cult: of Bulgakov, 83n30; of personality, 131, 186, 258 (see also Stalin, cult of); of physics, 124; of Vysotskii, 65n11; of World War II, 47–48
Cultural life, 167–68
Cultural Revolution, Chinese, 70, 166, 259
Culture, 56, 209, 218; Latin, 205; Soviet, 6, 72n17
Cyprus, 109
Czechoslovakia, 244n15; family ties to, 190; invasion of, 20, 21, 40, 47, 67, 107, 137, 145, 198, 202, 236, 248, 263–64; travel to, 66–68

Dacha, 189, 204
Daily life, 9, 22, 218, 260, 265
Damansky Island crisis, 42, 259
Dancing, 76
Daoism, 209, 210
Darchenko, Arkadii Olegovich, 120–21, 122, 131, 263, 279
Death, 115, 267
Debt, 274–75
Dekulakization, 118
Democracy, 54, 97
Demonstrations, 40, 236
Denunciations, 165, 184, 242–43
Deportation, 124
Despair, 145–46
Détente, 99, 176

Development: cultural, 148; economic, 44, 81–82, 177, 245, 260; path of, 240; socialist, 234
Dewey, John, 3
Diakov, Boris, 168
Dickens, Charles, 180
Dikson (Siberia), 173, 180
Disarmament, 205
Discipline, 104, 145, 158; school, 92
Discrimination, 81, 223
Disease, 36, 274; heart, 189
Dissertation, 86, 88, 100, 101, 139, 171, 189; defense of, 105, 110, 119
Dissident movement, 20, 33n5, 107, 175, 202. See also Literature, dissident
Dissidents, 6, 18, 41, 83, 100, 198, 264
Divorce, 21, 39, 46, 73, 79, 105, 155, 169, 171, 201, 261, 263
Dizzy with Success speech, 261
Domestic help, 37, 190
Donetsk (Ukraine), 169, 170–71
Dostoevsky, Fedor, 40, 44
Double burden, 188, 201, 202
Draft, military, 162, 222, 264
Dress code, 130, 159. See also Uniforms
Drinking, 79, 238. See also Alcohol
Drug addicts, 267, 270, 274
Dubček, Alexander, 244n15
Dubna (Russia), 121, 127, 133, 136, 137, 139–42, 144–45, 149
Dunaevskii, I., 235n11

East Berlin (Germany), 150
East Germany, 44, 45, 111, 142, 213; travel to, 42, 108–109, 149–50, 175
Eastern Chinese Railway, 64n10
Eastern Europe, 4, 42, 44, 136n18; travel to, 21, 244
Echberger, Vera Filippovna (school principal), 66, 92, 158–59
Economy, 17, 21, 82, 112, 148, 246n17, 268; decline of, 243; market, 5, 54n33
Education, 5, 14–15, 61, 77, 157; American, 3; costs of, 86, 186; graduate, 21, 43, 77, 100–101, 110, 241; higher, 7, 19–20, 55, 105, 232, 240; importance of, 61, 125; musi-

cal, *see* Music, study of; quality of, 78, 93, 159, 191. *See also* College; Instruction; School; School No. 42; University

Egypt, 186

Ehrenburg, Ilia, 72n17

Eisenhower, Dwight D., 3n6

Eisenstein, Sergei, 260n9

Elections, 53, 274; American presidential, 205

Elite, 218; Communist Party, 31, 114, 189, 194, 207, 255–56

Emancipation, women's, 108, 119

Embroidering, 60, 68

Emigration, 11, 21, 39, 182, 220, 221, 242, 250; reasons for, 248–49

Emirates, 186

Employment, 36, 58, 100, 105, 169, 204, 206, 223, 230, 241, 246, 251, 264–65, 271; changes in, 98, 115, 173–74, 249–50, 275; foreign, 204. *See also* Career; Profession; Unemployment; Work

Engels (Russian city), 125n7, 246

Engels region, 268

England, 98–99, 109, 133; and English, 265

English language: importance of, 29, 66, 99, 100–101, 121, 127–28, 162, 244–45, 265; instruction in, 7, 64–65, 92, 160, 228, 230–31; reading in, 43, 224; speaking of, 125, 126, 129, 135, 161, 194; study of, 14, 19, 61–62, 95, 102, 162; teaching of, 40

Enisei River, 121, 123

Environment, 147–48

Equality, 226, 245, 247

Erevan (Armenia), 209

Ethnicity, 9. *See also* Nationality

Europe, 54, 186, 187; travel to, 278. *See also* Eastern Europe

Exams, 139, 227, 246; candidate, 100–101; entrance, 19–20, 62, 65, 136, 154, 197, 240; Ph.D., 171

Expectations, 17, 119

Factories, 13, 225, 237

Fadeev, Aleksandr, 269n20

Family, 32, 80, 87, 88, 90, 104, 105, 119, 155, 169, 172, 188, 201, 221, 251, 259, 260, 278; breakup of, 156, 157 (*see also* Divorce); influence of, 14, 162, 165, 191; international, 222. *See also* Grandparents; Marriage; Parents

Family history, 26–27, 36–37, 57–58, 88–89, 121, 123, 155–57, 162–64, 168, 189–90, 221–23, 254–55

Family life, 22, 51, 118

Famine, 164

Far North, 56, 61n7, 75, 156, 172

Farms, 268

Fashion. *See* Clothing

Fassbinder, Rainer Werner, 54

Fear, 38, 133–34, 217, 258, 270; of America, 212; of the Soviet Union, 4; of war, 56, 132, 216; of the West, 259

Federal Security Service (FSB), 53n31

Fedin, Konstantin Aleksandrovich, 164

Fellini, Federico, 208

Feminism, 176

Films, 26, 66, 124, 130–31, 146, 152, 202, 260; and clubs, 201, 207–208, 210; documentary, 71

Finland, 88

Food, 82, 132, 144, 248; shortages of, 181, 205 (*see also* Shortages, bread). *See also* Sausage

Food supply, 112, 206, 268

Foreigners, 38, 43, 236; contact with, 45, 56, 66, 71, 96, 112, 133, 250; treatment of, 207

Fowles, John, 210

Frank, Ilia Mikhailovich, 127, 140, 141

Freedom, 151, 167, 182, 238; deprivation of, 174; limits on, 54, 249; of movement, 247–48; of speech, 53

Friendship, 7n19, 73, 130, 202, 250, 251, 261; and gender, 80, 104, 170, 176; influence of, 29–30; school, 28, 63, 126, 134, 187, 192–193, 226, 228, 279; strains on, 145, 211

Furmanov, Dmitrii, 269n19

Gagarin, Iurii, 2, 13, 132, 167

Gaidar, Egor, 54

Galich, Aleksandr, 15, 139, 237

Games, 58, 224, 256

Gangs, 32, 254; Glebovrag, 261–62; Industrialists, 262

Gender, 22, 104, 113, 176; and identity, 79–80; and profession, 108, 143.
See also Relations, gender

Gender differences, 92, 93, 98, 114,
118, 130, 143, 199, 215, 264

Generation, 23, 148, 186, 199, 218,
276, 278; accomplishments of, 153;
lost, 153, 218, 277, 279; older, 278;
postwar, 4, 156; Sputnik, 4–7, 9,
11–16, 18–22; younger, 5, 18, 72

Generational differences, 38, 51,
72–73, 90, 94, 96–98, 129–30, 134,
151–52, 166–67, 198, 238–39, 251,
258, 275

Georgia, 109; and Georgians, 80n26

German Democratic Republic (GDR).
See East Germany

German Wave (Deutsche Welle), 19,
134

Germany, 84, 96, 143, 148, 161, 165,
259, 271; emigration to, 8, 39, 193;
and Germans, 145, 223, 273. *See also*
East Germany

Gilzin, Karl Aleksandrovich, 2

Glasnost, 21, 85, 114, 150–51, 188, 272

Glebuchev Ravine, 225, 237, 262n12

Goals, 83, 279; life, 278; spiritual, 217

Goods, 85; consumer, 68, 72, 82, 111,
132, 150, 205; supply of, 206

Gorbachev, Mikhail Sergeevich, 5, 12,
151, 183–86, 200, 250, 268, 269,
271, 272; attitudes toward, 84–85,
114, 146, 148, 179–81, 216, 276

Gorbachev era, 21, 46, 84, 178, 214,
267, 268, 272

Gorky, Maxim, 180

Graduation, 21, 78, 79, 119, 262, 263

Grandparents, 14, 36, 74, 123, 125,
156–57, 189–90, 191, 255

Great Britain. *See* England

Great Fatherland War. *See* World War II

Great Terror, 38n14, 53

Groznyi (Chechnia), 273

Guevara, Che, 235

Guitar poetry, 15

Gulag, 5, 18, 56, 102, 122, 132, 154,
168. *See also* Labor camps

Gulag Archipelago, 241

Gumilev, Lev Nikolaevich, 41

Gusinskii, Vladimir, 277n26

Hailey, Arthur, 203

Hairdos, 69, 159, 160

Hamlet, 131

Helsinki Group, 236n12

Herder (Canada), 150

History, 115, 127

Hitler, Adolf, 54, 252

Hobbies, 32, 60, 68, 86, 157

Holland. *See* Netherlands

Home economics, 15, 61, 93

Hooliganism, 38, 158, 262

Housing, 13–14, 125, 167, 213–14,
278; communal, 19, 132, 190, 224,
225; cooperative, 46, 172, 206; loss
of, 164; obtaining, 182, 264; purchase of, 277; sale of, 274; shortages
of, 14; single-family, 16, 190, 224,
225

Human factor, 114, 117

Human rights, 41n19, 47, 142, 147,
176, 247

Humanitarian aid, 209, 210

Hungary, 66

Hussein, Saddam, 276

Hypocrisy, 95, 178

Ice skating, 195

Ideals, 97, 175

Identity, 40, 108, 142, 176, 202, 242

Ideology, 71, 95, 97, 98, 251–52, 260;
Communist, 15, 136; and education,
20, 240; Israeli, 250

Illness, 102, 110, 116, 124, 157, 165,
168, 173, 216

Imperialism, American, 242

Income, 5, 159, 211. *See also* Money;
Salary

Independence, 202–203

Inequality, 37, 233

Influences, 136, 222; adult, 200; external, 113

Informants, 111, 247

Information, 19, 150–51, 168, 201, 214, 215, 216, 241, 242, 272

Inkeles, Alex, 6

Instruction: methods of, 92, 95, 230; politicized, 29, 65–66, 83, 98, 126–27, 129, 138, 194, 231. *See also* Education; School

Intelligentsia, 7, 8, 17, 83, 107, 179, 191, 193, 213, 218, 243; children of, 31, 91, 118, 191, 192, 194, 255

International Youth Festival (Moscow, 1957), 56, 70–71

Iraq, 266, 276

Ireland, 150

Iron Curtain, 175, 218, 245

Islam, 210, 276

Israel, 8, 126, 156n1, 182, 208, 220, 222, 230, 241, 244, 247n18, 248, 250, 251; emigration to, 242; travel to, 243, 249

Italy, 44–45

Ivanov, Gennadii Viktorovich, 13, 253, 257, 263, 279

Izvestiia, 34

Japan, 88; and Japanese, 273

Jeans, 30, 130, 138

Jewish, 21, 30, 222, 228n8, 243, 256

Jews, 9, 31, 81, 148, 222, 250

Jokes, 18, 178, 244, 247, 258. *See also* Anecdotes

Judaism, 276

Juvenile delinquency, 257

Kabzon, Iosif, 69

Kalinin. *See* Tver

Kamaiurova, Olga Vladimirovna, 187, 192, 195, 196, 263, 279

Kazakhstan, 1, 255, 273

Kazan (Russia), 30n4

Kennedy, John F., 4, 76, 99–100

KGB, 31, 35, 100, 243, 253. *See also* Federal Security Service

Kharbin (China), 64

Kharkov (Ukraine), 62

Khodorkovskii, Mikhail, 277n26

Khrushchev, Nikita Sergeevich, 2, 35n8, 72, 72n17, 94, 198, 227, 234n10, 258; attitudes toward, 102, 216, 233, 236; ouster of, 17, 33, 34, 72, 258; policies of, 14, 16–17; and Stalin cult, 33, 102, 131, 135, 154, 186 (*see also* Stalin, cult of)

Khrushchev era, 14, 16, 132, 167, 258

Khvalynsk (Russia), 254, 255

Kiev (Ukraine), 62, 170

Kitchen debates, 35n8, 234n10

Komsomol, 15, 18, 48–49, 59, 71, 96, 175, 197, 242n14, 260, 262

Konstantinov, Aleksandr Aleksandrovich, 24–26, 27, 30, 32, 33, 34n7, 39, 53n31, 63, 90, 126, 187, 191, 196, 220, 263

Korea, 114

Korolenko, Vladimir Galaktionovich, 36

Kosygin, Aleksei Nikolaevich, 46

Kozlov, Vladimir, 17, 18

Krasnoarmeisk (Russia), 273

Kreise, Bernard, 43

Kristalinskaia, Maiia, 69

Krupskaia, Nadezhda Konstantinovna, 36

Kruzhki. See Clubs

Kuibyshev. *See* Samara

Labor camps, 18, 27, 33n5, 61n7, 122, 156, 165, 168, 166, 174, 176, 218. *See also* Gulag

Laika (space dog), 2

Language, 67–68, 115, 125, 162, 231, 265; Chinese, 70, 128; conversational, 126; Hebrew, 245, 250; instruction in, 86, 159; knowledge of, 162, 194; literary, 64–65, 92; teaching of, 96. *See also* English language; Russian language

Latvia, 19, 40n15

Lavut, Aleksandr Pavlovich, 41

Lavut, Tania, 41

Law Academy, Saratov, 19, 90, 94, 96, 115, 156, 262, 264

Law Institute. *See* Law Academy, Saratov

Laws, 97, 247, 263, 277; moral, 118

Leadership, 53, 70, 83, 113, 146, 268–69, 276

Lebed-Kumach, V., 235n11
Lee, Harper, 208
Legality, 18, 53
Lenin, 34–35, 36, 71, 112, 122, 198, 227, 232, 233, 246, 260, 266n14
Leningrad (Russia), 20, 46, 100, 101, 142, 209; travel to, 62, 240
Library, 180, 208, 260
Ligachev, Egor, 185
Literature, 66, 129, 151, 160, 180, 185; dissident, 41, 75, 83 (see also Samizdat); English, 65, 92; world, 210
Living permit (propiska), 46, 127, 140–41
Living space, 132. See also Housing
Living standards, 16, 102, 116, 144, 146, 148, 149, 182, 203, 205, 213–14, 225; changes in, 18, 132, 164, 167, 245, 268; Eastern European, 44, 67–68; Western, 234
London, Jack, 260
Lumumba, Patrice, 235
Luna 1-3, 2
Lvov (Ukraine), 101

Machtet, Grigorii Aleksandrovich, 36
Magadan (Russia), 155, 171, 172, 173
Magadan oblast, 56, 168, 172, 174, 180
Magomedov, Muslim, 69
Mao Zedong, 70n14
Marijuana, 224–25
Markets, farmers, 206
Marriage, 38–39, 73, 78–79, 105–107, 139–40, 156, 162, 164, 169, 171, 172, 176, 201, 241, 264, 278
Marx (Russian town), 203
Marx, Karl, 137, 211, 244, 246
Marxism, 81–82, 137–38, 167, 244, 268
Marxism-Leninism, 18, 101
Mass media, 65, 83, 99, 100, 137, 151, 270
Material situation, 211, 217
Maupassant, Guy de, 260
May Day, 30, 192, 195, 212
Medical Institute, Saratov, 19, 27, 30, 73, 161n5, 191, 196, 201, 204, 255
Medicine, 86, 191, 211, 247, 263

Memory, 11, 56, 87–88, 193. See also Childhood, memories of
Men, 119, 143
Mensheviks, 267
Michurinsk (Russia), 57, 58
Microbe (anti-cholera institute), 36, 189
Military, 155, 221, 236
Military-industrial complex, 13, 98
Mines, Siberian, 121–22, 172, 181
Ministry of Education, 117
Ministry of Internal Affairs, 117, 271
Minsk (Belarus), 100
Missiles, 3n6; intercontinental ballistic, 1, 141n26
Mobility, social, 14, 232
Moldavians, 9
Money, 41, 105–106, 113, 150, 186, 209, 226, 236, 245, 250, 268, 271–72; and education, 86, 159; need for, 51, 171–72, 177 (see also Salary); and travel, 52, 111, 142, 211, 278; value of, 146, 248, 274–75
Mordovia, 264
Mordovia State University, 101
Morning Star, 162
Morozova, Boyarina, 74
Moscow (Russia), 7, 20, 24, 26, 34, 109, 127, 142, 144, 176; attitudes toward, 45, 78, 112, 144, 181, 236–37, 245; education in, 46, 61, 77–78, 100, 101, 110 (see also Moscow University); exhibits in, see American exhibition; explosions in, 53; festivals in, see Youth festivals; residence in, 8, 27–26, 36–37, 40, 63, 187, 251; travel to, 25, 41, 62, 82, 173, 178, 240, 245, 268
Moscow Conservatory, 51–52
Moscow Economic-Statistical Institute, 55, 77
Moscow News, 162
Moscow State Commercial University, Saratov branch, 55
Moscow (State) University, 19, 24, 26, 36, 38, 41, 43, 46, 139, 177, 187, 270; Dubna branch of, 137
Mothers, working, 14, 90, 91, 96, 223

Music, 26, 42, 51, 52, 69, 152, 195, 222, 256; rock, 38; study of, 28, 68–69, 102, 195 (*see also* Moscow Conservatory; School, music); Western, 19, 38, 139, 237, 238 (*see also* Beatles)
Myths, 37, 75; and crime, 270; political, 85; Soviet, 47–48, 85, 113, 214, 246, 269

Nabokov, Vladimir, 180
Napoleon, 144
Narcotics, 267, 274
National Aeronautics and Space Administration, United States (NASA), 3
National Defense Education Act, United States (NDEA), 3
Nationality, 22, 30–31, 71, 81, 125–26, 134, 136, 182, 222, 223, 243, 254, 273; German, 256; Polish, 256; Russian, 9, 256, 222; Ukrainian, 9
Nature, 58, 123
Naval Ministry, 184
Near East, 144, 277
Nekrasov, Nikolai Alekseevich, 176
Nemtsov, Boris, 111
Netherlands, 8, 265, 275
New Economic Policy (NEP), 163, 266
New Year, 91, 93
New York (United States), 223–24
Newfoundland (Canada), 150
Nine Days of One Year, 124, 130
Nixon, Richard M., 35n8, 234n10
Nizhnii Novgorod (Russia), 110
NKVD (People's Commissariat of Internal Affairs), 156
North Vietnamese, 242
Nostalgia, 33, 88, 95, 192–93, 210, 248
Novocherkassk (Russia), 17, 223
Novyi mir, 74, 75, 103, 168
Nuclear physics, 121, 127, 137, 143

October Revolution (1917), 4, 15, 57, 59n4, 107n15, 212
Odessa (Ukraine), 62, 101
Ogonek, 200
Oil, 246, 250, 277
Okudzhava, Bulat, 15, 139

Okunevskaia, Tatiana, 165
Old Believers, 74
Oligarchs, 186, 277
Openness, 18, 32, 38, 50, 142, 180
Opera, 195
Optimism, 7, 16, 56, 72, 73, 153, 183, 235, 248, 257
Oral history, 10, 24, 87, 120, 187
Organizations, youth, 15, 18, 59n6. *See also* Komsomol; Pioneers; Young Octobrists
Orlova, Liubov, 235n11
Orthodoxy, 210
Osho. *See* Rajneesh, Bhagwan Shree
Ostrovskii, Aleksandr Nikolaevich, 260
Oswald, Lee Harvey, 100

P., Natalia, 87, 88, 89, 103, 279
Pakistan, 267
Palestine, 251, 276
Palma, Olef, 99
Panfilov men, 269
Parents, 60, 91, 94, 96, 255–56; influence of, 36, 57–58, 108, 136, 191
Pashtuns, 267
Patriotism, 17, 18, 115, 242
Patronage, 173
Pearl Harbor, 273
Pedagogical Institute, Saratov, 19, 39–40, 65, 92, 93, 94, 95, 104–105, 116, 162
Pension, 96, 179, 182, 186, 274
Penza (Russia), 59
People's Democratic Party of Afghanistan, 266–67
Perestroika, 5, 21, 60, 83, 112, 128, 129, 150, 151, 180, 188, 198, 208, 211, 249, 267, 272; impact of, 97–98, 115, 152, 198, 201; reasons for, 84, 114, 148, 179, 216, 217, 250, 271; and travel, 52, 142
Petakh Tikva (Israel), 220
Pevek (Siberia), 155, 180, 183, 184
Piatigorsk (Russia), 101
Pioneers, 15, 48, 59, 63, 127, 197
Pitsunda (Georgia), 34
Poland, 44, 111, 142, 207; travel to, 42, 108–109

Political economy, 20, 88–89, 100, 101, 112
Politics, 32, 34, 48, 72, 100, 108, 114, 132, 236, 272; and crime, 275
Pollution, 148, 213, 248
Polytechnic Institute, Kiev, 169, 170
Polytechnic Institute, Saratov, 13, 19–20, 55, 66, 77, 88, 91, 100, 121, 162, 169, 171, 201
Pomerants, Grigorii, 41
Population, 17, 227
Potsdam Conference, 109
Prague (Czech Republic), 68
Prague Spring, 67n12, 244n15
Pravda, 145
Prestige, 48, 50, 157
Pride, 16, 167, 183
Prisoners, 124
Privatization, 248n20
Privilege, 31, 45, 60
Productivity, 183
Profession, 98, 99; changes in, 127–28; and gender, 108, 143; love for, 101. *See also* Employment; Work
Pronina, Natalia Valentinovna. *See* Altukhova, Natalia Valentinovna
Propaganda, 76, 85, 205, 212, 226–27, 232; effectiveness of, 231; Soviet, 2, 56, 234
Property: distribution of, 248; private, 246
Proust, Marcel, 26
Public opinion, 17, 248n20
Pugachev (Russian town), 123
Punishment, 60, 174
Pushkin, Aleksandr Sergeevich, 37, 129
Putin, Vladimir, 22, 53, 54, 83, 186, 276, 277n26

Radio broadcasts, 40, 41, 53, 65, 66, 134, 234, 236, 240, 241; Czech, 145; foreign, 19, 40, 47, 75–76, 103, 133, 166, 198, 204, 205, 257 (*see also* British Broadcasting Corporation; German Wave; Radio Liberty; Voice of America)
Radio Liberty, 19
Radio Moscow, 235n11

Rajneesh, Bhagwan Shree, 208, 209, 210
Rampa, Tuesday Lobsang, 208
RAND corporation, 1
Rationing, 102, 133. *See also* Shortages, bread
Reading, 16, 37, 40, 61, 75, 195, 202, 208, 224, 230, 234, 255
Reagan, Ronald, 204–205
Red Square, 40, 236
Rehabilitation, 156
Relations: family, 21, 116, 202; gender, 31, 76, 79–80, 94, 119, 237, 261
Religion, 27, 37, 73–74, 101, 111, 125, 194, 257; and age, 118; attack on, 17; banning of, 95; and conflict, 276; Eastern, 199, 209–10; revival of, 83. *See also* Atheism; Christianity; Church; Islam; Judaism; Orthodoxy
Repression, 38, 102, 156, 165, 166, 189, 197, 258
Resettlement, 273, 274
Resources, 17, 271
Responsibility, 94, 116, 276; criminal, 274
Retirement, 182. *See also* Pension
Reunion, class, 10, 94, 187–88, 192–93, 279–80
Revolution, 163, 266; Bolshevik, *see* October Revolution; Chinese, *see* Cultural Revolution, Chinese; Cuban, *see* Cuba, revolution in; world, 235
Riazan (Russia), 36, 37
Rolling Stones, 139
Romania, 204, 205, 206, 207, 208, 211, 213
Romanov affair, 107, 137–38, 241
Romm, Mikhail, 124n6
Rostov-on-the-Don (Russia), 221, 223, 224
Ruble, 153, 248
Rumors, 270
Russia, 54, 149, 150, 182, 188, 207, 226, 242, 248, 249, 250, 251, 259, 266, 271, 280. *See also* Soviet Union
Russian language, 61, 65, 67, 115, 127–28, 129, 130, 133–35, 161, 224

Russians, 1, 67, 81, 145, 149, 155, 174, 182; and living abroad, 64n10, 204, 207

Sakhalin Island, 56, 61n7, 255
Sakharov, Andrei Dmitrievich, 147
Salary, 91, 98, 102, 140, 151–52, 169, 171, 190, 248, 250, 271
Samara (Russia), 110, 262
Samizdat, 41, 107–108, 133, 142, 151, 176, 202, 240–41. *See also* Dissident movement
Saransk (Russia), 101, 264
Saratov (Russia), 8, 24, 25, 36, 87, 120, 144, 154, 167, 179, 230, 253–54; changes in, 88, 151, 180, 218, 275; as closed city, 7, 13–14, 37–38, 66, 96, 112, 133, 161, 177, 236–37; dissidents in, 20, 137; educational opportunities in, 100, 157; employment opportunities in, 212; family roots in, 57, 89, 121, 123, 141, 221, 251, 272; and foreigners, 38, 133, 161–62, 245; impressions of, 62, 124; industry of, 13; isolation of, 241, 242; move to, 27, 32, 45, 56, 58, 61, 78, 139, 156, 161, 172, 204, 222, 264; neighborhoods in, 28, 32, 125, 224, 237, 262n12 (*see also* Glebuchev Ravine); old, 124; outskirts of, 193; population of, 9, 12, 80; and sister city, 160–61; travel to, 187; and war, 89, 155
Saratov oblast, 12, 254
Saratov University, 13, 19, 20n43, 46, 121, 137–38, 139, 221, 240; arrest of students at, 20, 107 (*see also* Romanov affair)
Sartre, Jean-Paul, 40
Satellites, artificial, 1–2, 2n6, 3n6, 4. *See also* Sputnik; Sputnik II
Sausage, 96, 177, 178, 205, 206, 207, 268. *See also* Food
Sausage trains, 81, 144, 245, 268
Schiller, 50
School, 3, 33, 34, 59, 158, 188, 225, 226, 228, 257, 260; magnet, 7, 8, 8n21 (*see also* School No. 42); music,

28, 68, 102, 157, 195 (*see also* Music, study of); neighborhood, 8, 14, 25, 28, 61, 63, 90, 125; nursery, 223. *See also* School No. 42
School No. 42 (Saratov), 7, 15, 19, 20, 25, 26, 31, 39, 56, 93, 116, 118, 121, 128, 154, 157, 190–91, 220, 225–26, 240, 244, 255–56; admission to, 28; and Bristol, 236; choice of, 225; curriculum at, 14, 65, 160; description of, 158, 226; education program of, 63–64, 129, 160; enrollment in, 8, 90, 61–62, 125; preparation for, 64; quality of, 159, 230–31; student composition of, 9, 30–32, 63, 125–26, 255–56, 262
Scientific communism, 20, 138, 240
Scott, Walter, 180
Second economy. *See* Black market
Secret service, 96
Security clearance, 21, 142, 244
Security organs, state, 31, 53, 253. *See also* Federal Security Service; KGB; NKVD
Self-perception, 79, 104
September 11 (2001), 115, 251
Sewing, 60–61, 68, 93
Shalamov, Varlam, 201n16
Shannon (Airport), 150
Shcharanskii, Anatolii, 236
Shlapentokh, Vladimir, 19
Shock therapy, 54n33
Shortages, 177, 206, 243, 268; bread, 82, 132, 235–36, 258; food, *see* Food, shortages of; housing, *see* Housing, shortages of
Shostakovich, Dmitrii, 131n15
Show trial, 33n5, 165
Shushenskii (Siberia), 122
Siberia, 56, 61n7, 118, 121, 123–24, 129, 132, 141, 182, 268
Singing, 59, 71
Siniavskii-Daniel trial, 33, 34, 35
Slogans, 215
Slovakia, 13–14
Smoking, 238, 253
Smoktunovskii, Innokentii, 131
Social change, 5

Social class, 59, 80, 91, 115, 123, 125, 179, 191, 255. *See also* Working class

Social experiment, 23, 231, 239

Social status, 8, 98

Socialism, 5, 56, 137, 152, 153, 232, 244, 245, 250; belief in, 226; building of, 266; refashioning of, 17; transition to, 235. *See also* Communism

Socialist Revolutionary (SR) Party, 36

Soldiers, 34, 137, 216, 248, 271

Solidarity, 207

Solzhenitsyn, Alexander, 18, 41, 74–75, 83, 103, 122, 133, 147, 168

Songs, 76, 77, 139, 192

Soul, Russian, 88, 115

Soviet dream, 9, 22

Soviet power, 232, 233, 238, 244, 249

Soviet system, 5–6, 33n5, 56, 121, 221, 224, 243, 268; collapse of, 55, 56; decay of, 17, 81

Soviet Union, 1–3, 7, 14, 64, 100, 182, 188, 205, 207, 222, 238–39, 241–42, 244, 246, 247, 251, 271, 277; collapse of, 6, 21, 50–51, 88, 98, 115, 181, 217, 275; fate of, 9, 276; as superpower, 4, 5; travel in, 62

Space, 3; exploration of, 1–2

Space race, 3, 56

Space stations, 141n26

Speculation, 97

Spidola. *See* VEF radio

Spirituality, 47, 202, 217, 218

Spock, Dr. Benjamin, 3, 118

Sports, 142, 160, 224, 230, 255, 256

Sputnik, 1, 2, 2–3n6, 4, 6, 56

Sputnik II, 2

St. Petersburg (Russia), 62. *See also* Leningrad

Stability, 46, 95, 113, 115, 236, 247

Stagnation, 46, 84, 94, 113, 145, 146, 178, 207, 214, 247, 267–68, 272

Stalin, Joseph, 2, 5, 32, 33, 35, 48, 71, 72, 83n30, 109n18, 110, 120, 144n28, 154, 260–61, 273, 274; cult of, 33, 102, 166, 217, 231, 232–33, 258; death of, 49, 156, 258

Stalingrad region, 254

Stalinism, 5, 33n5, 72n17, 153, 272

Stamp collecting, 61, 68

Stavropol (Russia), 223

Stealing, 274

Stereotypes, 129, 218, 251

Students, 14, 137, 158; American, 3

Subjectivity, 87, 88

Surikov, Vasilii, 74n20

Susuman (Siberia), 180

Swedes, 266

Swimming, 195

Syria, 109

Tambov (Russia), 264, 268

Taraki, Nur Mohammad, 267n16

Tashkent (Uzbekistan), 209

Tatarstan, 30n4; and Tatars, 9, 30, 41n19, 262

Taubman, William, 17

Teachers, 160; favorite, 160, 193, 228, 256; foreign, 133, 161, 194; quality of, 28–29, 92, 126, 191

Technical University. *See* Polytechnic Institute, Saratov

Television, 16, 38, 53, 65, 66, 145, 167, 185, 218, 234, 236, 265; government control over, 276

Tempus Program, 110

Tereshkova, Valentina, 2

Terrorism, 276

Texas (United States), 277

Textbooks, 64–65, 92, 95, 127, 129, 160

Thailand, 274

Thatcher, Margaret, 109

Thaw, 2, 18, 56, 72, 94

Theater, 91

Third World, 2

Three Musketeers, 130

Tolstoy, Lev, 40, 180

Torres, Lolita, 167

Tourists, 21, 66–68, 108, 175, 185, 186, 213, 249, 274, 278. *See also* Travel

Trade unions, 161, 177, 178

Transformation, 5, 10, 153, 242

Transition, 235, 275; coping with, 97–98, 213, 238–39, 249; economic, 88; post-Soviet, 9, 22, 96, 114–15

Travel, 38, 62, 101, 128–29, 207, 213, 278; business, 52, 142; foreign, 44–

45, 52, 66, 108, 109–10, 133, 142, 148–50, 161, 186, 243, 249, 275; restrictions on, 182; youth, 165
Trubnikov, Aleksandr Vladimirovich, 76–77, 126, 220–21, 222, 227, 247n18
Truman, Harry, 109n18
Trust, 7n19, 50, 53, 243
Truth, 114, 134, 201, 235, 269
Tsar-Kolokol, 214
Turkey, 186, 265
Tver (Russia), 100, 101
Twain, Mark, 260

Ukraine, 124, 171, 181, 182
Unemployment, 98, 247
Uniforms, 69, 130, 159, 160, 227
United Nations (UN), 233, 258
United States, 3, 39, 50, 73, 82, 99, 105, 132, 159, 181, 182, 224, 230, 232, 250, 274, 276; democracy in, 54; emigration to, 8, 118, 119; influence of, 84; and Iraq, 266; and oil, 277; travel to, 52, 278
University, 14, 20, 35, 40, 42, 52, 95, 127, 140, 152, 232, 240, 241; administration of, 117; composition of, 45; and foreigners, 38; and friendships, 28. *See also individual names of institutions*
Urbanization, 5
USSR. *See* Soviet Union
Ussuri River crisis, 128n12

Vacation, 16, 26, 71, 91, 169, 195, 211, 228, 229, 248, 259, 278. *See also* Travel
Values, 94, 116, 152, 186, 221; changes in, 96–97; common, 106; Soviet, 6, 156n1
VEF radio, 19, 40, 40n15, 133
Verne, Jules, 180
Viatkin, V. S., 168
Vietnam War, 215, 242, 266, 248
Virgin lands campaign, 242
Voice of America, 19, 134, 166, 204, 231, 240, 241

Volga German Republic, 254, 272, 273; and Volga Germans, 9, 203n20
Volga region, 164, 275
Volga River, 12–13, 30n4, 124, 224, 273; pollution of, 147–48, 248; summer camp on, 16, 93, 134, 135, 139, 228–30, 259
Volgograd (Stalingrad) (Russia), 273
Volleyball, 230
Volsk (Russia), 255
Vorkuta (Russia), 156
Vysotskii, Vladimir, 15, 65, 77, 139

Wages, 13, 183, 225, 242, 248. *See also* Salary
War, 34, 56, 88–89, 97, 112, 205, 233, 261, 274; civil, 146, 216; class, 234; nuclear, 16, 22, 76n23, 132, 212; prisoners of, 26–27. *See also* Afghanistan, war in; Chechnia, war in; Civil War; Cold War; Fear, of war; Vietnam War; World War I; World War II
War and Peace, 130
Waugh, Evelyn, 208
West, 142, 176, 242, 268; attitude toward, 35–36, 41–42, 66, 98–99, 111–12, 128, 143–44, 166, 234, 237, 243, 259; depictions of, 35; influence of, 38, 97, 146, 154, 272 (*see also* Foreigners, contact with; Music, Western; Radio broadcasts, foreign); and material goods, 150 (*see also* Living standards, Western); travel to, 42, 52. *See also* Europe; United States
Wilde, Oscar, 92
Women, 22, 100, 114, 119, 143, 157, 162, 215, 223; influence of, 162–65; life of, 80, 202; as mothers, 113 (*see also* Mothers, working; Parents); role of, 203; and study, 107–108. *See also* Gender; Relations, gender
Work, 84, 96, 97, 116, 181–82, 213, 278; conditions at, 95, 156; cultural, 175; and gender, 108, 176 (*see also* Mothers, working); meaning of, 57, 107, 119, 152, 183, 223
Work assignments, 140

Work brigades, 20
Workers, 58n2, 80, 91, 179, 234, 243;
    white-collar, 57, 59
Working class, 8, 57, 234, 255
World Trade Center, 251
World War I, 12
World War II, 4, 5, 41n19, 88, 110n20,
    112, 121, 155, 216, 254, 273; com-
    memoration of, 13; effects of, 14,
    26–27, 143, 157, 161, 165, 221–23;
    and partisans, 39, 131, 196, 197; vic-
    tory in, 233

Wrestling, 256

Yeltsin, Boris, 54n33, 83, 114, 151,
    182, 186, 248n20, 276; attitudes to-
    ward, 53, 148, 181
Young Guard, 269
Young Octobrists, 15, 48, 59
Youth festivals, 70, 167. *See also* Inter-
    national Youth Festival
Yugoslavia, 115, 190

Ziuganov, Gennadii, 147

Donald J. Raleigh is Jay Richard Judson Distinguished Professor of History at the University of North Carolina, Chapel Hill, where he teaches modern Russian and Soviet history. He is author, editor, or translator of numerous books, including *Revolution on the Volga: 1917 in Saratov; Provincial Landscapes: The Local Dimensions of Soviet Power, 1917–1953;* and *Experiencing Russia's Civil War: Politics, Society, and Revolutionary Culture in Saratov, 1917–1922.*

1967   2005